Advance Praise for

Teaching Green

Green Teacher magazine has done an outstanding job of providing quality resources to environmental educators for over ten years. Having the best of those resources for middle grades in one volume is long overdue and will be welcomed by environmental educators everywhere.

— GRANT GARDNER, Associate Dean of Science, Memorial University

Teaching Green – The Middle Years provides a blueprint for many lessons and projects that develop critical thinking and decision-making skills in students. Included are many offerings for the innovative teacher who sees the environment as an opportunity to improve student achievement by using natural surroundings as a context for learning.

— SUSIE SHIELDS, Environmental Educator for the Oklahoma Department of Environmental Quality and past-president of the Oklahoma Association for Environmental Education

Developing a personal relationship with the environment, a true sense of place, is a crucial step towards forming attitudes that will lead young people to work for a more a sustainable future. *Teaching Green — The Middle Years* provides practical suggestions for helping children discover how they fit within this complex system called Earth.

— COLLEEN ELDERTON, Principal, Cove Cliff Elementary School, Vancouver, British Columbia, and VICTOR ELDERTON, Principal of North Vancouver Outdoor School and Director of Environmental Educators of BC

Teaching Green
The Middle Years

Teaching Green
The Middle Years

Hands-on Learning in Grades 6-8

Edited by Tim Grant and Gail Littlejohn

NEW SOCIETY PUBLISHERS

Cataloging in Publication Data:
A catalog record for this publication is available from the National Library of Canada.

Cover design by Diane McIntosh.

Printed in Canada.

Green Teacher acknowledges the support of The Ontario Trillium Foundation,
an agency of the Ontario Ministry of Culture.

THE ONTARIO
TRILLIUM FOUNDATION

LA FONDATION
TRILLIUM DE L'ONTARIO

New Society Publishers acknowledges the support of the Government of Canada through the
Book Publishing Industry Development Program (BPIDP) for our publishing activities.

Paperback ISBN: 0-86571-501-7

Inquiries regarding requests to reprint all or part of *Teaching Green — The Middle Years* should be
addressed to New Society Publishers at the address below.

To order directly from the publishers, please add $4.50 shipping to the price of the first copy,
and $1.00 for each additional copy (plus GST in Canada). Send check or money order to:

GREEN TEACHER
95 Robert Street, Toronto, ON M5S 2K5, Canada
2045 Niagara Falls Boulevard, U-7, Niagara Falls, NY 14304-1675, USA
1-888-804-1486 / 1-416-960-1244
www.greenteacher.com

or

NEW SOCIETY PUBLISHERS
P.O. Box 189, Gabriola Island, BC V0R 1X0, Canada
1-800-567-6772
www.newsociety.com

New Society Publishers' mission is to publish books that contribute in fundamental ways to building an ecologically sustainable and just society, and to do so with the least possible impact on the
environment, in a manner that models this vision. Green Teacher's mission is to publish resources
that help educators to foster young people's appreciation of the natural environment, understanding of the Earth's systems, and desire and ability to apply their knowledge in solving environmental
problems. Both organizations are acting on their environmental commitments by phasing out
paper supplies from ancient forests worldwide. This book is one step towards ending global deforestation and climate change. It is printed on acid-free paper that is **100% old growth forest-free**
(100% post-consumer recycled), processed chlorine-free, and printed with vegetable-based, low-
VOC inks.

NEW SOCIETY PUBLISHERS   www.newsociety.com

Table of Contents

Not the Final Word

Glossary

Index

Curriculum Index

About Green Teacher

Acknowledgments

More than 250 individuals have generously contributed their time and expertise to the publication of this first "best of Green Teacher" book in our *Teaching Green* series. In particular, we thank the dozens of contributing authors who share in these pages their wide-ranging knowledge, their diverse experience, and their passion for a new model of education. During the past year, all of them have volunteered their time to revisit and update teaching strategies and activities that they had previously contributed to *Green Teacher* magazine, and in many cases have developed them further in response to the helpful comments of reviewers.

We also owe an enormous debt to a group of educators who gave their time to review and critique the proposed contents of the book. Their detailed and thoughtful comments showed us where improvements were needed and helped to guide authors in their revisions. They also suggested many additional topics, some of which we incorporated in order to make the book a more complete and helpful resource. We thank the following reviewers:

CANADA:

Alberta – Karin Adshead, Sue Arlidge, Colleen Connolly, Aaron Domes, Ellen Gasser, Brenda Giourmetakis, David Gue, Mary Harding, Julie Jaffray, Rhonda King, Marie Meeres, Julia Millen, Sue Moleski, Rick Mrazek;

British Columbia – Garry Cotter, Colleen Elderton, Victor Elderton, Liza Ireland, Rick Kool, Calvin Parsons, Denise Philippe, Mary Gale Smith, David Zandvliet;

Manitoba – Bob Adamson, Ron Munro, Amanda Tetrault;

Newfoundland – Joy Barfoot, Grant Gardner, Jean Harding, Cheryl Donovan White, Craig White;

Nova Scotia – Joan Czapalay, Betsy Jardine, Susan Moran;

Nunavut – David Benton, Lori-anne Bond;

Ontario – Judith Arai, Brian Craig, John Hannah, Jane Hayes, Diane Lawrence, Charles Levcoe, Barrie Martin, Barb McKean, Patrice Milewski, Kim Mustard-Fenton, Susan O'Leary, Kate Oxley, Yafit Rokach, Constance Russell, Airin Stephens;

Québec – Michel-Yves (Mitch) Bailly;

Saskatchewan – Ken Boyd, Ali Sammel;

Yukon – Gregory Heming, Terry Markley, Lina Radziunas.

SCOTLAND:

Della Webster.

UNITED STATES:

Alabama – Francine Hutchinson;

Arizona – Dorothy Bentzin, Monica Pastor;

Colorado – Megan Baker, Marcee Camenson, Patti Corsentino, Michelle Finchum, Karin Hostetter, Sue Kenney, Mark Montgomery, Carol Silvas, Beth Simmons, Kirsten Springer, Steven Veatch, Tracee Vickery;

Connecticut – Jessica Anderson, Lars Cherichetti, Laurel Kohl, Heidi Rerecich, Melissa Sikes, Mary Lou Blanchette Smith;

Florida – Sabiha Daudi, Sabrina McCartney;

Georgia – Lynn McCoy;

Hawaii – Rachel Hodges Lau;

Iowa – Shelly Codner;

Indiana – Lisa Burkhardt, Lois Campbell, Sam Carman, Juli Fast, Cathy Meyer, Jim Rogers, Rick Towle, Bryan Wee;

Kansas – John West;

Kentucky – Kathryn Drinkhouse, James Roessler, David Wicks;

Massachusetts – John Hassan, Laura Rogers-Castro;

Minnesota – Dina Bizarro, Patty Gavin, Nalani McCutcheon, Jennifer Walker;

New Jersey – Rebecca Beer, Patricia Camp, Kathy Janes, Sue LeBeau, Laurie Pappas, Linda Ridinger;

New York – Mary Ford, Peg Goldman, Dan Rain, Kimie Romeo;

North Carolina – Liz Baird, Brady Rochford;

Oklahoma – Richard Bryant, Jeanine Huss, Christine Moseley, Susie Shields, Suzanne Spradling;

Pennsylvania – Amy Cohen, Cathy Stephenson;

Tennessee – Maurice Houston Field, Kim Cleary Sadler, Cindi Smith-Walters;

Vermont – Jimmy Karlan;

Virginia – Anita Bright, Adair Collins, Mary Lynn Everhart, Dott Fricke, Lee Teevan;

Washington – Kathy Jacobson, Michele Mohamed;

Wisconsin – Greg Bisbee, Mitch Burtard, Kay Domaszek, Doris Hayes, Jeanine Staab, Susan Streich-Boldt, Dennis Yockers;

Wyoming – Wendy Esponda.

Finally, we offer our heartfelt appreciation for those who labored behind the scenes to make this book a reality: a group of Ontario educators whose letters of support helped us obtain funding from a competitive grants program; the editorial staff and design team at New Society Publishers; and, last but not least, our editorial assistant, Lisa Newman. Her months of patient fact-checking, research, and assembly work were critical to the creation of this, our largest book to date.

— **Tim Grant and Gail Littlejohn**
Toronto

Introduction

by Tim Grant and Gail Littlejohn

Since 1991, we have had the pleasure of working with a great many inspired educators who have shared their innovative environmental education programs, strategies, and activities in the pages of *Green Teacher* magazine. This book is a selection of some of the best of those "green" teaching ideas for educators who are working with students in the middle school grades. Some are strategies for helping young people learn about local ecosystems and what is needed to protect them. Others explore what lifestyle changes may be required if we are to lessen our environmental impact and live more sustainably on the planet. Still others help students recognize global disparities in resource use and their own connections with other people and other species. Perhaps most important, many of the activities provide opportunities for young people to develop and reflect on their values and to consider how they might take an active role in solving environmental problems, both locally and globally. Virtually all of the more than 60 contributors have revised and updated their articles based on the comments and suggestions of reviewers. The result is a wide variety of up-to-date activities and teaching strategies designed to engage adolescents in learning the fundamentals of environmental citizenship in the 21st century.

But what exactly does it mean to "teach green"? While definitions and frameworks abound among environmental, global, and outdoor educators, most agree on a few fundamental principles:

Students should have opportunities to develop a personal connection with nature.

We protect what we care about, and we care about what we know well. If students are encouraged to explore the natural world — to learn about local plants and animals, to observe and anticipate seasonal patterns, to get their feet wet in local rivers — they are more likely to develop a lifelong love of nature that will translate into a lifelong commitment to environmental stewardship.

Education should emphasize our connections with other people and other species, and between human activities and planetary systems.

If young people understand our global interdependence and common reliance on having a healthy environment, they are more likely to take steps to reduce global inequalities, preserve biodiversity, and work together to find ways of lessening our impact on the Earth's life support systems.

Education should help students move from awareness to knowledge to action.

Awareness of environmental issues does not necessarily lead to action. When students have opportunities to act on environmental problems, they begin to understand the complexity of those problems, to learn the critical thinking and negotiating skills needed to solve them, and to develop the practical competence that democratic societies require of their citizens.

Learning should extend into the community.

Community partnerships and service learning projects provide authentic "real-world" reference points for classroom studies and help students develop a sense of place and identity while learning the values and skills of responsible citizenship.

Learning should be "hands-on."

The benefits of hands-on learning are widely acknowledged among educators, and, during the past 20 years, brain research has underscored its importance. Learning is a function of experience and the best education is one that is sensory-rich, emotionally engaging, and linked to the real world.

Education should integrate subject disciplines.

Environmental issues are complex and cannot be separated from social and economic issues. Addressing them requires knowledge and skills from all disciplines. Integrated learning programs, in which several subjects are taught simultaneously, often through field studies and community projects, help students develop a "big picture" understanding and provide opportunities for authentic learning.

Education should be future-oriented.

History helps us to understand the present, but to solve environmental problems we also need to think about the future. As British educator David Hicks has said, "The future is that part of history that we can change." Students should have opportunities to explore alternatives to our current paths of development, to envision the kind of world they would like to live in, and to think realistically about what is needed to achieve it.

Education should include media literacy.

Through constant exposure to mass media, our mental environments can become just as polluted as the natural environment. Media studies help students understand how advertising and other mass media foster dissatisfaction by creating false "needs" and contribute to the depletion of resources by promoting consumption as a goal in itself.

Education should include traditional knowledge.

It is important for young people to realize that the scientific, social, and economic models of Western culture reflect a worldview that is not held by everyone. Across North America, many educators invite native Elders to share aboriginal perspectives on nature and ecology, exposing students to a worldview that recognizes the intrinsic value and interdependence of all living things.

Teachers should be facilitators and co-learners.

The teacher's role is to facilitate inquiry and provide opportunities for learning, not to provide the "answers." Teachers do not need to be experts to teach about the environment. The natural world is an open book for endless discovery by all. As co-learners alongside their students, teachers both model and share in the joy of learning.

While "green" teaching is appropriate for education at any level, environmental education is particularly well suited to meeting the developmental needs of students in the middle school years. Young people between 10 and 14 years of age are experiencing major intellectual, physical, and emotional changes. During this time, the neural circuitry of the brain is strengthened and refined, and students become capable of more abstract and complex thinking. They are reshaping relationships and developing their identities. They are beginning to think beyond the personal sphere to the wider world. The National Middle School Association, in their 2003 report "This We Believe: Successful Schools for Young Adolescents," identified several characteristics of education that successfully meets the special learning needs of this age group. They include opportunities for active leadership; partnerships between schools and communities; curriculum that is relevant, integrative, exploratory, and developmentally appropriate; and the use of multiple learning strategies and interdisciplinary team teaching. The hands-on, multi-sensory, multi-disciplinary nature of environmental education fits this bill exactly.

Whether you are just beginning or are an old hand at environmental education, we hope you will find many ideas in this book to help you to enrich your teaching. On the first page of each article, you will find a handy summary that indicates the subject connections, key concepts, skills to be developed, and, if appropriate, the time and materials needed to carry out activities. At the back of the book, a glossary defines terms that may be new to some readers, and a curriculum index serves as a quick guide to subject links. Matching national curriculum standards — both American and Canadian — for each article and activity can be found at the Green Teacher website <www.greenteacher.com>.

With more than 60 individual contributors, the book includes a diverse mix of approaches and styles and a wide spectrum of environmental topics. It does not, however, directly address two topics that are central in many environmental education programs: climate change and the greening of school grounds. In response to the anticipated impact of climate change in the coming decades, and to the current interest in creating outdoor classrooms, we have published two separate books, *Teaching About Climate Change* (2001) and *Greening School Grounds* (2001), each one a collection of the best articles and activities on those topics from *Green Teacher* magazine.

The environmental and social problems bedeviling humankind will not be solved by the same kind of education that helped create these problems. It is our hope that this book — and the companion books for the elementary and secondary school levels that we will produce in 2005 and 2006 — will inspire educators to take a leading role in helping the next generation to develop knowledge, skills, and values that will enable them to enjoy and share the Earth's bounty while living within its means.

Learning About Ecosystems

Wilderness Awareness School

Teaching with the Seasons

Nature's daily and seasonal drama provides the textbook for this Grade 7 natural science course based on phenology

by Larry Weber

Subject areas: science

Key concepts: phenology

Skills: observation, awareness, writing, note taking

Location: indoors and outdoors

Time: year-long

Those of us involved in environmental education in the early 21st century face a formidable challenge. Environmental degradation continues even as we try to tell the next generations how unwise this is. Preaching the wrongs of environmental sins does not work, nor do environmental scare tactics or blaming the students for the lifestyle enjoyed by their families. And merely describing environmental problems and possible solutions is a boring way to teach and to learn. Underlying the difficulty of finding ways to foster concern for the environment is the fact that the majority of the youth we are trying to reach have less interaction with and awareness of the natural world than any previous generation.

Over my 35 years in teaching, I have seen a dramatic decline in the amount of time students spend outdoors exploring on their own. Pick up an interesting insect, leaf, or seedpod from your schoolyard and chances are that most of your students — and many of your colleagues — will be completely unfamiliar with it. "I never saw that before!" they might exclaim. Ask your students to name ten animals and most will name domestic animals or animals from other parts of the world. Given how little many of our students see or know of the natural world right outside their window, how can we expect them to care about environmental problems? Is it reasonable to hope that they will work to protect what they do not see or know about? I believe that part of our task

Larry Weber

as environmental educators is to fill this gap in students' education and awareness, and to give students a positive healthy view of their planet, starting with the abundance and variety of nature nearby. For the past 20 years, I have been teaching a natural science course to seventh graders that seeks to do just that.

The curriculum I have developed is based on phenology, which is, as Webster explains, "the study of natural phenomena that recur periodically, such as migration or blossoming, and their relation to climate and changes in season." Students learn about local flora and fauna, track the weather, and closely monitor the progression of the seasons. Through the year, they develop the skill of observation, gain an awareness of seasonal changes in local flora and fauna, and become more attuned to the environment generally. They come to see that nature is not "somewhere else" but a dynamic presence in their daily lives.

This phenology-based natural science course has been very successful and has been adapted in its entirety or modified by colleagues for use with elementary, middle, and secondary classes. Both students and parents have shared with me how observant they have become as a result of this class. They report that family outings are now enriched with comments about local plants and animals, and most remark that they never knew so much was so close by.

We and our students are living in a world of shrinking natural habitat and diminishing opportunities for interacting with nature. The phenology-based approach to natural science can help us counter this trend. By putting students in touch with nature on a daily basis, by encouraging them to become familiar with local flora and fauna, and by teaching and reinforcing their skills of observation, we can help them build the foundation of a lifelong appreciation of the richness of the natural world around them. Only then can we expect young people to care enough about the environment to make the effort that will be needed to save it.

Design of the course

This phenology natural science course operates around three unique conditions:

- We do not use a textbook.
- We regularly use the outdoors as a classroom.
- We follow the seasons' phenology as the curriculum.

Instead of using my alloted money to buy textbooks, I buy classroom sets of reference books — mostly the Golden Zim guides — which students use to research the weekly topics of study, to verify observations, and to identify finds. Students bring two notebooks to class. One stays indoors, while the other becomes a field journal in which students take copious notes and make sketches on our outdoor forays.

We go outdoors on a weekly basis (see A Typical Week sidebar, below). With the exception of two short bus trips, we make use of the school campus and nearby property for the entire year. The purpose of the outdoor walks is to find examples or evidence of the phenology topic we are exploring that week. To add spontaneity and excitement, students are encouraged to look for other interesting things along the way. Students observe and make notes on the phenology topic of the walk and some of these unanticipated finds, as well as on weather and ground conditions

While always rewarding, going outdoors weekly is not without its difficulties. Students do not always come properly prepared for weather conditions, and their energy levels outdoors can be taxing to a teacher. For these reasons, it is important to maintain a semblance of classroom structure. I have found that taking students outdoors regularly from the beginning of the school year establishes a routine. As in the indoor classroom, we have a strict code of conduct for how we act toward one another and how we treat organisms that we find. (See Tips and Rules sidebar.) Knowing what to expect from me and what is expected of them helps us to build a pleasant working rapport. Most students find that they enjoy the walks even when the weather is not ideal.

Class procedure

Regular class procedure revolves around five main components.

Weather: Temperatures and precipitation are recorded regularly; each day we plot the high and low temperatures. Being near Lake Superior, we often find huge variations in temperature within very short distances. As a result, we obtain the official weather from a local weather station but we also check our instruments. We compare monthly weather statistics to the norm, and measure and mark snowfall totals on a "snowboard" on the wall. For students who are unaccustomed to noticing or remembering the weather from one day to the next, this constant weather watch fosters an awareness of the newness of each day, of recurring patterns, and of links between weather and wildlife. Recalling the weather during the past week, students learn to predict what they are likely to find on our outdoor walks.

Months: At the beginning of each month, we list and discuss what will happen in nature during the coming month, including the timing of the full moon and other astronomical events. We also talk about the names of the months and try to come up with more meaningful ones that reflect events in the natural world, such as The Dark Month (December) or The Crusty Snow Month (March).

Fall and spring phenology charts: Each year, the class plots the dates of the last sighting in fall and the first appearance in the spring of common flora and fauna. Similar data are kept for such weather events as freezing, thawing, or snowfall (see example, page 5). The phenology charts are extremely valuable in documenting the change of seasons and the consistency of events from one year to the next. Kept over a long period time, such charts can even aid in detecting such long-term trends as global warming.

Students' discoveries: Students are regularly given time to share their own findings, either sights (critter news) or specimens caught and brought to class for observation. All collected organisms are returned to where they were found within a day of being caught.

Phenology topics: I have developed a sequence of 30 phenology topics (below), each of which is explored for a week or two, not more, so that the current topic is always pertinent to what is happening in nature at that time of year.

A Typical Week

These suggestions can be modified for longer or shorter periods.

Monday: discussion of present phenology, critter news, sharing of students' discoveries, weather news, introduction to the week's phenology topic

Tuesday: discussion of the week's topic, using classroom references and other sources as well as slides

Wednesday: outdoor walk to look for examples or evidence of the phenological topic, take notes, and make sketches

Thursday: go over findings from the walk and continue discussion of the topic

Friday: students hand in a written report summarizing the walk and findings, and then take a quiz on the topic, often done in cooperative groups

Tips and Rules

TAKING STUDENTS OUTDOORS

- Use the area near your school, regardless of its condition.
- Take students outdoors from the start of the school year, if possible in the first week.
- Don't wait for sunny weather, as clear warm days may not be suitable; cold cloudy days are great.
- Have a second walk planned in case the first has to be changed.
- Keep each walk structured and remind students that this is still school.
- Prepare students by talking about the walk the day before. After the walk, review all the findings and, if appropriate, have students write a report with labeled drawings.
- Explore and learn along with the students, and don't be concerned that you do not know everything.
- Catch and/or bring back finds so that everyone can have a closer look, but be sure to release captured creatures.
- Don't get hung up on names. Let students name discoveries by what they look like. Interested students can find names later.
- Don't overdo walks: students can get burned out by going out too often or going too far.

RULES FOR STUDENTS OUTDOORS

- Be prepared with notebooks and appropriate clothes.
- No running (an especially valuable rule in winter).
- Stay together: line up or form a circle around a find.
- No talking when a teacher or another student is addressing the class.
- No hurting of creatures: creatures that are caught are to be looked at and then released.
- In winter, snow stays where it falls: no throwing or kicking snow.
- In spring, anyone who picks a green plant should be prepared to eat it.

Larry Weber

Phenology topics by month

The timing of the 30 phenology topics described below may vary in some years, but this is a desirable sequence, as it reflects natural patterns through the school year. Teachers attempting to use phenology-based methods will need to become aware of their own local weather and phenology. This may be challenging, but it is a terrific learning experience and offers the joy of learning along with the students.

September: The Cooling Month

Mushrooms and other fungi: Mushrooms and other fungi abound nearly every fall, often on the school lawn. They are easy to find and lead to good discussions and activities.

Fall migration — raptors: Hawks and other raptors are the focus of bird migration in the fall. We visit Hawk Ridge, about 15 minutes away by bus.

Fall wildflowers: We go into meadows filled with asters, goldenrods, sunflowers, clovers, and many other wildflowers to learn about these often overlooked plants.

Deciduous trees: We learn trees by their leaves, fruits, and berries. In our region, deciduous trees spend more of the year without leaves than with them.

October: The Leaf Drop Month

Insects: On warm mild days, insects are very common in meadows. We catch, observe, and release many. We also find galls and leaf miners.

Spiders: Mild autumn days are excellent for catching, observing, and releasing spiders in meadows, lawns, and ballooning in the bare trees.

Ponds in fall: A visit to a nearby pond before freeze-up reveals the diversity of aquatic life. Many organisms are caught, observed, and released.

Small mammals: With leaves dropping, we look for signs of small mammals getting ready for winter. We live-trap, observe, and release a few.

November: The Cloudy Freeze-up Month

Non-flowering plants: With leaves off trees, we learn about small plants such as mosses, club mosses, and ferns, which are easy to see before they are covered by snow.

Animal signs: November is a good time to see (even in the snow) nests, gnawings, caches, droppings, and other indications of animal presence.

Animal tracks: In early light wet snows, many mammals are active and leave their stories for students to observe in lawns, meadows, and woods.

December: The Dark Month

Large mammals: Having been introduced to animal signs and tracks last month, students are on the lookout for large mammals. We rarely see many large mammals but we recognize their signs and tracks.

Larry Weber

"You taught me new and wonderful things!"
"It's cool to know what you're looking at when you're outside." — Students

Winter birds: With the advent of cold weather and snow, we observe birds at feeders as well as other birds that winter with us. We make and maintain a bird feeder at our school.

Natural lights: In the darkest week, in anticipation of the solstice, we look more closely at natural light and discuss colors of sky, ice, and snow.

January: The Cold Month

Wildlife in winter weather: In the cold and snow, we take time to look at how wildlife is able to cope with these conditions and survive.

Fall and Spring Phenology Charts

Fall Weather
First frost
First 20°F, 10°F, and 0°F
First Below 0°F
Last 70°F, 60°F, and 50°F
Ground frozen
Ice on puddles
Ice covering nearby pond
Ice covering nearby lake
First snow flurries
First snow of 2"
First snow of 4" or more
Last rain
Last thundershower

Fall Plants
Peak of mushroom growth
Peak of deciduous tree color
Peak of tamarack tree color
Leaves off trees
Last flower still in bloom

Fall Animals
First migrating geese
Peak of hawk migration
Peak of bald eagle migration
First snowy owl
First redpoll
Last snake
Last frog
Last butterfly
Last grasshopper
Last mosquito
Last chipmunk

Spring Weather
First 50°F, 60°F, and 70°F
Last below 0°F, 10°F, and 20°F
Last freezing
Last snowfall
Last snow to melt
First spring rain
First spring thunder shower
Ice off nearby pond
Ice off nearby creek
Ice off nearby lake

Spring Plants
Green grass
First lawn-mowing
Leaves on deciduous trees
Sap flowing
Pussy willow open
Silver maple in bloom
Dandelion in bloom
Crocus in bloom
Bloodroot in bloom
Marsh marigold in bloom
Hepatica in bloom

Gail Littlejohn

Spring Animals
First spring robin
First red-winged blackbird
First tree swallow
First killdeer
First great blue heron
First migrating geese
First grouse drumming
First bird's nest
First spring chipmunk
First woodchuck
First bear
First bat
First baby rabbit
First snake
First turtle
First frog
First frog calling
First frog eggs
First spring mosquito
First butterfly
First monarch
First dragonfly
First bumble bee
First jumping spider on wall
First orb web
First wood tick
First earthworm
Smelt running

Ponds in winter: With augurs, we drill through the ice covering the pond and sample the water to examine it for pond creatures. This is a good time to introduce the use of microscopes.

Conifers: Staying green all winter, evergreens are now easy to see. We learn different kinds of conifers and how they use their leaves and shape to deal with winter conditions.

February: The Dry Month

Humans in winter weather: With a little planning and understanding of winter conditions (i.e., wind chill, hypothermia, frostbite), students learn how to be outside safely.

Winter wildflowers: We learn about different perennial plants ("weeds") that persist throughout winter, often looking dead and stick-like, and how they differ in their methods of seed dispersal.

Deciduous trees in winter: Trees are bare but can be identified by their shape, color, bark, and various twig conditions. We make and use a simple dichotomous key.

March: The Crusty Snow Month

Sap flow: Quietly, the trees respond to the warmer and longer days. We tap sugar maple trees for sap and make enough syrup for everyone to taste.

Fish and streams in early spring: Streams break up before ponds and lakes, and several fish species are quick to spawn. We go to a small stream nearby to look for fish and other fauna.

Early spring events: As this is the time of micro-environments, we wander around the school searching for the first dandelions, earthworms, flies, and jumping spiders.

Tree flowers: We observe trees that flower early, responding to the longer days; pussy willow and aspen start the catkin season and several others follow.

April: The Thawing Month

Spring migration — waterbirds: Rivers now hold many waterbirds as early migrants. We learn common waterfowl and visit the St. Louis River to see them, a 20-minute bus trip away.

Frogs and other amphibians: With the thaw, ponds are the location of calling and mating frogs. We listen and look for common species, but do not collect eggs.

Ponds in spring: The water is still cold, but the spring pond is filled with life. We observe how eggs and larvae of many organisms are different from the adults we saw on earlier visits.

May: The Greening Month

Spring wildflowers: Since the trees are still leafless, sunlight penetrates to the forest floor. We seek out and learn many of the ephemeral wildflowers.

Spring and summer songbirds: Spring migration is at its peak and warmer weather brings myriad insects. We listen and look for songbirds, many of which nest here, as they return.

Less-loved critters: As the school year comes to an end, we go outside more often. We are more likely to come in contact with and learn about wood ticks, mosquitoes, and black flies.

Larry Weber has taught middle school natural science for more than three decades at The Marshall School in Duluth, Minnesota. He is the author of Backyard Almanac: A 365-day guide to the plants and critters that live in your backyard, *and two regional guide books,* Butterflies of the North Woods *and* Spiders of the North Woods.

RESOURCES

Bates, John. *A Northwoods Companion: Spring and Summer.* Manitowish River Press, 1997.

Bates, John. *A Northwoods Companion: Fall and Winter.* Manitowish River Press, 1997.

Borland, Hal. *Book of Days.* Alfred A. Knopf, 1976.

Borland, Hal. *Sundial of the Seasons.* J.B. Lippincott Co., 1964.

Borland, Hal. *Twelve Moons of the Year.* Alfred A. Knopf, 1979.

Gilbert, Jim. *Jim Gilbert's Nature Notebook.* Minnesota Landscape Arboretum, 1979.

Gilbert, Jim. *Through Minnesota's Seasons with Jim Gilbert.* Minnesota Landscape Arboretum, 1987.

Serrao, John. *Nature's Events.* Stackpole Books, 1992.

Teale, Edwin Way. *Circle of the Seasons.* Dodd, Mead, and Co., 1987.

Teale, Edwin Way. *A Walk Through the Year.* Dodd, Mead, and Co., 1987.

Weber, Larry A. *Backyard Almanac: A 365-day guide to the plants and critters that live in your backyard.* Pfeiffer-Hamilton, 1996.

Wilber, Jerry. *Wit and Wisdom of the Great Outdoors.* Pfeiffer-Hamilton, 1993.

The Biosphere Challenge: Developing Ecological Literacy

An adaptation of various professional attempts to sustain life in sealed environments, the biosphere activity challenges students to rethink their most fundamental ideas about nature

by Jimmy Karlan

Subject areas: science, mathematics, language arts

Key concepts: biodiversity, adaptation, sustainability, ecology, limiting factors

Skills: problem solving, observation, critical and creative thinking, research

Location: indoors and outdoors

Time: 6 one-hour classes, then short observations over many months

Create whatever you think has to happen so that multiple generations of spiders can live inside a sealed 20-liter (5-gallon) container.

These seemingly simple instructions present a challenge that has captivated hundreds of students. Called the biosphere activity, the exercise is an inquiry-based, hands-on, minds-on, problem-solving, student-centered curriculum that can help students of any age deepen their understanding of ecology. It is open-ended and messy. It can last as long as one class or one semester. Traditional tests will not assess what students learn from it. Rather, assessment is seamless with the rest of the instruction; it is authentic and action-oriented, and continuously reveals students' deepening ecological understanding. The exercise is not about arriving at predictable outcomes, or about having all students achieve the same understanding at the same time and in the same way. Rather, it is about challenging students to reflect on, to test, and to rethink their most fundamental ideas about nature.

The biosphere activity began in 1993 as one of two research instruments I developed to help study children's ecological concepts and theories. Working with 24 students in Grades 5 and 8 from urban and rural communities in New England, I began with a sketching activity that asked students to represent what they thought would have to happen to sustain multiple generations of foxes and a diversity of wildlife. This was followed by the biosphere activity, which challenged them to create an environment that would sustain multiple generations of spiders. The activity is an adaptation of various professional attempts to sustain life in sealed environments. For example, Carl Folsum sustained generations of algae for 20 years in a sealed flask.[1] The Biosphere II folks tried to keep eight humans alive for two years in an enormous greenhouse. And NASA now sells a desktop globe that they claim can sustain a few shrimp for more than eight years. Like the biosphere activity, all such models of sustainability require their developers to demonstrate their fundamental ecological concepts and theories.

During the last five years, I have transformed the sketching and biosphere activities into a powerful ecology curriculum that I use with environmental studies students at Antioch New England Graduate School who are becoming environmental educators and science teachers. The design of the biosphere activity as a curriculum is rooted in a constructivist instructional model in which teachers elicit students' current understanding, facilitate experiences that challenge students' initial conceptions, and support students in accommodating to new ideas.[2] Here's how I have designed the biosphere activity within this framework.

J.W. Karlan

Eliciting students' current conceptions

Ausubel states, "The most important single factor influencing learning is what the learner already knows; ascertain this and teach him accordingly."[3] The goal of the first phase of the biosphere activity is to deploy an "exposing event," an experience that elicits students' authentic understanding of a phenomenon. This is tricky. One's first tendency might be to ask students outright, How do you sustain non-human life? If you do, you will probably hear from fewer than ten percent of your students. And you will learn mostly about your students' ability to recite a definition of the word "sustain" rather than their conceptual understanding of it.

To deploy my initial exposing event I meet my students at a nearby public forest. I greet them with shovels, trowels, 20-liter (5-gallon) terrariums, plastic containers of different sizes, and the following challenge:

> Work with someone to create whatever you think has to happen in order to sustain multiple generations of spiders in a completely sealed container. You will seal your container in one hour. You will be able to observe what you've created throughout the semester.

Many students stand motionless for a few minutes, wondering what to do. Some assert that it can't be done; others murmur they don't know how to begin. Some do a construction blitz and insist they're done after ten minutes. By the hour's end, everyone is still collecting and arranging stuff in their container and sharing with their partners what they think will sustain life in their closed system.

While students are creating their biospheres, I wander around asking them what they are doing and why. I try to help them feel comfortable bringing forth all their ideas. I keep them company while they contemplate. I follow them through fields and brush, along a wood's edge, across streams, and down wooded ravines. I inquire into the reasons for their selections and intermittently ask them to clarify, elaborate, and respond to counter-suggestions. I let them know it's okay to move slowly, to sit quietly, to think aloud, and to modify their responses. They understand that their ideas can't be wrong since my only interest is in understanding what they think. At the end of this first phase of the activity, the students seal their containers, figure out where to place the biospheres in the classroom, and fill my ear with their initial story of sustainability.

This initial exercise allows students to express, both verbally and materially, their thinking about big questions: Is nature an object or process? linear or cyclical? monochrome or diverse? in balance or disequilibrium? cooperative or competitive? dynamic or steady? open or closed? inclusive or exclusive of humans? male or female? Ultimately, their story — manifested in their biosphere constructions and accompanying explanations — reflects their conceptual "thumbprint": their most fundamental ideas about nature.

Conceptions revealed by students

When I used this activity with students in Grades 5 and 8, I learned that many think nature is balanced, stable,

self-regulating, and purposeful. As compared with their Grade 8 counterparts, the students in Grade 5 tended to view nature as a series of discrete linear events that do not stray too far spatially or temporally from the "original" event. The children from both grades seemed to think of life as an object rather than as a process. Their notions of water, air, and food cycles were precarious at best. In their sketches, the children represented a greater diversity of vertebrates than invertebrates, more animals than plants, and few, if any, microorganisms, detrivores, and saprophytes. From the children's perspective, the primary relationship and activity in nature centers around eating and avoiding being eaten. The children almost always described wildlife in particular and nature in general with male pronouns — so much so that I began to wonder if they attributed male characteristics to nature.

In addition to gaining some insight into how these children think about nature, I learned a very unexpected lesson about teaching. I was surprised initially by a comment many of my research participants made at the close of the biosphere activity. They thanked me for teaching them. "But how?" I asked. "All I did was ask you what you think." I had had no interest in teaching them anything; I hadn't realized that elicitation and learning are flip sides of the same coin. The very act of constructing and articulating one's thinking about something compelling alongside someone who nonjudgmentally asks for elaboration, clarification, and reflection is a learning-full process. Listening rather than telling may be one of the most neglected qualities of good teaching.

Challenging students' initial conceptions

It is not enough just to elicit our students' ecological conceptions. We must also craft compelling experiences that effectively challenge ideas that conflict with current ecological understanding. I nourish such "discrepant events" by giving students ample opportunity to share their biospheres and their reasoning for what they've

A sketching activity elicits students' initial ecological concepts. This Grade 5 student's representation of "what has to happen to sustain multiple generations of foxes and a diversity of wildlife" depicts an ecosystem populated mostly by vertebrates engaged in eating and avoiding being eaten.

created, by giving them at least three opportunities to open up and redesign their biospheres, and by inviting them to observe an ecologist creating a biosphere.

When students share routine observations of their biospheres and discuss redesigning them during their three "windows of intervention," they shake up their own and each other's initial ideas. On these occasions, I search for opportunities to create cognitive dissonance. When I hear students paraphrase the original directions into "What does a spider need to survive?", I ask them if there's anything fundamentally different between their paraphrase and the initial wording of the challenge — "Create what you think has to happen so that multiple generations of spiders can live." I might ask them, Does it matter if people think of nature as objects or processes? When I observe a team of middle school students adding a saturated sponge as the only water supply for multiple generations of spiders, I ask them to share their plans with another group that is trying to figure out how to sustain their water supply in a different way. When I see students cutting the roots off of plants in order to fit them in their container, I ask them to compare what they're doing to another group that is transplanting roots fully intact. I take a similar approach when I see students creating food chains rather than food cycles, and omitting microorganisms, decomposers, and detrivores.

After the biospheres are sealed, I encourage students to analyze the biodiversity represented in each other's work. When examining the diversity of plants and animals we look for patterns:

- Are plants or animals more highly represented?
- What types of species seem most popular?
- What is the relative presence and importance of microorganisms?
- What do our biospheres reveal about our ideas about nature?

When I notice students describing animals primarily in terms of their efforts to eat and not be eaten, I challenge them to reflect on this and to generate other ways to explain interactions among organisms. When I hear students referring to the wildlife in their biospheres with male pronouns, I create an "exposing event" by posing

J.W. Karlan

Biospheres created by (top to bottom): graduate student, Grade 8 student, Grade 5 student. Students have opportunities to redesign their biospheres based on their evolving understanding of ecological relationships.

questions such as: I'm noticing that most of you are using male pronouns to describe the creatures in your biosphere. Why do you think that's so? How might you be attributing male or female characteristics to nature? Does it really matter?

Powerful discrepant events also occur when students have the opportunity to observe a professional ecologist creating a biosphere. My graduate students watch Tom Wessels, an ecologist at Antioch New England Graduate School, create his own biosphere, and then modify their biospheres based on what they learn. As a result of listening to Tom's musings while collecting and arranging materials, the students reconsider their designs and wonder how they can create a homeo-dynamic system — a system that does not experience wide fluctuations in the physical environment.

They reconsider their first inclination to saturate their soil and exchange some of their plants with species that have lower water demands. In order to prevent the wide fluctuations in carbon dioxide and oxygen levels that would result if their plants became dormant, they add perennial plants (e.g., mosses, lichens, and herbaceous plants that keep their leaves all year, such as evening primrose, yarrow, and plantain). In order to avoid too much carbon dioxide, they remove some of their soil to reduce the population of respiring microorganisms. They consider the second law of thermodynamics and contemplate how to minimize the rate at which energy in their biosphere becomes unavailable. And they return to their biospheres aware of an ecologist's effort to create a complex network of cyclical interrelationships and connections that are in constant transformation.[4]

Other discrepant events always emerge around the morality of the biosphere activity. Every class debates the ethics of an exercise that condones the confinement of organisms for the sake of education.[5] Even seemingly homogeneous groups like my science certification and environmental studies graduate students present a diversity of perspectives on this issue. This multiplicity blooms dissonance, which in turn increases students' moral breadth. Since students can return everything they collect at any time, they are faced continually with determining their own evolving

Guidelines and Tips for the Biosphere Activity

This is best undertaken as the first activity of a unit in ecology, environmental science, or life science in the fall or spring.

Time: 6 one-hour classes; then short observations over many months

Materials: (per group, 2 students per group recommended): 1–2 hand trowels, 1 shovel , 2–4 plastic food containers (250 ml to 1 liter / 8 to 32 ounces), 20-liter (5-gallon) clear plastic container with lid (available from most biology education supply companies), 1 sheet of plastic wrap big enough to seal top of container, duct tape, water (untreated and treated)

Creating the biospheres

1. Gather students to the area where they will collect materials for their biospheres, such as a school nature area or nearby woodland. Inform students: "Your challenge is to create what has to happen so that multiple generations of spiders can live in this container after it is completely sealed. You will also need to find the spiders you want to sustain."

   Note: Since the objective is to elicit students' current ecological concepts, let them begin the exercise without discussing as a group any of their ideas about sustaining life.

2. When students have finished creating their biospheres (allow about one hour), stretch a single piece of thin clear plastic wrap over the top of the containers. Seal the edges of the plastic on the outside of the container with duct tape.

Observing: The frequency of observations can vary, depending on your needs. Ask students what they think everyone should observe for. Invite students to compare their biospheres every three to seven classes.

Unsealing and modifying: At a minimum, allow students three opportunities to unseal their containers and apply

what they have learned about what has to happen to sustain life. This is best done soon after reading articles on Biosphere II, watching a film, and/or observing a guest ecologist create a biosphere. You can either return to the original collection area or ask students to bring in whatever they might need to modify their biospheres on a designated day.

Welcome students to return the contents of their biospheres back to where they were collected at any time they do not feel comfortable with continuing their biospheres. Ask students what they think they should do when their biosphere study ends.

Student tendencies and risks: Both younger and older students tend to provide their biospheres with too much water, too many plants that go dormant, too much soil, too much biodiversity, and too much sun.

- A dormant plant community risks wide fluctuations in carbon dioxide and oxygen levels.
- Too much water will lead to increased fungal activity.
- Too much soil contains too many respiring microorganisms that can produce too much carbon dioxide.
- Too much biodiversity can lead to unsustainable feedback loops.
- Too much sun can result in wide temperature fluctuations.

Students may also try to sustain orb spiders, but these spiders depend on flying insects that are difficult at best to sustain in a closed 20-liter container.

Optimal designs: An optimal biosphere experiences only minor fluctuations in the physical environment (i.e., it is a homeo-dynamic system). An unstable environment can cause a closed system to collapse. An optimal biosphere has relatively stable air, water, nitrogen, and nutrient cycles.

- The spiders should be webless ones (e.g., wolf or jumping spiders).
- The plants should be perennials, keep their leaves all year, and require little water (e.g., mosses, lichens, herbaceous plants such as evening primrose, yarrow, and plantain).
- The biodiversity should be minimal.
- There should be refuges for predators and prey.
- The biosphere should be placed in a semi-shaded area with a relatively constant room temperature of 20ºC (70ºF).

Can it be done? The value of this exercise is in the process of learning ecological principles, and not in the successful creation of a working biosphere. However, students may be interested to know that, according to one ecologist, the container would need to be the size of the Superdome to successfully sustain multiple generations of spiders over a period of a few years. A closed system will ultimately be destroyed by entropy, the second law of thermodynamics.

moral responsibility. Students who oppose the exercise on moral grounds are invited to collaborate with me in designing alternative ways to meet my curriculum goals without compromising their moral position. One conscientious objector became the class journalist. He observed and interviewed his peers as they were constructing and later modifying their biospheres, and then published a weekly newsletter summarizing both his own and his colleagues' reflections on the pedagogical value of the exercise and their evolving ecological understanding.

Supporting conceptual accommodation

The resolution of discrepancies is considered a learner's fundamental quest.[6] Creating discrepant events alone is not enough, especially in light of our tendency to make things fit our preexisting ideas. The third phase of this constructivist learning model is about supporting cognitive accommodation. Accommodating to new ideas requires students to change their conceptual framework in order to resolve the discrepancy between their original ideas and reasonable and plausible conflicting ideas. As their biospheres respond to interventions and students are faced with conflicting evidence from their peers, guest ecologists, films, and readings, they collect new data, reconsider their original thinking, and develop new understandings of ecology. I have designed a variety of ways to help students accommodate to three key ecological concepts that I think they need help understanding: processing, cycling, and biodiversity.

Accommodating processing

How can we help facilitate a process view? Whorf proposes that "Every language binds the thoughts of its speakers by the involuntary patterns of its grammar …. Languages differ not only in how they build their sentences but in how they break down nature into the elements to put into those statements."[7] English speakers, for instance, connect their verbs with a subject. Consequently, says Whorf, "English and similar tongues lead us to think of the universe as a collection of detached objects of different sizes …. Thus as goes our segmentation of the face of nature, so goes our physics of the cosmos." The Hopi, on the other hand, use more participles and gerunds. This is a reflection of a Hopi cosmology that focuses on relations, occasions, and events rather than the attributes of various substances. English speakers say, "A light flashed," setting up an actor, "light," to perform what we call an action, that is, "flashing." Yet the flashing and the light are one and the same! The Hopi language reports the flash with a simple verb *ri-pi* "flash (occurred)."[8]

Creating a process-based language requires tremendous diligence. I was reminded of this recently while doing house projects. When friends asked what I was up to, I found myself telling them, "I fixed up my mudroom and installed some doors." I reduced my efforts to simple objects. When I was more process-minded, I explained, "I created a process by which my dog and cats can choose where they want to be. That's why I installed a pet door in my mudroom." Similarly, converting a sliding screen door into a hinged door was not about creating a screen door; rather, I created a process by which my young children can come and go as they please without hearing me nag them to close the door and not rip the screen.

Ecology curriculum should sharpen our students' "process vision" — the ability to look at any seemingly discrete object and see a complex array of worldwide processes that play multiple roles in sustaining diverse communities of life. A pencil is no longer a pencil, but a synthesis of cellulose, lignin, rubber, metal, graphite — materials that are captured for the moment but undergoing constant transformation. Not long ago they were conceived by many processes that were not "pencil" and now they are already on their way to becoming something other than "pencil." Each of these resources is a story of transformations of matter and energy and how people interact with their environment.

> *Ecology curriculum should sharpen our students' "process vision" — the ability to look at any seemingly discrete object and see a complex array of worldwide processes.*

It's hard to break the habit of objectifying wildlife. I've slipped repeatedly with my children into the old and familiar, "That's an oak tree. There's an ant. It's a robin." My children will think differently if instead of naming nature I say, "I wonder what's going on. I wonder where that bird is coming from and going to and why. I wonder how it's helping to sustain life." Ecology curriculum should teach about life as a verb as well as a noun.[9] It should celebrate the fox as an individual object — a four-legged, reddish, bushy-tailed, dog-like predator that lives in the woods — while also maintaining that fox is both manifestation and raison d'être of innumerable processes — air, water, and inorganic and organic cycling — whose interactions with one another are the meaning of life.

Accommodating cycling

Chiras in *Lessons from Nature* states adamantly that "we need a co-operator's manual that teaches us how to fit into the cycles of nature's economy."[10] Cycling is one of the essential "lessons we can learn from nature [that] comprise the biological principles of sustainability."[11] Overemphasis on chalkboard representations of the water and air cycles does little to relieve the uncertainty expressed by 12-year-old Shannon, who said:

The trees have something to do with oxygen … I think. I've heard from people that if we didn't have trees we wouldn't have air. And I don't know the reason for that. I don't know if I believe it, because, I mean, I don't know enough about it to believe it or not believe it.

We need to challenge our students to create experiments and inquiries into questions about cycling: What happens to dead ants, spiders, houseplants, trees? What conditions facilitate and inhibit decomposition? What kind of class or schoolwide composting system can be used to nourish a class garden? What are the pathways — cradle to grave — of everyday objects, and how are their manufacture, use, and disposal part of a cycling system? We need to take them to landfills and ask, What in nature, if anything, resembles a landfill? We need to design curriculum that allows our students to witness cycling firsthand and come to know deeply how "a forest can eat itself and live forever."[12]

Accommodating biodiversity

I am concerned about the general absence of microorganisms and invertebrates in my research participants' biospheres. Without the doings of microorganisms and invertebrates, all biological activity would cease. Kellert elaborates:

> As invertebrates represent more than 90 per cent of the planet's biological diversity, they perform most of the critical ecological functions of pollination, seed dispersal, parasitism, predation, decomposition, energy and nutrient transfer, the provision of edible materials for adjacent tropic levels, and the maintenance of biotic communities through mutualism, host-restricted food webs, and a variety of other functions and processes.[13]

Curricula should expose students repeatedly to this magnificently diverse microworld living on and in their bodies, around their classrooms, detectable in almost every drop of water and soil. Observing and experimenting with microorganisms will broaden students' sense of biodiversity, and help them conceive of nature as something more than just who eats whom. Microorganisms are critical regulators of the Earth's atmosphere, hydrosphere, and lithosphere.[14] Challenging students to sterilize the soil in one of two otherwise similar biospheres can help reveal this invisible force.

We need stories for young children that reveal this parallel world. We need parents looking at decomposing leaves with their preschoolers and saying aloud, "It is hard to believe that there are more creatures living on this leaf than there are kids in your classroom." And we need in our elementary and middle school classrooms a tool that has been neglected since the computer's monopoly on technology: it's called a microscope. Students need to understand how their micro-neighbors are playing roles in sustaining life, and how human activities affect microorganisms.

Meaningful curriculum

The biosphere activity is a powerful way to deepen students' understanding of such big questions as, What has to happen to sustain non-human life? Creating meaningful ecology curriculum is particularly challenging in light of our culturally inherited nearsightedness. We are far from being "process fluent" and light-years away from being able to travel temporal and spatial scales with ease. Education devoted to ecological literacy may be the best fight against global warming, habitat destruction, and the loss of biodiversity. But ecology education that neglects children's current ecological ideas and isn't informed by an effective model for conceptual change may also be a significant part of the problem.

Jimmy Karlan is the director of the Teacher Certification Program in General Science and Biology and the academic director of the masters' programs in the Environmental Studies Department at Antioch New England Graduate School in Keene, New Hampshire.

Notes

1 K. Kelly, "Biosphere II: An Autonomous World, Ready to Go." *Whole Earth Review*, vol. 67, 1990, pp. 2–13.

2 J. Nussbaum and S. Novick. "Alternative Frameworks, Conceptual Conflict and Accommodation: Toward a Principled Teaching Strategy." *Instructional Science*, vol. 2, 1982, pp. 183–200.

3 D.P. Ausubel. *Educational Psychology: A Cognitive View*. Holt, Rinehart and Winston, 1968.

4 J.B. Callicott. "The Metaphysical Implications of Ecology," *Zygon Journal of Religion and Science*, vol. 8, no. 4, 1986, pp. 301–16; G.H. Lewes. *The Story of Goethe's Life*. J.R. Osgood, 1873; D. Oliver. "Introduction and Overview." *Process Studies*, vol. 17, no. 4, 1988, pp. 209–14; D. Oliver and K.W. Gershman. *Education, Modernity, and Fractured Meaning: Toward a process theory of teaching and learning*. State University of New York Press, 1989; and P. Shepard. "A Theory of the Value of Hunting." Presentation to 24th North American Wildlife Conference, 1957, pp. 505–506.

5 J.W. Karlan. "Aquariums in the Classroom — Sanctuaries of Diversity or Walls of Oppression?" *Connect*, May/June 1992, Teachers' Laboratory, Inc.

6 J.G. Brooks and M.G. Brooks. *In Search of Understanding: The Case for Constructivist Classrooms*. Association for Supervision and Curriculum Development (ASCD), 1993.

7 Whorf, quoted in Oliver and Gershman, 1989.

8 Oliver and Gershman, 1989.

9 L. Margulis and D. Sagan. *What is Life?* Simon and Schuster, 1995.

10 D.D. Chiras. *Lessons From Nature: Learning to Live Sustainably on the Earth*. Island Press, 1992.

11 Chiras, 1992.

12 B. Kingsolver. *The Poisonwood Bible*. Harper Flamingo, 1998.

13 S.R. Kellert. "Biological Basis for Human Values of Nature." in S.R. Kellert and E.O. Wilson, eds. *The Biophilia Hypothesis*. Island Press, 1993, p. 47.

14 Margulis and Sagan, 1995.

SUGGESTED READINGS ON BIOSPHERE II

Kelly, K. "Biosphere II: An autonomous World, Ready to Go." *Whole Earth Review*, 67, 1990, pp. 2–13.

Kelly, K. "Biosphere II at One." *Whole Earth Review*, 77, 1992, pp. 90–105.

Warshall, P. "Lessons From Biosphere II." *Whole Earth Review*, 89, 1996, pp. 22–27.

Surveying Biodiversity

*A framework for getting started on environmental monitoring
through plant and animal surveys*

by Roxine dePencier Hameister

Subject areas: computer technology, mathematics,
language arts, social studies, science

Key concepts: environmental monitoring

Skills: mapmaking, maintaining field notebooks,
manipulating data, identifying plants and animals

Location: indoors and outdoors

Time: several days over the course of a year

Materials:

For plant surveys: maps, field guides, field logs or
journals, pencils, graph paper, compass, plastic tubing or
hoops, wooden stakes, string, measuring tape or rope,
scissors, small rulers, plastic bags and damp paper
towels, labels (for collecting samples), camera, GIS
software (optional)

For bird surveys: binoculars, field guides, birdsong
tapes, maps, bird feeder (optional)

Young people are sometimes the first to notice
new and different things in the local environment. In one such discovery in the fall of 1997,
a group of Grade 4 and 5 students in an after-school
environmental club found a tiny and rare tailed frog at
a small stream near their school in West Vancouver,
British Columbia. When they learned that the stream
ran through an area scheduled for development, the
students set to work
researching the frog
and its habitat. And
when they discovered
that the tailed frog is
a vulnerable species
(*Ascaphus truei*), they
contacted the media,
made a presentation
to Vancouver's city
council, and succeed-
ed in having the
stream site protected.
In another example,
the discovery of
deformed frogs by
Minnesota school-
children in 1995 set
off alarms about the health of wetland ecosystems and
raised awareness of the need for environmental monitoring and protection in North America. In both of these
instances, students made observations that no one else
had made, recognized that change was needed, and
helped to make it happen. What better lessons to learn
at an early age?

Engaging students in authentic scientific activity
fosters a sense of empowerment and develops the ability
to participate in informed decision-making. Young
people often worry about the future, especially when
they are told that they will need to work hard to
improve the health of the environment. But rarely do
we give them the tools to determine what needs to be
done. Environmental monitoring projects put these tools
in students' hands. Knowing that they are assessing the
health of local ecosystems, they quickly come to see
their project as a way of obtaining information that can
be used to help make the world a greener place. As they
become knowledgeable about the plants and animals
they are studying, they also develop attachments to
them and become more vocal about protecting these
organisms and their habitats.

Whether your class is taking part in a national or a
local monitoring project, the frameworks for biodiversity surveys presented here can help you get started. The
first step in protecting an environment is to survey what
is in that environment. Carried on year after year, surveys generate data that can be used to analyze how the
composition and
diversity of local
ecosystems may be
affected by changes in
that environment.
Biodiversity surveys
offer a maximum of
field time and as
much curriculum
integration as you will
achieve with any class
project. In collecting
and analyzing data,
and communicating
their results to
others, students
find real-world
applications for their

Roxine dePencier Hameister

developing skills in communication technology, math, language arts, geography, and science. Such projects are not only good science, but good pedagogy, too.

Plant surveys

You can begin your own ongoing plant-monitoring project by establishing sampling plots, or quadrats, on one or more sites that represent typical ecosystems in your region. Since the project should extend over several months or years, it is very important to record the exact location of study sites — if possible, on a topographic map of the area. Be sure to ask permission of any landowners before you and your class visit. It is also helpful to go over the area to determine which plants are likely to be found and to review them with the class before going into the field. Ensure that students have some basic knowledge of botanical terms associated with flower parts, leaf shapes, and growth patterns, as well as familiarity with plant field guides. Determine before-hand if the students are going to use the common or scientific names of plants; most field guides give both, but if you are going to produce reports or compare your data with those from schools in other locations, it is advisable to use scientific names.

In all projects, it is very important to keep accurate and complete records of observations. The skill of accurately recording what is observed does not come easily. You might practice in the classroom by having students survey the contents of their desks and then generate group statistics. Make a master "desk list" to record the variety of objects in the desks, find the average length of pencils, determine the dominant brand of notebook, or calculate the percentage of space occupied by books. Such activities will familiarize students with the processes of gathering, recording, and analyzing data.

When in the field, have each student or pair of students record data in a field log or journal. Recording should be done in pencil on water-protected paper. There are some very nice field books available, but a student-made cardboard clipboard or notebook covered with a piece of plastic will do to keep the costs down. These field logs or journals become the source of all the raw data — all students' recorded observations — that can be referred to if something does not add up when statistics are being compiled.

Andrius Valadka

A grid constructed of lightweight tubing makes an easily moveable study plot.

Sampling methods

Divide your study site into sampling plots of at least 1 square meter (10 square feet) each. Plots can be laid out with string and stakes (and this will be necessary if your site has many trees and large shrubs), or you can make portable plot frames using lightweight plastic tubing with corner joints. Divide each square frame into smaller grid units by marking the sides of the frame at regular intervals and running string across the frame from side to side and top to bottom. You now have a movable grid that can be placed anywhere. A simple alternative is to borrow Hula Hoops from the gym and secure strings around them at regular intervals using masking tape. Such grids are not the traditional squares — but they are acceptable and cheap.

Another way to survey plants in the field is to run a transect line (a tape measure or a piece of string) from a fixed point, walk along the line for 5 meters (15 feet), and record all the plants within 10 centimeters (4 inches) on both sides of the line. This results in a study plot of about 1 square meter (10 square feet). Then move the string and repeat the transect every 5 to 10 meters (15 to 30 feet) to cover a large part of the study site. This is a good variation for large groups working in pairs, since one partner can observe and the other record.

It is useful to do a practice plant survey before going to the field. Areas of the schoolyard that have a limited number of plants can be surveyed quickly and still give sufficient practice in both plant identification and data recording.

Field observations

Create a master map of the site that has all of the sampling plots or transects marked and numbered, and assign the plots randomly by having students pick a number from a hat. In the field, begin by having students record the date and time, the exact location (obtained by compass, topographic map, or global positioning system), the names of the recorder(s), and the weather conditions, cloud cover, and temperature. Then have them sketch a map of the entire site on graph paper, using a scale that enables them to fit the site on one sheet of paper. Add letter and number codes at regular intervals along the two axes of the map to provide the coordinates of the individual plots to be surveyed. In addition to trees, woody shrubs, and herbaceous plants, have them record the location of rocks, bare ground, water, or other landmarks.

Next, ask students to stand outside their assigned study plot and sketch a map of it on graph paper, again using a scale that enables them to fit the entire plot on one sheet of paper. Their maps should show the grid lines within the plot and note the coordinates of the plot (from the site map). Then have students count, identify, and map all the plants in the plot. In addition, have them estimate and record the percentage of the total area that each species covers. In plots where there are trees, have students measure the circumference of the trunk in order to calculate the diameter at breast height, which is a standard measure taken 1.3 meters (4.5 feet) from the ground. Small rulers are useful if you also wish them to gather data on plant height or leaf size. Students usually need about half an hour to identify all the plants they can and to mark their locations on the graph. For identification, field guides are essential; it is also a good idea to invite a local botanist or other naturalist to assist in identifying plants. Students who wish to can make additional sketches or take photographs of the site, their sampling grids, and individual plants — taking care to keep accurate notes of the subject of each photograph.

When all plants have been recorded, have students carefully collect samples of any plants they cannot identify, *being sure not to remove any rare or endangered specimens.* It is the teacher's job to ensure that rare plants are left undisturbed — another compelling reason to seek the assistance of a botanist or naturalist. The usual practice in plant collecting is to take the entire plant, including roots, but the stem and leaves should be sufficient for identification in the classroom. Cut specimens with small scissors and place each in a plastic bag with a damp paper towel to keep it moist. Label every bag with the date, the plot number or location, and the plant's position on the plot grid. If you have reviewed plant and flower parts, students should be able to key out most of the specimens they collect.

Handling data

When you have returned to the classroom and identified all the plants, transfer the data to a master plant list and a master map. The master plant list is a record of all plant species identified, regardless of their abundance in the plots. Students can add to the list as new species are found in the field and, over time, the master list may reveal changes in the composition and diversity of plant communities.

On a transparency of an enlarged topographical map of the study site, students can mark the plots and locations of features such as large trees, paths, and boulders. A side chart for each plot can list the plants identified there. If you have the means to do mapping with Geographical Information System (GIS) software, you can put the map on a computer and input the plant data directly on to it; if you do not have this capability, consider a joint project in which a high school or nearby college produces the base map and your students provide the groundcover data. You can add digital photos of the site and the plants found there to both the online and print versions of the study results.

Data on the numbers or percentage of cover of plant species are the raw material for activities such as estimating the number of plants in the entire site, calculating percentages of the different types of plants, or determining the total area covered by vegetation. For instance, dividing the number of plants by the area of the plot gives the density. Dividing the number of species by the area gives a measure of the biodiversity. Plants can also be dried and weighed to obtain an estimate of total biomass; however, as this method

Roxine dePencier Hameister

requires that you destroy the plants, it renders the plot unusable for long-term monitoring.

Statistics should be generated three times a year: in early spring, late spring, and in early fall when you are back in class with a different group of students. Areas that are green year round can also be surveyed in January after the holiday break. Students can publish a report of the data they have collected, with photographs and drawings that record each season. Maintained and added to year after year, these reports will soon become the basis for a multi-year comparison. The information can be shared with others by putting it on your school's website or presenting it at a science fair or community event.

Alternative plant surveys

If you are in an urban area with no natural spaces, all is not lost. Consider doing the project on empty lots or other areas where plants grow untended. The results will be different but interesting. In an urban area, it is difficult to maintain surveys of plant life over several years, as the environment can change quickly; but similar areas can usually be found, even if your original site is paved over.

For young students, phenology studies provide a good introduction to plant observation and monitoring. Have successive classes of students record dates of such events as the opening of the first blossoms, the release of seeds, and the first leaf drop, along with temperature and weather conditions. Alternatively, you can participate in an organized phenology program such as Plantwatch, which has students in all parts of North America monitoring the dates that selected plants bloom.

Bird surveys

As your class becomes better able to use field guides, consider adding a bird survey to your ecosystem studies. As with the plant survey, choose several study areas within your site. Then have students take field guides and binoculars to the site, sit, and try to remain quiet. It is very helpful to have a birdwatcher along on these trips, as many birds are small, fast, and very similar in appearance to the untrained eye.

Students can also create a bird sound map. At first, have them sit very quietly and record on graph paper the sounds and the direction from which they come. As students become attuned to birds, play tapes in the classroom to introduce them to the songs of common birds in your area. (Many birdwatching websites also offer birdsong audio clips.) When students return to the study site, have them work in pairs to note any birds they can identify by sound. The information can be recorded on topographical maps of the site in the classroom.

If you wish to participate in a formal bird monitoring program, there are several feeder watch programs. (See Monitoring Programs and Resources) Most programs have students set up bird feeders in the schoolyard and monitor and report the number and species that visit between November and March. Results are tallied, reported to participating schools, and made available on the Internet. This project can be done in an urban area by mounting the feeder on a classroom window or in a protected school common area. If vandalism is a potential problem, have a parent who lives near the school volunteer his/her yard as a site. A few students can accompany the parent to the feeder each day to refill the feeder and record the birds.

Survey of insects and other animals

Similar activities can easily be conducted to survey insects and other small animals in your area. It is sometimes hard to see insects, as they may be under litter or observable for only a short time. Have students look for such evidence as tracks or small trails, chewed leaves or fruit, or egg cases. If you find egg cases, record the location of the site so that students can make return visits until the eggs hatch. If this is not possible, collect some eggs and keep them in a secure container in the classroom until they hatch; be sure to provide a habitat as close to natural as possible and to release the hatched insects into the area where they were collected. Similar activities can be conducted with mammals, reptiles, or amphibians. Several excellent international projects, such as Monarch Watch and Frogwatch allow students to participate in formal monitoring programs. (See Monitoring Programs and Resources.)

Sharing data and findings

Ideally, your project will continue over several years and contacts can be made with local universities or conservation authorities to make students' data available for research. Students may have difficulty understanding why others would, for many years, collect the same kinds of data in the same area. To illustrate how long-term data can be used to determine trends, have students obtain and compare weather records for particular months for several years past. Ask them to identify trends in precipitation and temperature: Are summers getting hotter? Are springs getting rainier? Are winters getting drier? Have them make weather predictions based on the trends they identify. Your class could become one of the school weather watchers for the local media.

With the changes in technology in the last few years, many schools have websites that can be linked to national environmental monitoring programs. You may choose to participate in a formal project, such as one of the watcher programs, or you might choose to develop your own focus area to monitor. This is an excellent project to do with a buddy class at another school.

Whatever you choose, your students will be at an advantage when it comes to dealing with global change and the decisions that informed, knowledgeable citizens must make. Doing these projects and sharing the results with your school community, the local community, or the world through the Internet is a positive contribution to the baseline knowledge needed for protecting local and national habitats. It is a win-win situation for all concerned.

Roxine dePencier Hameister teaches social studies at Wellington High School in Nanaimo, British Columbia.

REFERENCES

Binder, Deanna. *Backyard Biodiversity and Beyond*. British Columbia Ministry of Forests and Canadian Heritage, 1995 (available from Project Wild, 1005 Broad Street, #300, Victoria, BC V8W 2A1).

Forests in Focus: A British Columbia Exploration. British Columbia Ministry of Forests, 1997.

Hunken, Jorie, and the New England Wild Flower Society. *Botany for all ages: Discovering Nature through Activities for Children and Adults*, 2nd ed. The Globe Pequot Press, 1993.

Penn, Briony. *Canada's Rainforest: From Maps to Murrelets*. Sierra Club, 1998.

Perdue, Peggy, and Dianne Vaszily. *City Science*. Good Year Books/Scott Foresman/Harper Collins, 1991.

Ritter, Bob. *Soil and Plant Ecology*. Nelson Science, 1997.

Sobel, David. *Mapmaking with Children*. Heinemann, 1998.

Stansbury, Gladys, and Cathy Ready. *Soil Secrets: An Integrated Intermediate Science Resource*. British Columbia Agriculture in the Classroom Foundation, Pacific Edge Publishing, 1995 (Site 21 C50, Gabriola, BC V0R 1X0).

The Straitkeepers Handbook: A Teacher's Guide to Discovering the Ecology of Georgia Strait. Save Georgia Strait Alliance, 1993.

MONITORING PROGRAMS AND RESOURCES

United States

<www.uwex.edu/erc/gwah> Give Water a Hand watershed education and monitoring program.

<www.monarchwatch.org> Monarch Watch, University of Kansas Entomology Program.

<www.usu.edu/buglab> National Aquatic Monitoring Center "Buglab" watershed monitoring program supported by U.S. Bureau of Land Management and Utah State University.

<http://plants.usda.gov> Natural Resources Conservation Service plant identification site.

<www.plt.org> Project Learning Tree provides workshops to assist teachers in forest biodiversity studies.

Canada

<www.oiseauxqc.org/feuillets/cbcp_can.html> Canadian Bird Checklist Program invites birdwatchers to report sightings and maintains a database for species and sightings by province.

<www.cnf.ca> Canadian Nature Federation sponsors Project FeederWatch and Frog Watch.

<www.eman-rese.ca/eman> Environment Canada's Canadian Community Monitoring site has protocols and suggestions for monitoring projects.

Worldwide

<www.ciese.org/collabprojs.html> The Center for Improved Science and Engineering Education runs international collaborative science projects for students, including biodiversity studies and monitoring programs.

<http://archive.globe.gov> The GLOBE Program has information and protocols for just about everything to do with environmental monitoring.

<http://birds.cornell.edu/pfw/> Project FeederWatch is a joint project of Bird Studies Canada, the Canadian Nature Federation, and the Cornell Lab of Ornithology.

Monitoring Wetlands

Join in the effort to monitor local frogs and assess the health of wetland habitats

by Patrick Stewart

Subject areas: science, mathematics, social studies

Key concepts: amphibians, indicator species, biomonitor, bioindicator, wetland, acidity, microclimate, environmental assessment, environmental monitoring

Skills: measuring, observing, note taking, organizing data, interpreting data, teamwork, mapping

Location: indoors and outdoors

Nova Scotia Museum of Natural History

Early each spring, schoolchildren across North America perk up their ears to listen for the wake-up calls of frogs and toads, important dwellers in wetlands everywhere. The young listeners are participating in education and awareness programs dealing with the health and fate of reptiles and amphibians. In northeast North America, the object of their attention is often the northern spring peeper, a tiny tree frog whose voice is too big for its size. The peeper and various other species have been players in nature's spring pageant since soon after the last ice age — and possibly long before. For many people in the northeast, it is a sure sign of spring when the peepers break into song after spending the winter frozen beneath leaf litter in nearby woods.

Apart from the recreational and educational nature of the activity, it is concern about declining amphibian populations that draws volunteers to lurk at roadside ditches on spring evenings and listen for their calls. A decade ago, biologists first sounded the alarm about what appeared to be rapid and serious declines in numbers of frogs and other amphibians. Then, in 1995, reports from Minnesota described large numbers of frogs with deformities that had not been observed before. Since then, malformations have been found in more than a dozen species. Some species have disappeared, and even previously abundant species are becoming less common in many areas. There is no question that the loss of wetlands due to human activity is a major factor in declining populations of amphibians, but other environmental changes, such as global warming and ozone depletion, may also be contributing factors.

Patrick Stewart

Frogs and other amphibians are good indicators of environmental change for two reasons. First, they live both in water and on land, and disturbances to either of these habitats can affect their health and abundance. Second, frogs live in almost seamless contact with the environment. Because their skin is permeable to water and oxygen, contaminants can be transferred directly from the environment into their bodies; and because the skin lacks protective scales or hair, it is directly exposed to damage from such environmental factors as high levels of ultraviolet radiation. The eggs, too, are generally delicate and unprotected and therefore vulnerable to contaminants and environmental disturbances. Many biologists regard frogs as an ecosystem's canary in a mine: when amphibians begin to disappear, it is a clear warning that all is not well in their environment.

Several volunteer monitoring programs have been developed in recent years in response to worldwide concern about amphibians. By participating in frog monitoring, students can make a valuable contribution to research on amphibian decline and such associated issues as unexplained malformations and deaths of large numbers within a short time. Findings made by students are most useful as part of a larger project or network of observation; but even if there are no organized monitoring programs in your area, students can submit their reports to a local museum or archive for use in future programs that may develop.

Patrick Stewart

The following projects have students monitor the spring occurrence of a local species of frog and perform a mini-environmental assessment of a wetland. Both are easy to carry out and can be adapted for use in most areas. The simple skills that students develop can provide a basis for pursuing further environmental studies.

Frog monitoring

The aim of a frog monitoring program is to have students listen for and record the first calls of a local species of frog. There are certain basics to starting such a program:

Choosing a species

Most areas of the continent have frog species that call when breeding and are ideal for this project. The spring peeper is itself fairly widespread, being common throughout northeastern North America. For school projects, the main requirement is that the species selected be active during the school year. A local biologist, museum staff person, or university professor or student could assist your class in choosing a likely candidate in your area.

Introducing the topic

Aim at least one class session on environmental issues such as amphibian decline, global warming, ozone depletion, and wetland disappearance. Consider inviting a representative from a government wildlife agency or local naturalists' group to talk to your class about the characteristics of and potential stresses on amphibians in your region.

Give the students information about why we should be interested in making observations of frogs (or any

organism). Frogs are particularly good candidates for environmental monitoring because they are sensitive to changes in the environment, they are large enough to observe readily, there are not too many species to misidentify, and most make mating calls at certain times of the year.

Introduce the concepts of bioindicator and biomonitor. A bioindicator is an organism that functions as a signpost or calendar, indicating environmental factors such as seasonal change or proximity of a vital resource (e.g., a clump of lush green plants in a sandy desert is a bioindicator of a hidden underground pocket of water). A biomonitor, on the other hand, is an animal or plant that is sensitive to changes in the environment and, thereby, helps us to assess the overall health of its habitat. Whereas bioindicators give us a single piece of information, such as the presence of water, biomonitors help us to measure long-term trends.

Frogs can be both bioindicators and biomonitors. The calling of frogs is closely linked to temperature and weather, and in many regions the spring peeper is a bioindicator marking the arrival of spring. On the other hand, changes in abundance of spring peepers in a particular location over time might indicate loss or deterioration of their habitat; and an increase in malformations could indicate higher levels of ultraviolet adiation or chemical contaminants. In such cases, frogs are functioning as biomonitors.

Deciding when and where to monitor

The period of study should be ten days to two weeks during the breeding season of the species you are monitoring. Local wildlife managers and biologists can direct you to the best frog-listening spots in your area. To avoid surprises in the night, it is best to do your listening in familiar places and, where necessary, get landowners' permission before entering their properties.

Any ponds, roadside ditches, or wet places near woodlands are good places to start. If you are in a city, look for frog populations in parks with ponds, zoos, wildlife management zones, or other green areas. In urban environments, parents may be able to escort students to suitable wetlands nearby. Some species of frogs live in streams and along river edges. If you are monitoring an early species such as the spring peeper, the best way to hear the very first calls is to visit spots that are more exposed to the sun and therefore likely to thaw early.

Frogs become most active at night, especially on warm wet evenings, so the best time to begin listening for them is at dusk. Since monitoring will take place after school hours, parents or other interested adults should be recruited to accompany young students, and no one should go out without a partner. You might prepare a brief set of written instructions to be taken home.

Patrick Stewart

Warmth (warm or cold). "Other Observations" may be anything that catches students' attention or interest.

Put your map, or an enlarged version of it, on the wall. This will be the reporting center. Next to the map, post a sheet of paper that has numbered lines. When students first hear frog calls, have them sign on an empty line and put the corresponding line number beside the location on the map where they heard the calls. This provides a permanent record of students' observations.

Going out every night adds a sense of excitement for students; it can also show them the development of the breeding frenzy — particularly with peepers — and may reveal the coexistence and patterns of other species at your site. If, after the frogs have first peeped, there is a cold spell, they might not peep again for a while; this in itself is an interesting observation for students. Remember, too, that not hearing frogs at a chosen location is an acceptable result: it shows where frogs do not occur and may indicate an environmental problem such as pollution.

Mapping monitoring sites

Location is a key element of any environmental observation and must be recorded in enough detail to enable others to return to the same place. Typically, this information is reported by making a map and/or providing the location's geographic coordinates. If you have a map of your area, use latitude and longitude or military grid coordinates for the site. Learning how to determine coordinates from a map is a good parallel activity, the fundamentals of which you can easily pass on to your students. If you have only a city street map, use the grid system on the map. A further step is to have each student write a short description of the location of their site in relation to the nearest well-known landmark. Alternatively, have them draw a map of their listening spot, with streets and other features.

Keeping records

Making and recording regular observations is important in monitoring any natural event. Have each student make a record sheet on lined paper that has columns for the following observations: Date, Time, Heard Frog Call (Y/N), Number of Calls per Minute, Air Temperature, Weather, and Other Observations. Weather observations should include the "Three Ws": Wind (calm or windy), Water (rain, snow, drizzle), and

Variations

Everywhere — even in an area as small as a subdivision — you are likely to see significant variability in the observations that your students make. Emphasize that variability is an important feature of the natural world, and that all observations are equally important. There's no right or wrong observation.

From their records, students can find the range of values — sometimes considerable — for time of frog calling, as well as the average. Use these simple statistics to summarize the class's efforts. As a demonstration of geographic variability, try twinning your students with a class in a distant part of your province or state and have them try to explain differences or similarities in the observations.

Keep a record of these measurements year by year so that each class can see how its findings compare with those of earlier groups. Over many years, this will become a valuable record of natural change.

Wetland project

Whether on its own or in conjunction with frog monitoring, a wetland study increases awareness of issues surrounding wetland loss and acquaints students with the basics of environmental assessment. The following project involves classroom work and one or more class trips to a wetland. In the classroom, students learn techniques for proper measurement of temperature, acidity, and microclimate. In the field, students make observations of temperature and water quality, biological life, and physical characteristics of a wetland as well as some of the characteristics of the watershed. The project is also a simple environmental assessment. No major industrial or development project can take place without some form of assessment to identify its possible effects on the environment and to recommend ways to mitigate those effects. The information students gather and record is similar to but simpler than what is usually required. The wetland project requires only basic skills in math, science, and other disciplines.

Patrick Stewart

Background

In the classroom, give the students an overview of environmental issues related to wetlands, focusing on the local wetlands the students will visit. Background information may include:

Importance of wetlands: Wetlands are among the most biologically productive ecosystems on the planet. Like other ecosystems, they are occupied by biological communities that use them to capture solar energy and maintain life. Wetlands have plants of various kinds, from microscopic single-celled algae to larger plants, such as cattails, reeds, and even trees. They also provide habitats for a host of other organisms, from bacteria to higher animals such as mammals (e.g., raccoons and rodents), snakes, and amphibians. In addition to their biological importance, wetlands act as settling basins for silt eroded and transported by watercourses, and generally help to slow the rate of erosion farther downstream. Wetlands can remove some contaminants from water and can hold water for use in dry periods.

Problems facing wetlands: The main problems facing wetlands are loss due to human activity such as urban development and conversion into farmland, and contamination resulting from activities on adjacent lands. If possible, obtain some old maps of your study area to see the changes that have occurred over time, such as expansion of housing development, wetland infilling or drainage, or road construction. In some areas, global warming may lead to loss of wetlands, as increased temperature and shifts in precipitation patterns tip the delicate balance between inflow and evaporation.

Mapping

A map documents the location of the study site, helps determine relationships between the wetland and nearby human activities, and is useful in interpreting information collected. To prepare students for making simple grid maps of a wetland in the field, try having them map your classroom using grid paper with intervals corresponding to a unit of distance (e.g., 1 meter / 3 feet per grid interval).

Measuring temperature

There are two components to measuring temperature: understanding how thermometers work and using them correctly; and knowing that temperature often varies significantly with location. The following classroom activities can help students learn the tricks and complexities of temperature measurement.

THERMOMETER RESPONSE TIME

Have students estimate the time it takes the thermometer to reach its temperature measurement (usually one to several minutes); this is the thermometer's response time. The response time is a property of a thermometer and each thermometer is different.

Materials: a beaker of ice water, several thermometers, paper towel or cloth, masking tape, a watch or clock with a second hand

Procedure:

1. Using a small piece of masking tape, label the thermometers #1, #2, #3, and so on.
2. Place the beaker of ice water on a desk and have each student take the temperature of the water using one of the thermometers. Instruct students to start timing as soon as the thermometer enters the water and to stop and remove the thermometer when they think the thermometer fluid has stopped going down.
3. As each student finishes, record the elapsed time, along with the student's name and the number of the thermometer.
4. Dry each thermometer and allow it to return to room temperature before the next student uses it.
5. When all have finished, write all the numbers on the blackboard and invite students to calculate the average response time for each thermometer. This average is the length of time to wait when measuring temperatures at the wetland with that thermometer. Try to use the same thermometers when you visit the wetland.

TEMPERATURE VARIATIONS

This activity demonstrates that there are temperature variations in any environment.

Procedure:

1. Divide the class into five groups and give each group

a thermometer. Assign one group to each corner of the classroom and send one into the hallway.

2. Have students go to their specified location and take and record the air temperature as high as they can reach, and again at floor level without letting the thermometer touch the floor. Then have each group calculate the average temperature for its location.

3. On the blackboard, have each group record the upper-level, floor-level, and average temperatures at their location, and then have the class calculate the overall averages for each level and for all of the measurements together.

4. Discuss possible reasons for differences in average temperature in different corners of the room and hallway, and between the higher levels and the floor.

Measuring acidity

An important measurement for natural waters is the acidity, or pH. Students can easily become familiar with pH by testing different liquids using pH paper purchased from a laboratory supply house.

Preparation:

1. Prepare labeled containers of several common liquids: tap water, rainwater, a cola soft drink, vinegar, a baking soda solution, a milk of magnesia solution, and a salt solution. You might also include a mixture of soil in water that has been allowed to settle.

2. Place the pH strips and color chart on the table nearby.

Procedure:

1. Explain that pH is the notation chemists use for "concentration of the hydrogen ion" and can be used to measure the acidity of a solution.

2. Have students list the solutions to be tested and then dip a pH strip into each liquid to a depth of about 5 mm (¼ inch). (This procedure allows each strip to be used twice, once at each end.)

3. Have students compare the color on each strip to its corresponding color on the pH chart, and record the results.

4. When all the liquids have been tested, record everyone's readings and have students determine the highest, lowest, and class average for each liquid.

5. Have students account for variations in readings, if any.

Wetland field trip

A wildlife, conservation, or environmental organization — or even a university — may be able to assist you in finding a nearby wetland and coordinating a field trip. Marshes, swamps, bogs, fens, sloughs, artificial ponds, and temporary pools such as snowmelt ponds are all wetlands that may be suitable for your study. Roadside ditches are often good wetlands if they haven't been recently dredged; but for safety reasons, choose ones with access off the road. An accessible shoreline is essential for observations. An ideal study site is within walking distance of the school, but if you have transportation, you may be able to visit a distant one in a park or managed wildlife area. A wetland survey will take about two hours, in addition to travel time. Consider visiting the site several times in the year to obtain a seasonal perspective. Be sure to ask permission from landowners, if appropriate, and alert them of days when your class intends to visit.

Materials and equipment: map, thermometers, pH paper, glass or clear plastic sampling jars for tests and for looking at plants and animals, dip nets for capturing wetland creatures, field guides, copies of a prepared form for recording observations and measurements, notebooks or clipboard and paper, tape measure, graph paper, and pencils (ink tends to run when it gets wet). You might also want to bring a compass and camera. Students should wear outdoor clothing and rubber boots.

Preparing for the field trip: Before the trip, locate the wetland on the map, have students determine its geographic coordinates, and make observations about human activities likely to affect it, such as nearby roads, quarries, farm fields, subdivisions, or houses.

Survey procedure: It is recommended that students work in teams. Either divide the work so that each team looks at separate components of the environment, or have each team do a complete survey on its own. Before letting the students loose, emphasize that they can harm the wetland if they are not careful. Choose a limited number of observation and sampling points to minimize your class's impact. Include the following basic steps in the students' wetland survey.

1. GET YOUR BEARINGS. Which way is north and where is the wetland in relation to your school and other familiar features, such as roads or buildings?

2. WHAT DOES THE WETLAND LOOK LIKE? Have the students take a good look at the wetland and its surroundings to try to determine what type of wetland it is. Have each group sketch the shape of the wetland on graph paper, using arrows to indicate direction. The students can estimate dimensions by pacing (i.e., mark a known distance with a tape measure, walk the distance with normal steps, and then convert steps to distance). Remind students to mark the scale on their map (e.g., one grid square = one meter). On the map, put in plants, water, and bare ground. With arrows, note any significant features that are just off the map (e.g., railroad tracks, ocean, quarry).

3. HOW DOES THE WETLAND FIT INTO THE LANDSCAPE? What do the students see around them (i.e., forest, farmland, buildings, a parking lot)? Is the wetland beside a wood, close to the ocean, in a housing

development, or on the outskirts of a city? In particular, can they determine what human activity (if any) is likely to have the greatest effect on the wetland?

4. **MEASURE AND OBSERVE.** It is often easiest to prepare a photocopied form for recording information in the field and then have students transcribe their data back at school. Basic measurements to include are weather (the Three Ws), and time and date of observation. In addition, groups should measure or observe the following:

Temperature: Have each group measure temperature at a number of different locations in the wetland — in the water, in the air just above the water, and at the highest point of land in the immediate area. The object is to show microclimate, or the tiny changes that occur within an area. If all the students take measurements, the results can be tabulated and an average calculated. Keep the thermometers sheltered from the wind and out of the sun. Discuss what factors affect the temperatures observed.

Water quality: Have students fill a small jar with water from the water's edge, taking care to exclude mud or debris. Observe whether the water is clear or cloudy, and if there is any color to it. Cloudiness, or turbidity, often results from suspended material in the water, frequently from erosion. Many waters are naturally colored and it is useful to record this. Using the same water samples, have the students measure the pH or acidity of the water, as pH is one of the most important factors for sustaining life in wetland ecosystems.

Signs of life: Students should note any animals or plants they see. To help them focus, have individuals go to random spots along the shore and look at the plants within 45 centimeters (18 inches) of their feet. Similarly, have them concentrate on a single spot on the wetland bottom at the water's edge and note anything they see. This is an opportunity to look for egg masses of frogs and other amphibians. Also note any major types of vegetation surrounding the pond (e.g., forest, willows, cultivated lawn). Use a dip net to collect a few samples of pond organisms. Once these organisms have been observed, return them to the pond. Look for such animal signs as tracks, feathers, and scat (animal droppings).

Surroundings: The wetland is part of a much larger ecosystem. Let the students go a short distance from the wetland to observe the surroundings. Is water moving through the wetland and, if so, from where to where? Can they find adjoining wetlands or water bodies? What drainage system is the wetland a part of? (If this is not obvious during your site visit, it can be determined from a map.)

Signs of pollution and human disturbance: Note indications of pollution, such as mats of algae at the water surface, cloudy water full of suspended particles, an oily sheen on the water, an odor, garbage, areas of bare soil or erosion. Sadly, you can expect to find some litter in most wetlands you visit.

Reporting

Back in class, have students prepare a report that includes a brief description and map of the site, as well as their observations and photographs, if any were taken. Records such as this are extremely important for documenting change at natural sites. Suggest to the students that they keep their reports and visit the site in future to see if the wetland, or their perception of it, has changed.

Environmental studies today require many kinds of knowledge — from physics, chemistry and biology to sociology, anthropology, and even archeology. But the basic approach involves simple skills such as measuring, observing, note taking, organizing, and becoming aware of aspects of the greater whole, the big picture into which it all fits. Projects such as environmental monitoring and assessment carried out in a natural environment where all these factors come into play help students develop that greater picture. They leave an impression more lasting than any classroom project. The hundreds of student reports that I've seen — some really quite amazing — give me hope for upcoming generations and for the environment they'll be living in.

Patrick Stewart is a biologist and environmental consultant, and was a partner in developing and implementing the Frogwatch and Froglands programs in Nova Scotia in the 1990s. He lives near Brooklyn, Nova Scotia

ON-LINE FROG MONITORING PROJECTS

Many of these sites include sound files for frog and toad calls.

<www.nwf.org/frogwatchUSA> FrogWatch USA is a long-term monitoring program managed by the U.S. National Wildlife Federation.

<www.eman-rese.ca/eman/naturewatch.html> FrogWatch Canada is an amphibian monitoring program coordinated by Environment Canada's Ecological Monitoring and Assessment Network (one of four Nature Watch programs).

<http://cgee.hamline.edu/frogs> A Thousand Friends of Frogs offers extensive teacher and student activities, including the monitoring of amphibians across the United States.

<www.carcnet.ca> Canadian Amphibian and Reptile Conservation Network has profiles and information on every amphibian species in Canada, including calls.

<www.cnf.ca/naturewatch> The Canadian Nature Federation, a partner in FrogWatch Canada, has an on-line teacher's guide for Grades 7-12 and many resources for frog monitoring and study.

<www. pwrc.usgs.gov/naamp> The North American Amphibian Monitoring Program (NAAMP) is part of an international initiative known as the Declining Amphibian Populations Task Force, established in 1991 to determine the extent and causes of amphibian decline worldwide. Operating through the U.S. Geological Survey, NAAMP conducts volunteer amphibian monitoring programs in Canada, the United States, and Mexico, and is a useful source of information.

A Constructed Wetland: From Monitoring to Action

A water quality monitoring project evolved into an experiment using constructed wetlands to treat the toxic legacy of an abandoned gold mine

by Dan Kowal

Subject areas: science, mathematics, language arts

Key concepts: acid mine drainage, constructed wetlands, phytoremediation, pH, heavy metals, adsorption, precipitation

Skills: using the scientific method, observation, taking scientific measurements, data synthesis and analysis, presentation skills

Location: outdoors

Time: 1 day per month to prepare gear, go to the site, and complete sampling; 1 hour of class time per week

Materials: water quality monitoring equipment

Colorado, as its name implies, is washed in the color red — from its mountains to the willows along its riverbanks in the fall. And it was the color red that attracted a group of students to a small stream in the mountains near Denver in 1991. "The rocks in the stream look rusty," said one. "It looks like the fender on my dad's old car," said another. Their observations were correct. It was iron oxide — in other words, rust. But where did it come from? Was it bad for the stream? If so, could anything be done about it? Fueling the curiosity of student and teacher alike, these questions led to a river-monitoring course for 12- to 14-year-olds and an innovative eight-year-long experiment using a constructed wetland to treat acid drainage from an abandoned mine.

Dan Kowal

In 1992, students at The Logan School for Creative Learning in Denver began monitoring the stream through a program called Rivers of Colorado Water Watch Network, or River Watch. Sponsored by the Colorado Division of Wildlife and supported by funds derived from state fishing licenses, the program provides schools with water quality testing equipment, a computer, and laboratory analysis of heavy metals. In return, students collect data on stream or river sites in their watershed, following strict sampling and testing protocols.

While their class sessions at school focused on the interpretation of the tests and analysis of data, River Watch students visited the stream site each month to test for heavy metals, pH, alkalinity, hardness, temperature, and dissolved oxygen. After two years, students' sampling data indicated that concentrations of zinc, copper, and iron in the stream surpassed state standards for supporting aquatic life. Aware of the gold mining operations of yesteryear in the area near Denver called Gamble Gulch, students became suspicious of an abandoned mine upstream. Further investigation confirmed their suspicions: the water coming from the mine had a pH of 3.0, and an aquatic survey showed species diversity dropping from 28 to 1 after the stream's headwaters passed the mine.

Convinced that they had a problem on their hands, the River Watch students began looking for possible solutions. A workshop on acid mine drainage by the U.S. Geological Survey introduced the class to a low-tech but labor-intensive treatment process using limestone to raise the pH and constructed wetlands to remove heavy metals. The process had been developed by the Colorado School of Mines, and the success of their experiments inspired Logan students to begin designing a wetland system to test whether it could be an effective means of removing heavy metals from the stream. School of Mines faculty and graduate students assisted in the design process, the Colorado Division of Wildlife provided financial help, and in-kind support came from the Colorado Division of Minerals and Geology.

The River Watch students broke ground in 1994 for the construction of four wetland treatment systems. With summer and fall work brigades of parents, students, and teachers, as well as families from another school downstream, the project was completed by the summer of 1996. Throughout this time, the class continued to collect data at several stream sites, log the data on a computer, and send it to the Colorado Division of Wildlife. Besides writing analytical reports of their findings, students wrote and secured a grant from the 319 Task Force, a committee coordinated by the Colorado Department of Health that funds nonpoint source pollution cleanup projects. This money enabled them to finish the project.

The wetland system

The main components of the wetland system were a culvert, a settling pond, and four wetland cells. Where the mine water emanated from a collapsed mine adit (an entrance that is almost horizontal), the treatment system began with a water diversion through a culvert filled with crushed limestone (see diagram). This culvert, lined with Hypalon (pond liner material), was approximately 7.5 meters long, 60 centimeters wide, and 30 centimeters deep (24 feet long, 2 feet wide, and 1 foot deep). As the effluent passed through the culvert, the calcium carbonate in the limestone raised the pH of the water above 4.0. This increase in pH enabled bacteria to catalyze the adsorption of heavy metals into the wetland substrates of manure and compost.

Emerging from the culvert, the effluent collected in a Hypalon-lined settling pond, about 4.5 meters (15 feet) in diameter and 1 meter (3 feet) deep. This reservoir allowed for the precipitation of iron oxides before the effluent entered the wetland cells, thus preventing iron oxide precipitates from

clogging the system. The pond was equipped with an overflow pipe to prevent spills during the snowmelt in spring or in the event of a blockage by debris in the pipes leading to the wetlands. A plumbing system comprised of ¾-inch PVC pipe drained the pond by gravity feed into four separate wetland cells.

The walls of the wetland cells were constructed of railroad ties, metal sheeting, and Hypalon liner. Each cell was 2.5 by 2.5 by 1.2 meters deep (8 x 8 x 4 feet) and held 5.5 cubic meters (200 cubic feet) of either manure or composted manure. Bacteria in the manure reacted with the water to remove heavy metals from solution. Crushed limestone was also added — 6.4 cubic meters (25 cubic feet) to each wetland cell — to assist in raising the pH level. Valves controlled the rate of flow into each cell at 3.8 liters (one gallon) per minute. This predetermined flow rate increased the longevity of the substrate, which stayed reactive for at least one year.

From the outset, students wanted to test the efficacy of different wetland configurations in filtering heavy metals. To test differences in reactivity between substrates, two of the cells held manure and two held composted manure. Students also wanted to find out if the direction of water flow through the substrates would influence the removal of heavy metals. Therefore, two different flow regimes were configured for each substrate. In upflow

Wetland System Design

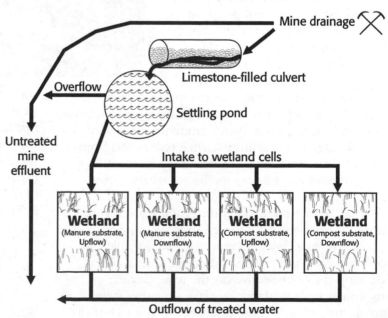

Mine drainage

Limestone-filled culvert

Overflow

Settling pond

Untreated mine effluent

Intake to wetland cells

Wetland (Manure substrate, Upflow)

Wetland (Manure substrate, Downflow)

Wetland (Compost substrate, Upflow)

Wetland (Compost substrate, Downflow)

Outflow of treated water

Dan Kowal

systems, water entered through perforated pipe at the bottom of a cell, rose up through the substrate, and left the cell through an outlet pipe. A bed of pea gravel surrounded the perforated pipes and outlet pipes of upflow cells to filter out debris. In downflow systems, water entered at the top of the cell and trickled down through the substrate. Water pressure sent the treated mine effluent through perforated pipes on the cell floor up through a solid outlet pipe. A covering with 15 centimeters (6 inches) of straw insulated each cell.

Results

Students found that the constructed wetlands significantly reduced the concentration of heavy metals. According to data collected from September to December 1996, each artificial wetland lowered the amounts of zinc, iron, and copper well below toxicity thresholds for fish and other aquatic life. The pH rose to more favorable levels of between 6.0 and 8.0. In the fall of 1997, the students presented these preliminary findings to the 319 Task Force, and the following spring the class provided an update on its progress to the Water Quality Control Commission of Colorado. Meanwhile, students maintained their monthly sampling schedule.

Developing perspectives

After data collected over several years demonstrated that the wetlands technology might be a viable approach to detoxifying acid mine drainage, many River Watch students asked, "Why can't we clean up this stream?" However, it was clear that processing the water from the entire stream would require a much larger wetland system than the small-scale study site; it would also require expertise, funding, and cooperation from a variety of stakeholders with different perspectives. Further, there was uncertainty about whether such an endeavor would succeed on a large scale. The issue of cleaning up the stream was therefore selected as the central question in a project aimed at gathering more information and developing perspectives. In this project, the River Watch students cooperated with computer and cognitive science researchers from the University of Colorado at Boulder who were seeking to pilot a computer-mediated collaborative learning model.

The students were divided into four groups representing government, landowners, mining companies, and environmentalists. For one year, the groups collected information and interviewed adult mentors in order to develop their perspective on the feasibility of using constructed wetlands to clean up entire streams contaminated by acid mine drainage. At the end of the

Dan Kowal

year, students expressed their viewpoints in a lively debate. The result was a consensus over two findings:

- Artificial wetlands alone are not the sole solution to the problem of acid mine drainage, but are part of a strategy that could be combined with other approaches.

- The U.S. environmental law that protects water resources (the Clean Water Act) should be amended so that "good Samaritans" who attempt to clean up waterways cannot be held responsible should their cleanup efforts fail to work.

Project conclusion

At the end of the 2000 school year, the constructed wetlands project ended, but not before it had spawned a number of interesting studies along the way.

Documentation

Dick Frazer, a youthful miner in his nineties who was still working his claim farther up Gamble Gulch, stopped by often to check the students' progress. Since Dick knew the entire mining history of the gulch, his visits gave students a rich historical context for their work. They planned and filmed an oral history interview with him, and, with the help of a local film production facility, produced *The History of Gamble Gulch*. The film was donated to the Colorado Historical Society.

Soils and phytoremediation

In the final phase of the project, the River Watch class secured another 319 Task Force grant to conduct soil and plant experiments on all four wetland treatment cells. As part of the closing down of the wetland system, soil sampling was done to determine whether the heavy metal content of the substrate surpassed federal and state guidelines, in which case the manure or compost would have to be taken to a hazardous waste treatment facility. (Fortunately, the cells' substrate did not have to be removed, as the sampling results were well below safety standards.) Soil sampling also provided the students with background information for plant experiments involving phytoremediation, the process of using plants to clean up pollution. Students were interested in two questions:

- How well do wetland plants absorb heavy metals?

- What parts(s) of a plant — roots, shoots, or fruits — are most effective at concentrating heavy metals?

In the summer, students planted cattails, sedges, and slough grass in the cells. In late fall, they harvested these

What is Acid Mine Drainage?

While acid rain has grabbed headlines during the past few decades, a less publicized form of acid had been steadily killing streams on this continent for more than a century. Acid mine drainage, an effluent produced by mining operations, has polluted upper watersheds in the Rocky Mountains since the earliest explorations for silver and gold; and in coal mining areas such as Pennsylvania, it is the most serious environmental problem affecting aquatic ecosystems.

Acid mine drainage typically consists of very acidic water with high concentrations of heavy metals. The process begins with excavation of rock containing sulfur compounds, the most common being iron pyrite or "fool's gold." When exposed to air and water, the sulfides oxidize to form sulfuric acid, which dissolves heavy metals in the rock such as iron, copper, lead, zinc, and cadmium. The resulting effluent, or acid mine drainage, finds its way to rivers and streams through underground seepage or surface runoff. Its acidity and high concentrations of heavy metals create a stream environment that is toxic to fish and other aquatic life.

Enormous quantities of waste rock — the culprit in acid mine drainage — are generated in mining operations because the metal being extracted for use may constitute as little as one percent of the material excavated. Canadian government statistics in 1991 indicated that mining in Canada was generating nearly two million metric tons of waste rock and tailings per day, all with the potential to cause acid mine drainage. If left exposed to air and water, this rock continues weathering for decades. It is estimated that, in the United States, acid drainage from abandoned mines has polluted 19,300 kilometers (12,000 miles) of streams and rivers and 73,000 hectares

Dan Kowal

Dan Kowal

(180,000 acres) of lakes and reservoirs.

Given the magnitude of the problem, acid mine drainage is not going to be cleaned up easily. Neutralizing the effluent with lime reduces its acidity and precipitates metals, but results in a toxic sludge that is itself a pollution problem. Completely submerging waste rock stops the acid-forming oxidation of sulfides, and containing tailings in impervious ponds can halt seepage into waterways; however, both of these methods require the perpetual maintenance of containment structures. Another strategy — that of covering mining waste with till and soil — is no guarantee against surface water percolating through acid hot spots and contaminating groundwater.

In the search for ways to treat acid mine drainage, the potential for constructed wetlands to neutralize and remove metals from mine effluent has been attracting interest over the past decade. Trials have been conducted on a small scale only, and much research remains to be done. But as self-sustaining ecosystems, wetlands may offer the long-term remediation needed for this long-term environmental problem.

— *Gail Littlejohn, co-editor*

REFERENCES

Environmental Mining Council of British Columbia. "Acid Mine Drainage." On-line in March 1998 at <www.miningwatch.org>.

Mills, Chris. "An Introduction to Acid Rock Drainage." On-line in January 2004 at <http://technology.infomine.com/enviromine/ard/Introduction/ARD.HTM>.

Sobolewski, André. "Wetlands for Treatment of Mine Drainage." On-line in January 2004 at <http://technology.infomine.com/enviromine/wetlands/welcome.htm>.

---

plants and had parts analyzed by a local environmental laboratory. Students worked in five groups, each focusing on a different heavy metal, to analyze the performance of each plant. The outcomes were presented in a report to the 319 Task Force.

A repeatable project?

Dedication, perseverance, and a willingness to learn are key ingredients in taking on a project of this magnitude. As in any school project that spans several years, the teacher is the key to ensuring continuity, keeping the aims of the program fresh, and directing student activity toward the small milestones that lead to ultimate goals. Fortunately, in the River Watch class, there was usually a core group of students who took the course for two years. These repeat students taught newcomers the water

quality testing procedures and introduced them to the overall scheme of the project. The opportunity to take leadership roles gave students a sense of ownership and responsibility.

The wetland project demonstrated a community effort that could not have been completed by the school alone. Its success was initially secured by identifying potential sources of technical expertise and monetary and in-kind support. Partnerships with state agencies and mentor support through local universities proved invaluable. In particular, the Division of Minerals and Geology, a state agency responsible for mine reclamation, put the school in contact with the landowners to begin the project in the first place. Scientists from all institutions were accessible and responded to questions in a timely fashion. With this kind of assistance, we never had the feeling that we had to be experts to carry out the project. All it took was a lot of drive. Having 60 or more volunteers — students, families, teachers and a host of others — helped the class to complete the project relatively inexpensively. The cost of the wetland treatment system was well within $6,000. The expensive part of the project was time.

Every year, a different learning opportunity emerged for the River Watch class. While planning new material was daunting at times for the teacher, the annual change kept the project intriguing for everyone involved. Its longevity and unintended inquiries pulled students into an active learning process that will serve them in years to come. One former River Watch student, for instance, has spearheaded a major effort to have his college campus go "green" with energy-efficient devices for existing buildings and rigorous environmental standards for new buildings.

> *We never had the feeling that we had to be experts to carry out this kind of project.*

The first group of River Watch students who worked on the design and construction of the wetlands did not have the chance to see it to completion. But their investigative spirit built the foundation for future inquiries. For this reason, I always asked successive River Watch classes if they ever noticed a sight, a smell, a sound, or a taste that seemed out of place. Did they investigate or ask questions? I then told them that the constructed wetlands had begun with the curiosity of a few students who noticed the color red in a mountain stream.

Dan Kowal, a former teacher at The Logan School for Creative Learning in Denver, Colorado, now works as a Web programmer for the National Oceanographic Atmospheric Administration's National Geophysical Data Center where his skills continue to support environmental education.

Tracking and Stalking the Wild

"If it's not flat, it's a track." — *Tom Brown, Jr.*

by David Kowalewski

A simple fact is indisputable: tracks are the single most common body of evidence available about animal behavior on Earth. They are — literally — everywhere, and you do not even have to leave your home to find them. Most environmentalists, biologists, zoologists, and other natural scientists act as if this motherlode of scientific data does not even exist. Yet, as trackers say, walking on a landscape without knowing how to track is like walking through a library without knowing how to read.

This situation is changing, however. Courses on tracking are appearing across North America at universities, wilderness schools, scout camps, state parks, and elsewhere. Tracking has caught the attention of popular media such as *Field and Stream*[1] and weightier publications such as *National Geographic*.[2]

Stalking in full camouflage is a technique that humans have learned from other animals.

[vertical caption: Wilderness Awareness School]

Uses and values

Certainly some of this popularity can be attributed to a neo-romantic faddism deriving from New Age and Primitive Renaissance movements. But do the skills of tracking and stalking have a more lasting value? I believe so. In fact, it appears that their uses and values, which are many and profound, are being rediscovered.

> *... walking on a landscape without knowing how to track is like walking through a library without knowing how to read.*

Surviving: Tracking and stalking are, in the first instance, survival skills. When a Kalahari Bushman was asked what made him such a good tracker, he simply replied, "Hunger."[3] Tracking assists survivalists in countless ways, from locating water to following game. It is used by search-and-rescue teams and law-enforcement agencies to find children, hunters, hikers, and escaped convicts.

Intimate understanding of the animal world: Trackers have an adage that tracks are a window into an animal's soul. Imagine following the footsteps of another human for an entire day; you would easily get an intimate picture of the person's habits, interests, and feelings. Trackers soon realize that each animal has a unique personality, a fact that most scientists stubbornly resist. More broadly, the skills teach about the web of life, that everything in nature affects everything else. In particular, trackers learn how profoundly the human species impacts wildlife. Ultimately, they discover their own place in the web.

Environmental planning: Tracking is increasingly being used in government programs as part of environmental assessment. State agencies in Florida, Massachusetts, and Washington, for example, employ trackers to find endangered species, estimate wildlife populations, and locate animal corridors.[4] Tracking a locale for several years provides detailed models of predator-prey cycles and other ecosystemic relationships.

Preserving ancient skills: Environmentalists and other scholars are increasingly turning to primitive skills to discover truths about nature. Yet most of us would agree that it is far better to keep such skills alive in the young than dead in museums and libraries. Tracking is also a useful tool for anthropologists and sociologists to understand indigenous peoples.[5] It is undoubtedly *the* oldest profession. Keeping the skills alive enables humans to better understand themselves: our hunter-gatherer ancestors account for over 99 percent of hominid evolution — they are literally in our genes. In fact, we can say that modern humans are hunter-gatherers with only a thin veneer of modern civilization. So, in the last analysis, humans are tracking and stalking themselves.[6]

Replacing hubris with humility: Trackers soon realize their human inadequacies upon encountering the powers of wild animals — powers such as strength (martens climb vertically in a flash), smell (squirrels can find where 95 percent of their nuts are cached), and hearing (foxes hear the ticking of a watch several meters away). Above all, they see the huge difference between the awareness of wild animals and that of domestic ones, including humans. They realize that, in terms of awareness, civilization is not all it is cracked up to be, and that they have much to learn from "all their relations" in the wild.

Photographing wildlife: Tracking enables us to find the best times and places for photographing wild animals in their natural settings, while stalking allows for those up-close-and-personal shots.

Educating about the wild in the wild: Given preparation to ensure a reasonable degree of comfort, tracking is simply the most enjoyable way to learn about nature.

Identifying claw marks in tracks along a riverbank.

Participants in tracking courses often comment, "I just had to get out of the office (or house, dorm, store, etc.)." Kids love competitions to "find the raccoon trail" and even grownups like making casts of tracks. Classroom lectures on ecosystemic variables may be enlightening, but how much fun are they? There is some truth to the mountain man's saying that "If you cain't do it in the woods, it ain't worth doin'."

In sum, tracking is a practical, enjoyable, and enlightening skill. In fact, some scholars speculate it may be the origin of science itself.[7] Whatever the case, it is a science — and certainly an art — worth preserving for the survival of species, including our own.

David Kowalewski is a professor of environmental studies at Alfred University in Alfred, New York, and the author of Deep Power: The Political Ecology of Wilderness and Civilization (Nova Science, 2000). He is currently writing a textbook on tracking and is available for teacher training in tracking skills.

Notes

1 Sam Curtis, "Jim Halfpenny: Master Tracker," *Field and Stream* (July 1997), pp. 59–61.
2 Tracking Project, *Newsletter* (July 4, 1999).
3 "Tracking: A Wild Discovery Program Special," Discovery Channel, 1999 (videotape).
4 Paul Rezendes, *Tracking and the Art of Seeing*, Camden House Publishing, 1992; and author's interviews in 1996 and 1998 with the Tracking Project in Corrales, New Mexico, and the Wilderness Awareness School in Duvall, Washington.
5 Neville Agnew and Martha Demas, "Preserving the Laetoli Footprints," *Scientific American*, vol. 279 (September 3, 1998), pp. 44–55.
6 Hannah Nyala, *Point Last Seen: A Woman Tracker's Story*, Beacon Press, 1997.
7 Louis Liebenberg, *Art of Tracking: The Origin of Science*, David Philip Publishers, 1990.

Recommended Tracking Resources

FIELD GUIDES

Brown, Tom, Jr. *Field Guide to Nature Observation and Tracking.* Berkley Publishing Group, 1983. This great guide to tracking and stalking outlines Brown's system and contains everything from fundamentals to techniques for awareness, track aging, and comparing and classifying tracks, including measurements.

Elbroch, Mark. *Mammal Tracks & Sign: A Guide to North American Species.* Stackpole Books, 2003. Winner of the 2003 National Outdoor Book Award for "Best Nature Guidebook," this is the most thorough treatment of the subject ever published; includes track and trail data and illustrations for 135 species, range maps, over 1,000 full-color photographs, and much more.

Halfpenny, James. *A Field Guide to Mammal Tracking in North America.* Johnson Books, 1986. This well-written and illustrated guide covers basics, techniques, ten animal families, and Halfpenny's well-respected system of measurement and gait morphology.

Levine, Lynn, and Mitchell, Martha. *Mammal Tracks: Life Size Tracking Guide.* Heartwood Press, 2001. A sturdy, weatherproof, and easy-to-use tracking guide for beginners, with a life-size key to 29 species.

Murie, Olaus. *Animal Tracks.* Houghton-Mifflin, 1982. A Peterson field guide: the original North American tracking field guide.

Rezendes, Paul. *Tracking and the Art of Seeing.* Camden House Publishing, 1992. This photographic tracking guide is a work of art and includes an important introduction to "What Tracking Means" and "Tracking as the Art of Seeing."

STORIES AND AUDIOTAPES

Brown, Tom, Jr. *The Tracker.* Berkley Publishing Group, 1978. This was the first book written by this famous tracker and author. Filled with stories of Brown's early mentoring, it is an extremely influential work for many of today's trackers.

Corbett, Jim. *Jungle Lore.* Oxford University Press, 2000. Stories of Jim Corbett's life and career in the rainforests of India.

Ingwe. *Spirit of the Leopard.* Redhawk Productions, 1997. This audio-cassette is a collection of short stories from Ingwe's youth among the Akamba people of Kenya, East Africa.

Young, Jon. *Learning the Language of Birds* (1 cassette, 1996); *Advanced Bird Language: Reading the Concentric Rings of Nature* (6 cassettes, 1999). Owlink Media. In these two audiotape series, Jon Young shares the secrets of bird language. Learning to understand this "forest alarm system" will help your students see and experience more wildlife and enhance their stalking and tracking abilities.

Young, Jon. *Tracking Pack One* (2 cassettes): *What Tracking Can Do For You & What All Great Trackers Have In Common* and *Spirit Tracking & Other Feats of Native Awareness.* Owlink Media, 1995. These audio recordings by renowned tracker and storyteller Jon Young are perfect for listening to in the classroom.

— compiled by David Kowalewski and Dan Rain

Teaching Tracking and Stalking

by Dan Rain

Subject areas: mathematics, science,

Key concepts: gait pattern, biomechanical movement, stride, straddle, ecological relationships

Skills: tracking, stalking, sensory awareness, pattern recognition, observation, deductive reasoning, patience, concentration

Location: indoors and outdoors

Time: varies by activity

The following activities can be incorporated into many courses to introduce students in middle school to the art and science of tracking and stalking. They are good additions to any educator's repertoire for field trips, class retreats, or other outdoor excursions. You do not need wilderness at your doorstep to start tracking; some of these activities, however, do require an area with at least minimal wildlife presence. If you don't have access to a woodlot, try going to a nearby park or even your schoolyard. Suburban and urban areas will usually offer the tracks of common wild mammals and birds, as well as domestic dogs and cats. Several of the activities will work without any animal tracks and, if necessary, most of the activities can be done indoors.

Wilderness Awareness School

Learning to move like the animals is important in tracking and can help you maneuver in nature. Here students practice a bipedal deerform — great for traveling quickly through the forest over logs and bush.

Tracking activities

Getting started

Begin by inspiring students about tracking through telling your own stories or sharing others' adventures. (See Recommended Tracking Resources at end of previous article.) Then go outdoors to see what you can find. Even a seemingly commonplace set of tracks can become exciting if the right questions are asked. Try to encourage students' curiosity, rather than giving answers — especially when just starting. Ask such questions as:

- What animal might have made these tracks? How do you know?

- How many toes do you see?

- Was this a big animal or a small one? How can you tell?

- What was it doing?

- Where did it come from? Where did it go?

You'll be amazed by how quickly students grab the field guides you produce.

Trail detectives

Materials: blank paper, writing utensils, scissors, tracking field guides, notebooks and pens for recording conclusions

1. Indoors, have groups of two to five students each draw and cut out two dozen or more paper tracks of four or more different local species. Any tracking field guide can be used to create the paper tracks. For wonderfully accurate track stencils, visit <www.AnimalTracksBySteve.com>.

2. Have each group lay its set of tracks either in different places in your classroom, or outdoors in an ecotone area (i.e., the border between two different ecosystems, such as where field and forest meet). Remind students to place special emphasis on the interactions among species (e.g., a coyote meets the path of a cottontail, turns, and starts trailing it for breakfast).

3. When everyone is ready, send each group to visit the other groups' areas to try to identify the animals and figure out the stories told by the paper tracks. Ask each group to record its findings.

4. Indoors, have the groups share their explanations and conclusions.

Magic tracking stick

Blindfold activities teach the use of senses other than sight and how to move quietly in nature.

Wilderness Awareness School

Materials: tracking stick with moveable markers, measuring tape (2 meters / 6 feet or longer), tracking field guides for reference.

1. Prepare a "magic tracking stick": a relatively straight stick about 1 meter (3 feet) in length with a diameter of about 2.5–5 cm (1–2 inches) that you have decorated by carving or painting it and adding beads or feathers. Use colored rubber bands or colored pieces of yarn to create differentiated markings that indicate the average length of stride and straddle of common mammals in your area (i.e., squirrel, deer, rabbit, fox, housecat).

2. When you bring the stick to class, try to spark students' interest in the stick by being secretive about it. When they ask what it is, say only that that it is "a magic tracking stick." If they want to know how it works, maintain their curiosity by stating that you can't explain but only show them.

3. Outdoors, locate some animal tracks, measure the stride, and mark the stride on the stick by adjusting the rubber bands or yarn.

4. Demonstrate how the stick "magically" helps you to find the next track. To find the next track, hold one end of the stick above the last track and slowly pivot it; the next track should fall within a range close to your stride mark.

5. Once you have measured and marked a few different animals, ask students how correspondence with your average stride measurements can help to identify the animal you are tracking.

6. This is an excellent time to start sharing the concepts of straddle, track length, and track width (see Basic Tracking Measurements sidebar). You can also demonstrate that a perfect print is not necessary to identify an animal.

Trailing

By pretending they are part of a wildlife research project or search-and-rescue operation, students can learn a great deal about the art of "trailing" — that is, discovering where an animal (or a person) has gone.

1. While out tracking, have a fellow teacher or other accomplice — wearing boots with a distinctive tread — slip away unnoticed and become "lost." To make trailing less frustrating for beginners in difficult tracking conditions, the adult could make the trail more visible by dragging his/her feet or a stick.

Basic Tracking Measurements

Stride: The distance from one track along an animal's trail to the next track made by the same foot. Always record stride from the exact same point on each track, e.g., the "trailing edge" — or rearmost point — of the first track to the trailing edge of the next track.

Straddle: The width of an animal's trail, measured perpendicular to the line of travel at the widest point of a group pattern, including the width of the tracks. (Some authors call this measurement "trail width" and do not include the width of the tracks themselves when measuring straddle.) As a general rule, as speed increases, stride increases and straddle decreases.

Track length: The length of a track, from the leading edge of the foremost toe pad to the trailing edge of the track — not including claws, as their length can change with the animal's activities.

Track width: Measured at the broadest part of the track.

These definitions are from *A Field Guild to Mammal Tracking in North America* by Dr. James Halfpenny. Tracking authors differ widely with respect to measurement and gait terminology. Teachers may wish to compare tracking guides to see which terms make the most sense to them and their students. Simple conversions allow for calculating equivalent measurements from guide to guide. For example, some authors measure "stride" as half of Dr. Halfpenny's stride (what he calls a "half-stride" or "step"); to convert, multiply their stride by two or divide Halfpenny's in half.

— Dan Rain

2. After allowing enough time for the adult to set the trail, ask students to try to find the adult by looking for boot prints, recently overturned leaves, or broken twigs. (For a greater challenge, find an area where students can find at least 25 animal tracks in a row and have them trail the animal.)

Cast collecting

Casts of animal tracks are wonderful tools for studying tracks and interactive additions to your classroom's natural history collection. Casts can be made of either plaster of Paris or Dentstone. Dentstone is a material used by dentists, preferred for cast making for its durability, attractiveness, clarity of detail, and the fact that it works in wet conditions. (Ask your dentist for a free sample, or order it in 50 lb. quantities from <www.IDSDental.com> or any dental supply company.) To given an even outside shape to casts, use plastic rings about 2 cm (½-1 inch) high to form their boundaries. A ring cut from the top of a plastic yogurt container will work, or PVC pipe with a large diameter can be cut into rings that can be reused. To make cast removal possible, cut a slit in each ring.

Materials: plaster of Paris or Dentstone in resealable container, plastic rings, full water bottle for mixing and rinsing, plastic container with lid and utensil for mixing. The materials for cast making must be carried into the field, as plaster sets up too quickly to mix ahead of time. It isn't as encumbering as it sounds, however, as everything will fit in a daypack.

Procedure:

1. In the field, look for deep impressions in mud or sand, as they are the easiest to cast.

2. Place a plastic ring around each track or set of tracks to ensure adequate coverage of the track. Mound dirt or sand around the outside of the ring to prevent leakage.

3. Mix plaster of Paris or Dentstone with water to the consistency of pancake batter (i.e., neither runny nor too thick).

4. Pour the plaster into the ring to overfill each track well on all sides. Leave the cast to dry completely: an hour to a couple of days, depending on conditions. Collect the cast when it has hardened.

Firekeeper — the ultimate stalking game.

Wilderness Awareness School

Animal forms relay

Moving like different animals, or practicing their "gait pattern" or "animal form," enhances students' ability to interpret tracks and is an activity that most enjoy. When they have a kinesthetic understanding of an animal's movement, students are better able to relate to the creature and, in the field, determine approximately how fast it travels during different activities or what motivates its course. I recommend showing students videos of animals moving as a source of ideas and inspiration.

1. Using pictures of animal tracks as a guide, have students move on all fours in a manner that reflects the pattern in the tracks. For example, students can hop or gallop with their legs landing past their hands like a squirrel or rabbit, or lumber forward on one side and then the other to imitate a bear. Keep in mind that there is no one right way for a biped to imitate the movements of a quadruped, and students' enthusiasm is the most important thing. Group members can help one another to improve.

2. After practicing movements of different animals, organize a relay race with the groups — to be non-competitive, if you wish. Stand to one side and periodically call out a new animal that participants must switch to at that moment. If students are moving too fast, try throwing in "rabbit" or even "snake" to see what happens!

Stalking activities
Firekeeper

This is the ultimate stalking game.

1. Have the class form a large circle seated on the ground, and place three pieces of "firewood" (anything from sticks to less challenging sets of keys) in the center of the circle.

2. Ask for a volunteer to be the "firekeeper." The firekeeper is blindfolded and sits in the center of the circle with the "firewood" in front of him/her. The firekeeper can occasionally reach out to check on the firewood but cannot guard or protect it. Tell the group that they must be very quiet during the activity.

3. Point at one student in the outer circle to begin. The student tries to sneak slowly and quietly into the

center to steal the "firewood" and return to the circle without being detected.

4. When the firekeeper hears or senses the "thief," he/she points in that direction. If the firekeeper points at the student, the would-be thief must return to the circle, and a new "thief" tries to steal the firewood. If the firekeeper points near, but not at, the thief, the thief must freeze and wait for your signal to keep going. (I have found it necessary to limit the total number of times that firekeepers can point to prevent them from pointing too often or at random. If they use up their allotted number of points, they can then catch thieves only by touching them at the moment of theft.)

5. A student who successfully steals the firewood and returns to the circle becomes the new firekeeper.

For more challenging versions, select an area with noisy groundcover (i.e., dry leaves), or choose two or more students to stalk into the center simultaneously. The entire class must remain quiet for this activity to work well: they usually do — hushed with anticipation!

Grazing deer

This stalking activity focuses on sight rather than sound and is a little like Red Light — Green Light. A couple of volunteers on all fours pretend to be deer grazing in a field or meadow. While their heads are down munching, other students try to stalk them very slowly from quite a distance away — preferably crawling on their bellies or hands and knees, but at least very slowly walking. When the deer look up, anyone they see who is still moving has to go back and start again. (You can help referee.) Students who reach the deer without being noticed become ungulates themselves and join the herd. Advanced stalking techniques can take into account the wind's movements and may employ mud, debris, and other camouflage.

Wilderness Awareness School

Tracking teaches concentration and focus.

Sneaking

There is no better way to get a group of adolescent students to pay quiet attention and learn from nature than to warn them that their classmates will be trying to sneak up on them! Of course, they will want to sneak up on others as well, which is excellent stalking practice. You'll be surprised at the natural mysteries discovered on the way. If you ask a group of middle school students to "go sit quietly by a tree for 15 minutes and study nature," they'll last about 30 seconds before losing focus. But ask them if they want to hide and wait to ambush their friends, and they'll wait quietly and intently for ages. They'll also start to observe and learn about the tree they're leaning against, the snail crawling along the ground, the plants at their feet, the birds and sounds in the air.

While two or more groups of students are out tracking, you can secretly arrange with another group leader for a pre-appointed ambush to keep the excitement flowing, or see if the groups can avoid being seen by each other the whole time they are in the field. If you don't want them to be sneaking the entire day, introduce this partway through and establish some ground rules, such as etiquette on- and off-trail.

Teaching bird language and behavior fits perfectly into this exercise, as students can learn to recognize another group's approach from what the birds are telling them. An excellent follow-up activity is to allow the students to share their stories with the class afterward — what their group discovered in nature, how they surprised their friends — so that the day's excitement can be relived in the retelling.

Dan Rain is with the Wilderness Awareness School, a national non-profit environmental education organization based in Duvall, Washington (<www.WildernessAwareness.org>). He lives in Delmar, New York, where he enjoys tracking with his three-year-old son.

Attracting and Studying Hummingbirds

Invite the dynamos of the bird world into your schoolyard and curriculum

by Kim Bailey

Subject areas: science

Key concepts: habitat, migration, adaptation

Skills: inquiry/investigation, problem solving, observation, technology

Location: indoors and outdoors

Time: ongoing throughout school year

Materials: hummingbird feeders, flowers to attract hummingbirds, red ribbons, observation journals, field guides, computers with Internet connection; see also activities below

After months of winter cold and the illusion of lifelessness, spring is a season full of expectation and excitement. More than anything, I eagerly anticipate the return of hummingbirds. Each day I impatiently check the Internet to see how much progress the tiny birds have made on their miraculous journey northward. I hang my feeders early and hope that maybe this year I'll be lucky enough to sight and report the first hummingbird to arrive in my area. (By submitting the date and location, I can document my discovery with a dot on the on-line migration map at <www.hummingbirds.net>). Every year, someone else nearby has beaten me to that first hummer sighting by at least a few days, but eventually the hummingbirds arrive in my yard, too. For me, spring and another opportunity for learning arrive with them.

Of the approximately 340 species of hummingbirds, all of which live in the western hemisphere, 17 have been known to breed in Canada and the United States. Hummingbirds are found in every Canadian province and American state, except Hawaii. Their spectacular beauty, fearless personality, and astonishing powers of flight captivate our attention and make them among the most beloved of all birds. Because they are relatively easy to attract,

Kim Bailey

these exceptional birds can be an endless source of interest for students and teachers. This article presents some of the remarkable adaptations behind hummingbirds' beauty, grace, and precision, and suggests a variety of ways to invite them into your schoolyard and your curriculum. Students will be spellbound as they experience hummingbirds up close and observe firsthand their special interactions with plants and natural surroundings.

Hummingbird facts and feats

Pollination: Uniquely adapted for feeding from flowers, hummingbirds are more efficient at dispersing pollen than many insects. Pollen dusted on the bird's bill, throat, or forehead is easily transferred from flower to flower. Hummingbirds are also more reliable pollinators: while insects become inactive on cold or rainy days, hummingbirds visit flowers regardless of the weather. Flowers adapted to pollination by hummingbirds are often red because this color is not visible to most insects. They also lack a fragrance, since hummingbirds have little or no sense of smell. A tubular shape and the absence of a landing platform are among other adaptations designed to help reserve the flower's nectar for hummingbirds and to discourage insects.

Flight: Hummingbirds are so adept at flying that they have no need to walk. Their small feet serve mostly as retractable landing gear used for perching. They are the only birds that can hover and fly backward, forward, sideways, straight up or down, and even upside down. Their wings can beat 70 to 80 times per second, giving them an average flight speed of 40 to 48 kilometers (25 to 30 miles) per hour. Hummingbirds must often eat more than twice their weight in nectar and insects every day as fuel for flight. A human with a weight-specific metabolic rate equal to that of a hummingbird would need to take in an estimated 155,000 calories a day!

Migration: To escape intense competition in the tropics, several hummingbird species migrate to the United States and Canada to breed each spring. It is amazing they make it here at all! Ruby-throated hummingbirds travel all the way from Central America to breeding grounds throughout the entire eastern United States and most of southern Canada. For most, the migration includes a remarkable nonstop flight across the Gulf of Mexico, a trip of 800 to 1,000 kilometers (500 to 600 miles). Weighing only about six grams when they set out (about twice their normal weight), and with a brain the size of a BB pellet, they are somehow able to complete this journey and return year after year to the same territories. Females have even been known to return to the same nest several years in a row. Rufous hummingbirds, which breed as far north as southern Alaska, have the longest migration route of any hummingbird, travelling up to 4,800 kilometers (3,000 miles) from Central America.

Preparing for hummingbird visitors

Just before the spring migration, hummingbirds gorge themselves on tropical nectar and insects. Some even double their body weight to store enough energy to make the journey north. When they arrive, they survive on insects, the nectar of early-blooming flowers, and even tree sap which they lap from holes made by woodpeckers known as sapsuckers. During this critical time, you can provide food for hummingbirds — and maybe even entice a few to stay — by hanging feeders and planting early-blooming trees, shrubs, and wildflowers that are indigenous to your area.

Hummingbird Feeder Tips

- Use feeders designed to exclude wasps, bees, and ants.

- If spring mornings are cold where you live, use a feeder without perches. Hovering while feeding helps hummingbirds stay warm.

- Always keep feeders clean, and nectar fresh.

- To make nectar, use one part sugar to four parts water. Use ordinary white cane sugar. Do not use brown sugar, honey, artificial sweeteners, flavorings, or anything but 20 percent sugar water! Do not add food coloring to nectar.

- To slow the rate of spoilage, boil the nectar for up to two minutes. Cool the nectar before adding it to the feeder.

- Store unused nectar in the refrigerator for up to two weeks.

Hummingbird inquiry ideas

Hummingbird gardens and feeders arouse curiosity and enable students to design experiments to answer their own questions about hummingbird behavior. Here are some questions and mysteries to get them started.

Which type of feeder is most attractive to hummingbirds?

Test several different types of commercial feeders or make your own. Hang the feeders in similar areas or the same area. Observe birds feeding and measure how much nectar has been consumed from each feeder. Be aware that one dominant bird may guard the feeder it prefers and force others to feed at less preferable feeders.

Rusty Trump

Do hummingbirds feed more or less often at feeders placed near nectar flowers than at feeders placed far away from them?

Place one feeder in or near the hummingbird garden. Place another feeder of the same type in a distant but easy-to-view location. Observe birds feeding and measure how much nectar has been consumed from each feeder.

Do hummingbirds really prefer red?

Obtain colorless feeders or make your own. Color the feeders with non-toxic paint or tie colored ribbons on them. Place the feeders in similar locations or the same location. Observe birds feeding and measure how much nectar has been consumed from each feeder.

Which flowers are most attractive to hummingbirds?

Observe hummingbirds feeding at different times of the day. Use a stopwatch to record the amount of time a bird spends feeding at each type of flower. Graph and compare feeding times, showing the favorite flowers in order of preference.

Do hummingbirds prefer nectar made from purified water to nectar made from ordinary tap water?

Make two batches of nectar, one using purified water and one using tap water. Use two identical feeders placed at the same location, just a few feet apart, each with a different batch of nectar. Record daily observations. Reverse the feeders and keep recording. Compare results with those at <www.naturalinstinct.com/hummingbird_master.html>.

Caution: Be careful not to set up an experiment that could possibly harm the birds. For example, never experiment with providing nectars of different concentrations or nectars made from different sugary substances.

— by Kim Bailey

To prepare for your first hummingbird visitors, teach students to use field guides or Internet resources to find out which species are found where you live (see list of websites, page 43). If ruby-throated or rufous hummingbirds migrate through your area, students can predict the first bird's arrival by checking the Journey North website and the <http://hummingbirds.net> site to view previous years' and current migration data and maps.

Ideally, feeders should be hung where they can be observed and where they are safe and accessible to hummingbirds. Have students survey the schoolyard to determine the most sheltered places for hummingbirds to feed and how the birds will get to these areas (e.g., whether there is a corridor of trees or shrubs leading to the area). To help attract the attention of hummingbirds, hang red ribbons on the feeders and nearby shrubs. If you live in an area where mornings are chilly, use feeders without perches, as hummingbirds can become hypothermic if they drink very cold sugar water while perching. By hovering while feeding, they warm their bodies and avoid hypothermia.

After the feeders are hung, students can learn more about hummingbirds, come up with additional questions, and plan other ways to make the schoolyard a better hummingbird habitat. They could, for instance, research flowers to be planted to increase the food supply and help catch a hummer's eye. Flowering plants are especially important to sustain the hummingbird habitat over the summer if feeders are not maintained during that time.

Spring is an ideal time to start a hummer habitat project, but hummingbirds can be a terrific curriculum tool at other times of the year. Why not start off the school year with observations of the peak of the southward migration in your area? Fall is the best time to plant many of the perennials, shrubs, trees, and vines that hummingbirds will seek out on their return. In winter, you can engage students in planning habitat areas or even propagating plants from seed indoors. No matter what time of the year

Hummingbirds' spectacular beauty, fearless personality, and astonishing powers of flight captivate our attention and make them among the most beloved of all birds.

you start a hummingbird garden, always avoid using pesticides. Chemicals sprayed on flowers could be ingested by the birds and could kill small insects that are an important source of food for hummingbirds.

As in any schoolyard habitat for wildlife, in addition to food, you should provide shelter and water. Do you need more trees or shrubs to create cover, nesting places, or perching spots near feeders? (Hummingbirds spend about 80 percent of their time perching.) How will you provide water? In nature, hummingbirds prefer showers to baths and can often be observed streaking back and forth in the fine spray of a waterfall in order to clean their feathers. Commercial bird misters are available from birdwatchers' supply stores for this purpose. Similar devices that attach to a garden hose are also sold as plant misters or poolside "personal cooling systems" and are often less expensive. All use a very small amount of water and can be set on a timer: the birds have even been known to learn a misting schedule and regularly appear just in time for their morning or afternoon shower. Hummingbirds will also bathe in flight by brushing against or sliding around on wet leaves — what a sight that is! To create this bathing alternative, simply make a small hole in the bottom of a bucket, fill the bucket with water, hang it above a leafy branch, and refill as needed.

When the hummingbirds do arrive in your outdoor classroom, encourage students to make careful observations, keep records of all the hummer happenings, conduct investigations and inquiry projects, continue to improve and expand habitats, and celebrate the hummingbirds in your schoolyard. Explore all the ways hummingbirds can provide natural motivation for learning and integrate all areas of the curriculum. Draw on the ideas, activities, and resources here to get started. If you and your class are lucky enough to attract an early arriver, don't forget to report your sighting on-line. Maybe you can earn that coveted dot on the hummingbird migration map that has always eluded me!

Kim Bailey

Territorial Tactics game

Territorial Tactics is an energetic tag game in which students simulate the territorial behavior and survival strategies of hummingbirds. It is designed to teach students tactics used by dominant territorial hummingbirds to guard a feeder or patch of nectar plants, and tactics used by other hummingbirds to try to feed from that protected food source. (The game is like Capture the Flag with a few adaptations.)

Subject areas: science

Key concepts: behavioral adaptations, intra-species competition

Skills: teamwork, problem solving, physical fitness (movement)

Location: outdoors

Time: 20 to 30 minutes

Materials: a rope 6 meters (20 feet) long or large hoop 1.5 meters (5 feet) in diameter; boundary markers (e.g., rope or traffic cones); at least 5 food tokens (e.g., red poker chips, red cutouts from laminated paper or foam place mats, or other small objects) per student

Preparation: Near the center of a wide flat outdoor area, lay down a hoop or rope to form a circle about 1.5 meters (5 feet) in diameter that will represent the food source. Place the food tokens inside this circle. Place boundary markers 15 to 30 meters (50 to 100 feet) away from the food source.

Procedure:

1. Choose one student to play the role of the territorial hummingbird who guards the food source by tagging competitors.

2. The rest of the students are competing hummingbirds who try to grab one food token at a time (no handfuls) without stepping inside of the food circle and without being tagged by the dominant hummingbird. (The food circle is large enough that students won't bump heads as they lean in to grab food tokens, but remind them to be careful.)

3. Students who are tagged must give up one food token, go outside the territorial boundary, and count to 30 before returning inside the boundary. (This represents a competitor being chased away from the feeder or flower.)

4. The first player to collect five tokens shouts "Territory Turnover" to signal that this round is over. All of the players return their food tokens to the circle. The winner becomes the dominant hummingbird in the next round.

Wrap-up: Ask students to explain the strategies and tactics they used to protect or obtain food. One strategy used by territorial hummingbirds, which students may also use, is to stay very close to the food source. A tactic used by competing birds is "strength in numbers": if many birds feed at once, the dominant bird has a harder time fighting them off. What other tactics did they use? Do hummingbirds use these as well? In nature, do flowers produce a continuous and endless supply of nectar? How might territorial behavior help hummingbirds to survive?

Adaptations:

- Play the first round with only one competing hummingbird, and then play with five, then with ten, and keep increasing the number of competing birds each round. (This increase in competition happens in nature during peak migration periods and toward the end of the breeding season when young birds become mature enough to feed at flowers and feeders.) Ask students how their tactics differ or change.

- After a few rounds, require competing birds to return to the boundary after picking up each token. This will reduce the number of birds feeding at the same time and may be a useful trick for playing the game with larger classes. Ask students how their tactics differ or change.

- After a few rounds, add a second feeding area some distance from the original. (People who wish to accommodate more hummingbirds hang a second feeder out of sight of the dominant bird. It is much harder a for dominant bird to defend two feeders, and often a second dominant bird will claim the other feeder.)

Extension: After playing the game, observe the behavior of hummingbirds feeding at a feeder or patch of flowers. What behaviors do students recognize from the game? If you cannot observe live hummingbirds feeding, several videos are available that include footage of feeding behavior (e.g., *Dances with Hummingbirds*, 1995, Nature Science Network, Inc., 61 min.; and *Watching Hummingbirds*, 1998, Nature Science Network, Inc., 33 min.).

Design a hummingbird flower

In this activity, students design and create a flower adapted for pollination by hummingbirds.

Subject areas: science

Key concepts: physical adaptations, pollination, competition

Skills: problem solving, creative thinking, teamwork/cooperative learning, oral communication, observation (if real flowers are examined)

Location: indoors

Time: One hour +

Materials: chalk and chalk board for planning meeting; real hummingbird flowers or pictures of hummingbird flowers (optional); paper, pencils, and miscellaneous art supplies for creating a flower prototype (e.g., markers, colored pencils, paint, construction paper, poster paper, pipe cleaners, beads, modeling clay, glue, tape)

Preparatory activity: It will be helpful to teach or review the parts of a flower (pistil, stamens, petals, sepals, etc.) using fresh flowers, dissecting tools, and a magnifying lens or microscope. One method that is memorable and fun is to have the students "build" a flower, with students posing and acting as the various parts and functions. For example, ask one student to raise her arms to represent the pistil; this student could also chant "Sticky, sticky, sticky" to demonstrate the sticky stigma which collects pollen at the top of the pistil. A small group of students representing stamens could encircle the pistil and hold their fists in the air to represent the pollen-bearing anthers at the tips of the stamen; these students could chant "Pollen, pollen, pollen" in deep macho-male voices. A larger group of students could encircle the stamens to represent the petals. Facing outward, these students should act very attractive by waving, smiling, and saying welcoming phrases to passing birds, bees, and insects. Finally, a last group of students could represent the sepals that hold the parts of the flower together and attach it to the stem. These students can encircle the petals, hold hands, and act and sound as if they are working very hard to hold the flower together. After acting out the flower parts, students can dissect real flowers as a hands-on way to identify all the parts. A magnifying lens or microscope can be used to examine each flower part in more detail.

Presenting flower designs at a teachers' workshop.

Procedure:

1. Announce to the class that today they are all designers for a product development and marketing company. Since they are so good at their jobs, Mother Nature would like them to do some work for her. She has hired the class to design a new species for her upcoming Spring Plant Kingdom line. Because of the high demand and buying power of her hummingbird customers, the new species should appeal specifically to hummingbirds. The flower should be fashionable to catch the hummingbirds' attention and functional to meet their needs. Since hummingbirds pay for the product with pollination, the flower should also be designed to make as much profit as possible. In addition, Mother Nature has one other special concern that needs to be considered in the flower design. Since her store is so large (the Earth), she doesn't have time to monitor the shoppers very closely and, unfortunately, shoplifting has become a problem. Certain insects have found ways to steal nectar from flowers without paying in full or at all. They simply take the flower nectar and do not pay by pollinating. Therefore, the new flower should be designed to deter and exclude these shoplifters.

2. Conduct a planning meeting. Have students brainstorm factors to consider before starting the project. List all aspects of the "customers," "shoplifters," and "market appeal" that the flower's design must address, but not actual ways to address them. The following are possible topics.

(a) Consider the customers and their shopping style and needs:

- Flight: they can hover.
- Size: they are small but most flowers cannot support their weight.
- Color: they are brightly colored.
- Sight: they have good eyesight and see longer wavelengths of light (red) best.
- Beak: they have long narrow beaks with a long tongue inside.
- Smell: they have a poor sense of smell.
- Behavior: they can be territorial and prevent other birds from feeding.
- Nutrition: they need large amounts of nectar, they need water, and they need protein from insects.

(b) Consider the shoplifters:

- Sight: most insects see shorter wavelengths of light best (blue, violet, ultraviolet); insects are also attracted to the color yellow.
- Mouth: they have shorter tongues than hummers but some have mouthparts that can pierce the base of the flower to steal nectar.
- Smell: they have a strong sense of smell that guides them to flowers.
- Size: they are light and often land on flowers they feed from.

(c) Consider ways to maximize profit:

- How to get the hummingbirds to transfer pollen most efficiently and effectively
- How to achieve cross-pollination
- How to attract customers
- How to reward customers
- How to prevent theft
- How to crush the competition (outcompete other flowers)

3. After the brainstorming session, divide the class into teams of designers. To ensure participation and cooperation, teachers sometimes find it helpful to assign specific design roles to team members (e.g., materials specialist, idea note taker, presenter, advertising manager, customer satisfaction specialist, theft-prevention manager). Each team must present an oral report about its proposed flower to explain its advantages. As part of the report, each team must also present a model or full-color drawing of its flower as a prototype.

4. As teams are developing their ideas, walk around and ask questions to stimulate students' imaginations and to remind them of factors they are omitting (e.g., how to exclude "shoplifters").

With its tubular, nectar-rich flowers, trumpet honeysuckle is a hit with hummingbirds.

Kim Bailey

Characteristics of Flowers Adapted to Pollination by Hummingbirds

- Often the petals of hummingbird plants are fused to form a tubular shape. This excludes many insects that do not have tongues long enough to reach the nectar hidden inside.
- Most birds do not have a well-developed sense of smell, so many hummingbird-pollinated flowers lack a fragrance. As bees and other insects are guided in part by scent, they are not attracted to these flowers.
- Hummingbird flowers often hang away from the plant, leaving space where birds can maneuver. Many also hang pointing down or to the side rather than up and the nectar inside is less likely to be diluted by rainwater. They are also easy for hummingbirds to hover around but difficult for insects to land on.
- Many hummingbird-pollinated flowers have a thickened covering at their bases, or the bases are grouped tightly together in an inflorescence. This prevents bees from piercing the base of the flower to reach the nectar.
- The stamens of hummingbird-pollinated flowers are often positioned to deposit pollen efficiently onto a hummingbird's throat, beak, or head.
- Many of these flowers are red. Most insects do not see longer wavelengths of light (red) at all or as well as they see shorter wavelengths of light (blue, violet, ultraviolet). Red may appear as a dark or black color to insects so they are not particularly attracted to it. However, red is easily seen and distinguished from other colors by birds. Note that a garden does not have to be full of red, orange, or pink flowers with the characteristics listed above in order to attract hummingbirds. Hummingbirds are extremely curious and opportunistic birds that will feed from almost any flower with nectar to which they can gain access, no matter what its color, shape, or size.

Wrap-up: Ask each team to present its flower model or drawing and to point out or demonstrate its fashionable and functional features. Each team should explain how its flower will attract hummingbirds, how pollen will be transferred, how hummingbirds will be rewarded, and how nectar will be protected from "shoplifters." Finally, congratulate the teams on a job well done.

Extension: As part of the activity you may want to study hummingbird-pollinated flowers using either real flowers or pictures (Mother Nature's current line!). If you are concerned that this might squelch students' creativity and cause them simply to copy real flowers, you could do it at the end of the activity. If you study actual flowers, note how the stamens on cardinal flower, Indian paintbrushes, and many penstemons are positioned to tap pollen onto the hummingbird's head. Columbine and many other dangling-down blooms get pollen all around the base of the bill. Many of the larger trumpet-shaped blooms deposit pollen on the hummingbird's throat. Other characteristics to note in the real-life flowers are their color (typically red or orange), tubular shape, lack of scent, thickened base, sideways or downward orientation, etc. Use the chart "Characteristics of Flowers Adapted to Pollination by Hummingbirds" (at left) as a reference.

Migration Mishaps game

Migration Mishaps is a game that helps to demonstrate why animals that migrate, such as hummingbirds, are threatened by habitat destruction.

Subject areas: science

Key concepts: habitat, migration, survival, competition, limiting factors, population dynamics

Skills: graphing (extension activity)

Location: outdoors

Time: 20 minutes

Materials: 2 paper plates or pieces of cloth ("habitat havens") for every 3 students, migration cards (next page); 3-5 soft foam balls (adaptation); wipe-off board and marker (extension activity)

Preparation: Review with students the definition of habitat (food, water, shelter and space suitably arranged) and explain that many factors limit the survival of populations of hummingbirds, including changes in the two habitats on which they depend. Have students research wintering and breeding habitats of hummingbird species in your area. (Ruby-throated hummingbirds winter mainly in Mexico and Central America, while their nesting habitat is in eastern United States and southern Canada).

Procedure:

1. Select a large area up to 20 meters (70 feet) in length. Designate one end of the area as the wintering grounds and the other end as the nesting grounds. Distribute the "habitat havens" (paper plates or cloth pieces) equally in the wintering and nesting grounds.

2. Begin the activity with all students at the wintering grounds, assigning no more than three players to each habitat haven. Explain that at your signal they are to migrate to a habitat haven in the nesting grounds.

3. For the first round, select a migration card that requires removing habitat havens. Read the card aloud and remove habitat havens in the area to which the hummingbirds will be migrating (in this round, the nesting grounds).

4. Give the signal to migrate. If players cannot find space at the new habitat (remind them that only three birds can share one habitat haven), they must die and move to the sidelines temporarily. These "dead" birds may re-enter the game as hatchlings when favorable conditions make more habitat havens available in the nesting grounds.

Safety note: Even though hummingbirds are aggressive and territorial, caution students that there should

Hummingbird True or False

This quick quiz highlights some little-known facts and dispels some misconceptions about hummingbirds. Use the quiz as a pre- and post-assessment. As your class learns more about hummingbirds, let them add their own items to the quiz or create a whole new quiz for another class to take.

Time: 10 minutes

____ 1. Hummingbirds eat only flower nectar.

____ 2. Hummingbirds can fly upside down.

____ 3. Hummingbirds suck nectar from flowers.

____ 4. Hummingbirds migrate on the backs of Canada geese.

____ 5. A hummingbird's heart beats over 1,000 times per minute.

____ 6. Hummingbirds search for nectar only from red flowers.

____ 7. Leaving up a hummingbird feeder late into fall can slow or prevent migration.

____ 8. Hummingbirds are most attracted to flowers with strong fragrances.

____ 9. Each hummingbird species makes a different "humming" sound.

____ 10. Hummingbirds will attack larger birds such as crows and hawks.

Answers

1. *False.* As hummingbirds need protein, they eat small insects and spiders. They also feed on tree sap and sugar water in hummingbird feeders.

2. *True.* Hummingbirds can fly upside down briefly, by doing a backward somersault.

3. *False.* Hummingbirds do not suck nectar. They lap up the nectar at about 13 licks per second!

4. *False.* Hummingbirds and Canada geese migrate at different times, live in different habitats, and migrate to different areas.

5. *True.* A hummingbird's heart beats 1,260 times per minute, or 21 times per second!

6. *False.* Hummingbirds are most attracted to red but will feed from any nectar-producing flowers.

7. *False.* Hummingbirds migrate based on changes in day length, not availability of food.

8. *False.* Hummingbirds do not have a well-developed sense of smell. They locate their food by eyesight.

9. *True.* The rush of air created by the wings makes a different humming, buzzing, or whistling sound in each species.

10. *True.* Hummingbirds are fiercely aggressive and are not intimidated by size. They have been observed attacking crows, hawks, and other larger birds.

Migration Cards for Migration Mishaps

 A large habitat was designated as a wildlife preserve. Gain 3 habitat havens.

 A wetland is filled so a new highway can be built. Lose 2 habitat havens.

 Pollution severely damaged a riverside habitat. Lose 2 habitat havens.

 The construction of a new subdivision and golf course destroys a forest habitat. Lose 3 habitat havens.

 A concerned school group improved a damaged habitat by creating an outdoor classroom and garden. Gain 2 habitat havens.

 A neighborhood creates backyard wildlife habitats. Gain 2 habitat havens.

 Drought killed some flowering plants. Lose 2 habitat havens.

 An apartment dweller plants hanging baskets with humming-bird-attracting flowers. Gain 1 habitat haven.

 Tougher laws are passed to protect bird habitat. Gain 1 habitat haven.

 A homeowner plants a row of trees for shelter. Gain 1 habitat haven.

 Pesticides contaminated the flowers' nectar. Lose 2 habitat havens.

 A late frost killed the first spring flowers. But sap is available through a sapsucker's holes in some trees. Gain 1 habitat haven.

 Insecticides killed insects needed for protein. Lose 1 habitat haven.

 A school hangs up hummingbird feeders. Gain 2 habitat havens.

 Trees used for shelter and nesting are cut down to make paper. Lose 2 habitat havens.

 A city-dweller hangs up a hummingbird feeder. But there are no trees for shelter in the area. Sorry, no habitat haven.

be no pushing or shoving over habitat. You may want to make a rule that students migrate in slow motion by walking instead of running.

5. Play several more rounds, beginning each round by reading a migration card, and adding or removing habitat havens in the habitat to which students will migrate.

Wrap-up: Ask students to summarize what they have learned about some of the many factors that affect migrating birds and their habitat. Discuss what students can do about habitat loss and degradation. What can they do to improve hummingbird habitat?

Adaptation: Hummingbirds face perils along the migration route as well as in wintering and nesting grounds. Soft foam balls can represent such perils as storms or running out of energy. Let students in the "dead bird"

Kim Bailey

zone take turns tossing the balls into the path of "migrating" students. When a ball makes contact with a migrating student, he/she becomes a "dead bird."

Extension: Use a wipe-off board and marker to graph the shifting hummingbird population after each round. Students in the "dead bird" zone can help with this while they are waiting to re-enter the game.

Kim Bailey is a regional editor of Green Teacher *magazine and the coordinator of the Environmental Education in Georgia on-line clearinghouse. At its website (<http://EEinGEORGIA.org>), educators can find more hummingbird activities as well as other lesson plans and resources for environmental education.*

The Migration Mishaps activity was adapted from "Migration Headache," Project WILD *Aquatic Activity Guide.*

RESOURCES

Newfield, Nancy L., and Barbara Nielsen. *Hummingbird Gardens: Attracting Nature's Jewels to Your Backyard.* Houghton Mifflin, 1996.

Osborne, June. *The Ruby-throated Hummingbird.* University of Texas Press, 1998.

Sargent, Robert. *Ruby-throated Hummingbird.* Stackpole Books, 1999.

Stokes, Donald, and Lillian Stokes. *The Hummingbird Book: The Complete Guide to Attracting, Identifying, and Enjoying Hummingbirds.* Little, Brown & Company, 1989.

Tyrell, Esther Quesada. *Hummingbirds: Their Life and Behavior, A Photographic Study of the North American Species.* Crown Publishers, 1985.

Williamson, Shed L. *A Field Guide to Hummingbirds of North America.* Houghton Mifflin, 2001. (A Peterson Field Guide.)

HELPFUL HUMMINGBIRD WEBSITES

<www.hummingbirds.net> This site lists hummingbird species by state and province, and provides spring migration maps and much more.

<www.portalproductions.com/> The Hummingbird Web Site includes approximate migration dates by species for the United States and Canada.

<www.mbr-pwrc.usgs.gov/> The North American Breeding Bird Survey provides hummingbird species distribution maps.

<www.learner.org/jnorth> Journey North records hummingbird migration tracking and other resources for the study of hummingbirds and other migratory animals.

<www.rubythroat.org> Operation Rubythroat provides cross-disciplinary hummingbird activities and inquiry project ideas for teachers (K–12).

<www.naturalinstinct.com> Natural Instinct is dedicated to collecting and distributing information on the flora and fauna of North America's backyards (includes hummingbird investigations).

<www.hummingbirdsplus.org> Hummer/Bird Study Group is a non-profit organization focusing on the study and preservation of hummingbirds and other neotropical migrants.

<www.hummingbird.org> The Hummingbird Society is a non-profit corporation dedicated to encouraging international understanding and conservation of hummingbirds.

<www.nanps.org> North American Native Plant Society includes a list of state and provincial native plant societies that may help you to identify the indigenous plants preferred by hummingbirds in your area.

Discovering Our Temperate Rainforests

Activities to explore species adaptation and forestry issues in North America's coastal temperate rainforests

by Anne Lindsay

Subjects: ecology, social science

Key concepts: adaptation, habitat needs, environmental issues (forestry)

Skills: creativity, problem solving, role playing

Location: indoors

Home of giant conifers, some of them more than 90 meters (300 feet) tall and 1,000 years old, the temperate rainforests of the Pacific Northwest support the greatest diversity of wildlife on the North American continent. The study of these ancient forests provides students with an opportunity to examine the ways in which living things adapt to a specific habitat, and the environmental issues that arise from human activity in a complex ecosystem.

These activities are designed to introduce students to the temperate rainforests of North America and to the unique climatic conditions that produce an environment conducive to plant and animal species found nowhere else. For example, the threatened marbled murrelet is a small seabird that nests on the highest branches of old-growth trees, where the moss creates a thick pad. The nest site of this species, which spends most of its time on the Pacific Ocean, was not discovered until

Gail Littlejohn

Coast redwoods of Northern California.

1901. Another bird, the Rhinoceros auklet, digs deep burrows in the root systems of large trees in remote coastal islands of the rainforest. To date, 80 species have been found to be dependent on this ancient ecosystem for their survival. The activities could form part of a more comprehensive unit of study of temperate rainforests, complement a classroom or school-wide study of rainforests or endangered species, be used as Earth Week activities, or form the basis of an independent study or research project. The Create a Creature activity could also serve as a culminating task, for evaluation, at the end of a study of adaptations to habitats.

How old is ancient?

The largest western red cedar ever recorded was about 2,000 years old, and Douglas firs may be more than 1,000 years old. To help students grasp the age of some of the trees in the temperate rainforest, have them plot major events in history on a timeline that spans the lifetimes of these oldest trees. You could begin by asking students to bring to class the oldest object in their home. (Caution them to ask permission, and not to bring anything living, fragile, or valuable.) The age of these objects can be plotted on the timeline first. Other information for plotting could include students' birth dates, the date on which their town was founded, the birthdates of historical figures, the dates of inventions, or other dates of interest to the class.

Adaptations to Life in an Ancient Temperate Forest

Characteristics of the Forest	Adaptations	
Large cone-bearing trees form a canopy over the forest. As a result, the plants on the forest floor and in the understory receive little or no sunlight.	Animals:	• some eat bits of moss and lichen that fall from branches of large trees (e.g., Roosevelt elk) • some burrow under the extensive root systems of the large trees for nesting (e.g., Rhinoceros auklet)
	Plants:	• plants on the forest floor have a higher than average concentration of chlorophyll • some plants have eliminated the need for roots and hang from the branches of large trees so that they can gain greater exposure to sunlight (e.g., lichens, mosses, and ferns)
Large standing snags or decaying trees	Animals:	• some use snags as nesting sites, shelters, and as a food source (home of many insects)
	Fungi:	• grow on decaying trees (e.g., bracket fungi)
Nurse logs (fallen logs on the forest floor)	Animals:	• use nurse logs for shelter, as nesting sites, and as a food source
	Plants:	• use nurse logs as a source of nutrients, moisture and warmth, especially for new seedling trees (hence the name "nurse log")
Large logs lying in streams	Animals:	• use slower water for protection (e.g., insects and young salmon)
Dry summers	Plants:	• broom-like branches of large trees "sweep" moisture from the air
Cold wet winters	Animals:	• warm coats of some mammals provide protection from cold (e.g., fox)
	Plants:	• evergreen conifers carry out photosynthesis in the winter
Green lush environment	Animals and Plants:	• camouflage (e.g., three-toed salamander)

Fast Facts about North America's Coastal Temperate Rainforest

• Coastal temperate rainforests comprise only two to three percent of the world's rainforests. Half of the world's temperate rainforests are in the Pacific Northwest; other major tracts are in Chile, New Zealand, and Australia.

• North America's temperate rainforest once covered 25 million hectares (62 million acres) in a coastal strip running from California north to Alaska. About 55 percent of this original forest remains undeveloped; almost all of these old-growth sections are in northern British Columbia and Alaska.

• Temperate rainforests are defined not by their vegetation but rather by their unique climate. The conditions for temperate rainforests are created by high coastal mountains that trap moisture-laden clouds moving inland from the ocean. Abundant rainfall (as much as 200 centimeters / 80 inches per year) and mild temperatures year-round promote the rapid growth of vegetation. Fog and clouds provide moisture for the growth of lichens and mosses in the forest canopy.

• Constant moisture from rain and fog means that coastal rainforests are rarely disturbed by fire. Trees are long-lived and many grow to enormous sizes. Windfall trees create openings for new growth, and decaying logs and litter on the forest floor provide a diversity of habitats.

• The rainforest of the Pacific Northwest supports more than 30 tree species and 250 species of mammals and birds. Rainforest streams are the spawning grounds and nurseries of seven species of Pacific salmon and trout.

• The dominant tree species of the Pacific Northwest rainforest are conifers. They include the gigantic redwoods of California, western hemlock, western red cedar, Douglas fir, Sitka spruce, and mountain hemlock. Different species dominate at different latitudes.

• Coastal temperate rainforests store more organic matter than any other forest type, including tropical forests — from 500 to 2,000 metric tons of wood, foliage, leaf litter, moss, and soil per hectare.

• For more than 5,000 years, the rich resources of the Pacific Ocean and the inland rainforest watersheds supported one of the largest and most diverse populations of aboriginal peoples in North America. More than 65 languages were spoken, and an extensive trading network linked villages and cultures.

Source: Edward C. Wolf, Andrew P. Mitchell, and Peter K. Schoonmaker, *The Rain Forests of Home: An Atlas of People and Place,* Ecotrust, Pacific GIS, and Conservation International, 1995, <www.inforain.org/rainforestatlas/>.

Create a Creature

Time: two 45-minute periods

Materials: class chart of "Adaptations to Life in an Ancient Temperate Rainforest" (page 45); 1 large piece of paper (or Creature Information Sheet, below), modeling clay (optional) per student, student journals

In this activity, students create an imaginary plant or animal that is adapted for life in an ancient temperate rainforest.

Goals:

- to review the habitat needs of plants and animals and how these needs are met
- to reinforce, in a concrete way, the ways in which living things interact and adapt to their natural habitat
- to promote creativity and problem-solving skills
- to introduce the concept of food chains and food webs

Background: The wet winters, short dry summers, and dense coniferous canopy of the temperate rainforest create a unique environment found nowhere else in North America. The plants and animals that are indigenous to the rainforest have adapted to this environment, often in remarkable ways. The chart "Adaptations to Life in an Ancient Temperate Rainforest" outlines some of the physical characteristics and conditions of a temperate rainforest and gives examples of how various species have adapted to each of these conditions. The first four characteristics are common to all ancient temperate rainforests of the Pacific Northwest. This summary chart can be used as a reference or can be produced as a class chart for students when you introduce this activity.

Ray Cromie

Procedure: Explain to students that they are to create a plant or animal that is adapted to living in an ancient temperate rainforest. They are to include a colored drawing of the creature in its natural environment, and they are to complete the information sheet about the creature.

Creature Information Sheet

1. Animal or plant?_____

2. Name of creature: _____

3. Drawing of creature:

4. Creature's source of water: _____

5. Creature's space or territory: _____

6. If creature is an animal:

   (a) Food: _____

   (b) Shelter: _____

7. If creature is a plant:

   (a) Source of light: _____

   (b) Soil type: _____

8. What species, if any, uses your creature as a food source?

_____

_____

9. How does your creature protect itself?

_____

_____

_____

_____

10. Name three ways your creature is adapted to life in a temperate rainforest.

_____

_____

_____

Rainforest debate

Time: two 30-minute periods

Materials: role-playing cards (provided: 1 per student), outline of debate format (on chart paper), costumes and props (optional), student journals

This activity encourages students to consider issues raised by human activity, particularly logging, in an ancient temperate rainforest. Students assume the roles of a variety of people who would be affected in different ways by plans to log an area of forest. By considering many perspectives, they can begin to understand the need for cooperative resolutions to environmental problems. The activity requires two days to complete (one to prepare, and one for the debate).

Goals:

- to introduce current issues relating to ancient temperate rainforests of the Pacific Northwest
- to encourage students to consider the various needs of different groups when discussing an environmental issue
- to provide a forum for presenting ideas and opinions
- to encourage cooperative group work
- to involve students in considering how natural resources can be used in a sustainable way

Procedure:

1. Read to students the following scenario:
   "TreeCut Company has placed a proposal before government seeking permission to harvest an area of ancient temperate rainforest called Orca Sound. Many people, as well as the forest itself, are likely to be affected by the government's decision to permit or turn down the proposal. Some of them have asked the government committee for an opportunity to present their views about the logging proposal in a debate. The people can also make suggestions about guidelines that TreeCut Company will have to follow if logging is allowed. At the end of the debate, the government committee will vote to recommend that the legislature either refuse the logging plan or approve it with guidelines."

2. Inform students that they are to play the roles of the people in the debate. They will tell the government committee what they think about the logging proposal and why. It is important to explain that they are role-playing a point of view with which they may not agree, and that the purpose is to present and consider all points of view involved in deciding how an ancient temperate rainforest should be used.

3. Divide the class into nine groups. Give each group a role-playing card and give the students time to prepare their group's positions. At this point, you may wish to allow time for students to research the issue in greater depth, perhaps by learning about perspectives presented in real-life logging controversies that have occurred in such areas as British Columbia's Great Bear Rainforest, Clayoquot Sound, and Stoltmann Wilderness, and the Tongass National Forest in Alaska. The group playing animals and plants may wish to research the needs of particular species that can survive only in old-growth forests. All groups should consider a range of options and compromises: clearcutting, sustainable logging, no logging of old-growth trees, no logging in protected areas, or no logging at all. The group playing the government committee representatives can write the names of the participants in the debate and discuss what position they think each will present on the logging plans, as well as one argument each might make to support that position. Ask each group to choose one representative to be the speaker at the debate.

   Note: Students may wish to dress for the parts they are playing.

4. For the debate, have the groups make their presentations one after the other in an order determined by you. Each group has 1 to 3 minutes to state its position on the logging proposal and to explain why. Then hold an open question period of 10 to 15 minutes in which members of any group may ask a question of any other group. Finally, allow each group to give a brief summary statement (30 seconds each).

5. Have the government committee members discuss the debate and make their decision either to refuse the logging plan or to approve it with guidelines. If they vote for approval, they should present the guideline that TreeCut should follow.

While the government is making its decision, ask the other students to write individual journal entries to answer these questions:

- Why do you think that we had this debate?
- Before the debate, what was your view on the logging proposal? Has your view changed since the debate? Explain why.
- Did you agree with the position that your group had to present? Explain why. If you didn't agree with your group's position, how did you feel about preparing it?
- Explain the importance of considering the views of others, even if we don't agree with them.

Wrap-up: After reviewing all of the reasons given for and against logging in the ancient temperate rainforest, invite students to vote again, but this time giving their personal opinions. Ask the students whether they changed their minds during the debate and, if so, which facts, arguments, or opinions influenced their decision.

Anne Lindsay is an environmental science specialist who teaches in Huntsville, Ontario.

Rainforest Debate Role-Playing Cards

Animals and Plants of Orca Sound:

You wish to remain in the ancient temperate rainforest, which is one of the few places where you can find your natural habitat. You believe that you have the right to shelter, food, clean water, and space. You know that logging — particularly clearcut logging (a method that removes all the trees in an area) — will destroy your habitat and you will probably die.

Aboriginal Elder:

You are Nuu-chah-nulth and your people have lived in the Orca Sound area for thousands of years. You believe that your people should have the final decision about what happens to the forest in your ancestral homeland. Your people have used the forest respectfully, but you would consider some logging if the profits help to improve life for your people.

TreeCut Company President:

You have been in the forestry business for more than 50 years, providing jobs for thousands of people. You admit that some of the logging practices used in the past were irresponsible and you are taking steps to improve them. If the government does not allow logging in Orca Sound, your company will start to lose money and might have to lay off some long-time workers in several towns.

Tourist:

You are planning a trip to the Orca Sound area next summer for sea kayaking, and hiking and photography in the forest. You will spend a lot of money to hire a guide and to fly yourself and your equipment to Orca Sound. You are against the plans for logging, as it would ruin your chance to experience the beauty of an ancient temperate rainforest.

Business Owner in Logging Town:

You own a restaurant near a TreeCut Company mill, the biggest business in town. People who work there and their families enjoy meals at your restaurant. If TreeCut's proposal to log the Orca Sound area is not allowed, many of the people in your town might lose their jobs and have to move to find work. Without their business, your restaurant might have to close.

Environmentalist:

You are an environmentalist who has lobbied government for a long time to protect ancient temperate rainforests in Orca Sound from all industry, including logging. Already, large areas of the forest have been destroyed by clearcutting. You believe that replanting trees only provides another crop of trees for the logging company to cut; it can never replicate the complex ecosystem of a true ancient temperate rainforest or replace the habitats that will be lost.

Logger:

You are the third generation of loggers in your family who have worked for TreeCut Company and you have three children to support. You are not trained for any other type of work and other jobs are hard to find in your community. If TreeCut is not allowed to log the Orca Sound area, you might lose your job. You understand that saving the old-growth trees is a good thing, but you have to make a living for your family to survive.

Inn Owner near Rainforest:

You own a small hotel that is often used by sea kayakers and people who hike in the ancient temperate rainforest. You have stayed in the Orca Sound area where you grew up so that you can spend your free time enjoying the forest. If the rainforest is logged, tourists may no longer have a reason to visit the area and stay in your inn. You may have to close your business and leave the area.

Government Representatives:

You are newly elected and depend on everyone's support to stay in office. You must recommend to the legislature either to refuse or to approve (with guidelines) the logging proposal. Environmentalists want you to pressure the legislature to preserve what remains of your area's ancient temperate rainforest. Loggers and others fear that they will lose their jobs and businesses if logging is not allowed in Orca Sound's rainforests.

RESOURCES

Books

Parkin, Tom. *Green Giants: Rainforests of the Pacific Northwest.* Douglas & McIntyre, 1992.

Wilson, Eric. *Spirit in the Rainforest.* Harper Collins, 1985. (fiction)

Wolf, Edward C., Andrew P. Mitchell and Peter K. Schoonmaker. *The Rain Forests of Home: An Atlas of People and Place.* Ecotrust, Pacific GIS, and Conservation International, 1995. <www.inforain.org/rainforestatlas/>.

Zuckerman, Seth, *Saving our Ancient Forests.* Living Planet Press, 1991.

Websites

<www.cotf.edu/ete/modules/temprain/temprain.html> This NASA-sponsored features a series of interdisciplinary learning modules on temperate rainforests and other environments.

<www.cofi.org> The site of the Council of Forest Industries gives the point of view of the forestry industry in British Columbia.

<www.focs.ca> The Friends of Clayoquot Sound site has basic background information on temperate rainforests, and photos of rainforest plants and animals as well as logging practices and protests.

<www.wildernesscommittee.org> The Western Canada Wilderness Committee site has news and articles on current issues related to temperate rainforests of the Pacific Northwest.

<www.eco-portal.com/Land/Forests/Types/RainLand/Forests/Temperate_Rainforests/welcome.asp> This "Eco-Portal" site has links to environmental groups working on issues related to temperate rainforests in North America.

Gail Littlejohn

Clearcutting on the road to Carmanah Valley on Vancouver Island.

Learning About Ecosystems

Zoning Out: Getting the Most out of a Beach Walk

by Terry Parker

Subject areas: science, biology, ecology

Key concepts: zonation, interrelationships, community ecology

Skills: observation, sampling, data collection

Location: ocean shoreline

Time required: 2 hours to a full day for field trip

Materials: outdoor clothing, buckets, shovels, tape measures, ropes, large plastic hoops

David Denning

"The time has come," the Walrus said,
"To talk of many things: Of shoes — and ships —
and sealing-wax — Of cabbages — and kings —
And why the sea is boiling hot —
And whether pigs have wings."

Lewis Carroll,
"Through the Looking Glass"

Just as Lewis Carroll's walrus knew, seashores are filled with stories waiting to be discovered. Stories of habitats organized with clockwork precision but at the mercy of random brute forces. Stories of animals and plants coping with life between two worlds, and of the ongoing struggle between predators and prey. Stories steeped in the legends of peoples worldwide.

Schools located near a seashore are blessed with an open-air classroom of almost boundless potential. Many teachers seize that opportunity by taking classes on a beach walk. With the time and effort that go into organizing such an event, you will want to turn the day into something more than a stone-turning search-and-destroy mission. While finding as many animals as possible from a checklist provides plenty of excitement, it often falls short of the full potential of the trip as a learning experience. Introduce a theme or story, however, and give the students the clues they need to do their own detective work, and your beach walk can easily become an intensive, enjoyable, whole-learning experience.

Later on, I touch on some of the themes you might use for your beach walk. Before that, though, let's consider some of the basic logistics of the trip itself.

Trip planning

To conduct a beach walk you must have a low tide. For long-range planning, tide tables are available at most boat supply stores and dive shops. Tide tables are also available on-line (see Resources). For last-minute planning, the weather section of newspapers usually contains daily tidal information. Long-range planning is best, however. In some areas, such as the Strait of Georgia in British Columbia, the time of the year plays a major role in the daily timing of the tides. In others, such as the Bay of Fundy in the Maritimes, the extremity of the tides requires careful consideration.

Not just any low tide will do for a beach walk. Some "low" tides will uncover barely half the shore — usually the less interesting half. Tides are measured in absolute vertical height above a theoretical lowest tide called "chart datum," which is set as the zero (meter or feet) level. Positive numbers are above this level and negative are below it. The best low tides — at 0.6 meters (2 feet) or lower — unlock most of the shore's hidden biological treasures. Tides close to zero, especially the rare tides below the zero mark (called minus tides) are sheer magic.

Chase the tide down. If you can afford the time, arrive on the beach two hours before the lowest tide of that day. Tides can move distressingly fast, and, especially on gently sloping shores, your stretch of low intertidal can be reclaimed by the sea while you stand expounding on the virtues of a burrowing existence. Chasing the tide down allows the sea to unravel its mysteries to the class; the farther down you go, the more alien the environment. Intrigue grows as students move from the terrestrial into the marine world. It is much more dramatic for students to start with small crusty barnacles and move their way down to powerful rock crabs, florally bright nudibranchs, and feathery seaweeds than it is to set up an anticlimax.

Site selection

Try to survey your site before the trip. Selecting the best type of shoreline depends on what you are looking for. Clams, sand shrimp, and worms are most likely to be found in a protected bay on a very flat sandy or muddy beach, preferably with some stones and with a freshwater stream running nearby. Stones provide a variety of habitats, and this increases the diversity of species to be found. Freshwater streams often carry nutrients that can add to the richness of the area. The beach should be well away from areas frequently used by humans. The shifting weight of sunbathers and heavy foot-falls of volleyball players can wreak havoc on burrowing communities.

David Denning

For a rocky shore beach walk, look for a gentle slope and fairly large cobble and stones, about 0.3–1 meter (1–3 feet). Beaches with small cobble tend not to support as rich a community because the cobble is rolled around too much by the waves, while larger boulders are difficult to walk on and even more of a problem to turn over. Shorelines with large low-lying expanses of exposed bedrock are very good, especially those with plenty of crevices and tidepools. Shores with a steep slope dry out more quickly between tides, keeping many of the animals and plants lower on the shore and out of students' reach. Exposed rocky headlands are often biologically rich but typically have steeply sloping, slippery rocks and are not worth the safety risk.

On any type of shore, be aware of the wave exposure of the area. Extreme open coasts are hazardous at best. Waves themselves are unpredictable and their undertow unforgiving. Sandy shores exposed to heavy surf are almost devoid of observable life because of the constantly shifting sand. On rocky shores, it is best to visit areas that receive moderate wave action. Very calm, protected embayments are good for sandy and muddy beaches, but their rocky areas usually have a low species diversity and are unrewarding.

Shoreline safety

Once you have selected a suitable site and day, arrange for a sufficient number of adult helpers to watch for the students' safety. You and your helpers should become familiar with the site before the walk. Often, rocky shores will have a variety of potential traveling paths with a variety of inherent hazard levels. Make a mental — if not paper — map of the safest routes. Brief the students on the potential dangers of waves and of walking on unstable rocks. A fall could be serious or even fatal, should someone's head hit a protruding rock. Ensure that your students know that the algae covering the rocks can be more slippery than ice — even if the rock looks dry and the algae is barely visible. When walking on the shore each foot should be settled before the next step is taken. Running is definitely to be avoided.

When the class is on the shore, make sure that at least one person is always watching the water for unusual waves. This could be a rotating job among your students. No matter what wave pattern you think you see, waves are unpredictable and the phenomenon of "rogue waves" is very real. At any time (and certainly not every seventh wave as many local superstitions have it) a wave much larger than any of the others can roll in. Because waves travel silently, the only defence is to see it coming. If you do get surprised by a wave, never run. The safest thing is to drop low, hang on to a rock until the wave recedes, and then crawl up the shore. On an exposed shore, watching for unusual waves can be a lifesaver. Even on calm shores it can save students from wet socks. As an added benefit, the wave watcher is also in a position to sight any off-shore activity from birds and marine mammals and point that out to the group.

Equipment

As far as equipment goes, the indispensables are rubber boots, shovels, some kind of identification sheet (prefer-able to the more cumbersome and delicate books), and magnifying glasses and buckets for viewing your finds as they were meant to be — immersed in seawater. Optional equipment includes thermometers, tape measures or pre-measured and -marked ropes for study transects (described below), and large plastic hoops to define sampling areas. Sheets of acrylic, masonite, or similar hard material that have been roughened with medium-grit sandpaper make washable, reusable notepads that can be written on with a soft pencil in any weather, and even under water.

As resources for background information and animal identification, several excellent books about marine life for non-biologists can be found in the natural history sections of larger bookstores. Try to find one that is specifically for your region; for the sake of generality, the texts that try to encompass large geographical areas often cannot include many key local species. Laminated identification sheets are indispensable on the walk itself.

Exploring shore life

Finding animals on a sandy or muddy beach can be challenging. For burrowing, sand-dwelling organisms, suggest that students take a few moments to inspect the beach visually before their feet wipe out all of the evidence. What they are looking for is small holes in the sand. The more the better, for under them lie the animals. When digging, it is best to use a full-size garden shovel, as many sand dwellers can outdig the fastest work with a small trowel! Plunge the shovel in as deeply as possible and then quickly bring up a shovelful and dump it into a bucket. Tease through the sample carefully to see what is there. When done, return the material to the hole it came from to minimize disturbance to nearby organisms.

Tidepools are special treasures. Because they never completely drain, they can be subtidal refuges, housing many plants and animals that normally are seen only by divers. Generally, the larger and deeper the tidepool, the better. If your shore has tidepools, use a tape measure or pre-measured and -marked rope to determine the distance from the low water edge to each pool. Have students identify organisms in the pools, take the water temperature, and estimate the volume of the pools. Students should be able to establish relationships between the variety, abundance, and size of organisms in a tidepool and the pool's size and distance from low water. The general pattern

The fantastic adaptations of animals and plants that inhabit this zone between two worlds provide a storyline that unites biology, physics, and chemistry.

is that larger pools that are lower down the beach present more stable ocean-like environments supporting dense and diverse communities, while smaller and higher pools present more physical extremes (i.e., salinity, temperature) and therefore usually have less diverse communities.

On rocky shores, look for large rocks to turn over. Flat rocks are often the best, as they have ample room underneath for larger animals. A thick cover of seaweed usually provides habitat for many creatures, both mobile and sedentary. Look in and around the bases of the plants rather that at their tips. When you have finished observing the underside of a rock, slowly and carefully replace it in the position you found it.

Observing organisms

If students want to get a closer look at beach organisms, they will often have to temporarily remove them from their immediate habitat. As any such disturbance is potentially destructive, remind students to be careful and sensitive to each organism's needs. If your beach walk is within a park, check with park personnel to see if park rules permit this type of activity before proceeding.

Regardless of where you get them, seashore animals are best observed in a clean container of fresh seawater. When submerged in water, most will become more active, and softer-bodied ones will show their natural form. As even high-shore creatures spend part of their life submerged, a few minutes in a bucket is unlikely to be harmful. Do be alert to temperature shock: if you take a creature from a warm tidepool, put it in water collected from that pool and not in chilly water taken directly from the ocean. Remind students that, once they have finished their observations on any creature, they must return it to where they found it.

If you want to remove an organism from a rock for closer observation, here are a few guidelines. Never remove permanently attached organisms such as algae or barnacles, as they are unable to reattach once removed. If you want students to observe these under water, try to find a smaller rock with them attached and submerse it.

David Denning

Sea anemones can move themselves around, but their attachment is so firm that you are almost sure to damage them if you attempt to remove them; so leave them in place, too. For firmly attached organisms, such as seastars, limpets, chitons, and snails, stealth and speed are critical. As soon as you announce your intentions by touching one of them, they will clamp down as hard as they can. In the resulting tug-of-war, either you will lose or the animal will be critically injured. The best way to remove these creatures is to grab, twist, and pull in one rapid and smooth motion. Do this by surprise without touching them first. If they beat you to the draw and clamp down, leave them alone and move on to the next animal. Never pry any of them loose by inserting a blade underneath them.

Sampling techniques

An excellent non-destructive sampling technique is to use a study transect, which is simply a line along which data are collected. To make a shoreline transect, run a tape measure (or pre-measured and marked rope) from the water's edge to the top of the shore. At intervals along the line place a large plastic hoop and have students identify and count every species present inside the hoop. For each set of data, have students record the location on the transect line. If they have a thermometer, they can also record the temperature. To get a measure of what the creatures themselves are experiencing, the temperature can be taken under the seaweed, in between or under the rocks, or in nearby tidepools. To make sure that students don't miss gathering data from the lowest shore, do the sampling in the second half of the field trip after they have done a general survey following the tide down. Students should start their measurements low on the shore near the time of the lowest tide and then work up the shore.

Possible themes

Once you have found the perfect beach, a good tide, and all the proper equipment, it is time to consider a theme for your walk. Having an overriding theme or story provides a framework for learning, and just about any topic will do as long as it fits into your curriculum.

Shoreline Humanities

Science isn't the only subject that can be enriched by a beach walk. Here are some suggestions that may spark your students' creative use of the shoreline.

- Write a story or poem about the lives of shoreline creatures.
- Write a story or poem from the point of view of a seashore animal or plant.
- Draw or paint local scenery.
- Draw or paint details from different tide zones.
- Visit a shoreline that was previously occupied by an industry or shipping dock and examine traces left by that former use.
- Collect all the garbage from a stretch of shoreline and then try to identify sources of the refuse and hypothesize how it got there and what impacts it might have.

Whatever your activity, do not base it on the collection of things from the shore. Even the dry vacant shells of dead organisms provide shelter or raw material for living ones.

Introduce the theme in class prior to the walk and provide students with background information they will need to make their own investigations. Their day on the beach should be given largely to the collecting and viewing of evidence for the theme, either as a class or in small teams.

Biological zonation is a major theme that is wonderfully suited to beach walks. On a good low tide, students should be able to recognize distinct areas, or zones, on the shore by noting the sizes and types of animals and plants present at different heights. In the intertidal, the drastic transition between marine and terrestrial conditions compresses many zones into a few vertical meters, or even centimeters. Your class could try sampling within hoops on a transect (as described above). From the data they collect, they will be able to distinguish whole communities later in class. The theme of zonation does not begin and end with the tides. Look to coastal mountains for zones characterized by snowfields, alpine meadow, scrub forest, and coastal forest. Beneath the waves this vertical patterning continues to the abyss. On land and in the sea, these zones cover hundreds or even thousands of vertical meters. The reasons for such a ubiquitous phenomenon could be explored in class before and after the walk.

As a topic, sex is an undeniable hit. The three most common questions I am asked about invertebrates are — in this order — How big does it get?, How long does it live?, and (usually rather furtively) How does it, you know, … do it? The most common mode of reproduction among invertebrates is broadcast fertilization; that is, the eggs and sperm are released into the water and the rest is left to chance. While hardly romantic, it is a good option for many of the creatures who spend their lives firmly cemented to one spot. There are, however, some strikingly notable exceptions. The natural history books that you use to prepare for your beach walk may have information on the sexual habits of species in your area. Encourage students to see if there are patterns in the habitats, lifestyle, and reproductive mode of the species that they find. The best time for a "sex on the shore" beach walk is spring. Have your class explore why it is that so many of these animals and plants reproduce in this one season.

The fantastic adaptations of the animals and plants that inhabit this zone between two worlds provide a story line that unites biology, physics, and chemistry. Intertidal animals have to cope with extremes of temperature, moisture, salinity, wave shock, and other factors. They are also subject to both terrestrial and marine predators. With careful observation and hypothesizing, students can observe the effects of these pressures in the designs and behavior of the shore's inhabitants.

The intertidal is also an abundant and dynamic community unto itself. Extremely rich and productive, the density of life on a healthy shoreline sets the stage for competition and predation. In a neverending race of evolutionary one-upmanship, predators and prey must constantly outdo one another. More effective defenses against predators increase the survival of prey. These defenses in turn select for more effective predators. If an adaptation by a competitor is not matched or exceeded, the penalty may be extinction. Serious evolutionary scientists have referred to this process as a "biological arms race." These high stakes have led to some interesting predator-prey relationships, competitive advantages, and even mutually beneficial relationships. With a little background information, a good eye, and an active imagination, students can delve into the Hows and Whys of adaptation in the intertidal.

Even human legends and creation stories are reflected on the seashore. Stories from all maritime cultures involve the seashore. If you or your class can uncover these gems from libraries and oral traditions available to them, your students' appreciation of the seashore — once a place of slippery, slimy rocks that smell funny — can grow.

As part of your beach walk preparations, become an artist and weave these themes, stories, and more into the tapestry of your class curriculum. By showing students real-world examples of classroom theory, and by encouraging them to be active participants in the search for evidence and hypotheses to flesh out the theme, you involve them in their own education. This involvement empowers them to see themselves as learners, scientists, and investigators. Education can't get any better than that.

Terry Parker teaches science at Frances Kelsey Secondary School in Mill Bay, British Columbia. He also designs educational programs and websites with Gracious Moon Studio (<www.graciousmoon.com>).

RESOURCES

A wealth of resources is available on-line to enrich a beach walk. The only caution is to separate regionally specific from general information. The following sites may provide useful starting points.

<http://co-ops.nos.noaa.gov> Tide and current tables for the United States are provided by the National Oceanic and Atmospheric Administration (NOAA).

<www.lau.chs-shc.dfo-mpo.gc.ca> Canadian tide and current tables provided by Fisheries and Oceans Canada.

<www.uri.edu/artsci/bio/rishores/> The Field Guide to the Shores of Rhode Island, hosted by the University of Rhode Island, illustrates the common seashore creatures in several types of Atlantic Seashore habitats.

<www.beachwatchers.wsu.edu> Beach Watchers, an organization administered by Washington State University, has a resource-rich website with general information applicable to all coastal areas, and with identification information applicable to the Pacific Northwest.

<http://oceanlink.island.net/oinfo/intertidal/intertidal.html> Exploring the Intertidal: An On-line Intertidal Field Guide is produced by the Public Education Department of the Bamfield Marine Sciences Centre in Bamfield, British Columbia. This information is applicable throughout much of the Pacific Northwest.

<www.enchantedlearning.com/subjects/ocean/Intertidal.shtml> The Enchanted Learning site has general information on intertidal animals and zonation, and printable blackline graphics.

<www.keepersweb.org/Shorekeepers> Shorekeepers is a program of Canada's Department of Fisheries and Oceans Pacific Region that involves citizens in shoreline monitoring and stewardship. Much of the information on the site is applicable anywhere.

Sustaining Ecosystems

Gail Littlejohn

Protected Areas:
Arks of the 21st Century

The designation of protected areas may be our last chance to rescue many species from extinction. Whether we are willing to make sacrifices to save them is a question of values.

by Sue Staniforth

Subject areas:
social studies,
language arts,
mathematics,
science

Key concepts:
values clarification,
ecological sustain-
ability, protected
areas, biogeoclimatic
maps, special
interests

Skills: negotiation,
values analysis

Location: indoors
and outdoors

Materials: chalk or
surveyors tape,
maps and biogeoclimatic maps for a region

Rick Searle

they embody many aspects of ecological sustainability, values clarification, and character education. This article explores some of these concepts and provides some background to this complex topic. Activity ideas for students of all ages examine daily acts of protection and how these relate to land and resource use.

Thousands of tired, nerve-shaken, over-civilized people are beginning to find out that going to the mountains is going home; that wildness is a necessity; and that mountain parks and reservations are useful not only as fountains of timber and irrigating rivers, but as fountains of life.
— John Muir (1954)

Like the "nerve-shaken" people of John Muir's day, North Americans head out in vast numbers each weekend to find refuge from the frenetic pace and human-built surroundings of "over-civilized" urban life. Most of us seek this respite in protected areas such as national, provincial, state or regional parks, wildlife management areas, recreation area, wilderness areas, ecological reserves, marine and aquatic conservation areas, and nature sanctuaries. Yet the protection of these natural areas is increasingly controversial, given the growing competition for the planet's land and resources. The issues and concepts surrounding land use and the protection of nature are important ones for educators, as

A look back: Protected areas in context

The establishment of parks and wilderness areas for recreation, nature conservation, and spiritual renewal is a relatively new concept in North America. In Eastern cultures, special places were set aside to meet spiritual needs as early as 500 B.C.; the Bo Tree shrine in Sri Lanka, for instance, has protected nature and provided a place for contemplation for more than 2,000 years. In Europe, the first official lands to be set aside were the royal forests and game preserves of England and France, documented in 1086. Some of the earliest lands to be called parks were formal gardens, such as Hyde Park, established in 1536. In North America, Boston Common is often cited as the first designated public open space (in 1634).

A major milestone was reached in 1864 with the establishment of Yosemite, a state park of 20 square kilometers (7.7 square miles) in California. This was followed, in 1872, by the world's first large-scale preservation of wilderness, the designation of 8,000 square kilometers (3,088 square miles) of northwestern Wyoming as Yellowstone National Park. That event seemed to spark a global interest in parks. In 1879, the

Royal National Park was established in Australia; in 1885, Banff National Park was created in Canada; and in 1894, Tongariro National Park was dedicated in New Zealand. At the same time, major cities throughout North America were designating large tracts of land as public parks and gardens.

Today, the International Union for the Conservation of Nature (IUCN) lists over 102,000 protected areas in more than 130 countries. Together, these areas encompass 18.8 million square kilometers (7.3 million square miles) and represent about 11.5 percent of the Earth's land area and 0.5 percent of the oceans. While these numbers are impressive, and growing, it is worth noting that more than 58 percent of the protected sites worldwide are less than 10 square kilometers (3.9 square miles) in area — in other words, small islands in a sea of human-altered landscape. Only 6 percent of the sites, representing 1.4 percent of the Earth's land area, are designated strict nature reserve or wilderness areas, the categories that afford the highest level of protection.

Rick Searle

Why protect natural areas?

If we managed resources in a sustainable fashion, with regard for the intrinsic value of nature and the future generations of all species, we probably would not need protected areas. Unfortunately, we have not done so. In the past 50 years, humanity has indulged in a spree of resource consumption that has used up more of the Earth's resources than our ancestors used throughout the past 300,000 years. For short-term gain, we have driven thousands of species to extinction and destroyed entire ecosystems. Our population has grown to more than 6.3 billion, a figure that increases by over a million every five days, or more than 8,000 every hour. (Check the World Population Clock on-line for updates.) The longer these unsustainable trends continue, the more they endanger the life-support systems and the future well-being of every living thing on Earth.

At the present rate of population growth, resource consumption, and environmental degradation, little of the mantle of life enfolding the planet will survive the 21st century. By actively consuming our own roots and foundations, we are destroying our heritage. Establishing a network of protected lands will help offset this destruction. Yet as communities, regions, and nations struggle to stretch dwindling resources to meet the demands of increasing population, the protection of natural areas will become more controversial, and those areas that are already established will be more at risk.

How much is enough?

The World Parks Congress estimated in 1992 that in order to preserve a representative sample of the world's ecosystems, at least 10 percent of the area of each of the planet's 14 terrestrial biomes should be protected. However, many people saw this percentage as a "ransom" that would allow industry to argue that, if 10 percent were zoned as protected, then the other 90 percent could be devoted to conventional multiple use. Obviously this would not protect biodiversity. To do so, there must be a concerted effort to care not only for the lands and waters inside parks but for the total environment of which the protected areas are a part. This effort would require a shift in conventional values.

Islands of wilderness

A current map of almost any region of the planet shows only isolated pockets of wilderness — sometimes protected as parks or nature reserves — where once there were continuous expanses of forest or prairie. In Europe, with the exception of northern Scandinavia, wild lands have vanished and the opportunity to experience wilderness simply does not exist. In the United States, excluding Alaska, only 1.7 percent of the land is designated wilderness; an additional 5 percent is called "roadless," meaning areas that are more than 10 miles (16 kilometers) from a public road. While northern Canada has vast wild lands, competition for their use is intense. Many areas are under pressure to serve economic goals through increased tourism and recreational facilities, and those that are already protected are constantly threatened by industrial activity and development. Researchers at the World Commission on Protected Areas, IUCN, predicted in 2002 that within the next decade most of the world's natural areas will be confined to protected areas.

Can these islands of wilderness support a variety of species and, if so, for how long? Biologist Reed Noss, editor of the journal *Conservation Biology,* cites habitat

A key aspect of wilderness protection is the recognition that people and societies differ in what they value and protect.

fragmentation as one of the most serious threats to conservation today. Ecological research supports his conclusions. A recent study showed that small forest patches can fail to support songbird populations, especially if they are adjacent to inhospitable landscapes. These island reserves may indeed become islands of extinction. One conservation strategy being considered is the preservation of wildlife, or green, corridors to connect otherwise isolated reserves. The idea is that plants and animals will travel from their habitat islands along these pathways to find new resources or mates. Some scientists are skeptical, however, arguing that the solution to habitat fragmentation lies not in the creation of corridors but in the protection of more habitat. There is also concern that corridors are being used as a quick fix by developers to make developed land look "green."

Rick Searle

We do not have forever to make choices about protected areas, as there will come a point when it is too late, when too much land and too many waterways have been developed or destroyed. We are probably the last generation with an opportunity to protect significant areas of the wilderness left on the planet, and the plants and animals they harbor. We must make these choices not only for ourselves but for future generations, as noted Canadian naturalist Doug Pimlott has stated: "Areas preserved from exploitation provide future generations the opportunity to make choices which should be their right to make, as well as ours."

Protection in the classroom

Protecting natural areas is consistent with the choices we make daily to protect things that we value. Exploring some of the values and beliefs associated with protection helps to clarify differences and to encourage reflection and understanding of different views. The following activities have been used with both elementary and secondary students.

Understanding protection

Have students brainstorm a list of things that they protect in their lives. Everyone spends time and energy every day in acts of protection, for example, taking care

of ourselves and our families, friends, pets, and possessions. Extend the brainstorming to include things and places that are protected in students' homes, at school, and in the community. For example, someone might protect a collection of hockey cards in a special scrapbook, the school library protects books, local museums protect art works and historical artifacts, and municipal parks and gardens protect habitat for wildlife and green space for the enjoyment of the community. After brainstorming, have students analyze reasons why each item on the class list might be protected. This values analysis provokes students to see the significance of some of the choices we make.

My special place

On a field trip or outdoor walk, have students explore a natural or urban setting and choose a special place in it that attracts them. They may feel drawn to an old tree, a gravestone, a brightly colored flower, or a monument. Alternatively, ask students to describe a special place where they go to feel safe (i.e., their bedroom, a fort, etc.) Have them draw this special place in their journals, and record their reflections on its characteristics and why they are attracted to it. Ask them to explain what makes this place special to them, what it reminds them of, and what actions they would take if their special place were threatened.

Protecting family treasures

Have students report on something that is important and treasured by their family: perhaps an antique clock, a family cabin, a photo album, a treasured story, or a song. Ask students why these treasured things are protected (e.g., because they have meaning to us, they are part of our heritage and culture, and they reflect our values and needs). By hearing what other students value and protect, students become aware of the differences in what people value and the decisions that were made to protect these treasures. A key aspect of wilderness protection is the recognition that people and societies differ in what they value and protect. These differences in values are often the basis for disagreement and conflict when it comes to protection decisions.

Yellowstone to Yukon

Conservationists in the United States and Canada are working to create a unique protected area, uncut by political boundaries, to run from Yellowstone Park to the Yukon. Known as the "Y2Y," this mountain ecosystem stretches 3,200 kilometers (2,000 miles) through the Rocky, Columbia, and Mackenzie mountains; it includes enough habitat to nurture populations of trout, salmon, raptors, grizzly and black bears, gray wolves, cougar, lynx, and wolverine. Existing national, state, and provincial parks and wilderness areas will anchor the system, while the creation of new protected areas and the conservation and restoration of critical segments of ecosystems will provide corridors and transition zones that are needed to complete it.

Canadian Parks and Wilderness Society

The Y2Y is a new type of protected area, linked to far-sighted biodiversity strategies that are based on protecting intact ecosystems — larger areas of habitat than anyone previously imagined. The task is challenging, for, to protect these larger areas, action must be taken locally, regionally, nationally, and internationally. Y2Y is a joint Canada–U.S. network of more than 80 organizations and institutions, and many concerned individuals. For information on educational materials or how to get involved, visit <www.y2y.net/> or e-mail The Canadian Parks and Wilderness Society at <cpaws_education@telusplanet.net>.

Schoolyard special interests

Setting aside land for a special purpose usually generates discussion and controversy. To experience some conflicts and compromises associated with such decisions, have students choose and negotiate special-use areas in the schoolyard. Divide the class into groups of four students. Have each group decide on a special interest in the schoolyard (e.g., a place for skateboarding or for basketball) and list the criteria of the area that meets the needs of that interest. Ask the groups to mark their special-use areas either on an outline on the chalkboard or outdoors in the schoolyard using chalk or surveyors tape. When students can see how their special-use areas overlap, encourage them to negotiate in their groups, so that their special areas are no longer in conflict and differing interests among the groups can coexist.

Making protection proposals

Provide small groups of students with maps that show protected natural spaces. Have students locate the boundaries of communities, roads, highways, and railroads, and then calculate the area of each protected space. Assign each group research using biogeoclimatic maps and natural history sources to find the specific habitat needs of a local plant or animal species. Have the groups report their findings. Then lead a class discussion on the amount of suitable habitat in the region for these species. Have the groups prepare proposals on what areas they would protect or rehabilitate, and whether wildlife corridors would help.

Sue Staniforth is a biologist and environmental education consultant who lives on Vancouver Island in British Columbia.

RESOURCES

Hummel, Monte. *Endangered Spaces: The Future for Canada's Wilderness.* Key Porter Books, 1989.

Muir, John. *The Wilderness World of John Muir.* Houghton Mifflin, 1954.

Oelbermann, Maren, and Michael Milburn. "Living on the Edge." *Nature Canada.* vol. 26, no. 1 Winter 1997. (Information on wildlife corridors.)

Staniforth, Susan, et al. *Protected Areas: Preserving Our Future. An Environmental Education Guide to Protecting Natural Areas.* British Columbia Ministry of Environment, Lands, and Parks, 1996. (ISBN 0-7726-2643-X. Available for $20 payable to Habitat Conservation Fund: 250–356–7111 or 800–387–9853).

ON-LINE RESOURCES FOR PROTECTED AREAS

<www.ahs.uwaterloo.ca/rec/parksoption/parkslinks99.htm> Website links to resources on Canadian parks and protected areas, compiled by the University of Waterloo.

<www.calacademy.org/research/library/biodiv/biblio/proareas> Protected areas website links for the United States, as well as international sites and general sites, compiled by the California Academy of Sciences Library.

<www.unesco.org//whc/index.html> The Protected Areas Virtual Library is an information service developed by the World Conservation Monitoring Centre in collaboration with the International Union for the Conservation of Nature (IUCN).

<www.iucn.org/themes/wcpa/index.html> The World Commission on Protected Areas has regional maps and reports and updates by the World Parks Congress on protected areas worldwide, including the *2003 United Nations List of Protected Areas* published by the International Union for the Conservation of Nature (IUCN) and United Nations Environment Programme.

Habitat Fragmentation and Genetic Diversity

In this simulation, students learn how difficult it can be to maintain a healthy gene pool in a fragmented habitat

by Gareth Thomson

Subject areas: science, social studies

Key concepts: genetic diversity, inbreeding depression, dispersal, habitat fragmentation, umbrella species

Skills: pattern recognition, deductive reasoning, developing empathy, clarifying concepts, critical thinking

Location: outdoors or indoors in open space where students can move about freely

Time: 30 minutes

Materials: several large pieces of fabric such as sheets; several ropes or lengths of brightly colored twine; two 30 cm (12-in.) boards; class set of blue, green, red, and black cards (or squares cut from poster paper)

> *The one process ongoing in the 1980s that will take millions of years to correct is the loss of genetic and species diversity by the destruction of natural habitats. This is the folly our descendants are least likely to forgive us.*
>
> — E.O Wilson, 1980[1]

Writing 150 years ago, naturalist John James Audubon spoke of the sky darkening for days as flocks of passenger pigeons numbering in the billions passed overhead. We may feel a pang of bitterness toward those who hunted this marvel of nature to extinction, but today the folly of over-hunting has been replaced by a more insidious and far more devastating folly: the destruction of natural habitats. Scientist E.O. Wilson estimates that loss of habitat is accelerating normal rates of extinction by several thousand times, and that we are, as a result, in the midst of an extinction spasm unrivaled since the dinosaur age came to an end 65 million years ago.[2]

One means of preserving the Earth's biodiversity has always been through the establishment of protected areas such as parks and wildlife refuges. Consequently, park planners and managers have in recent decades been shaken to the core by studies showing that most protected areas do not adequately protect many of the animals that live there. For example, in a 1987 study of 14 national parks in the western United States, conservation biologist William Newmark found that 13 of the parks had lost some of the mammals that previously inhabited those areas — simply because the parks are too small.

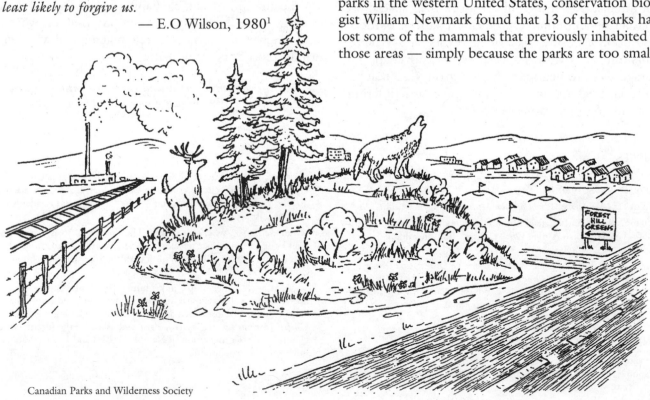

Canadian Parks and Wilderness Society

Surrounded by development, these protected areas are, in effect, islands of habitat. They cannot support stable populations of animals, especially large carnivores,[3] whose natural behavior is to disperse over wide areas, traveling far from their birthplace to find mates and new territories.

Consider the case of Pluie, a female wolf that was fitted with a satellite transceiver in northern Alberta. She proceeded to astound researchers by traveling deep into the states of Montana and Idaho, a journey of more than 1,000 kilometers (620 miles), crossing more than 30 jurisdictional boundaries and over an area ten times the size of Yellowstone Park. None of the parks in this region is large enough to protect such an animal; and current park designs, which include roads and town sites, further fragment the habitats within parks. As a result, populations of animals become isolated and, over time, begin to lose genetic diversity through inbreeding. This inbreeding depression, or loss of genetic fitness, often produces such harmful characteristics that animals can no longer reproduce and local populations go extinct.

There are two ways of solving the problem of local extinctions within protected areas. The first is to dramatically increase the size of such protected areas, an option that in most cases is politically impossible because of the uses of the land surrounding protected areas. The second is to connect protected areas by establishing wildlife corridors that allow animals to travel between refuges, giving isolated populations access to other populations of the same species. An example is the proposed Yellowstone to Yukon Conservation Initiative, a plan to link protected areas along the spine of the continent from Yellowstone National Park in western Wyoming to the Yukon-Alaska border, a distance of nearly 3,200 kilometers (2,000 miles). (See page 59) Changes on this scale will require a consciousness and desire for change that permeates society, from decision makers to the public they represent.

Bears of Banff is an active simulation in which students assume the role of grizzly bears in a protected area. As they try to survive and pass on their genes, they

We are in the midst of an extinction spasm unrivalled since the dinosaur age came to an end 65 million years ago.

find out how human activities can get in the way of a bear's plans for procreation. The activity focuses on the loss of genetic diversity that occurs when human activities make it impossible for animals to travel freely within or beyond protected areas. It helps students to understand that conservation of such animals as the wolf and grizzly bear will require unprecedented changes in the way we design and manage our parks

Bears of Banff simulation

Grizzly bears, the Great Bears revered in many aboriginal cultures, are today symbolic of wilderness and considered a valuable "umbrella" species, or indicator of ecosystem integrity. Grizzly bears were once found throughout the Canadian prairies and all the way down to Mexico, but in the last 150 years they have become extinct in more than half of their former range as their habitats have been lost and their populations have become inbred. Scientists have noticed the first signs of inbreeding depression in the grizzly bear populations in Banff National Park, even though the park is supposed to protect these animals.

Procedure:

1. Begin by inviting students into a large area that can comfortably hold the entire group. This could be arranged simply by moving all desks to one end of the room, leaving half of the classroom for the activity.

2. Inform the students that they are grizzly bears that have just entered a national park. Show them the boundaries of the park (this can be an imaginary line or some marker, which you identity to students). Tell them that the park borders are all impassable mountains and that all activities must occur within the park area you have defined.

3. Ask the students to name four things that every animal needs to survive (i.e., food, water, space, and shelter). Explain that, in this activity, they do not need to worry about meeting these basic needs, but they will be tested on their ability to mate and pass on healthy genes to new generations of grizzly bears.

4. Distribute four cards to each student: one each of blue, green, red, and black. To save time, ask four students to stand together, each holding all the cards of one color. Have the rest of the students walk past, taking one card from each.

5. Inform students that the long-term sustainability of animal populations requires the mixing of genes to keep the population healthy. Normally, individuals ensure genetic mixing by dispersing, that is, traveling long distances from their birthplace to mate with individuals from other families. Explain that the colored cards students are holding represent their genes. When you give the signal to disperse, their task is to trade cards with other bears until they have four cards of the same color.

6. Give the signal for dispersal. Students will likely need only a minute to finish trading.

7. Ask students to raise their hands if they were able to complete the task (usually, all or most will succeed). Congratulate them on their ability to disperse and their good genetic prospects.

8. Next, ask for a show of hands from students who were not able to collect four identical cards. (If there are none, postpone this explanation for the next round, when inbreeding is represented by four same-colored cards.) Tell these unfortunate individuals that they are the victims of inbreeding, or insufficient gene mixing caused by mating between animals that are closely related. Any bears that suffer from inbreeding in three successive rounds will be

diagnosed with incurable inbreeding depression; they will be so harmed by generations of inbreeding that they can no longer reproduce and will have to leave the game.

Note: If the students have studied genetics, explain that inbreeding can reduce the fitness of offspring because it increases the risk that harmful recessive alleles will occur homozygously. Inbreeding depression is one of the reasons that most human societies have taboos against incest.

9. For Round 2, place a piece of fabric in the center of the space to represent a town (it should cover no more than 20 percent of the total area of the park). Place a rope across the center of the fabric and extend it to the boundaries of the park to represent a road that bisects the park.

10. Explain to students that humans have come to live in the valley. They will be located in a modest town site in the center of the park, represented by the fabric. A simple road crossing through the park will supply essential services to the town. Warn students that towns and roads are dangerous for bears. Bears must not go into the town (fabric); and if any bear is seen in the town or stepping across the road, it will be killed by you, playing the role of a truck.

11. Inform students that when you give the signal to disperse this time, their task is to collect four cards of different colors. Then give the dispersal signal.

12. Play six or seven more rounds, incorporating the changes listed below and having students alternate

Canadian Parks and Wilderness Society

between trading for identical cards and trading for differently colored cards. At the end of trading for each round, ask for a show of hands so that the group can monitor the onset of deadly inbreeding depression.

Make the following changes as the activity proceeds:

- Round 3, divide the park into quarters by adding a railroad track, represented by a second length of rope placed perpendicular to the road.

- Round 4, double the size of the town by adding another piece of fabric to represent a commercial shopping area built to give people "something to do" when they come to the park.

- Round 5, build a large oil refinery by placing a sheet of fabric just outside the park. Then pull some of the fabric back over the boundary into the park. Explain that the fabric represents the zone of influence around a development that bears will not enter.

- Round 6, build an affordable housing complex and an airfield by placing pieces of fabric in two different places, each extending from the town site to the boundary. This causes yet more habitat fragmentation. Bears going into these areas will be killed.

- Round 7, pause to inform the bears that an environmental group has proposed building a wildlife overpass so that animals can cross the road. Place a board over the highway to show them what it would look like. Ask the bears if they are in favor of this proposal. Then take the board away and tell them that the government has turned down the proposal without asking the bears for their opinion.

- Round 8, pause again and tell students that the government has doubled the width of the road but has built two wildlife overpasses over it. In addition, a new environmental study recommends closing the airfield. Ask the bears if they are in favor of these changes. (Some dangerously inbred populations may be very happy about these changes.) Take out the airfield and place two boards across the rope on either side of the town site.

Wrap-up: The main intent of this simulation is to demonstrate how incremental development in the park makes genetic mixing more difficult. Ask students if they think it would get easier or more difficult for the bears in future rounds. Explain that things could go either way, but one thing is certain: even in a national park, humans often have a hard time saying "that's enough."

Extensions:

- Incremental development, in which human activities encroach on protected land in tiny increments year after year, is a major threat to natural areas. To reinforce this concept, place an empty box near the edge of a desk and explain that the box represents an intact ecosystem and your hand represents the impact of humans on the ecosystem. Ask students for examples of incremental impacts on ecosystems (e.g., highway expansions). With each example, push the container closer to the edge of the desk. Continue until the box is partially overhanging the desk edge. Point out that the box is still intact, but that it is at risk. Ask students if the ecosystem will survive unchanged if incremental development continues indefinitely. Discuss whether human activities should have limits.

- Like many protected areas, Banff National Park is the subject of debate between those who believe that parks are for people and those who believe that the first priority of a national park is to protect the animals and plants that live in it. Ask your students to discuss what they believe parks are for.

Gareth Thomson is Education Director of the Canadian Parks and Wilderness Society, Calgary/Banff Chapter. He lives in Canmore, Alberta.

The Bears of Banff activity is adapted with permission from the activity guide Grizzly Bears Forever!, *Canadian Parks and Wilderness Society, Calgary/Banff Chapter, 2000. It and other activities can be downloaded free at <www.cpawscalgary.org>.*

Notes

1 Edward O. Wilson. "Resolutions for the 80s." *Harvard Magazine* January-February 1980, pp. 22-26. cited in Edward O. Wilson. *Naturalist.* Warner Books, 1994, p. 335.

2 Edward O. Wilson. *The Diversity of Life.* WW Norton, 1992, pp. 280, 343, 346.

3 William D. Newmark. "A Land-bridge Island Perspective on Mammalian Extinctions in Western North American Parks." *Nature.* vol. 325, no. 6103. January 29, 1987, pp. 430-32.

The Race Against Desertification

Why it is important and what is being done about it

by Friederike Knabe

Subject areas: social studies, science

Key concepts: desertification, drylands, monocultural crops, cash-crops

Roger Lemoyne/CIDA

e moved to this village," said the old chief, "when I was a young man some sixty years ago. The hillsides around us, all the way down to the valley, were covered by a dense forest, so dense that you could get lost in it. It was full of wild animals and a wide diversity of trees and plants. It provided sustenance for people and animals."

"What happened?" asked the visitors. "How can such a forest disappear completely in such a short time and leave rocky, bare land without any soil for plant growth?"

"The rainfall decreased each year and so the trees did not have enough water to grow and they died."

"That's not all," added one of the chief's advisers. "Our people cut trees for wood and cleared land for planting crops. We never thought of replanting the trees. We saw the soil erosion but we did not know what to do to stop it. It had not happened before. And now it may be too late to reverse the situation."

This conversation could have taken place in many countries around the world. In fact, it happened in Mali in West Africa at the edge of the Sahara Desert in a region called the Sahel. The phenomenon being discussed is called desertification.

What is desertification?

Desertification is not simply the formation or expansion of deserts, nor is it the same as the natural fluctuations in vegetative cover at desert fringes. It occurs anywhere that the physical and biological characteristics of soil are progressively degraded to the point that the land is no longer productive. It can be caused by climate change, but it is mainly caused by human activities such as deforestation, overgrazing by livestock, and unsustainable agricultural practices.

The viability of many dryland areas of the world is endangered by desertification. Drylands — defined as arid, semi-arid, and dry subhumid areas — cover about 40 percent of the Earth's terrestrial surface and constitute 54 percent of the Earth's productive land. Because of their limited fresh water and widely varying rainfall, they are among the world's most fragile environments. Over centuries, the inhabitants of these regions developed a complex food production system to minimize the effect of recurring droughts. It included the use of local plant varieties, seed selection and storage, crop rotation and intercropping, as well as careful water management and soil protection techniques. Among cattle herders, the prevalence of a nomadic lifestyle ensured that the land was not overgrazed. To complement their staple diet, people also knew how to benefit from the wide variety of food sources from wild plants and trees.

Today, many species of wild plants and many varieties of carefully selected and adapted crops have disappeared or are threatened. Modern agriculture, introduced by many governments in dryland regions, has encouraged monocultural cash-crop production, often displacing the complex farming and resource management systems that maintained the land and the people for centuries. As traditional food crops and farming techniques have been replaced by those less suitable for delicate dryland conditions, soils have become exhausted and vegetation cover lost. Deforestation, overgrazing of land by animals, and increasing population pressure have compounded the problems. With less arable land available, conflicts arise among farmers and cattle herders; and, as farm families abandon marginalized land, indigenous knowledge of traditional farming practices disappears with them.

In addition to eroding the agricultural potential of drylands, desertification contributes to the loss of biodiversity. The drylands of the world have been an important source of genetic diversity in food crops and medicinal plants: some of world's main food staples, such as wheat, barley, and maize, have been cultivated from wild species indigenous to drylands. As the soils in these areas become unable to sustain either cultivated crops or the natural vegetative cover, more and more biodiversity is lost forever.

As traditional food crops and farming techniques have been replaced by those less suitable for delicate dryland conditions, soils have become exhausted and vegetation cover lost.

Extent of desertification

According to the United Nations, approximately 70 percent of the drylands used for agriculture around the world are already degraded, a situation that threatens the livelihood of the one billion people who live in these areas. People in Africa are particularly threatened by desertification because two-thirds of African lands are natural deserts or dry zones. Compounding this situation is the susceptibility to erosion of most African soils, and the comparatively high rates of population growth. Although the problem is most urgent in the developing nations of Africa, desertification is not limited to Africa or developing countries. According to the United Nations, the factors leading to desertification have already resulted in a dramatic degradation of the soil and environment in at least 110 countries. The latest studies suggest that as much as 41 percent of the Earth's terrestrial surface is seriously affected by desertification or at risk of becoming so.

In North America, drylands constitute a smaller portion of the land mass than on other continents, but a higher proportion of these lands is severely or moderately degraded. Many of us ignore the threat because desertification is not yet as dramatically visible here as in other parts of the world. We may know of isolated areas where soil erosion is severe, but we do not usually associate these with the broad problem of land degradation. This description of the process of desertification by Mamby Fofana, Director of USC Mali, may lead us to reconsider our assumptions:

Desertification is not the same as the advancing desert. Desertification usually starts in small pockets of land where, owing to a number of factors, the soil is seriously eroding. These small areas, if ignored, will grow and finally join. At that point the process of desertification is very difficult to reverse.

International action on desertification

Since the early 1990s, desertification has been increasingly on the agenda of international agencies and governments. The United Nations conference on environment and development in Rio de Janeiro in 1992 addressed the challenges to the Earth's environment in three draft conventions: biodiversity, climate change, and desertification. The United Nations Convention to Combat Desertification, adopted June 17, 1994, has been ratified by 190 countries, which recognize the global significance of the problem of desertification and the need for concerted action at the international, regional, and local levels. The convention is the first international treaty of its kind to emphasize the importance of bringing together traditional local knowledge of dryland management with modern science in the search for answers. It also recognizes that this information must be shared so that solutions can be tested in different circumstances and environments. The convention therefore encourages democratic processes that advocate participation by all sectors — including governments, non-governmental organizations, and affected populations, in particular women — in developing strategies and

USC Canada

In a market garden in Mali, a berm of soil around the growing beds conserves precious water and serves as a windbreak.

In a school arboretum in Gono, Mali, students raise a variety of trees that are adapted to dryland conditions.

action programs. This recommendation is based on the realizations that desertification cannot be addressed in isolation from socioeconomic conditions, and that reducing poverty is essential in the fight against desertification. For many governments in the affected regions, the collaboration with non-governmental organizations and community groups is new and poses its own challenges.

Community action

Experts and activists agree that the battle against desertification has to be fought at the front line — the community — because many of the people in the most affected regions are poor and have little choice but to exploit natural resources in order to survive. Realizing the link between degradation of the environment, poverty, and the pressure of increasing populations, programs designed to combat desertification must go beyond environmental protection to address the living conditions of the affected populations as well. For example, instead of telling people to stop growing crops on fragile land, programs need to focus on sustainable agriculture methods and on reducing extreme poverty by introducing income-generating activities and education programs. Two success stories from the African country of Mali illustrate some of ways in which soil and biodiversity can be restored in areas that have suffered severe land degradation. Programs like these are being implemented and replicated in many countries of Africa and Asia.

Gono, Mali

In Gono, a village in the Douentza region of northern Mali, at the edge of the Sahara desert, trees were an unusual sight; certainly, there were no trees in and around the schoolyard until a couple of years ago. The schoolteacher was encouraged by the local development staff of USC Mali to embark on a project to "green" the schoolyard. An arboretum was established where more than 50 varieties of local trees now grow and are looked after by the children. The trees are particularly adapted

to dryland conditions and serve different purposes, some being used in medicines, some as food for humans, some as fodder for animals.

Many of the tree varieties had previously disappeared from the region and it was difficult for the elders to pass on the traditional knowledge about their importance to the youth of the village. The school arboretum has provided a new framework for learning and appreciation of the trees' value for the community as a whole. The children are enthusiastic about their new responsibilities. The area around the school is green and visitors stop on the road nearby to see this unusual sight in the middle of a semi-desert. Other young people have started a second arboretum, and the model is being replicated elsewhere.

While planting trees is a vital component of the fight against desertification, villagers have introduced a number of additional techniques designed to protect the fragile topsoil and improve it over time. Farmers are constructing small dykes in their fields to conserve moisture when it rains and are planting hedges around their fields as windbreaks as well as for additional soil nutrition.

Badiari, Mali

Badiari is a small but dynamic village of 210 residents who participate in the Douentza Land Improvement Project, a program implemented by USC Mali. In this semi-arid area with a maximum annual rainfall of 400 millimeters (16 inches), trees are very precious commodities. For many families, there is no alternative fuel for such essentials as boiling water or cooking food. As recently as five years ago, because of the degradation and loss of agricultural land, the community faced chronic food shortages; many villagers, in particular the men, left to find work and survival elsewhere. The women and the children were left to eke out a living.

A student in Gono, Mali with 'his' tree.

In Badiari, Mali, nitrogen-fixing Acacia albida trees increase yields in the millet fields and help prevent the loss of fertile topsoil.

USC Canada

Understanding the serious environmental problems in the area, the villagers formed an environmental protection association they called Bême. One of the first concerns of Bême was the protection of the *Acacia albida*, a tree species that traditionally grows in the midst of millet fields. This tree fixes nitrogen, which contributes to the natural fertility of the soil. Villagers had noticed that where *Acacia albida* trees had been cut down, crop yields were seriously reduced. Bême took a twofold approach to reduce the loss of this particular tree. They educated residents, newcomers to the village, and passersby about the importance of eaving the *Acacia albida* in the fields. And they introduced a system of sanctions, including fines, against persons found cutting these trees.

Today, Badiari is flourishing and the livelihood of the people has improved substantially. Among the trees of the protected forest, fields of sorghum and millet produce a better crop than before. A further reason for this is the use of traditional local seeds that are adapted to local growing conditions. The seeds have been selected so that only the best performing varieties are planted. Traditional knowledge is passed on to the next generation. As a backup system for the protection of the seeds, a village gene bank has been established where different varieties are stored for future testing and use.

What can we do?

Wherever we live in North America, we can identify early warning signs of land degradation and study them to develop strategies that can reverse the trends. In southern Alberta, one of the driest regions in North America, for example, coordinated action has led to changes in agricultural practices designed to protect the fragile soil: no tillage, winter crops, fewer chemicals, and so on. Nongovernmental organizations concerned with desertification around the world often encourage communities, in particular schools, to learn about local land degradation and take actions such as planting native tree species in their neighborhoods. As more people become aware of the issues and the importance of local action, the United Nations World Day to Combat Desertification (June 17) is increasingly becoming a special date to undertake activities such as these in the community.

Friederike Knabe, of Knabe Konsulting, specializes in international dryland issues and sustainable development. She is the former Director of Canadian Programs at USC Canada in Ottawa, Ontario.

RESOURCES

<http://ag.arizona.edu/OALS/ALN/ALNHome.html>) *The Arid Lands Newsletter*, published semi-annually by the Office of Arid Lands Studies at the University of Arizona, features articles on resource use and environmental protection in drylands. (Issues published since 1994 are on-line)

Solidarité Canada Sahel provides information for schools in French (*information pour les écoles, en français*) (4837 rue Boyer, Suite 250, Montreal, QC H2J 3E6, 514–522–6077). See also Le Groupe Madie, "Documentation of the Desertification Process in Canada" (May 1998), a report prepared for Solidarité Canada Sahel as part of its program for Strengthening Civil Society in the Sahel financed by the Canadian International Development Agency.

<www.unccd.int> The United Nations Convention to Combat Desertification website offers background information on desertification, the text and list of signatories to the Convention to Combat Desertification, and up-to-date conference reports.

<www.iisd.ca/process/forest_desertification_land.htm> The International Institute for Sustainable Development: The Linkages website contains background information on desertification and links to the minutes of the meetings of the United Nations Convention to Combat Desertification.

<www.riodccd.org> The International NGO Network on Desertification and Drought/Réseau International d'ONG sur la Désertification (RIOD) is a network of non-governmental organizations around the world working to raise awareness of desertification and to assist people in dryland areas to achieve sustainable livelihoods. (In the U.S.: Michelle Leighton, Natural Heritage Institute, 114 Sansome St., #1200, San Francisco CA 94104, <mls@n-h-i.org>, or Robert Buchanan, National Coalition to Support the UNCCD, Washington DC, 202–234–3460; in Canada: Lyne Caron, Solidarité Canada Sahel, 4837 rue Boyer, Suite 250, Montreal, QC H2J 3E6, 514–522–6077.)

<www.usc-canada.org> The website for USC Canada includes information from the villages in Mali that are mentioned in this article.

Learning About Desertification

by Jackie Kirk

Subject areas: social studies, science,

Key concepts: desertification, soil degradation

Skills: brainstorming, experimentation, game board design, research

Location: indoors

Soil erosion experiments

The following experiments enable students to see for themselves the effects of soil erosion and some of the measures that can be taken to prevent or at least lessen it. The activities can be adapted for students of different grade levels and experience. Similar experiments could be set up on a much larger scale on a real slope in the school grounds; however, these "micro-scenes" are very visual, practical for the classroom, and allow the students to be actively involved in the experimentation.

Time: 2 hours

Materials: disposable baking tray(s), soil, water, small can, nail, small stones, wooden stir sticks, alfalfa seeds

Preparation:

1. Place dry soil in a large disposable baking tray and shape it to create a section of sloping land. You may want to set up several trays in order to try out different anti-erosion measures.

2. Use a nail to punch a number of small holes into the bottom of a small tin can, such as one used for tomato paste.

Procedure: This can be done as a demonstration or by students working in small groups.

1. Hold the small tin can over the soil, and fill the can with water. Explain that this is a source of rain or irrigation for the soil. Water the dry, loose soil just a little and have students observe the way the water runs off and what happens to the soil (likely some goes away with the water).

2. Encourage students to think of ways in which they could ensure that the water soaks into the soil, as rain or irrigation water is very precious in many dry regions.

3. Have students "plow" the land with their fingers, moving downward in the same direction as the slope. Water the land a little more and observe how the water runs off.

"Twinned" with Gono School in Mali, students in Lethbridge, Alberta, exchange news of tree-planting projects and share their learning about desertification.

4. Now have students plow the land across the slope, water it, and observe the difference in the water retention of the soil.

5. Brainstorm other ways in which to improve the soil's water retention, and recreate as many as these ideas as possible on the experimental slopes. For example:

   • Use a large number of tiny stones to construct a small wall across the slope. Then water the slope again and observe any differences.

   • Break a number of wooden coffee stir sticks in half and use them to construct a line of posts, all at the same contour height across the slope. Then water the slope and observe any differences.

   • Try planting rows of fast-growing seeds such as alfalfa across the slope to simulate a plantation of small shrubs or bushes in a region affected by desertification. Observe the effects of watering with the plants in place.

Wrap-up: Have students produce posters with drawings to share what they have learned about methods to reduce soil erosion.

Extension: These soil erosion experiments, along with other resource material on desertification, could form the basis of an interactive kiosk that students set up to mark the United Nations World Day to Combat Desertification on June 17. An on-line computer could enable visitors to do further research. These activities could be combined with tree planting, demonstrations of energy-efficient cooking techniques, and displays of local indigenous species which are hardy and well suited to local climatic and soil conditions. (See <www.unccd.int>).

Investigating local conditions

Soil exhaustion can be a serious problem in areas where people need to grow food crops and yet the soil is thin and of poor quality. Invite a local farmer or a knowledgeable gardener to describe how growers ensure that their soils retain both the minerals and structure necessary to sustain healthy crops. Discuss the merits of crop rotation, the careful positioning of complementary plants, and the choice of hardy indigenous species that are not too greedy — all of which are equally important in areas affected by desertification.

Saving the trees

In dryland areas that are at a high risk of desertification, many trees are cut down to provide wood for cooking on open fires. Ask students what measures they can suggest for reducing energy consumption when cooking, both in their own home and on an open fire. Measures such as keeping a lid on the pot and reducing the size of the flame are equally relevant anywhere. Special wood-saving equipment such as solar box ovens and high-efficiency clay stoves have been distributed in some areas affected by desertification.

Desertification board game

The Sahel is a dryland region of West Africa near the Sahara Desert that has experienced much desertification. (See "The Race against Desertification," page 64 for background.) In this activity, students work in groups to create a board game on the theme of "A walk in the Sahel."

Time: 2 hours

Materials: large sheets of paper, markers, paper and pencils, dice

Procedure:

1. Have students work in groups to brainstorm a list of activities that contribute to desertification and a list of all the measures they can think of to improve the situation for the people and land of the Sahel.

2. Have each group create a game board on a large sheet of paper, placing items from their lists on squares around the board. Squares representing harmful activities that promote desertification should require a forfeit (e.g., miss a turn, wait to throw a certain number), while squares denoting helpful activities should allow players to move ahead.

3. Have students decorate the board and test their game in their group. They can also play with younger students to introduce them to the concept of desertification.

Adopt-a-project

Have students find and contact organizations working in dryland regions to find out about projects aimed at stopping desertification. (The list of resources on page 67 is a good starting place.) Have each student select a project to research and report. Create a classroom display to show success stories.

Jackie Kirk is a consultant in global education in Montréal, Québec. Adopt-a-Project was suggested by Friederike Knabe, a consultant in Ottawa, Ontario.

Declining Fish Stocks: Pieces of a Puzzle

The case of the Northwest Atlantic cod provides a framework for examining the interrelated factors that are endangering fish stocks around the world

by Jeanette Winsor and John Goldsworthy

Subject areas: science, social studies,

Key concepts: sustainable resource management

In our parents' and grandparents' generations, fisheries and ocean ecology were never topics that came up in the classroom. People in coastal communities fished the waters around them, never suspecting that this abundant resource could ever disappear. Yet today fish stocks are disappearing. The Food and Agriculture Organization of the United Nations recently reported that more than 140 countries now fish the world's oceans, and that 13 of the 17 major fisheries of the world are in trouble because the stocks have been over-exploited. The World Wildlife Fund has asserted that the problem will worsen as fish harvesters move down the food chain to take less endangered species.

The collapse of traditional fisheries has devastated nations that rely heavily on that resource as a main industry and a major food source. The impacts range from loss of employment and poorer nutrition to the loss of entire economies and ways of life. And as fish quotas and territorial limits are set, conflicts arise between and within nations.

Today, environmental and scientific research organizations are raising public awareness of the threats to the world's fishery. However, if the world's fisheries are to be nurtured back to health and managed in a more sustainable manner in the future, today's young people — the future guardians of our ocean resources — must be aware of the complex puzzle of interrelated factors that have brought about this ecological and commercial disaster. Putting this puzzle together in the classroom is one step toward understanding the delicate balance between economy and ecology on which our aquatic resources depend.

One of the best case studies for learning what is happening to fish stocks around the world is the collapse of the cod fishery in the Northwest Atlantic Ocean around the island of Newfoundland, Canada. The following discussion examines the complex of interrelated factors that precipitated the decline in cod stocks, and serves as a framework for educators who wish to teach the importance of sustainable resource use and conservation of fish stocks and habitats worldwide. The suggested investigations

Jeanette Winsor

Curtis Fisher

Connie Pearce

Curtis Fisher

Gail Littlejohn

and activities that follow the case study can be used in a study of any fish species found locally, whether saltwater or freshwater.

Case study:
Northwest Atlantic cod fishery

> *There's lots of fish in Bonavist' Harbour,*
> *Lots of fish right in around here.*
> — Newfoundland folk song

For more than 500 years, Europeans have come to reap the ocean's rich harvest on the Grand Banks, an area of the continental shelf on the east coast of what is now Canada. The explorer John Cabot, sailing into these waters in 1497, reported a sea teaming with codfish. Throughout the centuries that followed, fishing crews found that the cod's abundance was matched by its size, some of them "as big as a man" and weighing as much as 82 kilograms (180 pounds).

Then, beginning in the late 1970s, people working in the Northwest Atlantic fishing industry noticed a decline in the cod stocks and a reduction in the average size of individual fish. By July 1992, the stocks were so depleted that the Canadian government declared them commercially extinct and called for a moratorium on fishing. When fisheries scientists, government officials, fish harvesters, and fish processors became aware that there were no longer "lots of fish in Bonavist' Harbour," or anywhere else in Atlantic Canada, they were forced to reflect on where the cod might have gone and how the stocks might be brought back to a sustainable level.

The government blamed overfishing, both foreign and domestic. Inshore fish harvesters blamed large companies, which allowed their huge trawlers to scrape the ocean floor during spawning season. Some fisheries scientists suggested that changes in the ocean environment could be a factor, while others pointed a finger at the burgeoning seal populations. It was apparent to most, however, that no single factor was responsible for the disaster. An intricate web of relationships maintains the balance of an ecosystem as diverse and dynamic as the ocean; assessing the cause of the depletion of one organism is like assembling a huge jigsaw puzzle.

Petty Harbour, Newfoundland

Puzzle piece 1: Foreign overfishing

Nations such as Spain, Portugal, and France have fished the Grand Banks for hundreds of years. By the late 1960s, the catches of cod reported by non-Canadian vessels amounted to more than 600,000 metric tons, compared to less than 200,000 metric tons caught from Canadian vessels. In 1977, in accordance with the United Nations Law of the Sea Conference, Canada declared a 200-mile (320-kilometer) exclusive economic zone around its coastlines, thereby claiming the right to regulate fishing in those areas. Foreign fishing vessels are excluded from this zone, which includes most of the waters on the continental shelf off the Atlantic coast. However, three areas of the continental shelf do not fall within the 200-mile zone: the Nose and Tail of the Grand Banks and the Flemish Cap. Because these areas lie outside of any one nation's jurisdiction, they are managed by the North Atlantic Fisheries Organization (NAFO), a partnership of 17 countries whose mandate is to investigate,

Petty Harbour, Newfoundland

protect, and conserve the fishery resources of the Northwest Atlantic.

One of the tasks of NAFO is to set Total Allowable Catch regulations for each species of fish. During the mid- to late 1980s, the European Community (now European Union) did not always agree with the Total Allowable Catches put forward by NAFO and so they set their own quotas, often well above those of NAFO — despite being aware of the cod crisis and the attempts by Canada to nurture the stocks back to health. The actual European Community catch between 1986 and 1991 far exceeded even the high quotas that the European Community had set for its member nations, and the catch was reduced only as the stocks being fished became severely depleted. Fish do not understand the concept of an exclusive economic zone, and, consequently, the excessive catches on the productive Nose and Tail of the Grand Banks and Flemish Cap contributed to a severe decline in the overall cod stocks and continues to affect their recovery.

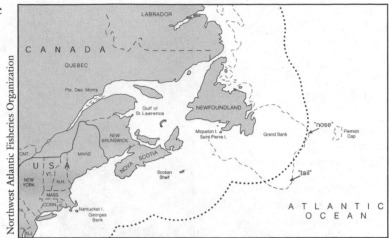

Petty Harbour, Newfoundland

Puzzle piece 2: Domestic overfishing

The Newfoundland domestic cod fishery consists of an inshore fishery and an offshore fishery. Before the decline in the cod stocks, the inshore fishery was conducted during the summer using such traditional methods as hook and line, gill nets, or cod traps. The offshore fishery was conducted from large vessels called trawlers during the winter when cod migrated to their spawning grounds on the northern Grand Banks. Trawlers could withstand the dangerous ice conditions and stay at sea for weeks at a time.

Improvements in fish-finding and navigation technology enabled ship captains to find the exact location of the spawning fish and then harvest them by dragging massive trawl nets along the ocean bottom. At the same time, large fishing companies found it more economical to keep their processing plants open year-round, thereby requiring a constant supply of fish. The northern cod — easily accessible on its spawning grounds — was the perfect catch for this new high-tech, year-round fishery. The offshore fishery proved to be a very profitable, but clearly

unsustainable, practice. The spawning biomass of the cod declined from 287,000 metric tons in 1986 to 22,000 metric tons in 1992.

Puzzle piece 3: More seals

Since the late 19th century, Newfoundlanders living along the northeast coast have relied on the annual harp seal harvest to supplement their income. In the years following the Second World War, for example, more than 250,000 seals were landed annually and nearly all of the pelts were exported to Norway. During the mid–1980s, the hunt slowed almost to a halt, owing to concerns voiced by animal rights activists and the subsequent decline in markets for seal products.

Since the 1980s, as a result of the sharp decrease in the number of seals being harvested, the total harp seal population off the northeast coast of Newfoundland has increased substantially. Fisheries and Oceans Canada estimated the harp seal herd to be in the range of 4.8 to 6.4 million in the 1990s, compared to a stable population estimate of 2 million in the mid–1970s. Studies of the harp seal diet estimate that each year the herd consumes 142,000 metric tons of cod around the Newfoundland coast and in the Gulf of St. Lawrence, 1.2 million metric tons of Arctic cod, and 1 million metric tons of capelin, which is the main food of the cod.

Many argue that the seals are merely eating cod that fish harvesters would have otherwise taken. However, scientists from Fisheries and Oceans Canada who examined the stomach contents of seals have suggested that seals usually eat smaller cod than fishing crews are allowed to take, thus destroying the potential breeding stock of cod. While attempts to quantify the contribution of seals to the demise of the cod stocks are not conclusive, indications are that the increased seal population is having a major impact on the recovery of the existing cod stocks.

Puzzle piece 4: Ocean changes

Cod tend to inhabit subarctic to cool waters of -0.5 to 10°C (31 to 50°F), a temperature range to which their metabolism is best adapted. If exposed to temperatures lower than this, the cod's cellular processes are impaired and the fish may freeze to death. At higher temperatures, the cod's metabolism speeds up to the point where the fish cannot get enough food energy to survive. It is also recognized that cod eggs will not hatch and larval cod cannot develop in ocean water colder than 2°C (36°F). Cod will naturally seek out waters that are within their optimal temperature range. Since 1987, water temperatures off Labrador and northeastern Newfoundland have been below average, and in much of the traditional offshore cod spawning region they have been below 2°C (36°F). Scientists agree that changes in ocean temperature may be influencing cod stocks; however, they caution that the influence of these conditions on cod distribution and mortality is not fully understood.

Ocean currents and light also affect the movement of fish. Fish such as salmon will sometimes head into

Jeanette Winsor

Quidi Vidi Village, Newfoundland

currents even when they are not being carried, and studies show that fish will often drift passively with the current in darkness but swim against it in the light. Currents also affect the transportation of eggs and prey. The full extent to which changes in ocean currents have affected cod stocks is as yet unknown. Scientists do know that the Labrador Current is a dominant physical feature of the Northwest Atlantic ecosystem. Yet there is much to be investigated, as Dr. Leslie Harris of the Institute of Social and Economic Research notes:

… the rate at which the great ocean river flows, the volume of water it annually receives from its Arctic and Hudson Bay sources, the extent to which its average width and depth may in an individual year be increased, the manner in which new eddies and swirls may be induced

Atlantic Cod Chronicle

COD FACT SHEET

Common name:	Atlantic cod
Scientific name:	*Gadus morhua*
Distribution:	Northwest Atlantic from inshore waters 5 m (16 ft.) deep to edge of continental shelf 200+ m (650+ ft.) deep, north to coast of Greenland and south to Cape Hatteras
Migration:	Most cod migrate extensively from a summer feeding range to their winter spawning range.
Stocks:	The population is divided into 10 separate stocks.
Average weight:	3 kg (6½ lbs.)
Average length:	70 cm (27½ in.)
Diet:	Young cod feed on zooplankton; Juveniles and adults feed on capelin, sandlance, herring, and shellfish (sea stars, crab, shrimp).
Reproduction:	A female cod over 6 years of age and about 80 cm (30 in.) long can produce more than 2 million eggs. As development is very complex, only 1 egg per million matures into an adult.
Spawning conditions:	Water depth of 200 m (656 ft.), temperature range 2.5 to 4°C (36.5 to 40°F)

COD FISHERY COLLAPSE TIMELINE

Year	Main events in cod fishery collapse
1968	Highest total catch, mainly by non-Canadian fishing vessels, recorded.
1977	Canada declared exclusive economic zone.
1978	Northwest Atlantic Fisheries Organization established to manage fishery outside exclusive economic zone.
1992	Canada declared a ban on commercial cod fishing in most Newfoundland waters (30,000 Newfoundlanders out of work).
1998	Committee on the Status of Endangered Wildlife in Canada declared Atlantic cod "vulnerable," and added cod to the national list of species at risk.
2003	Cod stocks still not recovering as expected; future remains uncertain.

ANNUAL CATCH IN NEWFOUNDLAND WATERS*

Year	Catch (tonnes)
1958	500,000
1968	810,000
1978	100,000
1988	250,000
1998	5,000

* Total catch, Canadian and non-Canadian, on open oceans, frozen seas, tidal seas, and coastlines

Jeanette Winsor

are all … matters for educated guesswork.[1]

Puzzle piece 5: Ghost nets

Among the many factors that may affect fish populations is the problem of "ghost" nets — nets or traps that have been lost at sea. Some nets separate from their buoys during storms and are impossible for fishing crews to find; some are cut accidentally from their moorings by other ships; and some are set and simply not retrieved. Most of these nets and traps are made from heavy nylon rope that is not biodegradable. They can drift in the oceans for decades, trapping and destroying untold quantities of fish and enticing sea birds and other marine life to their demise.

Change Islands, Newfoundland

Puzzle piece 6: Poor management

Fisheries and Oceans Canada is responsibile for managing all marine species, including the Atlantic cod stocks. The goal of this federal department is to allow for the maximum sustainable catch while maintaining the health of fish stocks. The department is also responsible for setting fishing quotas in Canadian waters, as well as the licensing of fish harvesters and vessels.

Throughout the 1970s and 1980s, fish harvesters and processors in Newfoundland were concerned that the average size of the fish they were taking was getting smaller and that the amount of fish landed per unit of effort was declining. Despite their repeated warnings to large companies, fishery scientists, and the federal government, no action was taken. This lack of effective resource management and communication also played a role in the decline of the stocks.

The closure of the Newfoundland cod fishery in July 1992 was the largest mass layoff in Canadian history, as 30,000 people were suddenly without work. Since that time, the fishing industry in Newfoundland has adjusted and recovered. The value of recorded landings is now greater than in years prior to the cod-fishing moratorium, mainly owing to an increased focus on shrimp, crab, and previously underutilized species. Unfortunately, the cod stocks are not recovering as expected and there is no commercial cod fishery along the northeast coast of the island.

Fishy classroom activities
Counting fish

An essential aspect of fisheries management is the calculation of fish stock populations. Counting fish is very difficult because they move around and hide. Instead, scientists tag some of them and use a method of estimation to reach a fair assessment of the number of fish in a given stock, as illustrated by the following experiment.

Procedure:

1. Have students cut a large number of small squares of paper and place them in a container. Explain that each square represents a fish and the container represents part of the ocean.

2. Ask students to remove a handful of squares from the container and mark an "X" on each, as if tagging a fish. Then ask them to prepare a record sheet by writing A, B, and C across a piece of paper. Have students count the squares they have tagged and record the number under A on the record sheet.

3. Return the tagged squares to the container and mix them up with the untagged squares.

4. Ask students to close their eyes and remove a handful of squares from the container. Have them count all the squares in this sample and record the sample size under B on the record sheet. Then have them count how many tagged squares are in the sample and record this number under C on the record sheet.

5. To estimate the total number of squares (fish) in the container (ocean region), have students multiply the number under A (total tagged fish) by the number under B (random sample size) and divide by the number under C (number of tagged fish in the sample).

6. Have students remove and count all the paper squares to determine the accuracy of their estimates.

Follow-up: Having established that counting and keeping track of the number of fish in a body of water is not an easy task, students will begin to understand the need for carefully controlling the number of fish taken. Have students research to find out:

- who controls the fish stocks in local waters

- what determines when people can fish

- what number and size of fish are allowed to be taken

- what kinds of equipment are allowed (e.g., fishing rods, reels, lines, jiggers, nets, traps, electronic fish finders)

- what penalties are imposed on those who violate the laws

Invite a local fisheries or conservation officer to visit the class to discuss the reasons for these regulations.

Based on Bruce Wyman, "How Many Fish in the Sea?," New England Aquarium, on-line in January 2004 at <http://www.neaq.org/scilearn/kids/fish.html>.

In a cod's ear

The foundation of fisheries management is accurate scientific data. The age of fish is one of the key factors scientists look for when trying to calculate the biomass of a population. But how do you tell the age of a codfish? It's quite simple: inside the fish's ear is the ear bone or otolith. A cross-section of this bone reveals rings. Just as we can count the rings of a tree trunk to determine the age of a tree, we can count the rings on the otolith to determine the age of a cod.

Investigating fish habitats

To increase students' awareness of the factors that affect a fish stock in your region, select a species to study and visit a body of water that it inhabits. Look for potential sources of pollution and disturbance nearby, such as factories, hydroelectric projects (dams, spillways, and reservoirs), logging, and roads.

If you visit a beach, go at low tide and study the marine life in intertidal pools. Examine and identify the kinds of creatures found in the pools. Discuss their position in their food chain, as well as the potential effect on your study species if these creatures are destroyed.

If you visit a river or lake, have students test the pH of the water, and remind them that fish and plants can live only in areas with a specific pH. Take samples from different locations and try to determine the reasons for any significant differences. Check the water temperature of the lake or river, noting that the colder the water, the higher the oxygen level. What temperature does your subject species thrive in? What effect might global warming have on the stock? What effect would heated water from a factory have on the stock's habitat? How will the reproductive cycle be affected by temperature changes? How will predators and prey of the study species be affected?

As a classroom activity, have the students create a wall mural to illustrate the food chain of your study species and how pollutants can affect the entire web of life.

High seas research

Since many fish migrate and fall prey to fishing vessels on the high seas (i.e., areas unregulated by any nation), declines in fish stocks are a problem for many nations. The following areas, where large numbers of fish are being taken and the possibility of decimation exists, are beyond national jurisdictions:

- the "Donut Hole" of the Bering Sea and the "Peanut Hole" of the Sea of Okhotsk (declining pollock stocks)

- the Challenger Plateau off the coast of New Zealand (declining orange roughy stocks)

- Argentina's Patagonian Shelf (declining hake, southern blue whiting, squid stocks)

- the coasts of Chile and Peru (declining jack mackerel stocks)

- the "Loop Hole" of the Barents Sea off the coast of Norway (declining redfish stocks)

- parts of the Atlantic and South Pacific oceans (declining tuna, dolphin, shark stocks)

Have students research fish stock depletion in one of these areas and develop a written report or display that focuses on the species ecology, the reasons for stock depletion, the present situation, and possible ways to ensure future conservation.

Ocean culture

Have students work in groups to collect ocean-inspired stories, songs, poems, pictures, and other artistic pieces. Each group could create a poster or bulletin board to display its findings and explain the importance of the ocean in the history and culture of a particular coastal community. Have students create their own essay, poem, or painting about life near the ocean.

Jeanette Winsor, a former adult educator in Bonavista, Newfoundland, now teaches at St. John's College in Belize City, Belize. John Goldsworthy has taught science and social studies at secondary schools throughout the northeast coast of Newfoundland, and now teaches in St. John's, Newfoundland.

Note

1 L. Harris, *The Newfoundland Groundfish Fisheries: Defining the Reality,* Institute of Social and Economic Research, 1993, p.3.

REFERENCES AND RESOURCES

Ackerman, Jennifer. "New Eyes on the Oceans." *National Geographic.* Oct. 2000, pp. 86–115.

Comeau, Pauline. "New Endangered Species Plan Unveiled." *Canadian Geographic.* July/Aug. 1998, pp. 28–30.

Fisheries and Oceans Canada. "Charting A New Course: Toward the Fishery of the Future." Report 4904, 1993.

Fisheries and Oceans Canada. *Department of Fisheries and Oceans Fact Book.* Document 4824, 1993.

Fisheries and Oceans Canada. "Northern (2J+3KL) Cod Stock Status Update." Department of Fisheries and Oceans Report and Canadian Scientific Advisory Secretariat Status Report 2003/018, 2003.

Fisheries and Oceans Canada. "Northwest Atlantic Harp Seals." Science Stock Status Report E1-01, 2000.

Guy, Ray. "Seal Wars." *Canadian Geographic.* Jan./Feb. 2000, pp. 37–48.

Harris, L. *The Newfoundland Groundfish Fisheries: Defining the Reality.* Institute of Social and Economic Research, 1993.

Kurlansky, Mark. *Cod: A Biography of the Fish that Changed the World.* Alfred A. Knopf, 1997.

Lanken, Dane. "Disappearing Cod: Too Cold for Comfort." *Canadian Geographic.* Nov./Dec. 1993, p.15.

Minty, Dennis, Heather Griffen, and Dan Murphy. *Finding the Balance for Earth's Sake.* Breakwater, 1993.

Pepper, Vernon, and Barbara Pepper. "Biology 3201: Fishery Module." Government of Newfoundland and Labrador, Department of Education and Training, 1994.

ON-LINE RESOURCES

Background Information

<www.dfo-mpo.gc.ca> Fisheries and Oceans Canada (DFO) provides links to science, management, statistics, regulation, and publications on the main page of its website.

<www.dfo-mpo.gc.ca/zone/under-sous_e.htm> Underwater World Information Series, DFO Canada, provides information on marine species including Atlantic cod.

<www.dfo-mpo.gc.ca/CSAS/Csas/English/Index_e.htm> Canadian Science Advisory Secretariat provides stock status reports for marine species, including northern cod and harp seals.

<www.gov.nf.ca> and <www.heritage.nf.ca> On the main page of its website, the Government of Newfoundland and Labrador includes links to its departments and publications. Memorial University's Heritage website introduces students to the history and culture of the province.

Teaching Resources

<www.education.noaa.gov> "Oceans and Coasts for Teachers" includes links to and descriptions of over 30 websites endorsed by NOAA about fish, marine mammals, and oceans.

<http://smithsonianeducation.org/educators/lesson_plans/ocean/main.//html> Interdisciplinary marine science by the Smithsonian Institute includes six lesson plans and activities focusing on the diversity and importance of the seas.

<www.pbs.org/saf/1306/teaching/teaching2.htm> PBS Scientific American Frontiers includes a complete teaching guide for an activity related to population sampling.

<www.eoascientific.com/oceanography/introduction/guide.html> EOA Scientific's "Oceanography in Atlantic Canada" includes lesson plans and guidelines for a mock community meeting related to the fishery collapse.

<www.wildeducation.org/programs/blue_school/oceneduc.asp> Canadian Wildlife Federation's ocean education program includes lesson plans, resources, and instructions for registering as a Blue School to carry out the Blueprint for Ocean Action.

<http://school.discovery.com/lessonplans/programs/oceans> Discovery Channel's "Understanding the Ocean" includes lesson plans for Grades 6 to 8 on oceans, ocean currents, and global weather patterns; Understanding Ecology" includes lesson plans on open oceans, frozen seas, tidal seas, and coastlines.

Living Sustainably

Henry Kock

Blowing Up Your World

An activity focusing on individual responsibility for the environment

by Jean Harding

Subject areas: science, social studies
Key concepts: carrying capacity, personal responsibility
Location: indoors
Time: 50 minutes
Materials: 1 balloon, pencils, paper, and safety glasses

The Blowing Up Your World activity illustrates that an individual's everyday decisions and behavior affect the environment. It can be used or adapted as a quick introduction to a variety of environmental topics, or as an opener for discussions of personal responsibility for protecting the planet's resources. It also can be used to demonstrate the concept of carrying capacity and our potential to exceed the Earth's limits.

This activity can be very moving — I have had students cry. Therefore, it is important during the activity that you release air from the balloon for good environmental behavior and, at the end, explain that the balloon is only a model. It is highly unlikely that our collective behavior could blow up the world.

Procedure:

1. Select one student to put on the safety glasses, stand in front of the class, and blow up the balloon to its ordinary full-blown size. Ask the student not to tie a knot in the balloon but to hold it closed with his/her fingers.

2. Tell the class that the balloon represents the Earth. Students should note that it is already tight with the environmental stress that their parents and grandparents have put on it. The planet we all depend on for survival is in danger of being stretched beyond its limit by our growing population's over-consumption of resources and pollution of the air, soil, and water. We need to see how good a job the students as individuals are doing.

3. Ask each of the questions below. With each response to a question, count the number of hands up and the number of hands down. For every three to five students whose behavior damages the environment, ask the student with the balloon to blow one big breath of air into the balloon. For every three to five students whose behavior is good for the environment, ask the student to let some air out of the balloon.

4. With each question, ask students to record their points, if any, on paper. Points are in brackets after each question.

Note: Suggest that students listen carefully to each question before deciding whether to raise their hands. To discourage students from repeatedly raising their hands in order to blow up the balloon, a hands-up response sometimes indicates good environmental behavior and sometimes bad.

Questions and discussion: These are sample questions; feel free to change them, add more questions, or have students make up some questions themselves.

1. *How many of you leave your bedroom light on when you are not in the room? (Hands down get 2 points.)*

   Discussion: Turning off lights saves energy as well as money. Ask where electricity comes from. The more electricity is used, the more rivers are dammed or more

Tom Goldsmith

fossil fuel is burned, causing air pollution and increased levels of carbon dioxide in the atmosphere. Explain and discuss the greenhouse effect.

2. *How many of you walked, cycled, or took public transport to get to school today, instead of coming by private automobile? (Hands up get 3 points.)*

Discussion: Our reliance on cars that burn fossil fuels is one of the major causes of increased levels of carbon dioxide in the atmosphere and is the primary cause of urban smog.

3. *How many of you, when you drink a soft drink, throw the container into the garbage? (Hands down get 3 points.)*

Discussion: Throwing away containers of any kind wastes energy and resources and adds to our waste problem. Many towns are running out of landfill space. Ask if a landfill site is a good use for land.

4. *How many of you eat potatoes grown in your own family's garden or by local farmers instead of mass-produced, canned, or frozen potatoes? (Hands up get 4 points.)*

Discussion: The average potato plant grown on a large farm has been sprayed up to ten times with different pesticides. Some pesticides are linked with cancer. Transportation also adds to pollution and packaging creates waste problems.

5. *How many of you use a hairdryer or other energy-consuming convenience appliance, especially in the morning? (Hands down get 2 points.)*

Discussion: Hairdryers use a lot of energy. In the morning, so much demand is put on our electricity grids that power companies often have to construct more power plants just to meet the peak morning demand. Students could wash their hair at a different time and let it dry naturally.

6. *How many of you, when you go to a store, get a bag for your purchases, even if you have only one or two small items to carry? (Hands down get 3 points.)*

Discussion: Making paper and plastic bags uses energy and resources. The bags add to our litter and waste problems, and plastic is not biodegradable. Recycling is not the best answer because collecting and recycling materials requires energy. Instead, carry a reusable cloth bag or a knapsack with you.

7. *How many of you carry your lunch to school in a lunch box or reusable container? (Hands up get 3 points.)*

Discussion: See the discussion on question 6, above.

8. *How many of you eat take-out or cafeteria food that is served in foam or plastic containers? (Hands down get 10 points.)*

Discussion: Polystyrene and other plastic containers are made from petrochemicals, do not decompose in landfills, and release toxic gases when they are burned in incinerators.

9. *How many of you use cloth towels instead of paper towels to clean up a mess? (Hands up get 2 points.)*

Discussion: Paper comes from trees. The more of it we use, the more trees are cut down. Ask why it is important to conserve our forests.

10. *How many of you have belongings that you do not use or need? (Hands down get 2 points.)*

Discussion: Before you purchase something, think carefully about whether you need it or are likely to use it for a long time. Shopping wisely and reducing our consumption are the first lines of defence in protecting the environment.

11. *Is your sewage treated before it flows into a lake or the ocean? (Hands up get 6 points; 0 points to those who don't know.)*

Discussion: Raw sewage running into a body of water pollutes it. Water is one of our most valuable resources, yet many towns still do not have waste treatment facilities. When we dump raw sewage, we are using lakes, rivers, and oceans as our toilets. Think of this the next time you drink a glass of water, milk, or pop: less than one percent of the world's water is drinkable and it is constantly being recycled. Every glass of water contains at least two molecules of water that at one time were part of someone else's body!

Scoring: Have students add up their scores, and then tell them how they did.

31–40 points	Very good: you're living an environment-friendly lifestyle!
21–30 points	Good: you're starting to save the world.
11–20 points	Lots of room for improvement.
1–10 points	You're exiled to the town dump!

Wrap-up: Did your balloon blow up? Point out to students that Earth is very resilient and will survive. It is *Homo sapiens* and other species that we endanger by damaging our environment. Discuss with the class what each of them can do personally to protect the environment. Ask students to choose one behavior for which they did not receive points to change within a given amount of time.

Jean Harding is Science Department Head at St. Paul's Junior High School in St. John's, Newfoundland.

Encouraging Global Awareness

Students examine their personal lifestyles to become more aware of the gap between industrialized and developing nations

by Donna Lyseng

Subject areas: social studies, language arts, art

Key concepts: per capita income, wants versus needs, developing countries, industrialized countries, food waste, quality of life

Skills: data gathering, organizing, analyzing, and interpreting

Location: indoors

Time: 5 to 6 periods (longer if action undertaken)

Materials: tarp, challenging images

I have always felt very strongly that, before students can understand global disparities and develop empathy toward others, they must examine and evaluate their own lifestyles. With this in mind, I developed a series of activities to challenge students to take a fresh look at their own habits, hopes, and aspirations. My hope is that these activities can lead students toward an awareness of the contrast between the wastefulness of typical North American lifestyles and the more limited means of millions of people elsewhere in the world. The unit includes an optional action component that encourages students to become more aware of their responsibilities as global citizens. As several of the activities require personal responses from students, it is important that the facilitator know the students well and that students have confidence in the facilitator.

What's my lifestyle?

This initial activity is aimed at stimulating students to develop an awareness of their own lifestyle. To begin, I ask students to:

- plan their most desirable menu for a day: breakfast, lunch, snacks, and dinner

- describe their ideal bedroom, including size, furnishings, and equipment

- identify five of their most valued possessions, ranking them in order of priority, and to choose the one they just couldn't live without

- identify five of their most cherished extracurricular activities and decide which one they couldn't live without

- estimate their personal (not their family's) disposable income

Having students describe their ideal menus and bedrooms sparks their interest and, more importantly, ensures that no one is embarrassed by having to divulge information about family eating habits or living arrangements.

I explain that disposable income is the amount of money that they personally have to use in any way they wish in a week, a month, or a year. They are to include money they receive from all sources (e.g., allowances, gifts, babysitting jobs, paper routes), but not money that they must use for specific purposes such as clothing and school fees. I emphasize that they do not need to discuss their income with anyone; our aim is to calculate the class's per capita disposable income so that we can use this information in our later inquiries. To protect confidentiality, I distribute small slips of paper on which students write down their incomes anonymously. Then I collect the slips, read the amounts, and have students calculate the class average. As this may be a sensitive topic, especially when significant income disparities exist among students, the teacher may wish to do the calculation of per capita income without reading the individual amounts aloud.

Next, I ask students to write a short essay (about 100 words) in which they summarize their lifestyle, comment on their level satisfaction with it, and explain why they feel that way. I tell them that their essays will be read aloud to the class and instruct them not to write their names on them and not to write anything personal that might embarrass them. A strategy I often adopt at this point is to let students discuss among themselves

Tom Goldsmith

what they think is expected of them. After a few minutes' discussion, they may ask a question or two for clarification; however, I intentionally refrain from giving specific instructions about what to include in the essays because I have found that students are more creative and candid when the assignment is open-ended. The essays can be completed in class or assigned for homework.

The essays are all handed in, numbered, and distributed so that no student has his/her own. Each student reads aloud the essay he/she has received, identifying it only by the number. As each essay is read, the rest of the class listens and each student writes a short phrase that briefly summarizes the essay. Example summary notes might include: "high expectations for the future," "is happy with very little," "would spend more money on hockey than anything else."

What's our class's lifestyle?

I then ask students to review their summaries of the lifestyle essays and write one paragraph that summarizes their observations of the lifestyles described by the class. Class discussions can take place before or after students compose these paragraphs. You could stimulate the class discussion with such questions as:

- Would these lifestyle choices be typical of all students your age in this community? in this province, territory, or state? in this country? Why or why not?

- Are these lifestyle choices mostly basic needs or mostly wants?

- Have some essential things been left out (i.e., basic needs)?

- What is the difference between basic needs and wants (or luxuries)?

- Many of the choices were beyond our means to have them. Where do such expectations come from?

- What does "quality of life" mean? What things besides basic needs do we include when we assess our "quality of life"?

Assessment of students' performance in this exercise may be based on their completion of the tasks. However, if you wish to evaluate compositions or summaries for specific skills, ask students to retrieve and identify their essays.

Broadening the view

Once students have had an opportunity to consider and evaluate their personal and the class's lifestyles, they are ready to broaden their investigation to the society around them. Students are assigned the task of gathering data that provides insight into the quality of life of a typical Canadian or American. Research topics are unlimited but might include life expectancy, infant mor-

tality, family size, per capita income, level of education, caloric intake per day, leisure activities, the number of televisions (or refrigerators, computers, or automobiles) per household, and other indicators that students think are important.

It may be useful to divide the class into groups of two or three, and assign each group one or more topics on which to collect data. Before students begin, discuss where they might find these data, including such sources as atlases, encyclopedias, library references, or government agencies, publications, or Internet sites.[1]

As students find information, each group can add their data to a large class chart. Teachers may also wish to use the data collected to prepare a fact sheet that can be regularly updated and used in this and related activities.

Once data have been collected, students can compare the class's lifestyle choices to those reflected in these data. Questions for discussion might include:

- How are the quality-of-life indicators you researched similar to and different from the lifestyle choices you gathered and analyzed for yourselves?

- What facts are not available from the data collected that would help in evaluating a person's quality of life? How important are these omissions?

- Did you find any data that have not yet been discussed? What was interesting about them?

How do we compare?

To widen the view further, students are assigned the task of gathering data on the quality of life in a developing country, using the same indicators researched for Canada or the United States. Each group can research a different country, and all of the information can also be displayed on a chart and analyzed through a class discussion. Some questions to stimulate discussion might include:

- How does the life expectancy of men and women in developing countries compare to ours in North America?

- How do people in developing countries meet their basic needs for survival? How does that differ from the way that you meet your basic needs? (e.g., how much time and what skills are required to obtain basic necessities such as food and water?)

- What material possessions, services, or activities are missing from people's lives in developing countries, by comparison to your life? How important are these things?

- Compare the per capita income in a developing country with that of a typical North American and with the class's per capita disposable income. (Students may discover that their own discretionary spending on entertainment and luxury items is higher than per capita income in many developing countries.) How do you think income might affect the quality of life of people?

- What activities and possessions could you live without if you had to live on the per capita income of people in a developing country?

To demonstrate their growing awareness, students could read a passage from a book or write and present a scene that reflects the lifestyle of a typical person in one of the countries they have been investigating.

One person's garbage …

After the students have begun to understand the wide differences in lifestyles between North America and developing countries, the following awareness-raising activity can be planned in cooperation with the maintenance and cafeteria staff in your school. Ask the staff to collect all the cafeteria garbage from one lunch hour and bring it to an open, non-traffic area where it can be displayed. To maintain the element of surprise, prepare the display without students' help.

1. Lay a large tarp on the floor and tip all of the garbage onto it. Above it, project a slide or place a large image of a malnourished adult or a child with hands outstretched. Surround the garbage pile with other challenging images that contrast with students' lives and that you feel sure will have an impact on your students.

Tom Goldsmith

2. Ask the students to enter with paper and writing and drawing tools. As they walk around the display, encourage them to share their feelings and comments. Open some of the lunch bags in the garbage and empty them. (Each time I have done this activity, money has been found in these bags.)

3. Ask students to illustrate the scene and to respond to it in an essay or poem. Display these illustrations and compositions in the classroom for all students to share. Most will be inspiring.

At this point, discussions can focus not only on the students' awareness of global disparities but also on students' roles in working toward solutions. I have found that these activities provoke thoughtful reflections — and actions — from many students who had not realized before just how unusual their lifestyles are when looked at from a global perspective. Two years after one lesson, a former student wrote:

> It is sad to say but it took such an extreme situation to make me aware of the problem. The picture of the starving children seemed closer to home when I became aware of the problem. My initial emotion was disgust and then I was ashamed to be a part of such a wasteful society. But the strongest feelings that have stayed with me are the feelings of anger and awareness. That day was my first move toward recycling, and believe me when I tell you that I never throw out half-eaten lunches!

Potential outcomes

Here are some outcomes from my experience of guiding this activity.

- This activity was scheduled to coincide with a parent-teacher conference so that parents and other teachers could see the extent of the waste. As a result, students and parents started to plan lunches together.

- Students organized groups to monitor garbage and persuade students to use recyclable containers.

- Students encouraged the cafeteria staff to set up an area where students could place lunch items that they did not want, such as unopened juices, sealed packages of food, and fruit. Anyone who was hungry was encouraged to take the food (as soon at some of the more popular students helped themselves, there was no stigma attached).

- More recycling bins were installed in the school, and a composting program was started by science and outdoor education classes.

Follow-up activities

Possible follow-up activities for students to become more responsible global citizens include:

- Through fundraising and other means, students could support organizations that help people in developing countries find sustainable ways to improve their standard of living.

- Students could learn about young people who have become activists, (e.g., Ryan Hreljac, who began a foundation that raises funds to drill wells in rural Africa <www.ryanswell.ca>, and Craig Kielburger who founded an organization that advocates for children's rights in developing countries <www.freethechildren.org>).

- Students could develop a directory of local organizations and businesses that sell fair trade crafts and food products from developing countries (e.g., Ten Thousand Villages <www.tenthousandvillages.com>, and Bridgehead <www.bridgehead.ca>).

- Students could collect eyeglasses that people no longer use and donate them to Operation Eyesight, which repairs them (if necessary) and sends them to developing countries for distribution at no cost.

- Encourage students to take some action: one person *can* make a difference.

Donna Lyseng is a retired junior high school social studies teacher who is an avid golfer, skier, and reader. She and her husband divide their time between Calgary, Alberta, and Big White, British Columbia.

Note

1 Useful demographic data can be found at the websites of the Canadian International Development Agency <www.acdi-cida.gc.ca>, the U.S. Census Bureau <www.census.gov>, the United Nations Children's Fund <www.unicef.org>, and the United Nations <www.un.org>.

How Big is My Ecological Footprint?

Measuring their dependence on nature on a typical day can give students a new understanding of the connection between personal lifestyle choices and the health of the planet

by Tim Turner

Subject areas: mathematics, science, social studies

Key concepts: ecological footprint, lifestyle, sustainability

Skills: lifestyle analysis, critical thinking

Location: indoors

Time: 1 hour

Materials: chart paper, colored markers (blue, green, brown, and black), copy of Personal Eco-Footprint Calculator for each student

Students calculating their ecological footprints at the Sea to Sky Outdoor School in British Columbia.

Each of us consumes some of the Earth's products and services every day. How much we take depends on the ways in which we satisfy our needs and wants — the many habits that together create our lifestyle. We can ask ourselves these questions to get a better sense of what these habits are: How much water do I use on a typical day? What do I eat and how much do I eat? How much food do I waste? How do I transport myself and how far do I go? How much clothing and footwear do I have and how often do I replace it? What and how much stuff do I buy? How much energy and materials are required to keep me dry and warm/cool? How much garbage do I produce? How much land and energy is used for my recreational activities?

Our answers to these questions reflect the demand that each of us places on nature. In the 1990s, sustainability gurus Mathis Wackernagel and Bill Rees coined the term "ecological footprint" to refer to the load or demand that we place on the Earth's resources. An ecological footprint is a measure of how much of the Earth's biologically productive land and water is needed to produce our food, material goods, and energy, and to absorb our waste.

Having students calculate their ecological footprint gives them a concrete understanding of their own personal impact on the Earth's systems and offers a means of assessing the sustainability of their lifestyles. More than that, engaging students in an ecological footprint analysis elicits curiosity, enthusiasm, and genuine interest in taking action to reduce the demand they place on nature. Students like the fact that the analysis focuses on their own lives, and they understand its clear message: that their choices — and hence they, themselves — can make a difference. Calculating one's ecological footprint reinforces the notion that sustainability is a journey and not a destination and that it is participatory, not a spectator sport. It serves as a simple guide to living, working, and playing in ways that don't cost the Earth.

How much Earth do we have?

Our "living" Earth has a surface area of 51 billion hectares, but less than one quarter of this — under 12 billion hectares — is biologically productive for human use. This is the amount of land available on the planet to provide all of the food, water, and other materials that we need to support ourselves. To help students visualize this, create a pie graph that shows how the Earth's surface area is divided.

1. Begin by drawing a large circle on chart paper. Explain that the circle represents the surface area of the Earth.

2. Draw lines to divide the pie into land and water: 28 percent of the Earth's surface is land and 72 percent is water.

3. Focusing on the 28 percent of the pie that is land:
   - color about two-thirds of the land area green to represent the 19 percent of Earth's surface that is biologically productive for human use (i.e., land that is fertile enough to support agriculture, forests, or animal life).
   - color the other third of the land area brown to represent the 9 percent of Earth's surface that is marginally productive or unproductive for human use (e.g., land that is paved, covered by ice, lacks water, or has unsuitable soil conditions).

4. Explain that processes such as desertification, soil erosion, and urbanization are constantly reducing the amount of biologically productive land on Earth. To show this, draw small brown tentacles reaching from the border of the brown segment into the green segment.

5. Now, focusing on the water realm:
   - color about one-twentieth of the water section blue to show that 4 percent of the Earth's surface is lakes and oceans that are biologically productive for human use (i.e., yield more than 95 percent of the global fish catch).
   - color the remaining section black to show that 68 percent of the Earth's surface is ocean that is marginally productive or unproductive for human use (i.e, yields only about 5 percent of the global fish catch).

6. Draw black "tentacles" from the unproductive-water segment to the productive-water segment to represent processes that contribute to loss of

fertility in lakes and oceans. These include the destruction of coral reefs, oil spills, overfishing (of both marine and lake species), and shoreline development.

7. This leaves a pie chart featuring four segments of varying sizes — an excellent picture of our "living" planet. Label the sections, noting the percentage of the Earth's surface that each represents and listing the forces represented by the "tentacles."

Wrap-up: Remind students that only the green and blue sections — about 23 percent of the Earth's surface — are biologically productive. This small percentage of land and water is all we have to produce all of our food, materials, and energy, and to absorb our waste. These precious slices of the Earth's surface are also needed by the other 10 million or more species with whom we share the planet.

Calculating a footprint

Have students complete the Personal Eco-Footprint Calculator to estimate how much of the Earth's biologically productive land and water is needed to support their own lifestyles. The calculator is divided into eight categories that represent the many ways that we "consume" nature each day. Explain to students that it is not a scientific survey, but it does give a good approximation of the impact of one's lifestyle on a typical day. More detailed lifestyle analyses include other considerations that usually increase the size of one's ecological footprint. Therefore, the calculation derived from this calculator should be seen as a simplification and an underestimate of reality.

Students may point out that some lifestyle choices, such as the size of their house or the number of family cars, are not under their direct control. Explain that the calculator is meant to provide a snapshot of their lives at present, and that the baseline information they gather will help them to monitor the impact of changes they make in their lifestyles. They may, for example, make different choices if they purchase their own house or car in the future. The connection between these lifestyle considerations and their future ecological footprints is an important learning outcome of using the Footprint Calculator.

Three Facts and One Inescapable Conclusion!

Fact #1: Of the 51 billion hectares of the Earth's surface, only 12 billion hectares are biologically productive and therefore capable of providing resources and treating waste. That's 10 billion hectares of land and 2 billion hectares of water.

Fact #2: The human population is 6.3 billion and climbing. Of the biologically productive land and water that is available, our average Earth share is 1.9 hectares per person (not including the needs of all other life forms). As our population grows, we must either reduce our average Earth share or find more Earths to inhabit.

Fact #3: The amount of biologically productive land on Earth is in decline owing to urbanization, overgrazing by livestock, deforestation, toxic contamination, poor agricultural practices, desertification, and global climate change.

Inescapable conclusion: Less is more: we all need to shrink our ecological footprint.

Personal Eco-Footprint Calculator

Procedure: Complete each of the charts for a typical day in your home community. Add the points on each chart to obtain a subtotal for that category, and transfer it to the summary chart. Use the grand total to calculate your ecological footprint.

Water Use   **My Score**

1. My shower (or bath) on a typical day is: _____
   No shower / no bath (0)
   1–2 minutes long / one-fourth full tub (50)
   3–6 minutes long / half full tub (70)
   10 or more minutes long / full tub (90)
2. I flush the toilet: _____
   Every time I use it (40)
   Sometimes (20)
3. When I brush my teeth, I let the water run. (40) _____
4. I washed the car or watered the lawn today. (80) _____
5. We use water-saving toilets (6-9 liters/flush). (-20) _____
6. We use low-flow showerheads (-20) _____
7. I use a dishwasher on a typical day. (50) _____
          Subtotal: _____

Food   **My Score**

1. On a typical day, I eat:
   Beef (150/portion) _____
   Chicken (100/portion) _____
   Farmed fish (80/portion) _____
   Wild fish (40/portion) _____
   Eggs (40/portion) _____
   Milk/dairy (40/portion) _____
   Fruit (20/portion) _____
   Vegetables (20/portion) _____
   Grains: bread, cereal, rice (20/portion) _____
2. ____ of my food is grown locally. _____
   All (0)
   Some (30)
   None (60)
3. ____ of my food is organic. _____
   All (0)
   Some (30)
   None (60)
4. I compost my fruit/vegetable scraps and peels. _____
   Yes (-20)
   No (60)
5. ____ of my food is processed. _____
   All (100)
   Some (30)
   None (0)
6. ____ of my food has packaging. _____
   All (100)
   Some (30)
   None (0)
7. On a typical day, I waste: _____
   None of my food (0)
   One-fourth of my food (100)
   One-third of my food (150)
   Half of my food (200)
          Subtotal: _____

Transportation   **My Score**

1. On a typical day, I travel by: _____
   Foot (0)
   Bike (5 per use)
   Public transit (30 per use)
   Private vehicle (200 per use)
2. Our vehicle's fuel efficiency is ____ liters/100 kilometers (gallons/60 miles). _____
   less than 6 liters / 2 gallons (-50)
   6–9 liters / 2–2½ gallons (50)
   10–13 liters / 3–3½ gallons (100)
   More than 13 liters / 3½ gallons (200)
3. The time I spend in vehicles on a typical day is: _____
   No time (0)
   Less than half an hour (40)
   Half an hour to 1 hour (60)
   More than 1 hour (100)
4. How big is the car in which I travel on a typical day? _____
   No car (-20)
   Small (50)
   Medium (100)
   Large (SUV) (200)
5. Number of cars in our driveway? _____
   No car (-20)
   1 car (50)
   2 cars (100)
   More than 2 cars (200)
6. On a typical day, I walk/run for: _____
   5 hours or more (-75)
   3 to 5 hours (-25)
   1 to 3 hours (0)
   Half an hour to 1 hour (10)
   Less than 10 minutes (100)
          Subtotal: _____

Shelter   **My Score**

1. Number of rooms per person (divide number of rooms by number of people living at home) _____
   Fewer than 2 rooms per person (10)
   2 to 3 rooms per person (80)
   4 to 6 rooms per person (140)
   7 or more rooms per person (200)
2. We share our home with nonfamily members. (-50) _____
3. We own a second, or vacation home that is often empty. _____
   No (0)
   We own/use it with others. (200)
   Yes (400)
          Subtotal: _____

Personal Eco-Footprint Calculator

Energy Use   My Score

1. In cold months, our house temperature is: _____
   Under 15°C (59°F) (-20)
   15 to 18°C (59 to 64°F) (50)
   19 to 22°C (66 to 71°F) (100)
   22°C (71°F) or more (150)
2. We dry clothes outdoors or on an indoor rack.   _____
   Always (-50)
   Sometimes (20)
   Never (60)
3. We use an energy-efficient refrigerator.   _____
   Yes (-50)
   No (50)
4. We use compact fluorescent light bulbs.   _____
   Yes (-50)
   No (50)
5. I turn off lights, computer, and television when
   they're not in use.   _____
   Yes (0)
   No (50)
6. To cool off, I use: _____
   Air conditioning: car / home (30 for each)
   Electric fan (-10)
   Nothing (-50)
7. Outdoors today, I spent: _____
   7 hours (0)
   4 to 6 hours (10)
   2 to 3 hours (20)
   2 hours or less (100)
                                        Subtotal: _____

Clothing   My Score

1. I change my outfit every day and put it in
   the laundry. (80)   _____
2. I am wearing clothes that have been mended
   or fixed. (-20)   _____
3. One-fourth of my clothes are handmade or
   secondhand. (-20)   _____
4. Most of my clothes are purchased new
   each year. (120)   _____
5. I give the local thrift store clothes that
   I no longer wear.   _____
   Yes (0)
   No (100)
6. I buy hemp instead of cotton shirts
   when I can. (-10)   _____
7. I never wear ___ % of the clothes in my cupboard.
   Less than 25% (25)   _____
   50% (50)
   75% (75)
   More than 75% (100)
8. I have ____ pairs of shoes.   _____
   2 to 3 (20)
   4 to 6 (60)
   7 or more (90)
                                        Subtotal: _____

Stuff   My Score

1. All my garbage from today could fit into a: _____
   Shoebox (20)
   Large pail (60)
   Garbage can (200)
   No garbage created today! (-50)
2. I reuse items rather than throw them out. (-20)   _____
3. I repair items rather than throw them out (-20)   _____
4. I recycle all my paper, cans, glass, and plastic. (-20)   _____
5. I avoid disposable items as often as possible.   _____
   Yes (-10)
   No (60)
6. I use rechargeable batteries whenever I can. (-30)   _____
7. Add one point for each dollar you spend
   in a typical day.   _____
   Today was a Buy Nothing Day (0)   _____
                                        Subtotal: _____

Fun   My Score

1. For typical play, the land converted into fields,
   rinks, pools, gyms, ski slopes, parking lots, etc.,
   added together occupy: _____
   Nothing (0)
   Less than 1 hectare / 2½ acres (20)
   1 to 2 hectares / 2½ to 5 acres (60)
   2 or more hectares / 5 or more acres (100)
2. On a typical day, I use the TV or computer   _____
   Not at all (0)
   Less than 1 hour (50)
   More than 1 hour (80)
3. How much equipment is needed for
   typical activities?   _____
   None (0)
   Very little (20)
   Some (60)
   A lot (80)
                                        Subtotal: _____

Summary

Transfer your subtotals from each section and add them
together to obtain the grand total.

Water use _____
Food _____
Transportation _____
Shelter _____
Energy Use _____
Clothing _____
Stuff _____
Fun _____

Grand Total: _____

My ecological footprint is:
Grand Total divided by 100 = _____ hectares
(To convert to acres, multiply hectares by 2.47)

Sharing Earth fairly

Once students have calculated their ecological footprints, they can compare their results with others and determine whether the Earth could sustain the human population if everyone lived as they do.

1. Have students consider how their results compare with the following average ecological footprints:
   United States: 10 hectares (24 acres) per person
   Canada: 9 hectares (22 acres) per person
   Italy: 4 hectares (9 acres) per person
   Pakistan: less than 1 hectare (2 acres) per person

2. Have students calculate how much of Earth's biologically productive land is available to each person on the planet. To do this, they divide the total area of biologically productive land (12 billion hectares) by the number of people on the planet (about 6.3 billion). This amount (1.9 hectares / 4.7 acres per person) is known as the Average Earth Share.

3. Have students calculate how many Earths would be needed if every human had an ecological footprint the size of theirs. To do this, they divide their ecological footprint by the Average Earth Share. (If the ecological footprint is in acres, divide by 4.7; if it is in hectares, divide by 1.9.) Discuss: How many additional Earths would be needed to meet human demands if everyone lived as we do? What insights come from this knowledge?

Wrap-up: To follow up, remind students that the limited amount of biologically productive land that supports us also needs to provide food, water, and shelter for more than 10 million other species. These needs were not factored into the Average Earth Share, which represents the needs of humanity only. Consider, too, the implications of living in a world where 80 percent of the human family use 20 percent of available resources, while 20 percent (i.e., those of us in wealthier countries) use 80 percent of available resources.

Extensions:

- An ecological footprint calculation provides a baseline from which to measure progress toward a smaller footprint and a more sustainable lifestyle. Challenge students to set goals for themselves in each lifestyle category (i.e., to eat less meat or to spend more time outdoors) and have them calculate their footprints again after an agreed-upon interval of time.

- The Personal Eco-Footprint Calculator assumes that the habits identified reflect how one always lives; however, we know that lifestyle is influenced by factors such as a person's age or time of year, and an ecological footprint will expand or shrink accordingly. Many residential outdoor and environmental education centers ask visiting students to calculate their ecological footprint twice: the first calculation is based on their activities on a typical day at the center, while the second is based on their daily routines and habits at home. Students often find that their ecological footprint is as much as 400 percent larger at home, yet most agree that the simplified living in the outdoor center ranks high on their quality-of-life index. This exercise provides a helpful comparison that debunks the myth that a person's quality of life is directly proportional to consumption.

Tim Turner is a sustainability educator with the Sea to Sky Outdoor School located on Keats and Gambier islands in Howe Sound, northwest of Vancouver, British Columbia.

RESOURCES

Wackernagel, Mathis, and William Rees. *Our Ecological Footprint: Reducing Human Impact on the Earth.* New Society Publishers, 1995.

<www.ecofoot.net> The most extensive site for educators interested in using the ecological footprint tool with their students.

<www.panda.org/news_facts/publications/general/livingplanet> WWF's Living Planet Report lists the ecological footprints of 150 countries.

<www.davidsuzuki.org> David Suzuki's Nature Challenge identifies the ten best things one can do to protect nature. This is an excellent follow-up project to helps students in their ongoing efforts to shrink their ecological footprint.

<www.seatosky.bc.ca> The Sea to Sky Outdoor School website provides access to such teaching resources as the Ecospherotron, Lifesavers, and Earth 100, which complement the ecological footprint.

Tim Turner

Simulation on Basic Needs

*A simulation game to highlight the challenge of
meeting basic needs with limited resources*

by Mary Gale Smith

Subject Area: social studies, science, home economics,
fine art, mathematics

Key Concepts: basic human needs, resource allocation,
survival, human rights

Skills: developing empathy, clarifying concepts, assessing
action

Location: indoors

Time: about 1 hour

Materials: 7 large manila envelopes, 4 pairs of scissors, 2
glue sticks, 2 rulers, 3 pencils, approximately 60 toothpicks
or ice cream sticks, sheets of colored paper (6 green, 6
pink, 4 gold, 7 white, 3 yellow, 4 blue), 7 copies of Basic
Needs chart (provided)

This simulation activity is designed to enhance
students' understanding of the uneven distribution of resources and how this affects families.
The aim is to develop empathy for other families and
their situations, and to promote social responsibility and
action in ensuring the welfare and fair treatment of
all families. The key
underlying values are
care, concern, coop-
eration, and com-
mitment. Students
form groups that
represent families
— either various
families within
one country or
typical families
from various
countries, rich
and poor. Note
that this activity
may not be suitable
for a class with a num-
ber of students who live
in poverty. You will need to
be sensitive to the feelings of
such students, perhaps asking
whether the simulation can be
undertaken without subjecting them
to feelings of inferiority.

Anna Payne-Krzyzanowski

Objectives: Students will demonstrate an understanding
of the uneven distribution of resources available to families in meeting basic needs, be able to describe some of
the effects of this uneven distribution on families and
society, and suggest actions to improve the ability of
families to meet their basic needs.

Preparation:

Prepare seven envelopes containing the resources for
seven families. Attach a Basic Needs chart (next page) to
the outside of each envelope, and label the envelopes
Family 1 to Family 7. Put the following materials in the
appropriate envelopes:

Family 1: 1 sheet of green paper, 3 sheets of gold paper

Family 2: 2 pairs of scissors, 1 ruler, 1 pencil, 1 glue
stick, 1 sheet of pink paper

Family 3: 1 pair of scissors, 1 glue stick, 2 sheets of
green paper, 2 sheets of white paper, 2
sheets of pink paper

Family 4: 1 ruler, 2 pencils, 2 sheets of yellow paper, 2
sheets of white paper, 2 sheets of blue paper

Family 5: 30 toothpicks, 1 pair of scissors, 2 sheets of
white paper, 2 sheets of pink paper

Family 6: 30 toothpicks, 2 sheets of blue paper, 2
sheets of green paper

Family 7: 5 sheets of paper, one of each of
green, gold, white, pink, and yellow

Procedure:

1. Divide the class into seven groups to represent seven families, so that Family 1 has
seven members, Family 2 has five members,
and Families 3 to 7 have two, three, or four
members (depending on the size of the
class).

2. Explain to students that they are part
of a group representing a family that
has to satisfy basic needs to survive. In
this activity, the basic needs required
for the well-being of each family member are food, clothing, shelter, water,
and education. In the real world,
resources vary from family to family. In
the simulation, they are to satisfy their
basic needs as best they can with the
resources available to them.

Basic Needs

Your family must attempt to satisfy these five basic needs.

Food   Make a pattern to represent the four basic food groups. Each food group must be a different color, one that approximates the color of food in that group. Each food group pattern must be at least 10 x 10 cm (4 x 4 inches).

Clothing   Make patterns to represent a piece of clothing for each member of the family. Each piece of clothing should use at least one-quarter of a sheet of paper.

Shelter   Make a three-dimensional shelter, no smaller than 10 x 10 x 10 cm (4 x 4 x 4 inches).

Water   Use a piece of white or blue paper to represent a water source.

Education   Make a four-page book to represent the education available to your family. Each page should be a different color and should use at least one-quarter of a sheet of paper.

3. Instruct the groups not to open their envelopes until you give them a signal. Distribute the envelopes and have students read the Basic Needs chart attached to their envelope.

4. Emphasize that students must meet the requirements on the Basic Needs chart but can use only the resources provided in their family's envelope.

5. Give the signal to begin and instruct the families to notify you when they have satisfied all their basic needs.

6. Observe the students' interactions. Note whether students cooperate within and between families.

Option: At some point, you can stop the simulation and check with the various families to see how they are doing. You could ask how this process could be changed. If students suggest sharing or trading, then that can be allowed. You could explain how people in real communities often work together to provide the basic needs for people other than their own family, and that this practice is acceptable for this activity.

7. Once the families have satisfied their basic needs, have each family explain how it managed to do so. Highlight creativity and cooperation. If any family was not able to meet its basic needs, ask the members to give reasons why.

Wrap-up: Discuss the students' reactions to the simulation. Sample discussion questions:

1. How did you feel when you discovered that resources differed from family to family? How does it feel to have plenty? How does it feel to have next to nothing?

2. Were you able to satisfy your basic needs without getting resources from other families? Why? How did this make you feel?

3. Why do resources vary from family to family?

4. Did you have resources that were wasted? Were any resources left after your family had satisfied its basic needs? What could you have done with these resources?

5. In what ways does cooperating with others help families?

6. Can you suggest actions in real life that can be taken to ensure greater fairness in resource distribution? What can governments do? What can community groups do? What can students do?

7. This activity concentrated on physical needs. Are there other human needs that might also be considered?

Extensions:

- Students could brainstorm reasons why people might be unable to meet their basic needs (e.g., unemployment, illness, family breakdown, war, lack of access to land or other resources, water or soil pollution). Then have students suggest actions that could be taken to address each situation.

Anna Payne-Krzyzanowski

- Have students research organizations in their community that work to ensure that people's basic needs are met (i.e., food banks, community gardens, service clubs, Coats for Kids, Breakfast for Learning, Red Cross, Habitat for Humanity).

- Invite guest speakers from community groups to explain the work they do locally or in other countries to help achieve a fairer distribution of goods and resources.

- Have students examine personal resource use or resource use in the school to recommend or make changes where resources are misused or wasted.

- Have students make a list of volunteer opportunities within their community where they can help to achieve a fairer distribution of goods and resources.

Interdisciplinary connections:

Vocabulary Development: Do a concept attainment activity related to needs (necessary for survival) and wants (things that are desired but not needed for survival). The differences between needs and wants in a relatively affluent country could be contrasted with those in a less affluent country.

Science: Students could research the environmental impact of human use of natural resources. This activity could be linked to ways in which animals in the wild cope with uneven allocation of resources.

Social Studies: Students could research the various ways that people of the world meet their basic needs, depending on availability of resources, cultural traditions, regional climate, and other factors.

Math: Students could gather and graph statistics on resource use, and then write a summary of the patterns that emerge.

Family Studies: Students could assess their food and clothing choices. They could host a "hunger banquet" or organize a group to recycle, reuse, or repair clothing. They could investigate local agriculture, the "slow food" movement, or child labor.

Fine Arts: Students could research some ways in which music and the arts have been used to express social issues.

Mary Gale Smith is a teacher in Surrey, British Columbia, and an Adjunct Professor at the University of British Columbia's Faculty of Education, where she lectures in Home Economics education, global education, and action research. This simulation is a modified version of Simulation of International Trade, presented by Margit McGuire at the International Social Studies Conference Pacific Rim, Vancouver, June 1988.

Population, Consumption, and the Environment

Making connections between population growth, lifestyle, equity, and environment

by John Goekler

Subject areas: social studies, environmental education, science, mathematics

Key concepts: carrying capacity; interconnectedness of lifestyle, population and environmental impacts; resource scarcity; geometric progression; exponential growth

Skills: critical thinking, web diagrams

Location: indoors

> *Population growth is the primary source of environmental damage.*
>
> — Jacques Cousteau

Environmentalists have long recognized that increasing human numbers and more consumptive lifestyles are the primary threats to the natural world. But how do educators deal with population issues? How can they approach a subject that is not only tremendously complex but also touches on highly charged issues and deeply ingrained beliefs?

Breaking the ice

One easy way to introduce students to population issues is with a quick round of "Population Jeopardy," asking such questions as

- What was the population of the world in 2003? (6.3 billion)

- What was world population in 1960? (3 billion)

- If current growth rates continue, what will world population be in 2050? (12.8 billion)

- What are the three most populous countries of the world? (China, India, and the United States)

- In what region of the world is population growing the fastest? (Africa by rate of increase, Asia by total number of people)

These questions help to establish a baseline of student knowledge about population, and the answers often bring head shakes and exclamations of disbelief.

The average North American consumes roughly 400 times the energy and is responsible for 400 times the pollution of a typical Ethiopian.

Gail Littlejohn

Anne Hansen

Gail Littlejohn

The carrying capacity debate

A discussion of carrying capacity is another excellent opening, because it asks students to internalize the issues of human needs, how those needs are met, and the resulting impacts. An easy way to introduce this concept is through the Carrying Capacity activity (see page 95). After doing that exercise, ask the students to quickly brainstorm indicators for how we will know when the Earth is "full," and then to list the ten most effective indicators. Next, ask how many of those indicators are apparent to some degree today. (This may be done as a collaborative group activity.)

It's important to look beyond the numbers and also to consider lifestyles and values. Instead of simply asking how many people the Earth can support, ask:

- How many people at what standard of living? Do we want to live like a typical North American, a typical Italian, or a typical person in India?

- For what percentage of the population? Does everyone get to enjoy this lifestyle, or only a small minority of the world's population?

- For how long can it support this many people at this standard of living? Is this sustainable?

- With what type of social and political institutions? Dictatorships may deal more effectively with resource scarcity than democracies, but are we prepared to live under that sort of regime?

- And with what values and tastes and fashions? Remember that rhinos are threatened with extinction today because people want their horns, and beaver were almost exterminated in North America during the 19th century because men in Europe wanted to wear fashionable hats.

Another tack is to ask students to define what they would consider a fulfilling lifestyle. Then ask them to consider the environmental consequences of six billion people living that lifestyle — or of ten billion people doing so. Also ask what the consequences (social, political, environmental, and ethical) might be of a few nations — or a small percentage of individuals — living that lifestyle, while the rest of the world lives a minimal existence.

Tracking the trends

It is important when exploring population issues that students understand key trends, including population growth rates and resource availability. Despite a global decline in birth rates, the human population is still growing by nearly 80 million annually — roughly the equivalent of adding another Germany every year. And this is projected to continue for the next 20 to 30 years.

Because of this growth, trends in food security are downward. Despite the Green Revolution in agriculture, per capita grain availability is down significantly from peak levels more than a decade ago. Nor was the Green Revolution "green" in an environmental sense: it resulted in huge production increases but also in massive habitat destruction — as open space was converted to farmland — plus significant erosion and topsoil loss, and water pollution from runoff of pesticides and fertilizers.

The amount of fresh water available per person is also declining. Because of population growth, world per capita water availability has dropped by about one-third since 1970. Some 80 countries currently experience some degree of water shortage, and it is projected that as many as five to seven billion people may suffer from water shortages by 2050. Major aquifers across the globe have been significantly depleted, and, because of dams and diversions, the Nile, Ganges, Huang He, and Colorado rivers run almost dry during parts of the year. As a result, the ecosystems and fisheries they once supported — and the communities dependent on them — also are in decline.

Economic inequity, both within and among nations, is also increasing. The World Bank estimated in 2001 that the average income in the richest 20 countries was 37 times the average in the poorest 20 nations, and that the gap between rich and poor had more than doubled in the past 40 years. The bank also reported that almost half of the world's people live on less than US$2 a day and that one-fifth live on less than US$1 a day. About 800 million are chronically hungry.

Typically, poorer nations and people have higher fertility rates. Children are assets in poor societies, being social security for their parents' old age; they also help to raise or gather food, haul water, collect fuelwood, and generate scarce cash by begging, by hiring out to sweatshops, or even by being sold.

Behind all these trends is the specter of scarcity, which can be expressed through the formula H = R ÷ P,

As human population and consumption grow, the resources available to the rest of the natural community decline.

The reasons for deforestation vary by region, but United Nations studies indicate that 79 percent of total deforestation between 1973 and 1988 was a direct result of population growth. By far the greatest cause of forest loss was clearing land for agricultural purposes in poor regions, followed by fuelwood harvesting in those regions — especially in Africa, where 90 percent of the population rely on wood for cooking and heating. Lacking access to arable land, poor farmers have little option but to clear forests to plant crops, just as people who cannot afford electricity or propane must gather fuelwood.

We can't simply blame deforestation on poor people, however. In many areas of Central and South America, forests are cleared to raise soybeans for cattle feed, or to graze cattle, to help meet the world's growing appetite for beef. In Canada, some 1 million hectares (2.5 million acres) fall to timber companies' saws annually, while in Russia that figure may be as high as 4 million hectares (10 million acres) annually — twice the deforestation rate of Brazil. The motive in these situations is profit — not survival — driven by consumer demand for large resource-intensive structures and huge quantities of paper and packaging.

Air pollution takes a number of forms, but the root cause is emissions from automobiles and industrial plants. Whether manifested as smog and soot, acid rain, ozone depletion, or global climate change, the largest proportion of atmospheric pollution is currently generated in the industrialized world. The average North American uses roughly 400 times the energy — and therefore is responsible for 400 times the pollution — of a typical Ethiopian. As both world population and the global economy grow, however, more people living more intensive lifestyles will consume more oil, coal, and natural gas — with a resulting increase in air pollution. Current projections indicate that by early in the 21st century, because of increases in population and consumption, rapidly industrializing regions will generate the majority of world carbon emissions.

Nowhere is the correlation between population and environmental impacts so clear as with habitat and biodiversity loss. In 1996, the World Conservation Union (IUCN) published a groundbreaking survey of the status of animal life on Earth. According to their estimates, 25 percent of mammal and amphibian species, 11 percent of birds, 20 percent of reptiles, and 34 percent of fish species surveyed so far are threatened with extinction. Subsequent work by IUCN in 2000 and 2002 indicates

in which H represents the human condition, R represents available resources, and P represents population. We can simply divide any essential resource — food, farmland, water, forests, housing, jobs, or health care — by the number of people in need to determine a trend. When finite resources must be divided by more and more people, the result is increasing scarcity, which can be compounded by inequitable distribution. In recent decades, both within and between nations, the rich have been getting richer, and the poor have been getting poorer.

Scarcity affects the environment in a number of ways. People facing scarcity will do whatever is necessary to survive — clear rainforests to sell timber or raise crops, overwork or overgraze farmland, deplete fisheries, and kill or capture endangered species to eat or sell. They may also migrate to cities or other regions, thereby inflicting greater stress on those environments. They may discriminate against other races, religions, or classes by denying them a fair share of resources. In rich and poor countries alike, women and girls are most likely to be denied a fair share of resources when those resources are scarce. (An excellent way to help students understand scarcity issues and impacts is through the Facing the Future exercise "Shop Till You Drop" at <www.teacherscorner.org>.)

Making connections

To help students internalize connections between population and environmental issues, it is essential to demonstrate these links. When students are asked to identify key environmental issues, they typically name rainforest loss, air pollution, and loss of wildlife habitat. If we examine these point by point, the connections to population and consumption are clear.

that the situation is as bad as or worse than originally estimated. The primary causes of these declines are human destruction of old-growth forests, wetlands, and other habitat, and overfishing in fresh and salt water. Increasing human population density correlates directly to decreasing habitat. As the human environmental footprint grows — from increases in both population and consumption — the resources available to the rest of the natural community will further decline.

Becoming part of the solution

Fortunately, we know how to solve these problems. Solutions must be humane, holistic, and culturally appropriate but generally follow prescribed patterns. We know that, as citizens of the industrialized world, controlling our own reproduction, reducing our own environmental impacts, becoming politically involved, and working to create a sustainable world are essential pieces of the solution. On a global basis, we know that accessible and affordable reproductive health care is key to population stabilization, because when people can reliably choose the number and spacing of their children, they have fewer of them. If reproductive health care were universally available and affordable, estimates are that world population growth would decline by nearly 20 percent almost immediately. Education and empowerment of women are vital components, because the more education a woman has, the fewer children she is likely to have. More highly educated women also have more economic options and more influence in their families and communities. And when women have disposable income, they tend to invest it in a better future for their children.

Community health care, education, and social justice — including land reform — are essential components of this restructuring, along with promoting sustainable livelihoods so that people can achieve economic security. Environmentally sound industries and technologies, such as renewable energy production, and their transfer to developing regions, are also vital pieces in stabilizing world population and sustaining the environment. Most important of all, we need to understand that each of us can and must make a difference, and that no effort takes place in a vacuum. Like touching a mobile — in which each piece moves in response to movement from any other — every contribution has a ripple effect that can spread across the planet and support other efforts.

We can stabilize world population at a sustainable level, protect and enhance the environment, create a vibrant economy, and redress inequalities among nations, individuals, and genders. We have the knowledge, the technology, and the capital available to do so. What we lack is a shared vision of the world that we would like to create and the political will to implement it. Making those connections and calling that vision into being may be the greatest challenge, and the most enduring legacy, of environmental education.

Classroom activities

Carrying capacity

This activity helps students to visualize the concept of carrying capacity, and to see that as the human population increases, habitat for Earth's other species deceases.

Goal: to create a visual model of the effects of population increase on carrying capacity

Skills: critical thinking

Time: 30 minutes

Materials: 2 clear containers (i.e., a salad or punch bowl that can hold at least 4 liters / 1 gallon), blue food coloring, measuring cups, towel or tray to catch spills

Procedure:

1. Fill one of the containers about half full with water and add enough blue food coloring to make the water quite visible. Fill the other container about two-thirds full with clear water.

2. Explain to the class that the container of blue water represents the Earth. The blue water is the human population and the air volume above it is the habitat for all other species on Earth.

3. Divide the class into two groups, one to represent births and one to represent deaths, and ask them to line up on opposite sides of the room.

4. Give one group a 250 ml (one-cup) measure and the other a 100 ml (one-third to one-half cup) measure to approximate the worldwide ratio of births to deaths. (This ratio was 22 to 9 per 1,000 population in 2003. Updated figures are available from the Population Reference Bureau's on-line Datafinder and World Population Datasheet at <www.prb.org>.)

5. Ask students from each group to come forward one at a time. Those representing births fill their cup with clear water and add it to the blue water (the human population). Those representing deaths fill their cup with blue water (the human population) and dump it into the clear water.

6. Repeat the process until the "Earth" container is dangerously full of human population, and any further increase will cause an overflow — or until a student points out that the habitat left is not enough to sustain life for other creatures.

Wrap-up: Lead a discussion of students' observations. As population increased, habitat for other species decreased. If population growth had continued until the water reached the top of the container, all other species would have been displaced. If population had increased further, the container would have overflowed. If the water were really the human population, its overflow would represent massive deaths from famine, war, and disease.

Ask what happened to the color of the water in the "Earth" container (it became lighter as it was diluted). Ask how this might compare to depletion of the Earth's resources as carrying capacity is approached. Ask students to describe possible impacts from this scenario on local environments, economies, and social institutions. How might their own lives be affected?

What's your favorite meal?

Skills: critical thinking, web diagrams

Time: 1 hour

Materials: poster paper, markers

Procedure:

1. Organize the class into three to five groups. Ask each group to agree on a meal they would like to share, and to list on the poster paper all of the components of that meal. (Alternatively, use the menu from the school cafeteria that day and/or break the meal into components and give each group the task of tracing an individual component.)

2. Have the groups discuss where and how they would obtain all the food for the meal they have chosen. Then ask them to suggest resources and technologies required to produce, process, package, deliver, and serve these foods (e.g., farmland, water, farm machinery, fertilizer, pesticides, fishing boats, petroleum fuels, electrical energy, transportation, refrigeration, grocery stores).

3. Ask students to identify some potential environmental impacts from the processes involved in obtaining their meals (e.g., soil erosion, pesticide runoff, overfishing, air pollution, freeway crowding, urban sprawl).

   Note: Allow 15 to 20 minutes and check regularly with each group to guide the discussion. Students may decide their food "came from the store," in which case you will need to coach them: Where did the store get the food? How did it get to the store? What was necessary for that to happen? Where was it grown, and what was necessary to grow it?

4. Have each group briefly report to the class on its meal and what is involved in providing it. After each report, open the discussion for other students' observations. You could ask the class what impacts they might expect if twice as many people lived in their community and enjoyed the same meals the students chose. What might be the implications if everyone in the world were to enjoy the same meals? Encourage students to suggest ways to obtain their food that might have fewer environmental effects (e.g., buying from local or organic farmers, growing it themselves).

Extension: Have students discuss what the implications (environmental, security, and ethical) might be if a small percentage of the world's people — perhaps some North

Americans — were able to enjoy such meals every day, while the rest of the world lived on bread and rice or went hungry.

When the chips are down

This exercise offers a way of viewing both the patterns of history and the underlying causes of the events that shape global issues today.

Time: 1 hour

Materials: 500 poker chips in various colors, several wide markers, sheet of butcher paper 2 to 2.5 meters (7–8 feet) long

Procedure:

1. Divide the class into three groups. (With larger classes, you may prefer to have six groups so that all students can participate more fully. In this case, double the materials listed.) Explain that each group will serve as the National Advisory Council for "their" country and will be responsible for all policy decisions. Have each group name their country and brainstorm the resources they want in it (e.g., farmland, forests, water, minerals, infrastructure, parks and wilderness) and the conditions under which they would like to live. Encourage students to consider the institutions and values they want for their country, including law, governance, and social values.

2. Assemble all three groups around a table or floor area on which the long roll of paper is laid out. Quickly create three "countries" by dividing the paper into three distinct areas with a marker. Hand out the markers, and ask each group to draw the features they agreed they would like to have in their country. (Alternatively, use separate sheets of butcher paper roughly 75 by 60 cm (2½ by 2 feet) in size so the groups can work in different areas of the room. Once the "countries" are finished, place them side by side. If using six groups, arrange the six countries in a grid pattern with three across and two down so that all countries are contiguous.)

3. Explain the concept of an ecological footprint: that is, that each person needs a certain amount of productive land to provide food, fiber, water, economic livelihood, and waste disposal. Larger populations have a larger total footprint because they require more resources. Affluent lifestyles also impose larger footprints. A diet high in animal protein requires much more farmland than a vegetarian diet. Having automobiles requires that roads, repair shops and parking lots be built, thus eliminating habitat. Manufacturing processes require resources and land and generate waste.

4. Place one poker chip on each country as a core population. Then have the groups model population growth and economic development over four generations, one generation at a time.

- The first group models a doubling of population, but with static economic development (like traditional agrarian societies). It receives 2 chips for its first generation, and 4, 8, and 16 chips for the subsequent generations.

- The second group models a 50-percent increase in population each generation, along with a doubling of consumption (like some rapidly industrializing nations). It receives 3 chips for its first generation, and 9, 27, and 81 chips for the subsequent generations.

- The third group models a doubling of both population and consumption each generation (a quadrupling of its ecological footprint), as the United States has over the past 50 years. It receives 4 chips for its first generation, and 16, 64, and 256 chips for the subsequent generations.

John Goekler

Hand out the appropriate number of pre-counted chips for each generation only after each previous generation is complete. Emphasize that people (i.e., chips) cannot be placed outside the borders of countries; that falling off the edge is death through famine, war, or disease; and that stacking of chips is not allowed!

Note: If you run this simulation using six groups, double the number of chips used while maintaining the same proportion, i.e., two groups model a doubling, two a tripling, and two a quadrupling.

5. Observe the progression of the models. The group modeling the doubling will finish its task quite soon. The group modeling a tripling will take somewhat longer, while the group modeling a quadrupling will take much longer and need much more room. As signs of stress appear, the groups will be forced to make difficult choices because all the chips won't fit in the faster growth models without overrunning the resource base. Ask students whether they see this occurring in the world today, and where. Situations that arise include deforestation, loss of habitat, migration, border incursions, "brain drain," and invasion of neighboring countries to support the population. Ask the groups what effect those decisions would have on the quality of life and social institutions they envisioned for their countries. How would they feel if wilderness and wildlife habitat were eliminated, for example? Would democracy survive in times of extreme scarcity or conflict?

6. Have the groups compare their models and discuss the results. Which decisions were most difficult? What alternatives did they consider? What solutions might they have implemented had they anticipated the outcome?

John Goekler is an organizational change consultant and the former executive director of Facing the Future: People and the Planet. He lives on Lopez Island in Washington.

The activity "Carrying Capacity" was inspired by "The Stork and the Grim Reaper," an activity developed by Zero Population Growth; an expanded version called "Splash But Don't Crash" is on-line at the teacher's section of the Facing the Future website <www.teacherscorner.org>. At the same website are expanded versions of "What's Your Favorite Meal" (called "Watch Where You Step") and "When the Chips are Down."

ON-LINE RESOURCES

<www.facingthefuture.org> Facing the Future: People and the Planet offers papers, overviews, and curriculum activities on population and related global issues. All Facing the Future curriculum materials, including expanded versions of these and other hands-on classroom activities, are available for downloading free of charge.

<www.census.gov/main/www/popclock.html> The U.S. Census Bureau's "Pop Clock" gives up-to-the-minute population estimates for the world and the United States.

<www.un.org/esa/population/unpop.htm> United Nations Population Division's latest population estimates and projections.

<www.prb.org> The Population Reference Bureau has technical data and reports. The Educators section of this website offers lesson plans and resource guides, while Quick Facts provides issue overviews on a variety of population-related subjects (Population Reference Bureau, 1875 Connecticut Avenue NW, Suite 520, Washington, DC 20009-5728; 800–877–9881; 202–483–1100).

<www.popact.org/resources/factsheets/index.htm> Population Action International's resources section provides fact sheets with technical data and analyses on population, environment, policy, and gender and society issues.

<www.pacinst.org/water_facts.htm> The Pacific Institute for Studies in Development, Environment, and Security has a good overview of water issues.

<www.wri.org/wr-98-99/econgrow.htm#overview> The World Resources Institute's article "Population and Human Well-Being: Economic Growth and Human Development" (from *World Resources 1998–99*) provides a good overview of population, economic, and equity trends.

Our Watery Planet

Studying water issues provides insights into a world of "haves" and "have-nots"

by Madeline Lunney

Subject area: science, social studies

Key concepts: conservation, resource distribution, pollution, developing countries, poverty, international aid

Skills: analysis, problem solving, decision making

Location: mostly indoors

Earth is a watery planet. Looking at a world map, we are struck by how much of its surface is covered by this element so essential to all life. Yet a closer look reveals that ours is a planet of fresh water "haves" and "have-nots." In many areas of the world, fresh water is in scarce supply, and making it available to people can be costly. In other places, water is more plentiful, but people's ability to gain access to the water they need may be determined by government policy, economic status, patterns of local resource use, and many other factors. In poorer areas of the world — those countries in the southern hemisphere where the majority of the world's population lives, or in rural areas in the northern hemisphere, for example — there are problems of both water quantity and water quality.

The availability of clean fresh water can determine the health of a people and the development of an entire region. Therefore, an exploration of its use and misuse is a good basis for studies of environmental and health issues, of rights and responsibilities, and of community participation in development and conservation. Studying water issues can also give students insight into the complex interaction of climate, topography, geography, population, and access to resources. The following discussion outlines some of the water-related issues that affect communities around the world and offers learning activities that explore some of these issues.

In North America, most problems of water quality are the result of chemical pollution from the dumping of industrial wastes, the runoff of agricultural fertilizers and pesticides, and drainage from mining and dumpsites. In recent years, deadly outbreaks of bacteria in the drinking water of towns such as Walkerton, Ontario, have made people more aware of serious problems with water quality even where facilities exist to treat water.

Chemical contamination affects water quality in developing countries, too, but it is not usually the most urgent problem. Many poor countries lack the infrastructure to provide potable water for everyone, and the resources that are available are typically spent in major cities. Rarely are rural communities — particularly those of indigenous peoples — the beneficiaries of water and sanitation projects. Nor are the shantytowns that have sprung up on the edges of major cities, as governments fear that providing services would legitimize these settlements as permanent communities. As a result, many people in Asia, Africa, the Caribbean, and Latin America rely on the water from rivers and streams for drinking, washing clothes, and bathing — water that can easily become contaminated with disease-causing microorganisms and parasites. In fact, 80 percent of disease in developing countries is related to poor sanitation and unhealthy drinking water. Making matters worse, diseases such as malaria, sleeping sickness, river blindness, and yellow fever are all spread by flies and mosquitoes that breed in or bite near water.

Lack of water delivery systems also means that the collection of water is a major preoccupation in large parts of the Africa, Asia, and Latin America. Children are often given the task of collecting water for their families, a chore that can take several hours each day and leave them too tired or with too little time to attend school except sporadically. Not surprisingly, when communities gather to discuss their needs, the availability of water is often the first thing mentioned. Various solutions have been tried, including massive investments in irrigation projects around the world during the 1970s and 1980s. In tapping previously inaccessible underground aquifers, such projects have allowed

Children in this community in the Philippines will live healthier lives because they have access to clean water.

A Nicaraguan girl drinks from a well in a community that was displaced by Hurricane Mitch in 1998.

for the expansion of agricultural lands. However, most large-scale irrigation schemes have proven extremely inefficient in that only about one-third of the water used actually reaches the crops. Some of it runs off immediately because the systems are built to distribute water by gravity flow through unlined ditches. Where soil is degraded or has poor drainage, its ability to absorb water is limited and much of it is lost to evaporation and seepage. The heavy demand for irrigation water, exacerbated by the inefficiency of these systems, often has the effect of lowering water tables and putting community water supplies at risk.

In seeking ways to curb misuse and waste of water, some scientists and planners propose tighter controls and true-cost pricing — arguing that, where water is free, it is wasted. Others suggest that it is unfair to charge those already struggling to get by for what little water they use; instead, they suggest that, if the real economic and environmental costs of water schemes were taken into account in planning new projects, only the most appropriate and sustainable options would be chosen in the first place. They point to foreign aid projects gone wrong, in which cement pipes lie unused and pumps no longer work because local people cannot afford the cost of repair parts that must be ordered from Europe or North America. In many cases, projects have been implemented without consultation with community members about their specific needs and their ability to maintain the systems once they are in place.

Many international and local organizations are working together to improve access to healthy sources of fresh water in developing countries. Increasingly, the solutions focus not on high-tech interventions but on more sustainable projects in which local communities assess their water needs and their own capacity to build and operate water delivery systems. This was the case with the community water project in El Tabón, Guatemala. The village's only water used to come from a

Fast Facts on Water

- Almost 75% of the Earth is covered by water.
- Of every 100 liters (26.4 gallons) of water on Earth, 97 liters (25.6 gallons) are ocean salt water and 3 liters (0.8 gallons) are fresh water. Of the fresh water, 2.5 liters (0.7 gallons) are in glaciers, ice caps, the atmosphere, soil and underground pools. Of the half a liter (half a quart) of fresh water that is available, only about 7 milliliters (half a tablespoon) is clean and accessible enough to be usable by people and animals.
- Around the world, only about 7% of the water used goes to households. The other 93% is used in farming and industry. In Canada, the ratio is almost 50:50, with 51% of water used going toward domestic uses.
- 70% of the human body is water; the body's blood is 83% water.
- The human body needs about 2 liters (2 quarts) of water per day in temperate climates; we can survive only a few days without water.
- Water helps humans and other animals digest food, take in oxygen, transport body wastes, and control body temperature.
- Our food is mostly water: tomatoes 95%, spinach 91%, milk 90%, apples 85%, hot dogs 56%.
- Around the world, approximately 34,000 deaths occur daily from water-related diseases.
- Toilets use more water than anything else in a North American home.
- Because water continually cycles through the environment, you could be drinking water that once fell in the Amazon rainforest, or that was once drunk by dinosaurs.

source located five kilometers (three miles) away. Since the water was contaminated, it had to be boiled and chlorinated to prevent illness. In the study preceding the project, the people of El Tabón identified a spring six kilometers (3.7 miles) from the village as the water source that would best meet their needs, for both quantity and quality. The whole community participated in the project by digging trenches and ditches, installing distribution pipes, and building water tanks. Today the people of El Tabón can draw water from any of 35 taps located along roads and footpaths throughout the village, and each family has a water filter to further improve water quality. Community leaders and health officials monitor the project to ensure that it meets the community's need for safe water.

In rural Malawi, where less than half of the population has safe drinking water, a community-built well frees women and children from long treks to collect water for their families.

Around the world, water pollution problems poignantly illustrate "the tragedy of the commons," in which a resource that we all share is misused without regard for others who depend on it. The activities that follow are classroom-tested ways to get students thinking about the importance of water for health and about our shared responsibility for protecting this vital resource.

Activities for exploring water issues

Bucket relay

Goals:

- to illustrate the difficulty of having to walk long distances to fetch water

- to encourage empathy for those who must perform this task daily

Time: 30 to 60 minutes, depending on number of participants (allow 30 minutes to set up the obstacle course)

Materials: for each team: 1 water-carrying pail (with volume of 2 liters / 2 quarts), 2 measured buckets (with capacity of 10 liters / 2.5 gallons or more), obstacles for obstacle course

Procedure:

1. Set up an obstacle course to represent the difficult terrain that many young people in developing nations must cross in order to fetch water for their families. (Found materials, such as old tires or boxes, or playground equipment can serve as obstacles.) For each team, place one of the large buckets (empty, as collection bucket) at the beginning of the course (home). Place the other large bucket (filled with water, representing a well) at the end of the course.

2. Divide the class into two or more teams and give each team an empty carrying pail. Explain that this is a race judged not by time but by the volume of water each team collects and delivers back to the starting point (home).

3. One at a time, team members run the course carrying the empty pail, which they fill with water from the full bucket at the end of the course. Holding the pails of water over their heads, students return through the course to home, where they empty their water into their team's collection bucket.

4. When every student has completed the course, the winning team is the one that has collected the most water in its bucket.

Wrap-up discussion: Explain that many people in the world spend as much as six hours each day collecting water. Have students consider the likely impact on their lives if they had to collect water for their families (e.g., it would interfere with school and they would have little energy left for other activities). Ask the teams to brainstorm any changes they would make in the way they use water if they had to walk long distances to obtain it. What conservation measures could they implement now (e.g., turning off the faucet while brushing teeth or washing dishes, collecting water in a rain barrel for watering houseplants and lawns)?

Waterlogged

Goals:

- to calculate how much water students use
- to consider ways to conserve water

Time: 30 minutes per day for several days (including at home)

Materials: large bucket, paper for student charts

Procedure:

1. Bring to class a bucket of known capacity (e.g., 10-liter / 2.5-gallon pail) to help students visualize different quantities of water.

2. In groups or in class discussion, have students estimate the total daily water consumption in their homes, or the daily consumption for specific tasks.

3. Over a three-day period, have students record the number of times each day that someone in their family performs an activity that requires water. To facilitate recordkeeping, prepare a three-day water log that lists activities requiring water (see chart).

4. Have students use the following chart to calculate how much water was used each day per person for the various activities, and how much was used in total. Students should add to their totals an additional 50 liters (13 gallons) of water per person per day to account for water that is typically wasted in distribution because of leaky pipes or dripping taps.

5. Discuss how the actual count compares to students' original estimates, and to the following national averages of daily per capita water use:

> Canada: 350 liters (93 gallons)
>
> United States: 375 liters (100 gallons)
>
> United Kingdom: 175 liters (46 gallons)
>
> Bangladesh: 45 liters (12 gallons)

6. Have students review their water logs and consider the changes that could be made most easily. As a class, brainstorm ways to save water in each of the tasks (e.g., keep a jug of drinking water in the refrigerator instead of running the tap until it is cold; save cooking water for making soup or watering plants).

7. If students (and their families) can agree on conservation measures they would be willing to try, they can use water log charts to monitor their progress over a week or month.

Oral rehydration therapy

The difficulty of obtaining clean water has fatal consequences in many parts of the world. Every year in developing countries approximately five million children die from dehydration as a result of diarrhea caused by contaminated water or food. Oral rehydration therapy is a simple inexpensive solution of water, sugar, and salts which replaces the water and essential minerals lost during bouts of diarrhea. Packets of glucose and salt, to which clean water is added, can be purchased for about ten cents each, but the solution can also be prepared at home from simple ingredients. At present, oral rehydration therapy saves half a million children annually, but it is estimated that it could prevent the deaths of more than three million each year, if more people knew about it. Health workers in developing countries often use posters to spread the word about oral rehydration therapy in communities where few people can read.

Goal: To support a discussion of preventable diseases and international aid to provide basic medicine.

Time: 30 minutes

Materials: measuring spoons, baking soda, sugar, salt, clean one-liter or one-quart container, water

Procedure: Invite students to try oral rehydration therapy for themselves.

1. Measure the following ingredients into the container: 2.5 grams (⅜ tsp.) salt, 2.5 grams (½ tsp.) baking soda, and 20 grams (5 tsp.) sugar.

2. Add 1 liter (or one quart) of clean water. Mix well and taste.

3. Have students design a poster that includes information on how to make oral rehydration therapy and why clean water is important for health.

Madeline Lunney has worked as a global educator for the Canadian Red Cross and Foster Parents Plan, among other organizations. She is currently a consultant to non-governmental organizations with environmental education projects in Canada and overseas.

These activities were adapted and condensed from Foster Parents Plan of Canada, "Kids Who Care," a global education kit.

Water Use for Daily Activities

Activity	liters	gallons (U.S.)
Brushing teeth, tap on	4	1.0
Brushing teeth, tap off	4	1.0
Shower	20 per minute	5 per minute
Bath	80	21.0
One flush of toilet	20	5.0
Washing dishes by hand	25	6.5
Using dishwasher	55	14.5
One load of laundry	200	53.0
Drinking/cooking (daily)	15 per person	4 per person
Wasted water	50 per person	13 per person

Adapted from Red Cross Society, "Waterlogged," World Day Handbook.

Water Across the Curriculum

Activities for integrating water topics into several subject areas

by Meredith Cargill

ater is everywhere on Earth, and everything on Earth depends upon it; yet we often overlook its importance. And while the subject of water fits into many science units, its relevance across the curriculum is rarely explored. Integrating this interdisciplinary topic into every subject area can help students understand that water penetrates every aspect of our lives and encourage them to become lifelong stewards of this precious resource. The following activities suggest ways to incorporate the topic of water into several subject areas. They can be used together as part of a water theme in an integrated curriculum, or selected as appropriate for subject-specific lessons.

Water in history and society

Water fates

Water shortages are increasingly common in many regions of the world. In this activity, students become more aware of their own use of water and of measures that could be taken to conserve it.

Key concepts: water use, conservation

Skills: calculating averages, setting priorities

Time: 45-90 minutes

Materials: Fate Cards, one per group (to be prepared), Water Use for Daily Activities chart (see page 101)

Preparation: Make four Fate Cards that describe

situations that could reduce the amount of water available for use; for example, "Unseasonably high temperatures and low precipitation. Water supply reduced by half." As students will be asked to change their water consumption based on the card they draw, most Fate Cards should require a reduction in use. However, creating one scenario, such as a flood, that results in an unexpected surplus of water can result in interesting discussions of whether and how to use surplus water (e.g., storing for future needs, selling or bartering water to another group).

Procedure:

1. Have students break into four groups and assign each group a season of the year. Ask students to brainstorm the primary uses of water during that season (e.g., watering lawns in summer) as well as the daily uses of water (e.g., drinking, washing, cleaning).

2. Have students research the quantity of water typically used for each activity on their list (see Water Use for Daily Activities chart, page 101). If they cannot find the amount of water used for an activity, they should make an educated guess based on the amount used in other activities. Finally, have students calculate how much water, on average, each person in their group would use during one week of their assigned season.

3. Regroup as a class to compile a list of activities that require water. Discuss what time of year water is in the most demand and for what activities.

4. Have students return to their groups and each group pick one Fate Card. Explain that they must adjust their previously calculated weekly water use in response to the situation described on the card. Each group is to set priorities for water use, determine the best methods for conserving it, and present its solutions to the class.

Extensions:

* Learn how communities plan for water-related crises such as water shortages, contamination of water supplies, and floods.

* Research real-life shortages and discuss reasons for them, such as droughts related to climate change, wastage, increasing population, and heavy draws for agriculture, industry, and residential landscaping.

David Dennings

It's epidemic

Throughout history, water has both helped and hindered the economic and social development of countries. The availability of fresh water makes crop production, manufacturing, and personal hygiene possible, but water is also a vector for diseases such as cholera, dysentery, hepatitis, typhoid fever, and giardiasis. In this activity, students work in groups to research a water-transmitted disease and then apply their research in creating an investigative game similar to the Project WET "Poison Pump" activity.[1] In Poison Pump, students learn the symptoms of cholera and are given a map of a fictitious community in which a cholera epidemic is underway. Victim cards, correlated with the map, show where each victim died and give clues to where each may have ingested contaminated water or food. Using critical thinking and analytical skills, students try to locate the source of the epidemic.

Key concepts: water contamination, waterborne disease

Skills: critical thinking, problem solving

Time: 45 minutes

Materials: large sheets of paper for community maps, cardstock for making victim cards, markers, scissors

Procedure:

1. Divide the class into small groups and assign each group a major water-transmitted disease (e.g., cholera, dysentery, hepatitis, typhoid fever, giardiasis). Have each group research and prepare an information sheet about the sources, pathways, and symptoms of the disease.

2. Ask students to draw on their knowledge of how the disease is spread to create an investigative game based on a hypothetical scenario of a community in which several people have contracted the disease as a result of water contamination. Each game is to include:
   - a map of the community
   - a set of cards that indicate where each victim died and give clues to where each may have ingested contaminated water or food
   - an information sheet on the symptoms and pathways of the disease

3. Have the groups exchange their games so that every group has an opportunity to play all of the games created. Encourage winners to state their evidence to prove the theory they believe to be correct.

Extension: Have students investigate the history of water treatment and plumbing.

Water and mathematics

Safe water: a limited resource

This activity helps students visualize how much of the Earth's water is available for human use. Water covers roughly 72 percent of the Earth's surface (and makes up 75 percent of our bodies). However, when we consider that 97 percent of the planet's water is in the oceans and 2 percent is frozen in glaciers and ice caps, we can begin to appreciate that the amount available for human consumption is very limited.

Key concepts: global distribution of water, water availability

Skills: measurement, conversion, percentages

Time: 45 minutes

Materials: aquarium with a volume of 20 liters (5 gallons), water, 6 plastic cups, 6 labels

Procedure:

1. Fill the aquarium with water and explain to students that it represents the Earth's water. Have students calculate, in milliliters or tablespoons, how much of the aquarium's water each water source represents. To do this, they multiply the percentages below by the volume of the aquarium (20 liters = 28,000 milliliters; 5 U.S. gallons = 1,280 tablespoons).

Water Source	Percentage
Oceans	97.2
Icecaps and glaciers	2.0
Groundwater	0.78
Freshwater lakes	0.009
Inland seas and salt lakes	0.008
Atmosphere	0.001
Rivers	0.0001

2. Have students label six clear plastic cups, one for each of the following water sources: icecaps and glaciers, groundwater, freshwater lakes, inland seas and salt lakes, atmosphere, and rivers.

3. Have students measure the appropriate quantity of water into each cup, using their calculations from step 1, above. (Most of the water will remain in the aquarium, representing the oceans.)

4. Have students draw conclusions about the availability of safe drinking water.

How little is too much?

Many chemical pollutants are invisible in water, although their presence, even in trace amounts, can be harmful. This activity integrates the use of fractions and decimals with the concept of how small a "part per million" and "part per billion" actually is.

Key concepts: parts per million/billion (ppm/ppb), dilution

Skills: fractions, decimals, ratios

Time: 45 minutes

Materials: per student: 9 white plastic spoons, eyedropper, water, food coloring

Procedure

1. Direct students to place different amounts of water and food coloring from an eyedropper onto each of the nine white plastic spoons:

    - Spoon 1: one drop of food coloring and nine drops of water to make a 1:10 solution.

    - Spoon 2: one drop of the solution from the first spoon and nine drops of water to make a 1:100 solution.

    - Spoon 3: one drop of the solution from the second spoon, and nine new drops of water.

    - Spoons 4–9: continue the process of taking one drop of the previous spoon's solution and adding nine drops of water until all nine spoons are filled.

2. Inform students that the first spoon represents one part per ten, the second represents one part per hundred, and the ninth spoon one part per billion. Have them determine the concentrations of the solutions in the third to eighth spoons.

3. Have students observe in which of the nine progressive dilutions the food coloring first becomes invisible. Ask them whether the fact that the food coloring cannot be seen means that it isn't there. Discuss what other invisible substances could be in the water.

4. Make a list of substances that, even in very small amounts, can make water dangerous (e.g., organic matter, human and animal waste, motor oil, antifreeze, pesticides, and fertilizers).

5. Discuss the ways in which dangerous substances can get into water and how they could be disposed of without endangering water supplies. Include in the discussion the need for water testing and precise monitoring.

Water and science

Where in the world is water?

In this activity, students investigate the sources of safe drinking water.

Key concepts: aquifers, wastewater treatment

Skills: research

Time: depends on depth of research

Procedure:

1. Inform students that safe drinking water comes from two sources: groundwater, which is stored in confined and unconfined aquifers, and surface water, which is in rivers, lakes, and reservoirs. Discuss the distinction between these two sources.

2. Have students find out the sources of their local water supply (surface water, confined aquifer, and/or unconfined aquifer) and how water is collected for human consumption.

3. Have students research methods used to treat water to make it safe to drink and find out which methods are used in their town or region.

Extensions:

- Create a water source map of the region, using shading or coloring to show areas that receive water from each specific source (i.e., reservoirs, wells).

- Have students create a water user's guide in which they present their research findings in the form of a brochure that can educate others.

Fountain of purity

Water from lakes, rivers, and reservoirs typically undergoes several processes at a water treatment plant before it comes out of the tap in our homes. This activity gives students an opportunity to observe some of the following steps in the purification of drinking water:

- *aeration:* the water is stirred to release gases and to introduce oxygen

- *coagulation* and *flocculation:* a chemical such as alum (potassium aluminum sulfate) is stirred into the water where it forms sticky globules called "flocs" to which bacteria and particulates become attached

- *sedimentation:* the water is put into a settling tank where flocs and other contaminants settle to the bottom

- *filtration:* the water is put through layers of coal, sand, and gravel to remove floc, particles, and microorganisms such as viruses and bacteria

- *disinfection:* any remaining microorganisms are killed, usually by adding chlorine to the water

Key concepts: water aeration, coagulation, sedimentation, filtration

Time: 45 minutes

Materials: per student: 250 milliliters of dirty water (add mud in a 1:10 ratio) in a container with a lid, 5 grams (1 teaspoon) of potassium aluminum sulfate (alum), stir sticks, clean 600-milliliter (20-ounce) plastic pop bottle, nylon (squares of pantyhose work well) and rubber band for a filter, 150 milliliters each of medium-sized gravel, coarse sand, and fine sand, clean water, clear plastic cup to catch filtered water, microscope and slides (optional).

Procedure:

1. Have students aerate about 250 milliliters (1 cup) of dirty water by briskly shaking it in a tightly closed

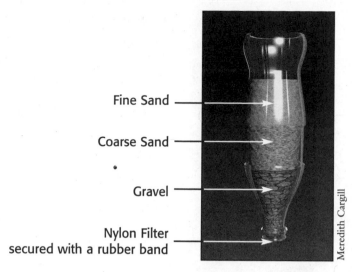

Fine Sand

Coarse Sand

Gravel

Nylon Filter
secured with a rubber band

Pop-bottle water filter.

container for 30 seconds. Have them note the appearance of the water.

2. Ask students to add 5 grams (1 teaspoon) of potassium aluminum sulfate (alum) to the dirty water and stir it slowly for 4-5 minutes. Then have them leave the water undisturbed for 20 minutes while they construct water filters.

3. Instruct students to make water filters, as follows. Put a nylon filter on the top of the plastic bottle. Stretch the nylon fairly taut across the opening and hold it securely in place with a rubber band. Cut off the bottom of the bottle. Invert the bottle so that it is like a funnel. Fill the bottom one-fourth of the bottle with medium-sized gravel. Fill the second fourth with coarse sand, and a third fourth with fine sand.

4. Have students hold the filter above a clear plastic cup and slowly pour clean water into it to flush out fine particles of sand and gravel. When the water comes out clear, the filter is ready to use.

5. When the dirty water has settled for 20 minutes, ask students to observe and record changes in its appearance (e.g., sedimentation and clarity). Then have them filter the water by holding the filter above the clear plastic cup and slowly, without disturbing the sediment, pouring the top two-thirds of the dirty water into filter.

6. Ask students to observe the water as it filters through the layers of sand and gravel. (Dirt particles are retained in the filter and visibly clean water is produced.) You may wish to analyze a sample of the filtered water under a high-powered microscope to look for microscopic organisms. With drinking water, you don't always see what you get.

Safety Note: Caution students not to drink their filtered water. While it will appear to be clean, filtration alone does not remove all contaminants. Water treatment plants use microfilters and chemical treatments to remove toxins and microbes that cannot be seen in a visual inspection.

Extensions:

• Discuss water purification products available for use in outdoor exploration and camping.

• Visit a wastewater treatment plant. This filtering activity leads readily into discussion of large-scale water purification and treatment systems used in municipalities.

Water in the arts

Water cycle drama

The states and pathways of water as it moves through the hydrologic cycle can be better understood by many students through performing arts. This activity introduces the water cycle through kinesthetics.

Key concepts: water (hydrologic) cycle, states of matter

Time: 45 minutes

Location: indoors or outdoors in an area clear of obstacles

Materials: index cards (1 per student)

Preparation: Prepare water cycle cards (one card for each student) by writing one the components or phases of the water cycle on each card: "heat from the sun," "evaporation," "condensation," "precipitation," and "infiltration."

Procedure:

1. Begin by discussing the different components and steps of the water cycle: heat from the sun, evaporation, condensation, precipitation, and infiltration.

2. Ask students to imagine themselves to be a water molecule and think about what the water experiences at each point in the cycle.

3. Distribute the water cycle cards, one per student, and ask them to keep what it says secret.

4. Signal all of the students simultaneously to start silently acting out what is on their cards. Without talking, they must then try to find other students who are acting out the same part of the water cycle.

5. Collect and shuffle the cards, and repeat the activity so that each student has an opportunity to act out different phases of the water cycle. End with a review of the phases of the water cycle.

Meredith Cargill

Acting out parts of the water cycle.

Water ambassadors

Challenge your students to combine persuasive writing with art to increase awareness of water quality and conservation in the school and community. This is a good culminating activity for a unit on water quality: it demands that students call on what they have learned and reinforces their sense of themselves as stewards of clean water.

Skills: communication skills, persuasive writing, dramatic and/or visual arts, depending on medium selected

Time: flexible

Procedure: Ask students to create succinct and engaging public service messages to inform others about the importance of water quality and water conservation. Students could work in small groups, each producing an announcement for a different medium, such as a poster, brochure, radio spot, short video, or quick skit to be performed in a school corridor or a local mall. The final messages can be broadcast or performed at school or on local radio or television stations. Posters can be displayed in school hallways and other public areas.

Meredith Cargill teaches Grade 5 in southern New Hampshire and is a teacher trainer in the Water in the Earth System program of the American Meteorological Society.

The activities Safe Drinking Water: A Limited Resource, How Little is Too Much?, Fountains of Purity, and Water Cycle Drama were adapted from Utah Nonpoint Source Pollution Education Activities for Grades 1–12, *by Kitt Farrell-Poe, available from Extension Publications, Utah State University, 8960 Old Main Hill, Logan, UT 84322–8960, 435–797–2251, on-line at <www.ext.usu.edu/publica/natrpubs/wqnopo.pdf>.*

Note

1 *Project WET: Curriculum and Activity Guide is provided to participants in Project WET workshops. Contact Project WET, 201 Culbertson Hall, Montana State University, Bozeman, MT 59717-0570, 406–994–5392, <www.montana.edu/wwwwet>.*

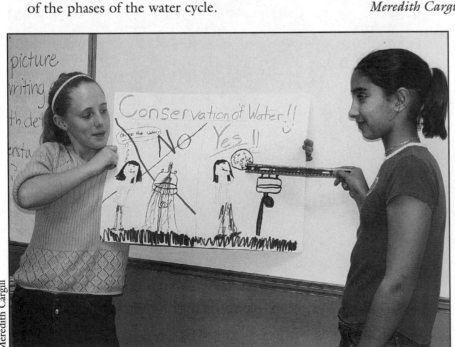

Meredith Cargill

As water ambassadors, students can educate others about protecting and conserving water resources.

Teaching about Food Systems

*As the product of an intricate web of natural factors and human actors,
food can nourish the mind as well as the body*

by Carmela Federico and The Sustainability Education Center

Subject areas: social studies, science, language arts

Key concepts: food system, sustainability, industrial/global food production, regional/organic agriculture

Skills: brainstorming, systems thinking

Location: indoors

Time: 3 class periods, or approximately 135 minutes

Materials: class copies of the handouts "Components of North American Food Systems" and "Guidelines for a Sustainable Food System" (provided), poster board, construction paper, and drawing materials or access to a computer graphics program (one computer per pair of students).

Schoolchildren eat lunch every day and rarely give it a second thought. They line up in the cafeteria and receive trays of food that materialize like magic, or open lunchboxes filled with their local supermarket's offerings. That lunchtime food, however, has a secret life, complex and multidimensional. Each mouthful is a product of a food system, an intricate web of human and natural actors, relationships, and events that nourish people's bodies and, with the right curricula, can also nourish your students' minds.

Integrated real-life issues

The study of food systems provides opportunities to learn about engaging, real-world issues that illustrate and illuminate crucial principles of ecology and sustainability. Around the world and throughout history, food production has depended on a dynamic interaction between human practices and geological, hydrological, and biological cycles and systems. It is easy, therefore, to reach out from a field or a meal to the natural laws and human behaviors that produce and support life. Food systems, moreover, can provide a tangible, bite-sized window into a troubling concern shared by scholars from many fields: whether modern industrial practices are damaging the life support systems of our planet irreparably. As we continue to learn the basic ground rules for sustainability, it is ever more apparent that our modern industrial food system — while increasingly productive and efficient by conven-

tional economic estimates — is rife with practices that are not sustainable. Modern technological methods of agriculture are intended to improve our food systems. But is industrial agriculture the best approach to adequately feeding all the world's people when even in the United States 11 percent of families are considered "food insecure"?[1] Do some of these practices threaten the biological systems necessary for life? Can a system so rife with losses — topsoil losses, soil fertility losses, arable land losses, losses to insect pests (despite of an ever-expanding arsenal of laboratory-concocted pesticides) — feed us unto the seventh generation, and beyond? And do these practices adequately address the real problems in our food systems? As you explore these questions with your students, in whatever context and depth are appropriate, you can help them fashion a deeper understanding of what sorts of human behavior and systems best safeguard the future of humanity, and which pose the gravest challenges.

Educational benefits

Teaching and learning about food systems can provide a feast of pedagogical and educational benefits:

- It is experiential and hands-on: everyone eats! Food systems are as tangible and immediate as the food on our plates and the living things around

Rowena Gerber

Students at Miami Country Day School in Florida have grown trees for hurricane victims, provided school-grown seeds to farmers in the tropics, and started a non-profit herb business to raise money for solar cookers in developing countries.

The Kids Growing Food garden at Minoa Elementary School in Minoa, New York.

us. Through exploring plants, examining eating habits, researching neighborhood supermarkets, and eating the foods of many cultures, students directly connect themselves with many facets of food systems.

- It supports multiple intelligences. Food is a subject with many pathways to student engagement. Students can explore food systems, for instance, through nurturing plants, studying the food myths and practices of other cultures, or exploring food in history, art, literature, and music.

- It is inherently interdisciplinary. Food systems are biological, in that they are composed of living soils, plants, and natural systems. They are cultural, in that societies develop different and special relationships to the land and its bounty. They are economic, in that most food systems involve the exchange of goods and services. Studying food systems can lead students on an integrated exploration of the world, one that naturally reaches beyond the boundaries of discrete academic subjects.

- It is topical and relevant. Each day, ideas and discoveries about how to feed the world arise from laboratories, are proposed by politicians, and are discussed in the media. Will

Small-scale, local, organic food systems put less stress on the planet's capacity to absorb wastes.

biotechnology feed the world? Are organic food systems better for the planet? Can food aid prevent famine? What is the relationship between free trade, the World Trade Organization, and world hunger? Decisions that societies are making right now about food systems will affect global climate and population as well as the contents of our kitchen cupboards.

- It is a pathway to diverse ideas and assumptions that are central to different worldviews: ideas about resources, progress, rights and responsibilities, and the meaning of life. Moreover, as food systems are complex and multidimensional, learning about them can foster systems thinking, an ability to understand the complex ways in which elements in real-life systems interact.

- It provides service-learning opportunities. Students can contribute to the larger community by growing food for local food banks or by working for more just and sustainable food systems.

- It's fun! Most of us really enjoy making things grow, eating, sharing yummy food, and learning about the secret life of the foods we eat.

There are as many worthwhile ways to educate about food systems as there are delicious foods to eat. The activities on the next pages aim to provide rich, meaningful, and enjoyable encounters with food systems and concepts of sustainability. Through organizing and creating a more sustainable food system, or through striving to attain the skills and assets needed to prosper as a subsistence farmer (see Tools of Hope Game, page 114), students can begin to envision true abundance and enduringly productive food systems.

Designing a sustainable food system

In this activity, students consider the sustainability of our food production and distribution systems and then design their own.

Procedure:

1. Brainstorm with students to generate a list of the components of food systems in North America. Organize them into the broad categories of inputs, natural resources, food production, food processing, food distribution, food consumption, and food waste and recycling (as in "Components of North American Food Systems," page 110). Draw lines to show links among these broad categories.

2. Have students work in groups of four to generate images to represent food system components. These can be cut from magazines or drawn by hand on squares of construction paper. Alternatively, students can use computer graphics programs to draw images and find computer clipart. If the computers are networked, students can compile a common pool of images that can be shared by the entire class. Each group of students needs a complete set of food system components.

3. Prompt the class with a basic definition of a sustainable food system (i.e., a food system that can nourish all people for generations to come). Give simple examples of unsustainable food systems, perhaps drawing on history (e.g., hundreds of years ago Mayan land, after centuries of overuse, could no longer produce sufficient food to feed everyone, leading

to a failed food system and a disrupted civilization). Continue with discussion of the requirements of a sustainable food system. Refer to the handout "Guidelines for a Sustainable Food System" for ideas on how to guide and inform the discussion. Note students' suggestions on the board, and elicit from them their reasoning for identifying something as a requirement of a sustainable food system.

4. Distribute the handout "Guidelines for a Sustainable Food System" and discuss sustainable food systems further in light of the requirements on the sheet. Explain that the guidelines on the sheet are a set of principles commonly used for making organizations and practices more sustainable.

5. For each requirement on the handout, brainstorm practical examples in a food system. What practices seem more sustainable, according to these requirements? What practices seem not to be sustainable? (For example, using fertilizer based on a fossil fuel is not sustainable, according to Requirement 1.)

6. Have students work in groups to build a model of a sustainable food system. Each group may use either its own drawings mounted and connected into a system on poster board, or computer graphic images linked in a graphics program.

7. Ask each group to present its food system to the class. Refer to the four requirements in "Guidelines for a Sustainable Food System" to determine which aspects of their group's food system are sustainable. Ensure that the discussion touches on both:

- the modern global, industrial food system (with human-made inputs, large-scale farms, food-processing factories, supermarkets, and lots of transportation along the way) and

- the growing number of local, organic food systems (with small-scale chemical-free farms, farmers markets, cooperatives, or community-supported agriculture, and much less processing and transportation).

The Heifer Project

Behind the housing projects on Chicago's west side, students in an after-school program called the Cabrini-Greens grow organic produce that they sell to local restaurants and supermarkets.

The study of food systems is inherently interdisciplinary. Food systems are biological, in that they are composed of living soils, plants, and natural systems. They are cultural, in that societies develop different and special relationships to the land and its bounty. They are economic, in that most food systems involve the exchange of goods and services.

Components of North American Food Systems

Natural resources to grow food:
These are the components of various interrelated systems of the planet, including weather systems, the water cycle, mineral cycles, energy cycles, and the web of living organisms through which nutrients flow, from plants to the animals that eat them, through waste products, to decomposers and soil microbes, and back into plants.

Food production: The process of making food from sun, soil, water, and seeds, or of feeding plant materials to domestic animals to create edible products. Food production requires energy, materials, and labor. Also, farmers sometimes add items to their farmland, such as fertilizers, pesticides, beneficial insects — collectively known as inputs — to increase food production.

Food processing: Processing creates new food products from basic food materials. For example, white sugar is refined from beet sugar or cane sugar. A cake is

Conservation Council of New Brunswick

processed from a combination of basic food materials such as eggs and dairy products, and processed foods such as wheat flour and sugar.

Food distribution: The process by which food gets from producers to consumers, possibly with stops at processing sites along the way. Food distribution includes packaging, storing, shipping, advertising, and selling. In our modern global food system, food reaches us from all over the world.

Food consumption: The eating or using up of food and food products.

Food waste and recycling: The material that remains after food is processed or consumed, or that is produced by food consumption. Food material becomes waste if no further productive use is made of it; however, food waste may be recycled into the food system as, for example, compost or animal feed.

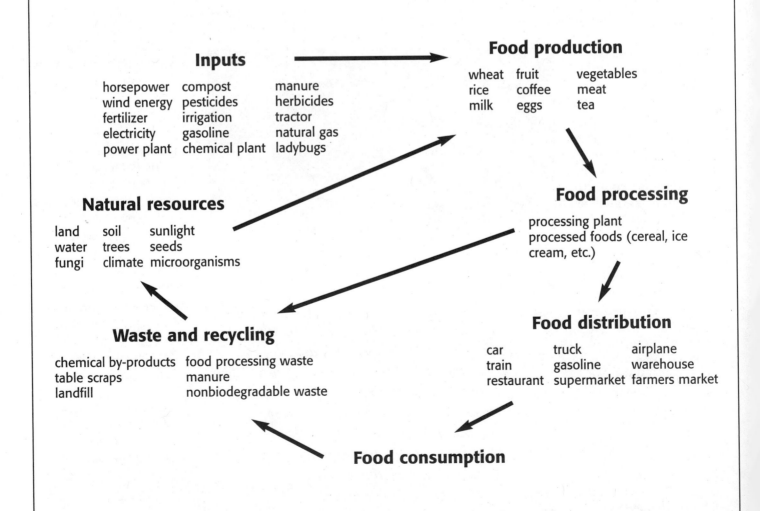

Inputs

horsepower   compost   manure
wind energy pesticides   herbicides
fertilizer   irrigation   tractor
electricity gasoline   natural gas
power plant chemical plant ladybugs

Food production

wheat fruit   vegetables
rice   coffee meat
milk   eggs   tea

Natural resources

land   soil   sunlight
water trees seeds
fungi climate microorganisms

Food processing

processing plant
processed foods (cereal, ice cream, etc.)

Waste and recycling

chemical by-products food processing waste
table scraps   manure
landfill   nonbiodegradable waste

Food distribution

car   truck   airplane
train   gasoline   warehouse
restaurant supermarket   farmers market

Food consumption

Guidelines for a Sustainable Food System

The Earth has a tremendous capacity to produce abundant food. In our current food system, however, we are both exceeding that capacity and leaving much of the world with insufficient food. By knowing and respecting the capacities of our land, our oceans, and our farms, and recognizing the importance of feeding the world fairly, we will be able to design a more sustainable food system.

Conservation Council of New Brunswick

Requirement 1: We cannot extract materials from the Earth's crust (i.e., fossil fuels, minerals, metals) faster than the Earth is able to absorb them. The Earth cycles these materials very, very slowly. If they are not recycled, they just pile up. Many of these materials, such as lead and mercury, become poisons when we extract them, concentrate them, and then introduce these high concentrations into our air, water, and soil.

Practical application: In designing your sustainable food system, try to use fewer fossil fuels, and encourage the use of only recycled metals and minerals when needed.

Requirement 2: We cannot destroy the ability of natural systems to provide the services that we and all living beings need to live — including the production of oxygen we breathe and the rich soil we need to grow food, the absorption of carbon dioxide, the maintenance of biodiversity, and the provision of abundant clean water.

Practical application: Your food system should protect or enhance biodiversity, enrich soil, and protect water quality. It should not have farming practices that harm rain forests, wetlands, or estuaries, which are treasure chests of biodiversity.

Requirement 3: We cannot produce "stuff" that accumulates. The Earth can absorb only so much garbage. Particularly troublesome are persistent chemical compounds, human-made substances that are not easily broken down by natural processes. As a result, they accumulate in the environment, sometimes damaging the air, water, soil, and living organisms, including humans. Remember that nothing disappears on our planet.

Practical application: In designing your sustainable food system, try to avoid using persistent human-made substances such as pesticides that stay in the environment longer than a few days. Try not to use a lot of plastic packaging for food, or figure out a way to recycle all packaging so it does not pile up in landfills.

Requirement 4: Resources must be distributed fairly and used efficiently to meet basic human needs globally. When poor people have enough food to meet their families' needs, they are less likely to take desperate measures that damage the environment and harm their neighbors. Fairness in food distribution, therefore, is not only morally right, but also helps to protect the environment. Meeting this requirement is a way to meet the other requirements.

Practical application: To be sustainable, your food system must feed people of all incomes and situations, use resources efficiently, turn waste into food or other resources, and not hurt one community to feed another.

These guidelines are based on principles of sustainability elaborated by The Natural Step <www.naturalstep.org>.

Extensions:

- Assign students countries or time periods, and ask them to research and construct models of a typical food system of that country or era. Encourage them to compare the sustainability of these food systems with that of the current large-scale food system in North America. Are any aspects more sustainable? What are the advantages and disadvantages of each system? Are people adequately fed in these food systems? If not, why not?

- Invite students to draw up a plan to make cafeteria food more sustainable, or to plan a one-time sustainable school lunch. Students can research local food options and decide on clear action steps in consultation with school food personnel. Students could contact local farmers markets, community-supported agriculture projects, food cooperatives, or local farm organizations for information and resources - some of them might even provide food! (See Resources for Food Systems Education, below.) The changes underway in the food system of schools in Berkeley, California, could serve as inspiration: see "You Learn What You Eat: Cognition Meets Nutrition in Berkeley Schools," on-line at <www.oriononline.org/pages/oa/index_01-3oa.html> and Carmela Federico, "Teaching about Food Systems," *Green Teacher*, issue 65, Summer 2001.

- Have students investigate how far the food their families consume in a week has traveled. Students can try to learn the origin of each item of food consumed and then calculate the average distance of all items. Share with students that food travels an average of about 2,400 kilometers (1,500 miles) in North America.[2]

Adapted by Carmela Federico and The Sustainability Education Center from a lesson in "Is Hunger a Global Problem?," a unit developed for the Center for a Sustainable Future in Shelburne, Vermont. Carmela Federico is Program Manager at the New Jersey Higher Education Partnership for Sustainability. The Sustainability Education Center develops multidisciplinary educational materials and professional development services that help individuals, school systems and organizations educate for sustainability; see <www.sustainabilityed.org>.

Notes

1 Mark Nord, Margaret Andrews, and Steven Carlson. "Household Food Security in the United States, 2001." U.S. Department of Agriculture, Food Assistance and Nutrition Research Report No. 29, October 2002. <http://ers.usda.gov/publications/fanrr29>.

2 Wayne Roberts, Rod MacRae, and Lori Stahlbrand. *Real Food for a Change*. Random House, 1999, p.10.

RESOURCES FOR FOOD SYSTEMS EDUCATION

Programs and organizations

Agriculture in the Classroom is a U.S. clearinghouse for state programs sponsored by the U.S. Department of Agriculture; an excellent resource for helping your class forge connections with farmers and food systems. <www.agclassroom.org>, 202-720-7925.

American Community Gardening Association has fact sheets and a curriculum guide on community gardening. <www.communitygarden.org>, 215-988-8785.

Center for Ecoliteracy's "Rethinking School Lunch" is an on-line guide to planning healthy farm-to-school lunch programs. <www.ecoliteracy.org>, 510-548-8838.

City Farmer promotes urban food production, including school gardens, and has published school resources on composting and nutrition. <www.cityfarmer.org>, 604-685-5832

Cooperative State Research, Education, and Extension Service offers grants and helpful resources for school food systems education. <www.reeusda.gov>, 202-720-6296.

Education for a Sustainable Future develops curricula on sustainable living. <http://csf.concord.org>, 802-985-0789.

Educational Concerns for Hunger Organization is a nondenominational Christian organization that works with farmers in developing countries to facilitate the exchange and provision of seeds, information, and ideas. <www.echonet.org>, 941-543-3246; in Canada, 905-844-3045.

Food First offers extensive, well-researched curricula on food security and reshaping local and global food systems. <www.foodfirst.org>, 510-654-4400.

Heifer Project offers educational resources, including curricula, about global hunger and the project's well-regarded grassroots efforts to eradicate the problem through grants of animals and other agricultural resources to needy farmers. <www.readtofeed.org>, 800-422-0474.

Kids Growing Food offers grants for school gardens in Delaware, New Jersey, Maryland, New York, and Pennsylvania. <http://cerp.cornell.edu/kgf>, 607-255-9255.

Curriculum resources

Castle, Jennifer. *Cookshop*. Community Food Resource Center, 1996. 212-344-0195. This is a rich collection of cooking curricula for the K-6 classroom, delivering nutrition, science, and multicultural education.

Cohen, Joy, and Eve Pranis. *GrowLab: Activities for Growing Minds*. National Gardening Association, 1990. A wonderful curricula for classroom gardens. <www.kidsgardening.com>, 800-538-7476.

Kids Can Make a Difference. *Finding Solutions to Hunger: Kids Can Make a Difference* A middle and high school program that includes a teacher's guide, newsletter, and kids' website at <www.kidscanmakeadifference.org>, 207-439-9588.

Lab's Alive! offers collaborative solar cooking and school garden science projects. <www.araratcc.vic.edu.au/users/web/labsalive/index.htm>.

Solar Cooking International features an extensive on-line archive of solar cooking information, plans, construction tips, and related curricula <www.solarcooking.org>.

Sustainability Education Center. *From Global Hunger to Sustainable Food Systems: Challenges and Choices, and the Sustainable Food Systems: Activity Guide*. This middle school curriculum and activity helps students construct a deeper understanding of what hunger is, why it exists, and how it could be ended; the activities develop systems thinking and foster connections to students' local food systems. <www.sustainabilityed.org>, 212-645-9930.

Composting

Appelhof, Mary, Mary Fenton, and Barbara Harris. *Worms Eat Our Garbage: Classroom Activities for a Better Environment*. Flower Press, 1995.

Appelhof, Mary. *Worms Eat My Garbage*. Flower Press, 1982.

Brooklyn Botanic Garden, Urban Composting Project. *The Complete Composter*. An on-line guide to composting at <www.bbg.org/gar2/topics/urban/composting>.

Living machines

Ocean Arks, designer of natural systems for wastewater treatment, works with schools to build classroom living machines; in-class natural systems that include living organisms from neighboring wetlands, ponds, ditches and other habitats; also, a manual for do-it-yourselfers. <www.oceanarks.org>, 802-864-4746.

Tools of Hope Game

*Players break the cycle of hunger by collecting
the tools they need for a better future.*

adapted by Carmela Federico

Subject areas: social studies, science, language arts

Key concepts: subsistence farming, equity, sustainable development, the role of women in development, the status of women in developing countries

Skills: awareness, empathy, analysis

Location: indoors

Time: 30 minutes for game, longer for follow-up

Materials: per group: 1 game board (see pages 116-117), 1 die, 4 different playing pieces; per player: 1 set of Tools of Hope cards

In the Tools of Hope Game, students explore challenges in the lives of farmers in developing countries in order to learn about the causes of hunger and the relationship between hunger and sustainable development.

Preparation: Make a set of Tools of Hope cards for each student. Write the Rules of the Game on the board or enlarge and copy them for each group.

Rules of the game:

- Players take turns rolling the die, advancing their playing pieces on the game board, and following the instructions on the squares they land on.

- Some squares direct players to return a Tools of Hope card. If a player does not have a card to return, he/she loses one turn.

- Each player is allowed to hold only one Tools of Hope card from each category at any one time.

- When a player has collected all six cards, he/she has broken the cycle of hunger.

Procedure:

1. Divide the class into groups of four, and give each group a game board, one die, four playing pieces, and four sets of Tools of Hope cards. Have students place the cards face up in the appropriate categories in the center of the game board.

2. Inform students that each player represents a farming village. Their aim is to break the cycle of hunger by collecting the tools necessary for a better future, represented by the Tools of Hope cards. Review the rules of the game.

3. In their groups, students take turns rolling the die and following the instructions as they land on squares on the game board.

Tools of Hope cards *(Copy cards and cut along dotted lines.)*

1 LAND SECURITY

Farmers need enough suitable land so they are not forced to overgraze it, destroy trees, or cultivate steep slopes that erode easily. When farmers know they have long-term use of their land, they take care of it.

2 PEACE

Hope of a peaceful future encourages farmers to make long-term plans and improvements, and ensures a safe environment for children to grow, play, and learn. Without peace, improving living conditions is extremely difficult.

3 WOMEN'S INVOLVEMENT

Women are responsible for much of the world's crop cultivation, fuel wood collection, food storage, and food preparation. Only if women are involved in decision-making will development projects meet the needs of the whole community.

4 COMMUNITY PARTICIPATION

Activities such as planting trees, creating fishponds, and digging wells are most successful when the whole community joins in. Community members must be involved in decisions and projects that directly affect them.

5 SUSTAINABLE AGRICULTURE

Farmers are knowledgeable about their land and environment, but sometimes need support. They need tools, farm animals, access to cheap credit, fair prices for their produce, and technical advice on tree planting, erosion control, terracing, and irrigation.

6 SUSTAINABLE POPULATION

Providing adequate food, schooling, and health care to a large population of young children is difficult for developing countries. Women's education, higher rates of child survival, and the security of support in old age tend to result in people choosing to have fewer children.

Follow-up:

1. After the game, lead a discussion by asking students: What things helped you break the cycle of hunger? What things prevented you? How true to life do you think the game is? What role does our country play in creating or ending hunger in subsistence farming villages in developing countries?

2. Analyze the many challenges faced by farmers in developing countries: poverty, inappropriate development, soil erosion, drought, deforestation, lack of health care, war, debt to other countries, being forced onto poor land, and powerlessness to set the prices for their goods. Explain why each challenge exists and how it contributes to hunger. Students could research some of these problems for discussion in future classes.

3. Discuss the factors that combat hunger: land reform, tree planting, community planning and decision making with involvement of women, good primary health care, population sustainability, and peace. Again, students could research these.

4. Invite students to make posters illustrating their understanding of the causes of and solutions to hunger in developing countries. Place the posters around the school to educate the rest of the school community on these issues.

Carmela Federico is Program Manager at the New Jersey Higher Education Partnership for Sustainability. The Tools of Hope game was adapted, with permission, from Church World Service, "We Can Do That, Too!," Hunger Education Activities That Work. <www.churchworldservice.org>.

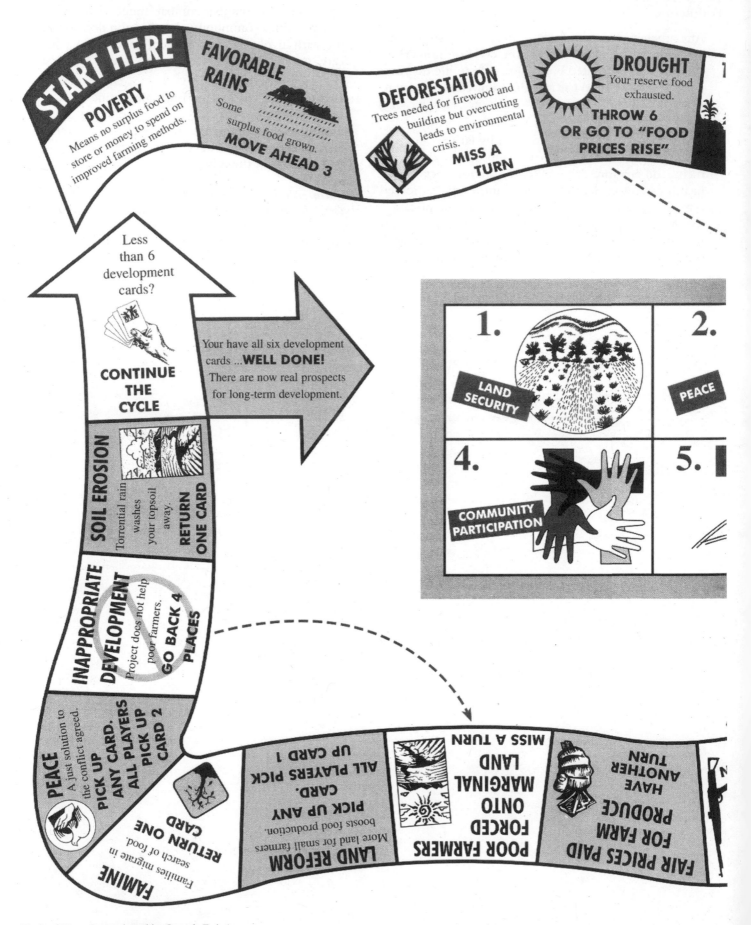

START HERE

POVERTY
Means no surplus food to store or money to spend on improved farming methods.

FAVORABLE RAINS
Some surplus food grown.
MOVE AHEAD 3

DEFORESTATION
Trees needed for firewood and building but overcutting leads to environmental crisis.
MISS A TURN

DROUGHT
Your reserve food exhausted.
THROW 6 OR GO TO "FOOD PRICES RISE"

Less than 6 development cards?
CONTINUE THE CYCLE

Your have all six development cards ...**WELL DONE!** There are now real prospects for long-term development.

SOIL EROSION
Torrential rain washes your topsoil away.
RETURN ONE CARD

INAPPROPRIATE DEVELOPMENT
Project does not help poor farmers.
GO BACK 4 PLACES

PEACE
A just solution to the conflict agreed.
PICK UP ANY CARD. ALL PLAYERS PICK UP CARD 2

FAMINE
Families migrate in search of food.
RETURN ONE CARD

LAND REFORM
More land for small farmers boosts food production.
PICK UP ANY CARD. ALL PLAYERS PICK UP CARD 1

POOR FARMERS FORCED ONTO MARGINAL LAND
MISS A TURN

FAIR PRICES PAID FOR FARM PRODUCE
HAVE ANOTHER TURN

1. LAND SECURITY

2. PEACE

4. COMMUNITY PARTICIPATION

5.

Tools of Hope Game adapted by Carmela Federico
All illustrations: Church World Service

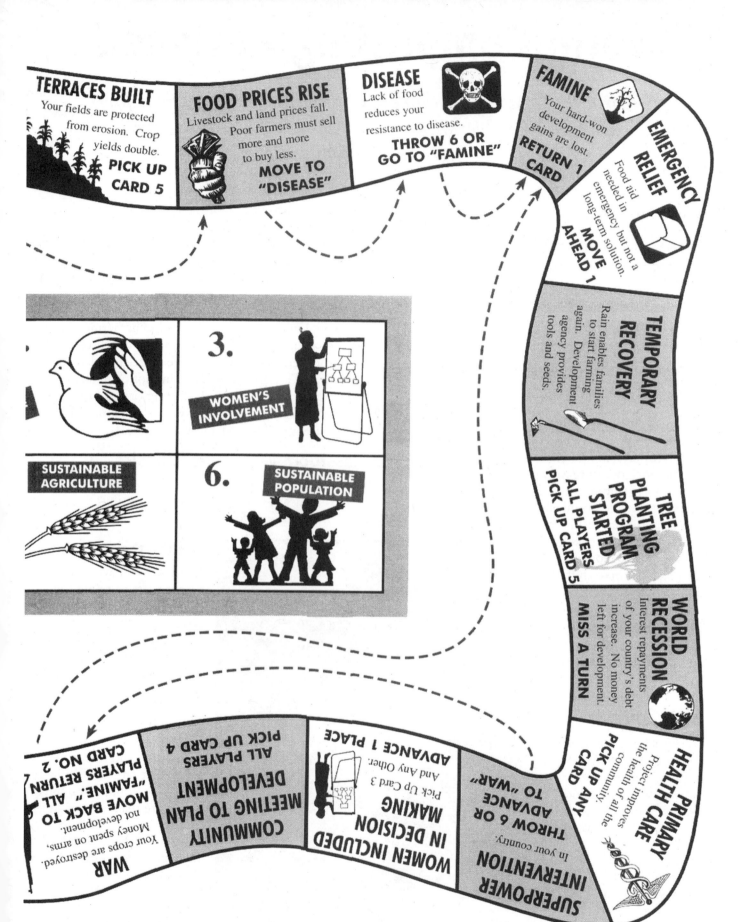

TERRACES BUILT
Your fields are protected from erosion. Crop yields double.
PICK UP CARD 5

FOOD PRICES RISE
Livestock and land prices fall. Poor farmers must sell more and more to buy less.
MOVE TO "DISEASE"

DISEASE
Lack of food reduces your resistance to disease.
THROW 6 OR GO TO "FAMINE"

FAMINE
Your hard-won development gains are lost.
RETURN 1 CARD

EMERGENCY RELIEF
Food aid is needed in emergency but not a long-term solution.
MOVE AHEAD 1

TEMPORARY RECOVERY
Rain enables families to start farming again. Development agency provides tools and seeds.

TREE PLANTING PROGRAM STARTED
ALL PLAYERS PICK UP CARD 5

WORLD RECESSION
Interest repayments of your country's debt increase. No money left for development.
MISS A TURN

3.
WOMEN'S INVOLVEMENT

SUSTAINABLE AGRICULTURE

6.
SUSTAINABLE POPULATION

PRIMARY HEALTH CARE
Project improves the health of all the community.
PICK UP ANY CARD

SUPERPOWER INTERVENTION
In your country.
THROW 6 OR ADVANCE TO "WAR"

WOMEN INCLUDED IN DECISION MAKING
Pick Up Card 3 And Any Other.
ADVANCE 1 PLACE

COMMUNITY MEETING TO PLAN DEVELOPMENT
ALL PLAYERS PICK UP CARD 4

WAR
Your crops are destroyed. Money spent on arms, not development.
MOVE BACK TO "FAMINE." ALL PLAYERS RETURN CARD NO. 2

Worm Composting Revisited

If "worm bin" makes you think of bad smells and pesky fruit flies, think again: new vermiculture systems and strategies make it easy to succeed with worm composting

by Jennifer Kusmanoff

Subject areas: science, art, math, language arts

Key concepts: vermiculture, worm compost, nutrient cycling, anatomy

Skills: journal writing, data collection

Location: indoors

Time: varies

Materials: worm bin(s) (purchased or classroom-built), red wiggler worms

Classroom composting with worms — or vermicomposting — is a unique way to capture the attention and interest of students while teaching them the importance of recycling. Vermicomposting has been used in agriculture for many years, with vermiculture farms worldwide producing large amounts of vermicompost as rich plant fertilizer. Many individuals use worms to compost leftover food scraps in their homes, perhaps placing a makeshift worm bin under the sink or in the garage. Only in recent years has composting with worms become a popular recycling activity in schools. In the beginning, rudimentary bins and such problems as fruit flies, rotten smells, and mold presented many challenges to teachers. Some were ordered to give up vermicomposting in their classrooms because entire schools became infested with fruit flies. Today, with new worm bins and new strategies for vermicomposting, these problems are eliminated.

Composting in the classroom continues to be a wonderful tool for introducing environmental education and for taking a hands-on approach to recycling. Worm composting activities have cross-curricular applications within science, math, language arts, home economics, and ecology. Through vermicomposting experiments, students develop skills in teamwork, observation, record keeping, reporting, and measuring. They also make the connection that they are aiding the environment by recycling leftover food scraps that would normally go to a landfill. Furthermore, students of all ages learn to use the nutrient-rich vermicompost produced by the worms as fertilizer for plants in outdoor and contained gardens, indoor plant stands, and science experiments. Overall, starting or restarting a worm composting program in your classroom can bring satisfying rewards to you and your students.

Classroom vermiculture basics

To begin, it's important to note the four basic needs of every organism: shelter (in vermicomposting, the worm bin), air, water, and food.

Jennifer Lippmann, Gateway Greening

Shelter: the worm bin

Great strides have made in recent years to refine the design of vermicomposting systems, so that many worm bins on the market today are wonderful to use. There are numerous styles of worm bins to choose from, ranging from complex multi-level bins to basic rectangular plastic bins; each has its own advantages and disadvantages. The larger multi-level bins — with built-in drainage and more than one feeding level — are well designed, sophisticated, and require little maintenance. In addition, they can process large amounts of food waste and are esthetically pleasing. The only disadvantages to educators of these larger bins are their size and higher cost,

Worm bins

The Cadillacs of worm bins are multiple-level models (e.g., the Can-O-Worms) that make it easy to separate the worms from the finished vermicompost at harvest time. Worms, bedding, and food scraps are initially added only to the bottom tray. Once the lower tray is full of rich castings, feeding shifts up to a second tray. The worms migrate upward in search of more food, leaving the vermicompost behind. As the worms reproduce and all the trays come into production, the system can handle 3 to 4 kilograms (5 to 8 pounds) of food per day and produce a full tray of vermicompost each month.

Many simpler, less expensive models are available commercially. Or teachers can make their own worm bins by drilling air and drainage holes in large plastic storage containers or a homemade wooden bin.

Reln Plastics Ltd., Australia

Gateway Greening

A new layer of bedding and food scraps has just been added to this multi-level bin at Crestview Middle School in St. Louis, Missouri.

given the limited space and small budgets of most classrooms. Smaller bins are usually simpler in design, cheaper, not quite as attractive, and require more maintenance than the larger bins, especially to drain and harvest the vermicompost. However, they work well where small amounts of food waste are produced, or where a simple and inexpensive way for students to experience recycling is preferable.

Our program uses two types of bins: a circular multi-level type and a simple rectangular bin with a lid. Both are available at some gardening stores, at vermicomposting specialty outlets, and through the Internet. However, teachers on a tight budget could use a simple plastic bin or construct a bin from wood.

Air

The worm bins available commercially have air holes to meet the worms' requirement for air. If you choose to design your own worm bin, you'll need to drill holes 3 millimeters (1/8 inch) in diameter in all sides and in the lid. Regardless of the type of bin you use, you may find some escapees on the floor near the bin until the worms are used to their new home.

Water

The skin of worms is a moist membrane through which they exchange air to breathe. It is crucial for this membrane to remain moist. If the inside of their bin becomes too dry, the exchange of air through their skin cannot take place and they will suffocate. Creating optimal moisture conditions in the worm bin is fairly easy to do. If you purchase a multi-level bin, the worms will live in a medium of coir (i.e., coconut fiber). With some bins you can buy, this coir comes prepackaged in the form of a dry brick; once soaked in a bucket of water, the coir becomes the moist bedding in which the worms live. A layer of wet newspaper strips is then added on top. Other worm bins will need only the wet strips of newspaper distributed evenly throughout. Keep a spray bottle near the worm bin to add moisture every day as the newspaper strips or the coir dry out. The bedding should be moist yet fluffy, not sopping wet or in clumps.

Food

As a general rule, vermicomposting worms will eat anything that is organic. In a classroom, however, this rule has to be adjusted to maintain a healthy bin with which students can be actively involved. It's best to feed worms in a classroom bin a diet of fresh fruit and vegetable scraps, such as banana peels, apple cores, lettuce, grapes, celery, carrots, and broccoli. You may also put coffee grinds, tea bags, and eggshells in a school worm bin. Foods that may spoil, smell, or attract mold, fruit flies, and other pests should not be fed to worms. (See table.) No teachers or students want their classroom to smell like rotten trash!

Worms will eat half of their own weight in food every day. So, when feeding worms, it's important to know the total weight of worms that you have in order to gauge how much food to put in the bin. As a general rule, start

Jennifer Lippmann, Gateway Greening

Through vermicomposting experiments, students develop skills in teamwork, observation, record keeping, reporting, and measuring.

a worm bin with 450 grams (one pound) of worms and feed them 225 grams (one-half pound) of food per day.

A worm bin tends to sustain itself, which means that, even with the worms reproducing, the population and the amount of food consumed will remain relatively stable. If the worms are eating more than half their weight in food, the easy solution is to add more food. You could invite students to calculate how much their original worm population will eat and how quickly they will consume the food provided.

Chop food for worms into small pieces — about 3 to 6 millimeters (⅛ to ¼ inch) — or use a blender or food processor to create "worm soup," so that worms can more readily consume it.

Another tip is to designate a different area of the bin for feeding each day of the week, using the four corners of the bin for Monday, Tuesday, Wednesday, and Thursday, and the middle of the bin for Friday. When adding food to the bin, bury it rather than laying it on top, and mark the area with a small flag indicating the day of the week. Feeding this way ensures that feedings are not skipped; it also allows students and teachers to observe what worms like to eat and how quickly they are consuming food.

Students in many classes construct charts and graphs to measure the amounts and types of foods consumed by their worms. One teacher had students in art class create an illustrated worm "cookbook" that included recipes featuring the worms' favorite foods.

With teachers' guidance to prevent harm to the worms, students can conduct experiments with organic and nonorganic items. For example, some educators have put nonfood items in the worm bin, such as cotton T-shirts (no dyes), leather items, and junkmail envelopes. One teacher in St. Louis put in the cardboard from the back of a battery package to see if the worms would eat it: they didn't. Another teacher placed a small leather purse in the worm bin and, over time, the worms ate everything except the plastic handle.

Maintaining a healthy bin

Maintaining a healthy worm composting bin is fairly simple if you follow a few easy rules.

* *Liquid drainage:* Drain the worm bin weekly of the liquid produced by the worms, which is frequently called worm "tea." Draining is fairly easy with models that have a built-in spigot for this purpose. With other bins, the easiest way is to hold back the moist bedding and tilt the bin to pour the liquid out. You can also siphon out the liquid with a turkey baster. While you wouldn't want to drink this "tea," it makes an excellent fertilizer for plants when it is diluted with water to produce a 50:50 solution.

Gateway Greening

Foods to Avoid Feeding to Worms

Food	Examples	Reason to avoid feeding to worms
meat	beef, chicken, fish, pork	They spoil quickly, smell bad, and may attract pests.
citrus rinds	orange, lemon, lime	The acidity is harsh on the worms' skin.
pineapple		It ferments over time into alcohol, which can poison worms.
starches	bread, potatoes, cereal	They can easily grow mold.
fruit stems	stems of apples, bananas, grapes	The stems could contain fruit fly eggs.
clippings	grass or leaves	They could contain pesticides or insect eggs.
condiments	ketchup, mustard, mayonnaise	They're not good for worms' skin; worms won't eat most of them.
dairy foods	cheese, milk, butter	They smell bad and may attract pests.

- *Mold:* Whenever you see any mold or slime in the bin, remove it immediately. You simply can't afford to let it get out of control in the bin if you wish to avoid smells and pests.

- *Fruit flies:* If at any time you observe fruit flies in or around the worm bin, take action immediately! Remove all food from the bin, and consider using fly traps in the room. If these strategies do not eliminate the problem, you may need to separate the worms from the bedding, rinse the bin with water, and start over with fresh newspaper strips. The easiest way to avoid fruit flies is to remove stems from fruit scraps and to remember to bury food underneath the newspaper or coir bedding.

- *Feeding:* Observe the consumption of food by the worms daily and adjust accordingly. Perhaps your 450 grams (pound) of worms are not big eaters, and 225 grams (half pound) of food a day is just too much. Do not be afraid to scale back or to increase the amount of food you put in. After the first couple of weeks, you should have a pretty good grasp of how much to feed to keep the system balanced.

- *Moisture:* Remember to keep the bedding in the worm bin moist.

Harvesting the vermicompost

Depending on the type of bin you have and how many worms your system is sustaining, the bin could be ready for harvest between three and six months after you added the original worms. In this time, all the bedding will have turned into a rich, dark, finely textured material called vermicompost. Essentially, vermicompost is the castings or waste from the worms. Students' responses

Beth Alseth, Gateway Greening

Gateway Greening

to finding out what vermicompost is usually range from disgust to amusement.

At harvest time, separate the worms from the vermicompost, and then rinse out the bin with water and add fresh bedding material. The worms can then be returned to the bin. Take care not to leave any worms in the vermicompost because it provides them no nourishment and, in time, can be toxic to them. Teachers can make arrangements for parents and other teachers to take surplus vermicompost to ensure that it will not be wasted.

Vermicompost and worm "tea" and are both valuable plant fertilizers because they are very rich in nitrogen, which aids in plant growth. In fact, they are so nitrogen-rich that they must be diluted before use or they will actually burn plants. It's best to dilute them by half, combining vermicompost in a 50:50 mixture with potting soil, and mixing worm "tea" in a 50:50 solution with water. These fertilizers can then be fed to plants as any other high-nitrogen fertilizer would be.

Students can design and carry out many experiments to investigate ways in which vermicompost helps plants to grow. An easy experiment would be to test the effects of three different treatments on plants: give one plant water only, another a 50:50 solution (i.e., worm "tea" and water), and the third undiluted worm "tea."

There is truly no age limit for classroom worm composting. In our program in St. Louis, the age groups span pre-school to college. While most of the activity and curriculum resources cater to K–8, there are many ways to incorporate vermiculture activities into curriculum for older students. One high school teacher in St. Louis keeps worm bins in his science classroom and encourages students to do independent studies and experiments with the worms, usually as a research project or for science competitions. Another teacher recycles all the food waste from the high school cafeteria using five circular multi-level bins. A home economics teacher uses a worm bin to dispose of food waste from each cooking class. A college horticulture professor uses vermicompost produced in her worm bins as fertilizer.

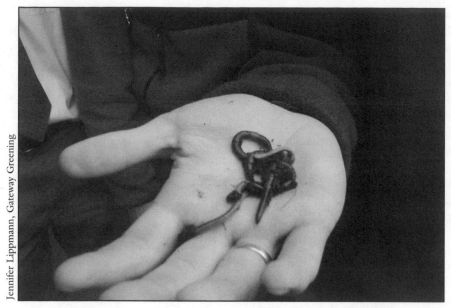

Jennifer Lippmann, Gateway Greening

For most middle school teachers, the worm bin is a wonderful teaching tool for units on decomposition or invertebrate biology. Educators who are not directly involved in science can bring the worm bin into their classrooms to teach the value of recycling. Regardless of what you teach, a worm bin is a truly valuable addition to any classroom, as vermicomposting holds limitless possibilities and rewards. As well as aiding in the teaching of required curriculum, vermiculture provides an opportunity for teachers and students to be environmentally conscious.

Jennifer Kusmanoff was an education coordinator for Gateway Greening, traveling throughout the St. Louis area for two years, teaching children of all ages the value and fun of vermicomposting. She now works as a grant coordinator for the Department of Biology at Washington University in St. Louis, Missouri.

RESOURCES

Books

Appelhof, Mary. *Worms Eat My Garbage.* Kalamazoo, MI: Flower Press, 1982.

Appelhof, Mary, Mary Fenton, and Barbara Harris. *Worms Eat Our Garbage: Classroom Activities for a Better Environment.* Kalamazoo, MI: Flower Press, 1995.

Kyle, Cori. *Worms are a Class Act.* Viscor Distribution Inc, 1996.

Websites

<http://stlouis.missouri.org/gatewaygreening> Gateway Greening in St. Louis, Missouri, has instructions and helpful links to other vermiculture sites; staff are available to answer questions about worm composting. 314–577–9484.

<www.composters.com> This site displays and sells many types of worm composting bins.

<www.wormwoman.com> Mary Appelhof's site has articles on worm composting and a catalog of excellent worm composting books, videos, and classroom guides, including her own Flower Press publications.

<www.worms.com> On this site, you can buy a variety of vermiculture resources, including worm bins and the live worms to go in them. The site also has information on do-it-yourself bins.

Building with Straw

A resilient and annually renewable material, the humble straw bale is enjoying a revival in building construction — and a debut in education

by Gilbert DiSanto

Subject areas: science, math, history, design and technology

Key concepts: renewable resources, sustainable building

Skills: measurement, carpentry and masonry skills, leadership

Location: any outdoor, high traffic location, except low-lying or wet areas

Time: 6 or 7 hours over 3 days

Materials: see activity below

If the three little pigs had had a lesson in straw bale design, they would never have needed to build the stick or the brick house. The Big Bad Wolf could have huffed and puffed until he turned blue and that house would have gone nowhere. In fact, the pigs would have been warmer in this better insulated structure and, if they had plastered the walls, it would have been fire resistant, too.

Straw was used for shelter by the earliest human nomads on the grassy plains of Africa and Europe, but it is not a widely used building material in these modern more technology-rich times. The focus of today's builders is on speed of construction and size of the house, not on preserving resources and conserving energy. Yet in an age of vast depletion of forests and massive burning of fossil fuels, straw bale construction offers a traditional solution to the modern challenge of creating sustainable communities. Straw bale buildings make use of a renewable and readily available material and they require less energy to heat and cool than typical woodframe structures. Straw bale structures have been built in many different climates, from semi-arid southern

Jeff Dickinson

Mexico to rainy and humid Alabama, and from wintry northern Alberta to the coast of Maine. Straw has also been built into a variety of forms to create elegant homes, art galleries, grocery stores, and barns.

While it is typical to associate straw bale design with large structures, the resource has many other potential applications and, on a smaller scale, it can be useful as a class project. Students can make anything from benches and bleachers to a gathering spot around a fire pit. One Grade 5 class even constructed a storage shed using rice straw.

A straw bale project can incorporate several subject areas into an interdisciplinary adventure with a tangible result. Being involved in the whole process, from planning and design to construction, is a great experience for students. Here, I provide background information and a basic framework for making a straw bale bench similar to one whose construction I helped to coordinate in 1997 at the Glen Helen Outdoor Education Center in Yellow Springs, Ohio. While this project is designed for students in Grades 6 through 8, the list of building materials and step-by-step directions could be adapted for more complex straw bale projects with older students. Because of safety issues, it is not recommended for younger students unless under strict supervision.

Six years after being built, the bench at the Glen Helen Outdoor Education Center remains, having weathered the elements and the persistent "concrete loaf of bread" jokes from colleagues. It has also survived at least 15,000 students running, pounding, jumping, and, of course, sitting on it. It is the ideal community-focused sustainable project. I wish you the best of luck with yours!

History of straw construction

Humans have used grass as a building material since the Stone Age. The enormous grasslands of the African and European continents provided ample materials with which to build shelters. The first documented use of the technology in the United States followed the Homestead Act of 1862, which facilitated the move of families to the Great Plains after the Civil War. On the prairie, settlers did not have a plentiful supply of wood, the traditional building material found in the east. Being resourceful and mimicking aboriginal cultures, they built "temporary" shelters from the cheapest and most plentiful resource they could find: straw. To eliminate drafts, they covered the interior walls with a layer of plaster.

Initially, these shelters were stopgap measures until the family could afford to build a "real" house. But it often happened that several years later, when the structure was weathered on the outside but showed no signs of age on the inside, this "temporary" shelter gained an exterior stucco veneer and became a permanent home. Although considered "a poor man's house," a straw home was practical, inexpensive, efficient, and sturdy. Some straw structures built more than 100 years ago still stand today.

Jeff Dickinson

Properties of straw bales

Straw is a by-product of renewable grass crops such as wheat and rice. After the edible seed heads are threshed from the mature plants, the strong fibrous stalks that are left are compacted and pressed into bales. Straw bales are renewable, resilient, and efficient insulators. The insulating value of any material — called its R-value — is a measure of its resistance to the flow of heat. The higher the R-value, the better the material is at keeping a building either cool or warm. Because of the thickness and density of straw bales, their R-value is very high; in optimal circumstances, it can reach R-60. In comparison, a woodframe wall with standard insulation reaches R-11 to R-19. The only insulating material that comes close to having the heat retention of straw bales is

Polyisocyanurate insulation, which in the average wall (15 centimeters / 6 inches thick) is R-48. However, in the production of this substance, fossil fuels are consumed and carcinogens released. Therefore, not only is straw an efficient alternative, it is also, by comparison, tremendously safe.

Building a straw bale bench

Goals:

- to provide an opportunity for hands-on, interdisciplinary learning while covering requirements in science, math, history
- to have students cooperate and complete a project that enhances the school or community
- to apply concepts of sustainability by constructing a bench using a renewable resource

Time: One one-hour planning session and three building sessions of approximately two hours each are needed to complete the project (six or seven hours in total). To allow time for the foundation concrete to set, schedule the second building session for at least two days after the first. The third session can be scheduled for the day after the second session.

Materials: 4 large straw bales, 1 roll 18-gauge wire mesh (chicken wire), 1 roll #30 asphalt roofing paper, 10 bags of Quickcrete (each 36 kilograms / 80 pounds) or another cement specifically designed for thick foundations, 23 kilograms / 50 pounds of gravel, 1 ton of sand, 2 bags of lime, 1 roll polypropylene twine, 2 x 6 lumber for framing the foundation, 6 lengths (each 45 centimeters / 18 inches) of #4 rebar, 1 bag outdoor plaster (optional), bale "needle" used to sew wire mesh to bales, hammer and nails (5 centimeters / 2 inches long), cement trowels, flat-edged shovels, level, sledgehammer, pliers and wire snips, pick (for breaking up ground beneath the bench), wheelbarrow, saw and hacksaw (if wood and rebar not pre-cut), water, safety goggles and heavy work gloves.

In an age of vast depletion of forests and massive burning of fossil fuels, straw bale construction offers a traditional solution to the modern challenge of creating sustainable communities.

Safety note: Ensure that students wear heavy-duty gloves, boots, and goggles whenever they work on this project.

In this project, students cooperate in the design and construction of a straw bale bench that can enhance the schoolyard or community for years. The materials listed will make a three-bale bench with two bales aligned end to end and one bale offset at a 45-degree angle. To prevent the project from seeming to be overwhelming, it is best to break it down into three main tasks: forming the base slab; placing the bales and covering them with stucco; and applying a finishing coat.

Gilbert Di Santo

A three-bale bench for the schoolyard is a great starter project.

Materials suggestions:

You can keep costs down by borrowing tools from parents and staff, and approaching civic-minded hardware stores and construction companies for donations of building materials. If you honor donors by writing their names in the side of the bench in wet stucco, their generosity will be marked forever. Here are some suggestions and tips.

- The bale needle must be several inches longer than the bales are wide. You can make your own from a rod with a diameter of 13 millimeters (½ inch) and about 1 meter (3 feet) long. Drill a hole through one end and make a point at the other end with a hacksaw. It's easiest to have someone at the hardware store do it for you.

- If you can pound the rebar far enough into the ground, you will not need to cut it with a hacksaw.

- We used straw bales of 0.5 x 1 meter (18 x 3 inches). Look for horse or dairy farms — even urban areas have some nearby — that might donate them.

- Chicken wire is available in most home repair stores. Here is a chance for students to apply math skills. The roll is 1 meter (or 3 feet) wide and you need enough to wrap around all three bales with room to spare. Students can also use math to calculate the amount of roofing paper needed.

- We used gravel straight from the driveway!

- To get the load of sand to your site, find a parent with a pickup truck or purchase it from a dealer who will deliver it free of charge.

- Use math again to calculate the number of boards needed for framing the foundation. (Our foundation was 18 inches wide by 108 inches long (3 bales, each 36 inches long). If possible, have the lumberyard cut the boards for you.

Planning session

Once you have obtained all the building materials, hold a planning session with students. Explain that they must decide on the location, design, and delegation of responsibilities. It is important to build the bench on firm ground and to avoid low-lying areas where water might collect or make the ground unstable. Ensure that everyone has a copy of the final design. The project becomes much more feasible for the coordinator when responsibilities are split among groups. For instance, delegate the gathering of materials to three groups and assign a leader to each group to ensure the tasks are done. This is a great team-building exercise.

Discussion and evaluation:

Math/geometry: What are the dimensions of the bench? How much of each material will you need? What will be the area of the bench?

Science/geography: What is the ground like where you plan to build? Will topography or slope have an impact? What about water? Will there be standing water when it rains?

Leadership and cooperation: Include students in developing an assessment rubric for these skills.

History: This is a chance to offer an overview of straw bale design history and the example that the class is setting by choosing this medium. What other materials could be used? Why use straw bale when there are other options?

Building session 1: Laying the foundation

The goal of the first building session is to frame and pour the concrete foundation for the bench. Divide the students into three work crews and assign one crew to each task. To ensure that everyone is involved, delegate specific responsibilities to each student, even if the job is to "help gather materials" or "get lemonade." Make sure that the crews rotate to avoid stagnation. Try to avoid having too many hands on one project, as it hinders concentration and can lead to an accident. For each crew,

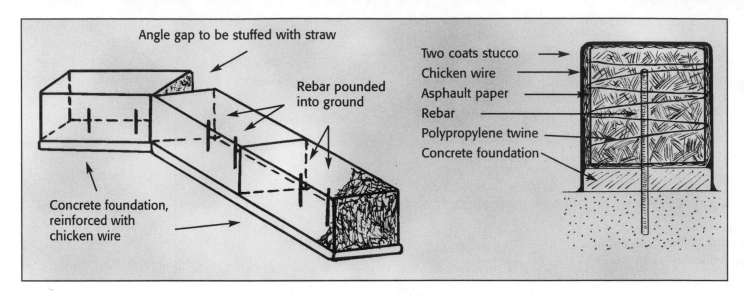

Angle gap to be stuffed with straw

Rebar pounded into ground

Concrete foundation, reinforced with chicken wire

Two coats stucco
Chicken wire
Asphault paper
Rebar
Polypropylene twine
Concrete foundation

there must be an adult available for guidance, safety patrol, and giving clear explanations.

Framing the foundation:

1. Assemble the 2 x 6 boards, hammer, nails, pick, and saw (if wood is not pre-cut). If you were unable to obtain pre-cut wood, cut the 2 x 6 boards to the size required for the foundation.

2. Nail the boards together to frame the base of the bench.

   Note: Make sure the dimensions of the foundation are exact multiples of the dimensions of the bales. For example, our bench was one bale wide and three bales long. With bales measuring 18 x 36 inches, this translated into a foundation of 18 x 108 inches. Refer to the design from the planning session.

3. Before placing the frame in position, use the pick to loosen the top two or three centimeters (inch or so) of soil. This helps the cement to "grab" and allows the site to be leveled as needed.

Mixing concrete:

1. Assemble the cement, sand, gravel, water, wheelbarrow, shovels, and cement trowels. Be sure to use cement that is specifically designed for thick foundations, because any other type of cement is likely to crack if you attempt to pour it to the thickness required for the foundation. Set aside three bags of cement for later.

2. Mix the cement, sand, gravel, and water according the manufacturer's instructions. In general, a concrete mix is a 1 to 3 ratio of cement to sand. Add water until the mixture is moist enough to ooze off a poured shovel. If it falls off in chunks, it is too thick and you must add water until it becomes thinner. If it pours off like watery soup, it is too thin, and you must add more concrete and sand at the 1-to-3 ratio until it reaches the desired thickness.

Laying the foundation:

1. Assemble the chicken wire, tools to cut wire, cement

trowel, rebar (and hacksaw to cut rebar if needed), sledgehammer, and level.

2. Within the borders created by the frame, pound two rebar poles deep into the ground for every bale (consult your design diagram). Pound until the rebar poles stand a few centimeters shorter than the height of the bales. If the ground is too hard to allow this depth, go as deep as possible and cut off the tops of the poles with a hacksaw.

3. Pour enough concrete into the form to cover the ground up to 5 centimeters (2 inches) deep.

4. Place the chicken wire on top of the concrete. The wire mesh should be at least 5 centimeters (2 inches) in from the sides and have no contact with the ground.

   Note: Traditionally, river reeds or bamboo were used to hold the foundation. You could substitute these for the wire mesh.

5. Cover the wire with at least another 5 centimeters (2 inches) of concrete, so that the slab is about 10 centimeters (4 inches) high. To make leveling easier and to minimize spilling, the concrete should be just shy of the top of the mold (the 2 x 6 boards).

6. Using the cement trowel and the level, smooth the surface of the concrete.

7. Rope off the project, post signs to prohibit playing around the foundation, and take any other precautions necessary to keep the foundation clean and undisturbed until it is set. The concrete slab will be set within two days.

Discussion and evaluation:

Science/chemistry: What happens to iron when it is in contact with water? What will happen to the bench if rebar or chicken wire is exposed? Why don't we use only concrete or only wire? Why are the two such a great combination?

Leadership and cooperation: Assess that they are exercised.

Building session 2: Constructing the bench

The second building session is to prepare the foundation for receiving the bales, and to set the bales in place, wrap them in wire, and cover them with a coat of stucco.

Preparing the foundation and positioning bales:

1. Assemble asphalt roofing paper, chicken wire, wire cutters and pliers, straw bales, bale needle, and polypropylene twine.

2. Cut the chicken wire and roofing paper to size by wrapping them around a bale to get a measurement. (Did it match the students' math?) The wire mesh must wrap around and overlap the bale by about 25 centimeters (10 inches). The roofing paper does not need to overlap, but it must cover the bottom and sides to repel moisture.

3. Lay the wire and then the paper down on the foundation slab.

4. (a) Impale the bales on the rebar and begin to pull the wire and paper up to wrap the straw tightly. It is essential to wrap the wire as tightly as possible around the bales and to bind the ends together with the wire tools; the overlap should give you leverage. You cannot wrap the bales too tightly.

   (b) If your bench has a 45-degree angle, as ours did, frame the angle with the chicken wire by tightly binding it on either side to the straw bales. Then stuff the corner as tightly as possible with straw from the fourth bale.

5. Thread the bale needle with polypropylene twine. Sew the wire snugly to the sides of the bale by zigzagging through the bale.

   Safety note: As it is very difficult to push the needle through the straw, especially for students, an adult may have to use a hammer. Be sure that everyone has on heavy gloves and goggles before starting this step.

6. Use more straw to fill any pockets that you find between the wire mesh and the bale. You know you are ready for the stucco when the class appears to have successfully restrained a wild bench with twine and fencing.

Applying stucco scratch coat:

1. Assemble the tools for the stucco scratch coat: 2 bags cement, 1 bag lime, 37 rounded shovelfuls of

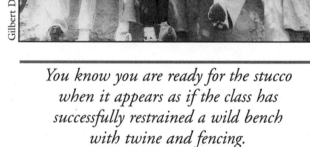

Gilbert Di Santo y

You know you are ready for the stucco when it appears as if the class has successfully restrained a wild bench with twine and fencing.

---

clean sand, water, wheelbarrow, shovels, and cement trowels.

2. Mix the cement, lime, sand, and water to a spreading consistency — neither chunky nor soupy.

3. (a) Use the cement trowel to spread the stucco on the bales and through the wire mesh, as if you were frosting a cake very aggressively. Press hard, spread evenly, and go all the way to the ground so that you cover the base slab. Having several trowels will give many students a chance to be involved.

   (b) If the bales are not exactly the same size as the support foundation and there is a ledge on the foundation, this is no problem. However, if there is a gap *under* the edge of the bales, fill it in. Do not expect the bales to form a perfect rectangle as the stucco is applied; the bench will likely have waves and bumps, which will give it character and an organic feel. If you have a chance to visit a straw bale house in town, take note of this feature.

4. Once the bales are covered with the stucco, have two members of the crew scratch the surface of the wet stucco by lightly dragging several twigs or the edge of a trowel over the entire bench. The purpose of this is to create a rough surface to which the final, brown layer can bond. The scratches must not penetrate through to the bales; the slightest roughness is all that's needed.

Discussion and evaluation:

Math: Compare the students' calculations of the amount of wire mesh and roofing paper needed with what was really needed. Did they match?

Science/chemistry: Why is lime used here but not for the foundation?

Building session 3: Applying stucco brown coat

Since the only task of the third session is to mix and apply the second coat of stucco, the challenge may be to assign everyone a job. Let each student take a turn spreading the stucco and schedule additional activities for the other members of the group.

Procedure:

1. Assemble the materials to make the second coat of stucco: 1 bag cement, 1 bag lime, 45 rounded

shovelfuls of clean sand, water, wheelbarrow, shovels, and cement trowels.

2. In the wheelbarrow, mix the cement, lime, sand, and water to a spreading consistency — neither chunky nor soupy.

3. Use the cement trowel to spread it evenly over the entire surface of the bench.

4. You can finish off this part by using a nail to etch a message, as well as the names of donors and participants, into the side of the bench.

5. With an additional hour's work and the optional bag of outdoor plaster, students can apply a topcoat of finish plaster to enhance the esthetic appearance of their bench. It is not essential to the structure.

Note: Students might like to try mixing separate buckets of the finish plaster with natural dyes from walnut hulls, pokeberries, or raspberries. It is better to mix pigments or dyes directly into the topcoat of plaster than to apply paint to the surface, as paint may trap moisture and peel. You can paint with the dyes, if you like, to complete the project with whatever design your class likes.

Gilbert DiSanto holds a Master of Arts degree in Environment and Community and teaches high school in Vienna, Austria.

REFERENCES

Black Range Films and Natural Building Resources. A good source of books and videos on straw bale construction and natural building in general; for a list, visit <www.StrawBaleCentral.com> or contact Black Range Films, Star Rt. 2, Box 119, Kingston, NM 88042, 505–895–5652.

MacDonald, Stephen O. "Straw Talk and Tech Tips." *The Last Straw.* Fall 1992, p. 7.

Magwood, Chris, and Peter Mack. *Straw Bale Building: How to plan, design and build with straw.* New Society Publishers, 2000. A recent how-to guide for both experienced and beginning bale builders that is well illustrated, with a special focus on building in northern climates.

Mcpherson, E. Gregory. "Benefits and Costs of Energy-Conserving Site Design." American Society of Landscape Architects, 1984.

Swentzell Steen, Athena, Bill Steen, and David Bainbridge, with David Eisenberg. *The Straw Bale House.* Chelsea Green Publishing Company, 1994. One of the classics on straw bale design and construction.

The Last Straw Journal. A quarterly journal sharing news and developments from around the world about straw bale construction and natural building. Contact The Last Straw at PO Box 22706, Lincoln, NE 68542-2706, 402–483–5135, <www.thelaststraw.org>.

The Power of Wind: It'll Blow You Away

Activities for exploring one of the oldest and cleanest energy sources

by Marcee Camenson and Michelle Finchum

Subject areas: science, social studies, mathematics

Key concepts: renewable energy, lift, Bernoulli's principle, convection

Skills: design, model testing

Location: indoors

Time: 1 hour (2 hours if convection box and wind farm model are constructed by students)

Materials: listed by activity

Capturing the wind's energy to do work is a practice as old as recorded history. The wind was harnessed more than 4,000 years ago to power the sailing vessels of early explorers and traders; and the first windmills were being used to grind grain and pump water in Persia in the 10th century. By the 14th century, windmills were draining fields in the Netherlands and moving water for irrigation in France. In North America during the 1800s, millions of windmills were built to pump water for fields and livestock, making it possible for settlers to move onto the semi-arid drylands of the west. Windmills designed to produce electricity — a Danish innovation in 1891 — enabled people in rural areas to make their own electricity for powering lights, tools, and, later, radios. Despite its long service to society, however, wind power's days seemed to be drawing to a close in the 1930s. As demand for energy grew and electrical grids were extended to rural areas, millions of small-scale windmills fell into disuse, replaced by large-scale generating plants burning cheap and abundant fossil fuels.

Few could have predicted the renaissance of wind power that is underway today. Due to technological improvements and declining costs, wind power is the world's fastest growing energy source. Worldwide, wind power capacity quadrupled

> *Due to technological improvements and declining costs, wind power is the world's fastest growing energy source.*

between 1997 and 2002, an average increase of 32 percent per year.[1] Utility-scale wind turbines are now supplying electricity to homes and industries in 32 American states and 7 Canadian provinces and territories. About 80 percent of the world's present wind power capacity is in Europe, however. In Denmark, one-fifth of all electricity comes from wind power, and Germany alone has twice as much wind-generated electricity as all of North America.

Wind power is an important renewable alternative to the burning of fossil fuels to generate electricity for our homes, businesses, and schools. Unlike conventional coal, oil, or gas-fired power plants, wind turbines emit no air pollutants or greenhouse gases. Apart from the materials needed to build them, they require no drilling, mining, transportation, or importing of resources. In addition, unlike nuclear power plants, wind turbines do not leave behind dangerous by-products. Gas, coal-fired, and nuclear plants use a tremendous of amount of water, a particularly significant factor in regions where water is scarce.

So why hasn't everyone switched over to wind power? One reason is that wind turbines produce an intermittent rather than a steady supply of electricity

NEG Micon Canada Ltd.

because the wind doesn't blow every-where all the time. However, wind power is easily supplemented with energy from other sources; and, as more wind turbines are built and wind power capacity expands, wind turbines can be networked so that energy produced on a slow day in one region can be supplemented with energy from other regions where the wind is blowing. Another limitation has been the high initial cost of wind power. Wind farms are generally located in rural areas, and transmission lines and substations must be installed to send the energy to the utility's customers. Despite the initial investment required, the cost of wind power has declined by 80 percent over the past 20 years as more wind turbines have been built and the technology has improved.[2] Proponents of wind power also point out that comparisons of the costs of wind power and non-renewable energy sources fail to take into account government subsidies for oil and gas development, as well as future increases in the cost of these fossil fuels.

As concerns about climate change and air pollution cause us to rethink our energy options, wind power offers a source of clean, non-polluting electricity that can contribute to the health of our planet. Exploring the topic with students is a fantastic way to get them interested in renewable energy and to introduce them to a not-so-new but increasingly important technology for the future.

Exploring wind power

In these activities, students learn some of the fundamentals of wind power, and design and test simple wind turbines. The segments can be used together as one lesson or selected as appropriate for adding a wind energy component to units on renewable energy.

Toronto Hydro

Introduction

Materials: pictures of wind turbines

The following brief introductory discussions and activities help to spark students' interest in wind power.

- Ask students what the difference is between renewable energy resources (e.g., wind, solar, geothermal, hydroelectric, tidal energy) and non-renewable energy resources (e.g., oil, coal, natural gas). Explain that renewable energy comes from sources that we will never run out of because they will last as long as the Earth does: the sun will always shine, the wind will always blow, the tides will always change, and Earth will retain its underground heat. Non-renewable energy resources are fuels such as coal or oil that we have a finite supply of; someday we will run out of them, or the few remaining supplies will be too difficult or expensive to extract.

- Show a picture of a wind turbine and ask students to guess the size of its three main parts: the tower, the rotor blades, and the central hub called the nacelle (pronounced nuh-sell). The nacelle sits on top of the tower and contains a gearbox, drive shafts, generator, controller, and brake. Write all of the students' guesses on the blackboard. You may choose to give the answers now, or wait until later in the lesson when discussing how turbines work.

Utility wind turbines are manufactured in different sizes for different wind conditions and electrical output. On a small 600- to 660-kilowatt turbine, which can generate electricity for about 250 homes, the tower is typically 30 meters (100 feet) or more tall. Each blade is about 20 meters (65 feet) in length. The nacelle, or hub to which the blades are attached, is as big as an average school bus, or about 11 meters (36 feet) long. Larger turbines may have blades as long as 30 meters (100 feet) and towers that are 100 meters (330 feet) or more high.

- Ask students if they know of places that are quite windy. Discuss the characteristics of these windy places. For example, they may be open spaces (wind coming across a lake or open plains) or hills (the higher you go, the more windy it is). Find out if there is a wind farm in your region. Discuss why the wind farm has been situated in that area. Students

Vision Quest Windelectric Inc.

may find wind maps of their continent or region on the Internet.

- In many municipalities, people have the option of obtaining their electricity from renewable sources such as wind or solar power. This does not mean that the utility company sends the wind-generated electrons to a specific home, as this would be impossible. Instead, customers agree to purchase a certain number of kilowatt-hours from renewable resources at a set price, and this enables the utility company to spend money to develop these resources. Many people are willing to pay more for this "green" electricity because it is better for the environment than burning fossil fuels. If your utility company offers "green" electricity, have students compare the cost per kilowatt-hour to the cost of conventional electricity. Students may calculate what it would cost their family to switch to green power (it usually adds only a few dollars a month to the energy bill).

- If coal-fired generators are used to produce electricity in your area, discuss why this is a problem for the environment (the burning of fossil fuels produces air pollutants and greenhouse gases). In one year, a 660-kilowatt wind turbine produces enough energy to replace 900 metric tons of coal and to reduce carbon dioxide emissions by 1,660 metric tons. If you can obtain a lump of coal from your local utility, pass it around the class. (Spray it with shellac to prevent smudging.) Have students weigh the coal and then calculate how many same-sized pieces would have to be burned to produce the amount of energy that one 660-kilowatt wind turbine produces in a year.

What makes wind?

Materials: candle carousel ornament or convection box (see sidebar)

Explain to students that wind power is actually a form of solar power. The sun heats the Earth's surface unevenly, so that it is warmer in some places than in others. (The equator, for example, receives more solar energy than the poles of the Earth, and land heats up more quickly than water.) When heat from the surface is transferred to the air, the molecules of air move further apart, making the air lighter and more buoyant. As warm air rises, colder and denser air rushes in to take its place, creating an air current. This process, known as convection, is what causes wind. Wind flow patterns are modified by the Earth's rotation, terrain, water bodies, and vegetation.

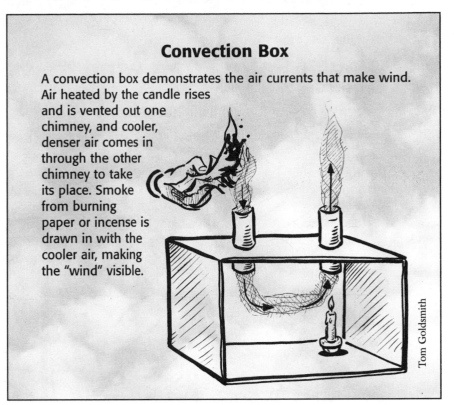

Convection Box

A convection box demonstrates the air currents that make wind. Air heated by the candle rises and is vented out one chimney, and cooler, denser air comes in through the other chimney to take its place. Smoke from burning paper or incense is drawn in with the cooler air, making the "wind" visible.

Tom Goldsmith

Open plains, mountain gaps, and shorelines are areas where wind is plentiful.

A quick way to illustrate that heat creates wind is to have students watch as you light a candle carousel ornament (found in Christmas supply stores). In these devices, hot air rising from burning candles creates a convection current that turns the blades on a fan-like carousel. (Remind students that turbines use wind; they do not make wind.) Another tool for demonstrating wind is a convection box (see sidebar). Instructions for making a simple convection box can be found on many science websites.[3]

How is the energy in the wind captured?

Wind turbines are machines that capture the wind's power. Moving air turns huge blades that spin a shaft connected to a large generator. The generator produces electricity through a process of electromagnetism: metal moves through a magnetic field and electrical energy is produced. This electrical energy travels into the electrical grid through power lines, just like electricity from conventional power plants.

Draw a simple schematic on the board to show students how electricity gets from a wind turbine into the electrical grid and then to homes. (See Power Path illustration, page 132.)

Wind farm model

To demonstrate the concept of a wind farm, a model can be made using small turbines with direct current (DC) motors, available from science supply houses (see Resources for supplier).

Power Path: From wind to washing machines!

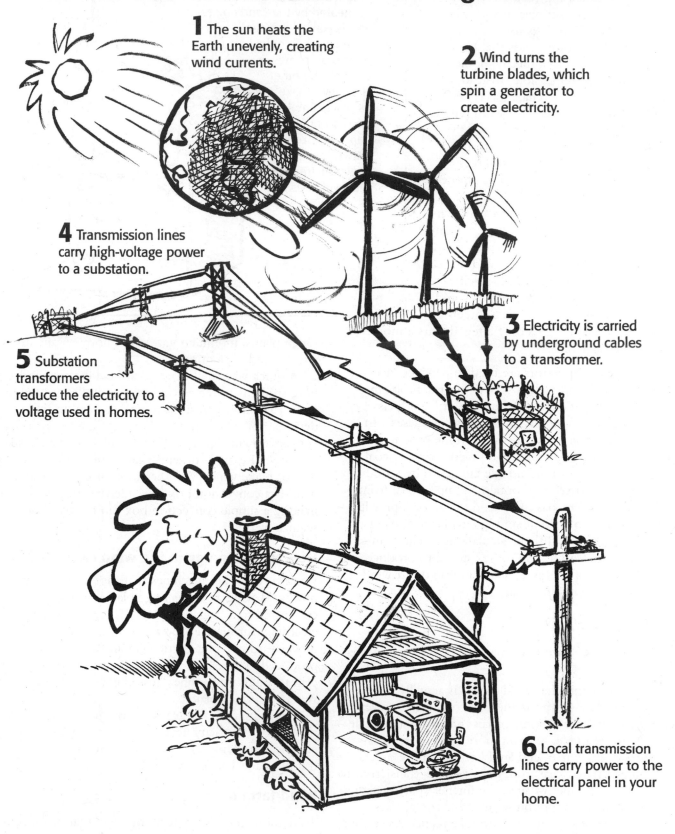

1 The sun heats the Earth unevenly, creating wind currents.

2 Wind turns the turbine blades, which spin a generator to create electricity.

3 Electricity is carried by underground cables to a transformer.

4 Transmission lines carry high-voltage power to a substation.

5 Substation transformers reduce the electricity to a voltage used in homes.

6 Local transmission lines carry power to the electrical panel in your home.

Materials: One length (approximately 30 centimeters / one foot) of 2 x 6 lumber, 4 or 5 model wind turbines, electric drill, voltmeter, #20 copper wire, wire snips, household fan

Procedure:

1. Mark positions for the turbines on the 2 x 6 board, offsetting them to ensure that each turbine will directly face the wind (the fan) and that there is enough space between them for the blades to turn.

2. At the positions marked in step 1, drill holes that are the same diameter as the base of the turbines.

3. Push the bases of the turbines into the holes so the turbines stand upright on the board.

4. Wire the turbines in series (positive to negative to positive to negative). Wire the first and the last turbines in the series to the voltmeter.

5. Turn on the fan. As "wind" is generated by the fan, the gauge on the voltmeter will show how much electricity the turbines are generating.

What makes a wind turbine turn?

Why does wind move the blades on a turbine, and how does the design of the blades affect the ability of the turbine to capture wind? In this activity, students investigate Bernoulli's principle and the force of lift.

Materials: One strip of paper (5 x 25 centimeters / 2 x 10 inches) for each student, flight feathers of birds (ask nature center or wildlife division for some), measuring tape

Marcee Camenson

Tom Goldsmith

Procedure:

1. Give a strip of paper to each student. Instruct students to hold the strip of paper just below their mouths, blow over the top of it, and observe how it lifts. Ask students if they can explain what is happening.

2. Explain that the air on top of the paper is moving faster than the air below the paper. This reduces the air pressure above the paper. The greater air pressure from below pushes up on the paper and forces the paper to "lift." This illustrates how the blades of a wind turbine are moved by wind. Wind causes the air pressure to be lowered over the top, curved portion of the turbine blade. The greater air pressure beneath the blade causes it to turn. You are actually exploring Bernoulli's principle, which states that gases (in this case, air) have less pressure when they are moving. The faster a gas moves, the less pressure it exerts.

3. If you have flight feathers available, have students experience lift by holding a feather at a slight angle (less than 45 degrees) between their thumb and index finger. As they move the feather back and forth in front of them, they should be able to feel the air pressure lifting the feather. Point out that wind turbine blades are shaped like a feather or an airplane wing; they are moved by the force of lift in a similar manner.

4. Recall that the size of a blade on a commercial wind turbine can be 20 meters (65 feet) or more in length. Use a measuring tape to measure out 20 meters in the classroom. Ask why the blades are so big. Big blades catch a lot of wind and produce more electricity than small blades, but they require a higher wind speed to turn. The optimal blade size depends on the average wind speeds and the desired electrical output.

Designing a wind turbine

Materials: large paper clips (5 centimeters / 2 inches), 1-3 electric fans; and:

for the nacelle: wine-bottle corks, or Styrofoam balls of 8-10 centimeters (3-4 inches) diameter. If possible, provide both. Styrofoam balls do not hold up as well as corks but allow students to experiment with the number and angle of blades.

for the turbine blades: wooden tongue depressors, small flat wooden or plastic spoons, popsicle sticks, or similar objects, at least 4 per turbine. Providing a variety of materials allows students to experiment with blades of different sizes and shapes.

Preparation:

Prepare corks ahead of time by making two cuts at 45-degree angles on opposite sides and drilling a hole in one end large enough to insert a straightened paperclip.

Procedure:

1. Ask students, "If you were going to build a wind turbine, what would you need to think about?" List their ideas on the board. Explain that their task will be to build the "best" wind turbine, but do not define "best." Let them discover what this means.

2. Give each student or group a set of materials. Show them how to straighten the paperclip and insert it lengthwise into the end of the cork or into the middle of the Styrofoam ball. The paper clip serves as a handle and allows the cork or ball to spin.

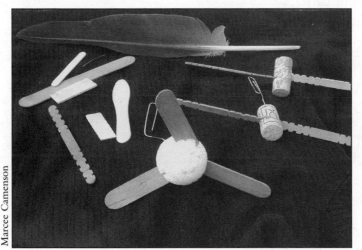

Marcee Camenson

3. If students are using corks, have them insert two turbine blades into the angled cuts in the corks. If they are using Styrofoam balls, have them push two or more blades into the foam.

4. Have students test their designs using the fan as a wind source.

5. Encourage students to experiment with different sizes and numbers of blades and, if possible (i.e., if using foam balls), varying the angle of the blades. They may also change the speed of the fan to see the effect of wind speed on turbines of different configurations.

6. After students have tested their designs, ask for their observations about what worked and what didn't. List the observations on the board.

Students should discover that all of the blades must be angled the same way in order for the wind turbine to work properly. They may also notice that varying the fan speed affects each design differently. For example, smaller blades will work better than larger blades at low wind speeds. Large commercial turbines require a certain minimum wind speed of about 8 to 16 kilometers per hour (5 to10 miles per hour) to begin to produce power, and they are designed not to begin to turn until the wind reaches that optimal "cut-in" speed. Similarly, they are designed with a maximum or "cut-out" speed of about 90 to 105 kilometers per hour (55 to 65 miles per hour). When the wind reaches the cut-out speed, the blades are stopped by a braking system and then rotated 90 degrees out of the wind. This ensures that they are not damaged in high winds.

There really is no "best" design; there are many acceptable designs, depending on the location and purpose of the turbine. For example, most utility turbines have large rotor blades designed to operate in fairly high-speed winds. A wind turbine for home use usually has a shorter tower and blades, and operates at a lower wind speed.

Review

Review the benefits of wind power. It is clean, efficient and renewable. Using wind power in place of coal offsets emissions of sulfur oxide, nitrogen oxide, particulates, and other air pollutants. It also reduces the accumulation in the environment of toxic metals and carcinogenic substances that are released from coal when it in burned.

Also discuss drawbacks of wind power. Because the wind does not blow all the time, a wind turbine is an intermittent rather than a steady source of electricity. However, it can be supplemented with other sources of electricity (including wind turbines in other places where the wind is blowing), and its power can be stored for times when the wind is not blowing. Wind turbines cannot be located just anywhere; they require open spaces that have sufficient wind to power them.

Review how wind is created and how electricity gets from a wind turbine to a home. Recall that there are many different kinds of wind turbines; the best one depends on the location and purpose.

Extension

Have students research an aspect of wind power that interests them. Topics may include different kinds of turbines, the history of wind power, the locations of wind farms in North America, or the benefits and drawbacks of wind power. Artistic students may wish to build models or make drawings of different types of turbines. Give students a variety of choices and see what they come up with. You can use their fantastic productions next year!

Marcee Camenson is the Education Coordinator and Michelle Finchum is an Education Specialist in Energy and Watershed Education for the City of Fort Collins Utilities in Fort Collins, Colorado.

Notes

1 American Wind Energy Association, Global Wind Energy Market Report, February 2003, on-line at <www.awea.org/pubs/documents/globalmarket2003.pdf>, January 3, 2004.

2 American Wind Energy Association, "Wind Energy FAQ," on-line at <http://www.awea.org/faq/cost.html>, January 9, 2004.

3 Instructions for making a simple convection box can be found at the following websites: <http://www.uncfsu.edu/msec/nova/timmod3n.htm>, Ronald A. Johnston, "Heating of Air by Convection," *Teaching Integrated Mathematics and Science, Module 3, Winds and Circulation*, Department of Natural Sciences, Fayetteville State University; and <http://www.air-infonow.org/pdf/CurriculaConvectionWithGraphic.PDF>, Pima County Department of Environmental Quality, "What's the Connection between Convection and Inversion?"

RESOURCES

Materials

Small turbines for use in model wind farms are available from Edmund Scientifics, 60 Pearce Avenue, Tonawanda, NY 14150, 800-728-6999, <www.scientificsonline.com>. Ask for item #3081713.

Books

Gipe, Paul. *Wind Energy Basics, A Guide to Small and Micro Wind Systems.* Chelsea Green Publishing Company, 1999.

Woelfle, Gretchen. *The Wind at Work: An Activity Guide to Windmills.* Chicago Review Press, 1997.

Organizations

American Wind Energy Association is a good source of information on all aspects of wind power. <www.awea.org>, 122 C Street NW, Suite 380, Washington, DC 20001, 202-383-2500.

BC Hydro provides a wealth of information about wind and other renewable energy. See their Wind Energy website at <www.bchydro.bc.ca/environment/greenpower/greenpower1754.html>, and green energy teaching modules at <www.bchydro.bc.ca/education/ index.html>.

Canadian Wind Energy Association has information about wind power development in Canada. <www.canwea.ca>, 3553 31 Street NW, Suite 100, Calgary, AB T2L 2K7, 800--922-6932.

Danish Wind Industry Association has a fun, interactive, and multilingual website for students aged 12-14; the "Wind with Miller" section explains the fundamentals of turbines and has an accompanying teacher's guide. <http://www.windpower.org/en/core.htm>.

National Wind Technology Center, National Renewable Energy Laboratory: the website. <www.nrel.gov/wind>, has a glossary of wind power terms, a wind resource map of the Unites States, and animated illustrations of how wind turbines work.

U.S. Department of Energy, Energy Efficiency and Renewable Energy. See Wind and Hydropower Technologies Program at <www.eere.energy.gov/windandhydro>; Wind Powering America at <www.eere.energy.gov/windpoweringamerica>; and the EERE Kids' pages at <www.eere.energy.gov/kids/wind.html>.

The Wind in the Schoolyard

In this activity, students measure and map wind speeds on the school grounds to determine whether there is enough wind energy to power to the school

by Jim Wiese

Subject areas: science

Key concepts: wind meters, wind barbs

Skills: measurement, mapping, use of protractor

Location: indoors and outdoors

Time: 3 hours

Materials: photocopies of protractor (provided on page 137 can be reproduced in the size shown, but enlargement to a width of 18 cm / 7 in. is recommended), sheets of thin cardboard the same size as the protractor, piece of string 15 cm (6 in.) long, ping-pong ball, ruler or paint stirring stick, glue, scissors, masking tape, nail or hole punch, paper, pencils (standard and colored), calculators, Wind Speed Conversion Table (provided), chalkboard or large piece of paper, household fan (optional)

Many factors come into play in deciding the best site for a wind turbine, but the most important factor is the power of the wind itself. Most commercial wind turbines are concentrated on wind farms, often located on hills near mountain passes, near oceans or other large bodies of water, or in other geographical areas that have a steady wind pattern. Wind speeds of about 13 kilometers per hour (8 miles per hour) are enough to turn the blades of most wind turbines, but winds of around 25 kilometers per hour (16 miles per hour) are needed to generate enough electricity to recover start-up costs quickly and make the wind turbine economically viable.

Tom Goldsmith

In this activity, students construct simple wind meters and determine whether there is enough wind on the school grounds to generate electricity for the school. The exercise provides students with a concrete example of how data is collected and presented when the wind-energy potential of a site is being assessed.

Constructing and testing wind meters

Begin by setting the context for the activity: before a new energy resource can be used, its potential must be explored. Explain that the most important thing in the operation of a wind turbine is whether there is enough wind to power it. Inform students that they are going to be using a simple wind meter to measure the speed of the wind around the school in order to determine if there is enough wind energy to power a wind turbine that could supply the school with electricity. The first step is to make and test the wind meters.

Procedure:

1. Prepare photocopies of the protractor; enlargement to 18 cm (7 in.) in width is recommended but not essential. Provide each student (or pair of students) with materials for making the wind meter.

2. Ask students to use scissors to cut out the protractor.

3. Next, have students glue the protractor onto the cardboard to strengthen it, and trim the cardboard around the outside borders of the protractor.

4. Demonstrate how to use a nail or punch to make a small hole at the center mark on the protractor, and then have students do this.

5. Have students tape one end of the string firmly to the ping-pong ball, and thread the other end of the string through the hole in the front of the protractor. Use masking tape to secure the string to the reverse side of the protractor.

6. Ask students to fold the top edge of the protractor back along the dotted line.

7. Have students tape the ruler or paint stirring stick to the back of the protractor under the folded edge to form a handle for the wind meter.

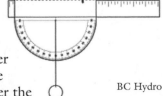

BC Hydro

8. Show students how to hold their meters so that the protractor is horizontal in front of them and the end of the handle faces the wind.

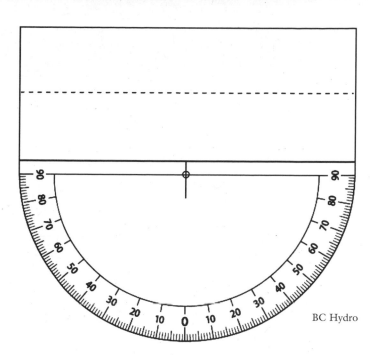

BC Hydro

9. Have pairs of students work together to test their meters. One student can simulate the wind by blowing toward the ping-pong ball, while the other student holds the meter and reads the deflection in degrees on the protractor. (Alternatively, a fan can be used as the source of wind, and the fan speed can be varied to obtain different readings.) Allow time for students to experiment with the meters by varying the wind speed and holding the devices at different angles to the "wind."

10. Have students determine the speed of the "wind" by converting protractor readings into kilometers or miles per hour using the Wind Speed Conversion Table below.

Discussion questions:

1. Why do you think a ping-pong ball was used in the construction of this device? Why not use a heavier ball?

2. Do you think it is better to hold the wind meter in front of you or off to one side? Explain your answer.

3. How could you use the meter outdoors to determine the direction of the wind? Explain.

Measuring and mapping wind speed

Explain to students that the data they will collect using their wind meters can be presented in a chart, a table, or a graph, but another way to present wind speed data is to use a map. The advantage of a map is that it will allow them to display the wind speeds measured at different locations on the school grounds at the same time.

Procedure:

1. Once students have made their wind speed meters and practiced their use, divide the class into teams of two or three students.

2. Work with students to draw a large map of the school on the chalkboard or on a large piece of paper. Put the school building near the center of the map, and leave enough room around it to note the locations of trees, shrubs, neighboring buildings, and other objects that might interrupt wind flow. Note any changes in elevation on the school grounds (e.g., hills and valleys). Finally, draw a compass showing north, south, east, and west.

3. Have each group of students make a copy of the map for their use.

4. Assign each group one or more locations on the school grounds where they are to take wind speed measurements. Have each group mark these locations on their maps.

Note: The locations you choose should take into account the safety of the students. For example, do not place them too close to a road, near water, or in locations where you cannot see them during the activity.

Wind Speed Conversion Table		
Protractor Reading (in degrees)	**Wind Speed (mph)**	**(km/h)**
0	0.0	0
5	5.6	9
10	8.1	13
15	9.9	16
20	11.8	19
25	13.0	21
30	14.9	24
35	16.1	26
40	18.0	29
45	19.2	31
50	21.1	34
55	22.9	37
60	25.4	41
65	28.5	46
70	32.2	52

5. Before going outside to collect wind data, discuss the ways in which wind speed and direction can be shown on a map. Wind speed and direction are usually marked on a weather map with a "wind barb" symbol that looks something like this:

The wind barb points in the direction from which the wind is blowing. The wind speed is shown by the number of lines coming off the main wind barb, with each full line representing 10 knots (1.9 kilometers per hour / 1.15 miles per hour) and a half line representing 5 knots (9.3 kilometers per hour / 5.8 miles per hour). The circle in the middle indicates cloud cover (open for clear skies, partly colored for partly cloudy, and all colored for cloudy skies). Thus the symbol illustrated shows wind blowing from the northeast at 15 knots, and 50 percent cloud cover. For this activity, it is recommended that you express wind speed in kilometers per hour or miles per hour to match the units in the chart that students use to interpret their wind meter readings. Thus students would use a full line to represent 10 kilometers (or 10 miles) per hour and a half line to represent 5 kilometers (or 5 miles) per hour.

6. Take the students outside to the school grounds, equipped with their wind meters, maps of the school ground, and pencils.

7. Ask each group to go to their assigned areas. At each location, have them take a reading of the wind speed and observe the wind direction, and then record this information in the appropriate locations on their maps.

8. When students return to the classroom, have them use the Wind Speed Conversion Table to convert their wind meter readings to kilometers per hour or miles per hour.

9. Have each team transfer its data to the large classroom map of the school grounds, using a wind barb to express the wind direction and speed at each location they tested.

10. Once all of the teams have entered their data on the class map, have the students complete their individual maps using wind barbs to indicate speed and direction at each location, and colored pencils to mark the locations with the greatest wind speeds.

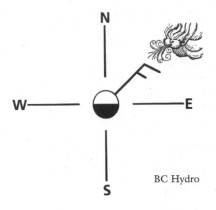

BC Hydro

A wind barb showing a wind of 15 knots blowing from the northeast, with 50 percent cloud cover.

Discussion questions:

1. In which location was the wind speed the greatest? the least? What might explain these differences?

2. For a wind turbine to make electricity, wind speed must be at least 13 kilometers per hour (8 miles per hour). According to your data, where on the school grounds could a wind generator be placed to make electricity? Explain your answer.

3. What are the limitations of the data that you collected in this activity? What other data would you need in order to be certain there is enough wind to generate electricity? Consider that a wind turbine would be 30 to 50 meters (100 to 165 feet) tall, and that its rotor (blades) would be about 47 meters (155 feet) in diameter. Also consider variations in wind speeds at different times of the day and in different seasons.

Extensions:

- Have students measure the wind speed at the same location on several different days or at different times during the same day. Graph the results and discuss any patterns that emerge.

- The Beaufort Wind Scale is another way that wind speed can be measured. Have students research the Beaufort Wind Scale and use it to measure wind speeds around the school. Are the results the same as in the wind speed meter activity?

- Have students find out how much electricity, in megawatt-hours, the school uses in a typical month during the school year. (One megawatt-hour equals 1,000 kilowatt-hours.) A small utility-scale wind turbine generates, on average, about 400 megawatt-hours per year. How many turbines would be needed to meet the school's monthly electricity demand? What factors would need to be taken into account in determining if wind generators would be feasible near the school? These can be economic (e.g., costs), environmental (e.g., amount of land required, positive and negative environmental impacts of wind generation), and social (e.g., safety for both humans and animals, such as migrating birds).

Jim Wiese is an author, educational advisor, and high school science teacher in Vancouver, British Columbia, who has won Teacher of the Year awards in both the United States and Canada.

These activities are adapted from material developed by Jim Wiese and published in Green Electricity Resources of British Columbia: Teaching materials for secondary school science and social studies, *BC Hydro, Vancouver, 2003; used with permission.*

Examining Values

Skid Crease

Living Within Earth's Means

Activities that help students separate wants from needs and develop a perspective on global disparities of wealth and resource use

by Barbara Duncan

Subject areas: social studies, consumer studies

Key concepts: basic human needs, wants versus needs, global disparities in wealth and opportunity

Skills: critical thinking, cooperative learning

A United Nations report in 1998 estimated that the richest fifth of humanity consumes 86 percent of all goods and services, while the poorest fifth consumes just 1.3 percent. Americans and Canadians consume much more than their share of the world's gasoline, paper, steel, aluminum, energy, water, and meat. This pattern of consumption is not sustainable, yet most North Americans don't know any other way to live. While "reduce, reuse, recycle" has become a familiar mantra over the past 25 years, the "reduce" part has been largely neglected because of the commonly held attitude that economic growth requires increased consumption of natural resources. Being a good citizen has evolved to mean being a good consumer, quite in contrast to the traditional definition of citizenship discussed in most civics classes.

Our failure to reduce consumption has also been exacerbated by our increasing urbanism. Fewer people than in the past have sufficient first-hand experience of nature to fully appreciate our dependence on natural resources; and few people are aware of the environmental cost of resource extraction, such as the clearcutting of forests, to feed our ever-growing appetite for wood and paper products. In addition, our culture of consumption is constantly reinforced by a bombardment of advertising. The Center for the Study of Commercialism reports, for example, that in the United States an individual's exposure to advertising averages one hour a day. Young people appear to be particularly susceptible to ads, as revealed by a 1995 Roper survey in which 93 percent of teenage girls named shopping as their favorite activity.

Helping students to evaluate their consumption and respond responsibly to commercialism in an increasingly wealthy society requires that teachers take particular care to be objective. Many parents' incomes are dependent on natural resource extraction or on people purchasing the goods produced by the companies they work for. In addition, frugality is no longer a common value in North American families. Instead, family attitudes vary along a spectrum from conspicuous to conscientious consumption: at one end is the attitude that "I've earned a good salary and I'll buy whatever I want"; at the other end is an environmental ethic, a belief that resources should be consumed in a sustainable manner.

Here in Vermont, the Vermont Earth Institute works with teachers to explore materialism and consumption with their students. We use a variety of curricula that help students to clarify wants and needs, and to develop a perspective on global disparities in resource use. Our goal is to help students define the components of sustainable living and the role of individuals in shaping a sustainable future. We hope that students will appreciate that the good life is more than having more stuff and more money. We also

Anna Payne-Krzyzanowski

Helping students to evaluate their consumption and respond responsibly to commercialism requires that teachers take particular care to be objective.

hope that they and their families will adopt sustainable lifestyles.

Among the many curricula that help teach about sustainable living, here are two of our favorite introductory activities. The first helps students differentiate between wants and needs; the second demonstrates global disparities of financial and natural resources, which, in turn, are linked to the ability of people to meet their basic needs. The material world offers countless enticements to young people. Activities such as these help them to realize that material goods are not the sole key to happiness, and that we must live within the means of this planet's natural resources, use them justly, and leave plenty for future generations.

What humans need

This exercise gives students an opportunity to make the distinction between basic human needs (e.g., oxygen, food, and education) and non-essentials (e.g., bottled shampoo, television, and cell phones). Having students adopt the perspective of someone in the less high-tech society of the early 1600s while ranking "wants" and "needs" helps them to appreciate the value of such basic needs as acceptance, fuel, and tools. It also helps to put a teen's desire for more CDs into perspective. It is interesting to follow students' ranking of needs and wants in the 1600s with a discussion of the value of these items in their lives. Items such as the car, computer, and telephone that had a low priority in the first ranking move up the list when the group turns to their everyday lives.

Time: 30 to 40 minutes

Materials: two 5" by 8" index cards per student

Preparation:

The 30 words below represent various needs and wants. Write the words on index cards, one word per card. Prepare one set of 30 cards for every 15 students (i.e., for 30 students, prepare two sets of 30 cards). If there are more than 30 students, add more words and cards so that there are two different cards for each student.

books	hot water	television
self-esteem	pets	clothes
shelter	shampoo	phone
heat	oxygen	fuel
electricity	health	acceptance
tools	air conditioning	computer
stereo	bike	medicine
bed	meat	refrigerator
education	car	toilet
food	friends	water

Having students make choices about "needs" is like having to choose what they'd like to have in their rooms: they will become very passionate.

Anna Payne-Krzyzanowski

Procedure:

1. Divide the class into two groups, each of which ideally should work around a large rectangular table.

2. Give two index cards to each student. Divide the long table into four sections marked "highest priority," "high priority," "low priority," and "lowest priority." Dividing the table in this way allows students, if needed, to create rows within any of these sections that more finely reflect their ranking of the importance of some needs and wants over others.

3. As a warm-up exercise, ask students to imagine that they are living somewhere on the planet in the year 1600. What would have been their most important needs and wants at that time?

4. Ask students who think they have cards that represent items of the highest priority to place them under the "highest priority" section. Allow a few moments for the group to peruse the placements made. Next, ask students who think they hold cards with items that are a "high priority" to place them in that section.

5. Continue these steps until all the cards have been placed in the four sections. There will be some obvious

low and lowest priority items, but students may feel that many needs vie with one another for the highest priority. While an item such as air conditioning would likely be deemed lowest priority — since electricity had yet to be invented in 1600 — this exercise helps students begin to separate basic needs from wants.

6. Ask students at each table to spend a minute examining the placements of the cards and then have them do a more complete ranking of the 30 items. With 15 people looking at 30 items simultaneously, the conversation may be a little chaotic. Having students make choices about needs is like having them choose what they'd like to have in their own rooms: they will become very passionate. Discussion is to be encouraged and will usually go somewhat like this:

Mark: Oh, we have "bed" higher than it needs to be.
Lisa: Well, it's important to have a place to sleep.
Joe: Doesn't it depend on what kind of bed we're talking about?
Jean: Yes, couldn't a bed be just a mat on the floor?
Lisa: Well, that's better than not having a bed.
Sue: I think we need to move "tools" up because they're needed to provide shelter.

7. Before their interest flags, allow each student to move one card up or down and give a short explanation in support of the move. This procedure allows everyone to have a say and mitigates the natural tendency for the most outspoken students to control the priorities. (Note that groups do not need to come to consensus; it is the process of prioritizing that is of value.)

8. Now ask students to rank the cards according to their personal (modern day) views of what are the highest and lowest priority needs and wants. Once again, allow each student to move one card up or down and give a short explanation in support of the move.

9. The group activity will take at least 20 minutes, which leaves time afterward for individual statements and discussion about current priorities.

Extensions:

- Ask older students to consider the contemporary trade-off between money and work: Is it better to work less and earn less, so as to have more time to enjoy life, or to work harder and longer to buy more stuff to be enjoyed in fewer available hours?

- Have students make a list of what they would take for a one-week backpacking trip, for which weight is a limiting factor. Ask them to rank the items according to their priorities.

- Have students make a list of what they need for a school day and then rank the items according to their priorities. Have them define how their lists might differ if they were students in a less wealthy country.

- Ask students to define how material and non-material needs are related: for instance, What makes them happy? What determines acceptance by others? What non-material needs can they think of (e.g., opportunities to learn, playing music, dancing, playing sports, spending time with friends)?

- Have students consider the role of advertising in creating a sense of need among possible buyers. What strategies are used by advertisers to create this sense of need for products?

Global resource bank

This activity builds on the previous one to help students appreciate the impact of global disparities of wealth, opportunity, and resources on the lives of most people around the world.

Time: 20 to 40 minutes

Materials: Human Needs credit cards (1 card per student; template provided); transparency of Global Resource Bank Menu (provided)

Preparation:

1. Prepare an overhead transparency of the Global Resource Bank Menu (page 144).

2. Use the template of Human Needs Credit Cards to prepare enough cards so that each student can receive one at the beginning of the activity. For a class of 30, you will need five 2-credit cards, twenty 10-credit cards, and five 25-credit cards. (If you make three copies of the template you will have more than enough of each). This distribution is roughly proportional to the distribution of resources worldwide, where one-sixth of the world is rich, one-half is very poor, and one-third are somewhere in between. Fold each card and place it in a container so that its value cannot be seen.

Procedure:

1. Ask each student to pick one card. Explain that the numbers 2, 10, or 25 on their cards represent the number of credits they have with which to purchase needs and wants from a Global Resource Bank.

2. Put the Global Resource Bank Menu transparency on an overhead projector. Clarify that students can select "luxury" items only after they have purchased their basic needs from the first four categories. Explain that, in this simulation, many will face choices similar to those faced each day by people around the world who do not have access to the conveniences enjoyed by most North Americans.

Anna Payne-Krzyzanowski

Human Needs Credit Cards

HUMAN NEEDS 2 credits	HUMAN NEEDS 10 credits	HUMAN NEEDS 10 credits
HUMAN NEEDS 2 credits	HUMAN NEEDS 10 credits	HUMAN NEEDS 10 credits
HUMAN NEEDS 25 credits	HUMAN NEEDS 10 credits	HUMAN NEEDS 10 credits
HUMAN NEEDS 25 credits	HUMAN NEEDS 10 credits	HUMAN NEEDS 10 credits
HUMAN NEEDS 10 credits	HUMAN NEEDS 10 credits	HUMAN NEEDS 10 credits

3. Ask students to make selections from each category of the Global Resource Bank Menu. They should write down their selections and the value of each, ensuring that they have enough credits to obtain those selections.

4. Once they have made their selections, ask two or three students with 2 credits to explain how they have chosen to spend their credits and why they chose as they did. Then ask students with 10 or 25 credits to explain their choices. You may want to seed the discussion with such questions as: Why might you want to avoid river water?

5. At the end of this activity, students who began with 10 or 25 credits may have a couple of credits left over. Students often raise the option of sharing those credits with those in need of them, a suggestion that can provoke a constructive discussion.

6. Lead a discussion about how students felt about their particular "lot in life." This is a good opportunity for a discussion about global disparities of wealth and opportunity. Students can examine how much is enough, whether they consider themselves well off, or the fairness of people's financial and environmental circumstances around the world.

Extensions:

- Ask students to consider the impact of their purchases on the environment. Do the purchases of those with more income tend to cause greater harm to the environment? Did the students consider their impact on the environment when they made their choices during the activity? (It is fair to conclude that all choices have an environmental impact, local or global, which is either negative or positive.)

- Referring to the What Humans Need activity, have students pick one of their needs and examine its environmental cost (e.g. production, transportation, disposal costs). There are good examples in *Stuff: The Secret Lives of Everyday Things* (see Resources).

- Locate maps or lists showing which

Anna Payne-Krzyzanowski

countries do and don't have the resources to meet the basic needs of their people. Choose two of the richer and two of the poorer countries, and research the main environmental problems in each of these countries. What similarities are there in the problems faced by the two richer countries? What similarities are found between the two poorer countries? What are the differences and similarities in environmental problems faced by the richer and poorer countries?

- Have students search for international stories in newspapers and magazines that describe the challenges in meeting basic human needs. Have students identify the needs and the challenges faced in meeting them.

Barbara Duncan is the Director of the Vermont Earth Institute in Norwich, Vermont.

"What Humans Need" and "Global Resource Bank" are adapted from Population Reference Bureau's Adventures on Earth *curriculum (see Resources below).*

Global Resource Bank Menu

Food

- Largely vegetarian diet, mostly home grown or from local sources (1 credit)
- Vegetarian diet with occasional meat from local sources (2 credits)
- Varied diets with foods from distant places; e.g., oranges in winter (6 credits)

Water

- Transported in buckets from a river (no monetary cost)
- Untreated well water 1 credit)
- Treated water (3 credits)
- Indoor plumbing with hot water (5 credits)

Energy

- Fuelwood from nearby forest (no monetary cost)
- Coal (2 credits)
- Oil (3 credits)
- Solar energy (8 credits)

Transportation

- Walking (no monetary cost)
- Public transportation/ bicycle (1 credit)
- Small, fuel-efficient car (6 credit)
- Sport utility vehicle (10 credits)

Luxury

- Radio (1 credit)
- Television (3 credits)
- Refrigerator (8 credits)
- Air conditioning (10 credits)

RESOURCES

Curricula

Center for a New American Dream. "Living in a Material World: Lessons on Commercialism, Consumption, and Environment," excerpt on-line at <www.newdream.org/discuss/living.html>.

Population Connection. "If Money Won't Buy It," activity in *People and the Planet: Lessons for a Sustainable World* middle school curriculum. Order on-line at <www.populationconnection.org> or by calling 800-POP-1956.

Population Connection. "Needs vs. Wants," activity in *A World of Six Billion Activity Guide.* Downloadable from <www.populationconnection.org>.

Population Reference Bureau. *Adventures on Earth: Exploring our Global Links,* 1997. Downloadable from <http://www.prb.org/pdf/aoe_lesson1.pdf>.

Videos

Affluenza. A humorous 56-minute PBS video, with mini-curriculum, on consumption and commercialism. Available from Bullfrog Films, 800-543-3764, <www.bullfrogfilms.com>.

The Cost of Cool. A 26-minute video, with mini-curriculum, on teenage consumerism. Available from The Video Project, 800-475-2638, <www.videoproject.net>.

Books

Brower, Michael, and Warren Leon. *The Consumer's Guide to Effective Environmental Choices: Practical Advice from the Union of Concerned Scientists.* Three Rivers Press, 1999.

Menzel, Peter. *Material World: A Global Family Portrait.* Sierra Club Books, 1994.

New Road Map Foundation. "All Consuming Passion: Waking Up From the American Dream." A 24-page pamphlet containing statistics on consumption. Available from The Simple Living Network, 800-318-5725, <www.simpleliving.net>.

Ryan, John, and Alan T. Durning. *Stuff: The Secret Lives of Everyday Things.* Northwest Environment Watch, 1997. Available from Northwest Environment Watch, 1402 Third Ave., Suite 500, Seattle, WA 98101, <www.northwestwatch.org>.

Anna Payne-Krzyzanowski

All Species Projects

*Using art, drama, and pageantry to build a sense of community
and a rapport with other species*

by Marty Kraft

Subject areas: art, science, anthropology, drama

Key concepts: biodiversity, consensus building, perspective

Skills: mask making, dramatic skills, negotiation

Location: indoors and outdoors

Time: 1 week to 2 months

Materials: student journals, research tools, mask, costume, and float-making materials

In *The Practice of the Wild*, Gary Snyder tells of riding in a pickup truck in Australia with an Aboriginal man. As they traveled along, the man was telling stories at an amazing pace — too fast for them to be told properly. Wondering why he would do such a thing, Snyder learned that the man's people remember and teach their ancient culture and relationship to the land as they move through the bush. Each feature of the landscape relates to a specific story or part of a story. At the speed of a moving pickup, the stories had to be told faster.

What does this say about the relationship between this man, his people, and the land that they inhabit — or that inhabits them? In North America, perhaps only aboriginal people can truly appreciate the significance of this relationship. Most of the rest of us have become disconnected from humanity's tribal community beginnings and multigenerational connections to land. Our children now grow up with television, the Internet, and games that offer electronic representations of reality. Walking outdoors, they see mostly asphalt, monocultural lawn, and ornamental shrubs — substitutes for rock outcrops, forest, or prairie. How can they form a relationship with something they rarely encounter?

Following the 2002 All Species Parade in Santa Fe, New Mexico, the "Ravens in the Genetic Corn" theatrical production drew attention to concerns about genetically-modified corn.

The systems we have developed to supply our basic needs further disconnect us from land. We flick a light switch and see the apparent consequence of our action. What we don't see is, for example, the strip mining of coal, the railroad cars, the mercury entering the atmosphere from a smokestack, the dumping of ash. These are also consequences of flicking that light switch.

All Species Projects offer a way to strengthen our connection with the Earth by making the needs of plants, animals — and the planet as a whole — more apparent to the human community. The idea was conceived in 1978 in San Francisco and further developed into an educational program for schools and community groups by Chris Wells, who had studied festival development and tribal celebrations in South America, and teachers John McLeod and Marty Kraft. The project invites students to adopt a favorite species and take on the role of that creature in activities that explore relationships and celebrate diversity. All Species Projects thereby make use of a powerful tool — children's innate rapport with other creatures — to help them come to understand community and to connect with nature.

Choosing a creature

Start by having each student select an animal, plant, or other part of nature to represent. Most will choose mammals and birds, but some might choose a tree, a dragonfly, or even an entire ecosystem such as a prairie or forest. Encourage the class to select a broad range of species, as this will give opportunities for learning about the dynamics within natural communities. Or, to gain a greater appreciation for the land where they live, encourage them to choose species from their own bioregion. If a student chooses an exotic creature such as a lion or gazelle, suggest that another student choose a related native species. The class can then study the similarities and differences between the distant and local species, and learn how each has adapted to its environment.

To help students identify with the species they select for study, read them the following (or paraphrase it in your own words):

> You may think of yourself as a person who is separate from others and from the rest of the world. While this is true in one way, thinking about yourself as part of nature might be just as true. Observing your own breathing is one of the best ways to recognize that each of us is part of nature. When you breathe in, you are breathing in some of the breath of everyone in this room — and of everyone and every creature that has ever breathed in this planet's atmosphere. You are also inhaling oxygen produced by a plant somewhere on Earth and exhaling carbon dioxide that can be used by a plant or a tree or, perhaps, plankton in a distant ocean.

Invite students to suggest other ways in which they are linked to all other organisms.

Have students research the creature they have selected and keep a journal to which they add newspaper articles, observation notes, haiku or other poems, raps, drawings, and facts about their chosen creature. To learn how their creatures move, students could find and watch relevant clips on film or websites; alternatively, you could take them to observe creatures on a field trip or in a zoo. Have them consider how it would feel to move like their creature, and whether that would help them to know more about that animal. Students can strengthen their rapport through these observations.

All species congress

When they have some knowledge about their creatures, have students form a creature congress or council of species to vote on a hypothetical human-initiated proposal that would affect them. Examples of proposals are:

- building a dam on a river
- trapping raccoons, squirrels, and coyotes and releasing them a long way from their city habitats
- cutting down trees at the edge of a town to build a large store

Chris Wells

Condors in an All Species theater production in Cayambe, Ecuador.

- poisoning prairie dogs, regarded as a nuisance by cattle farmers
- crossbreeding farm-raised salmon with wild salmon
- reintroducing wolves to a national park between mountains and prairie

Many other issues could be discussed; the key is to find a local or international issue that students find interesting. Through their own observations and information gathering on their selected creatures, students themselves might suggest good issues. Alternatively, local environmental groups and public officials may be able to suggest current local issues and provide the class with background information that will help them to develop their perspectives and clear away rhetoric.

In a class of 25 students, 22 could play the role of creatures and 3 could be humans. Invite students to devise the voting system beforehand. Encourage them to examine various systems, and remind them not to overlook consensus building, as they could learn much in the struggle to find unity, even when it seems to elude them. As the congress discusses the proposal before them, each member speaks in turn from the perspective of his/her creature. Typically, when it comes time for the creatures to vote, the results are rather different from conventional decisions made from a wholly human perspective.

Dramatic skits

As the students become comfortable in their roles, they could begin writing and performing short skits on environmental problems faced by their creatures.

1. Brainstorm to generate a number of topics.
2. Divide the class into groups of four to five students to ensure a mix of species, and have each group choose a topic to present as a skit.
3. Give each group ten minutes to create and prepare a skit to present to the rest of the class. Emphasize that it is quick thinking and creativity that is called for, not perfection. Often, students who have not done well at other activities shine here.
4. Have the groups present the skits in quick succession, and then lead a discussion. You might be surprised at the insight and wisdom that emerges. Once

Making masks, headdresses, and costumes to represent their chosen creature reinforces emotional ties and leads students to want to know more about their species.

students are familiar with this process, they may wish to repeat it using different topics.

Making masks and costumes

A very powerful way to foster students' rapport with their chosen creatures is to have them make masks and costumes to represent them. Mask making is a nearly universal human activity. Masks are used in celebrations all over the world — from Halloween in North America to New Year's celebrations throughout Asia to Carnival in Latin America. Making masks, headdresses, and costumes to represent their chosen creature reinforces emotional ties and leads students to want to know more about their species. It can also be part of preparations for an All Species Parade (page 148) in celebration of Earth Day.

Plaster-cast tape mask

Materials: Roll of plaster-impregnated gauze tape (from pharmacies and art supply stores) cut into strips about 3 x 10 centimeters (1 x 4 inches), petroleum jelly, bowl, warm water, scissors, paint, elastic string, headbands and old sheets for protecting hair and clothes.

Procedure:

1. Have students work in pairs. First, one partner smears the other's face with petroleum jelly so that the plaster will not pull hairs.

2. Dip plaster strips in warm water just long enough to wet them. Apply them to the greased areas of the face, with the plaster side facing outward. Spread the excess plaster to smooth and fill in holes in the gauze. Overlap the material well and build up about three layers.

3. Let the plaster dry for 15 to 20 minutes.

4. Pull the plaster mask off carefully, starting at the edges. Do not get petroleum jelly on the front of the plaster where paint and features will be added. Use crumpled newspaper to support the masks and set them aside for a day to finish drying.

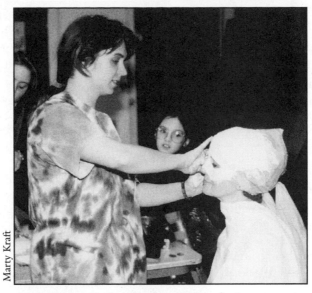

Art instructor Linda Wheeler applies plaster-gauze tape.

After completing their basic masks, students add horns, feathers, and beaks.

5. The next day, students can add ears, horns, or other features by building up layers of plaster tape over bases made of cardboard that are shaped as needed. Students could also add felt or other fabric, hot-gluing it in place. (An art teacher could help students with ideas and material choices.) Wherever possible, encourage the use of scrap materials.

6. When the masks are completely dry, students can seal the plaster with a primer such as Gesso and then paint them. I prefer to use latex paint, as it dries quickly and is waterproof (essential for an outdoor parade or other celebration). An art teacher can recommend paint products.

7. To hold the masks on, bore a small hole with the point of a pair of scissors on either side of the mask and thread a string of elastic through the holes.

Baseball cap headdress

This cardboard and papier mâché headdress uses a baseball cap as a base. It can be made without a cap, but the bill of the cap is useful: it can be cut to a desired shape, and it can be worn reversed so that the flap is at the back, or worn frontward to provide a built-in feature — like a beak — that is appropriate for the species.

Materials: Bristol board or other lightweight cardboard, baseball cap, stapler, tape, scissors, paper and paste for papier mâché, paint

Procedure:

1. Have students work in pairs. First, cut strips of cardboard of a variety of widths from about 1.5 to 5 centimeters (½ to 2 inches).

2. With the cap on the head, place a band of cardboard around the outside of the head and cap to form an exterior hatband. Overlap the ends of the band

slightly and mark where they meet.

3. Remove the cap and staple or tape the cardboard band firmly along the overlapped edges, as well as to the cap itself. To this hatband, staple, tape, or glue other strips of cardboard to create a basket that fits over the head.

4. Over several days, students can mold the features of the chosen species from papier mâché and attach it to the basket frame. Materials such as fake fur, feathers, and fabrics can also be incorporated. Some students might mold the entire body of their animal on the headdress, while others create only the form of the animal's head.

5. When the headdress is completely dry, it can be painted with latex or other waterproof paint.

Costumes

A costume can be designed to communicate what the species is or to suggest the environment in which it lives. Instead of a mask, some students might make a headdress of an entire animal, say a fish, and wear a costume with blue-green fabric to suggest water. Other costumes might attempt to create the body of the creature. Pieces of corrugated cardboard can be cut and placed under a costume to create the shape of a certain creature feature. Old clothes could be dyed or have pieces of fabric sewn on to complete an effect. Hospital or hotel laundries often have old sheets that they might donate for students to dye, cut, and sew. Fabric paint, available in many colors, can be used to create patterns on cloth that is difficult to dye. The ideas that students might generate in making costumes are endless, so encourage creative thought and trial runs.

All Species Parade

A parade, perhaps for Earth Day or some other celebration, is an

A culminating pageant such as an All Species Parade is a means of celebrating the relationships that promote our survival and of reminding ourselves of the values we share with fellow humans.

Heartland All Species Project

Heartland All Species Project

A fish joins in an Earth Day parade in Kansas City.

appropriate culminating activity for All Species Projects. Spring is a natural time to celebrate, just as plants and animals are re-emerging from winter dormancy or arriving back from their wintering grounds. The parade route can be around the halls of the school, it can be outside around the neighborhood, or students can participate in — or organize — a larger community event. Most communities do not require a permit if students stay on the sidewalk and you have monitors at corners. If the whole school gets behind the parade and wants a community event, then check local regulations before your planning gets too advanced; you may have to ask for official guidance.

Discuss with students possible parade entries and perhaps having a theme — for instance, having the sun go first, followed by plants, then herbivores, and finally carnivores as a linear model of energy consumption. Another approach is to replicate where organisms occur in the environment, with soil creatures and plants at street level, animals on the base of a float, and birds at a higher level on the float. A simple float can be built onto a child's wagon to represent an environment such as a prairie, a forest, or a coral reef. On the wagon place a lightweight frame made from used one-by-two lumber in the shape needed. Secure pieces of corrugated cardboard and fabric and color them with latex paint. (Tempera paint will run if it gets wet.) If you have funds, you can buy quarts of white, black, red, blue, and yellow paint to mix almost any color students might need. If the list of parade entries is short, consider including some short skits to be performed at intervals. Any way that students wish to organize the parade can promote learning and build rapport. Celebrations like these have been educating people in villages worldwide for thousands of years.

All Species events are very popular and photogenic, so be sure to invite local media to reach community members who cannot attend. Students could create and send media releases. By hosting or participating in a large community event, students receive public approval for their efforts. Beyond grades, they have an opportunity to communicate about issues they come to believe are important.

Until the advent of Earth Day in 1970, modern society had no celebration to strengthen our connection with the Earth. A culminating pageant such as an All Species Parade is a means of celebrating the relationships that promote our survival and of reminding ourselves of the values we share with fellow humans. Such events create community that does more than supply basic needs: if we choose, these activities can create neighborhoods that are friendly, supportive, and sustainable.

Building rapport with nature

In learning about nature, it is more important to know the relationship between the facts than to know the facts themselves. By building rapport with nature through All Species Projects, students are better able to shift their perception and take a larger view of the Earth, seeing it as a web of relationships and communities rather than a collection of isolated parts. By "becoming" their animals, they move from a self-centered perspective to one that includes other viewpoints. From there, you can help them look at the power of diversity. Start by considering how biological diversity helps every species to survive. Once the benefits of biodiversity are understood, students can consider the advantages of other kinds of diversity, such as economic diversity in hard times. It is a short step then for students to appreciate the advantages of cooperative relationships and cultural diversity.

The amount of time that is spent on these activities is up to each teacher: it could be one or two weeks, or it could be months with students doing a few activities a week. Some activities can be used alone. It would be wonderful, however, to transform an All Species Project into a total integrated curriculum touching on art, science, math, language arts, social studies, and other subjects. Like all good education, the All Species process is designed to educate the whole child and to foster a vision of a human society that is integrated seamlessly into the environment. Rather than being about filling a

Heartland All Species Project

human computer with thoughts, it is about engaging the whole person in a dynamic conversation with the world. It is about *being* a part of the whole, not about sitting apart and studying it. It is about us two-leggeds living in community with the wings, fins, four-leggeds, crawlers, and rooted folk.

Marty Kraft, a former science teacher, is co-founder and director of the Heartland All Species Project in Kansas City, Missouri, where he has organized eight citywide Earth Day celebrations. His efforts focus on promoting neighborhood gardens and other models of sustainable living. His 120-page study and activity guide Earth Day in Your School and Community: A Guide for Study and Celebration Creation *can be obtained from The Heartland All Species Project (5644 Charlotte, Kansas City, MI 64110, 816–361–1230) for US$15 plus $5 shipping ($7 to Canada). Marty Kraft, Stan Slaughter, and Chris Wells are available to help schools and communities implement All Species projects and perspectives.*

From Child Rights to Earth Rights

An activity to help develop students' concept of rights and responsibilities

by Alanda Greene

Subject areas: social studies, language arts, drama

Key concepts: rights and responsibilities

Skills: speaking, listening, brainstorming, summarizing, cooperative learning, comparison, evaluation

Location: mainly indoors

Time: see activities below

Materials: see activities below

The words "rights" and "responsibilities" are used often, and since they are spoken so frequently it is assumed that they are clearly and consensually understood. Yet demanding rights for oneself often means "Leave me alone to do what I want," while demanding responsibility from others often means "Don't be lazy, or unpredictable, or something other than what I want you to be." Such misuses result in many negative associations and, by narrowing the meaning of the words, make it difficult to extend the concept of rights and responsibilities beyond the personal realm. The activities below are designed to broaden students' understanding of rights

> *As we become more aware of the intimate connection between person and planet, our concept of rights and responsibilities must grow to reflect this connection.*

and responsibilities, starting with their personal experience and knowledge, and then building to a wider perspective that includes the entire Earth. As we become more aware of the intimate connection between person and planet, our concept of rights and responsibilities must grow to reflect this connection. Once students understand what rights and responsibilities mean on a personal level, they can begin to apply this understanding to the wider concept of human rights and, wider still, "Earth rights."

Some of the activities offer students an opportunity to express ideas non-verbally through music, art, or drama. Such activities add an important dimension to learning. By engaging many areas of the brain, they increase students' involvement and allow concepts to be internalized, not just intellectualized.

The activities include both individual and group work, and presuppose that students have certain skills of working cooperatively in groups. Before beginning, it will be helpful to review group skills, such as offering ideas, staying with the group, actively participating, listening to one another, speaking kindly, and building trust. A review of the ground rules of the brainstorming process might also be helpful: all

Anna Payne-Krzyzanowski

ideas are accepted, no ideas are criticized, ideas can be repeated, ideas that are similar or close can be offered again as one idea stimulates another, ideas are not edited or analyzed until later.

The time allotments for the activities will vary with class size and students' past experience, grade, skills, prior knowledge, and unique qualities. The topics for personal reflection allow some variability in timing to be absorbed, and can also be used for group discussion.

Personal Declaration of Rights

Time: 20 to 30 minutes

Procedure:

1. Ask students, working individually, to list examples of what they consider to be their rights (3–5 minutes).

2. Divide the class into groups of 3 to 5 students and have each group choose a recorder and reporter. Ask each group to brainstorm to create a list of what they believe to be their rights, while the recorder records the ideas (5–10 minutes).

3. Ask the reporters to read the brainstorming list aloud to the others in their group. Then ask each group to select the ten most important rights on their list. Some ideas may be grouped under a single heading; for example, "the right to not let my little brother use my bike" and "the right to not have my books stolen when I leave them in my desk" may be grouped as "the right to have my own property." Many other summary groupings are possible and probable. The goal is for members of the group to agree on a list of ten, which becomes "Our Group's Declaration of Rights" (10–15 minutes).

4. Have a reporter from each group read the group's list aloud to the class (3–4 minutes).

Wrap-up: Have students reflect on the activity by recording in their journals what they personally consider to be the most important right and giving their reasons for selecting that right (3–5 minutes).

UN Declaration of the Rights of the Child

Like the Universal Declaration of Human Rights, the United Nations Declaration of the Rights of the Child is a significant document that has been ratified by the governments of all members of the United Nations. Even though abuses and negligence of the rights laid out in them are rampant, these documents give reference points or agreed standards to which actions and omissions may be compared. Having the opportunity to examine the Declaration of the Rights of the Child and compare it to their own declaration contributes to students' deeper understanding of the concept of rights.

Materials: copy of the Principles of the United Nations Declaration of the Rights of the Child (1 per group); paper and pencil for recorder

Time: 20 to 30 minutes

Procedure:

1. Have students work in the same groups as for the previous activity, but ask each group to choose a different recorder and reporter.

2. Ask students to read the United Nations Declaration of the Rights of the Child.

3. Explain that each group is to compare the United Nations Declaration to their own group's declaration of rights from the previous activity. As a group, they are to determine which rights, if any, appear in both documents; which ones on their list are missing from the United Nations Declaration; and which ones in the United Nations Declaration are missing from the group's list (8–10 minutes).

Principles of the United Nations Declaration of the Rights of the Child

- The right to affection, love and understanding.
- The right to adequate nutrition and medical care.
- The right to free education.
- The right to full opportunity for play and recreation.
- The right to a name and nationality.
- The right to special care if handicapped.
- The right to be a useful member of society and to develop individual abilities.
- The right to be brought up in a spirit of peace and universal brotherhood.
- The right to enjoy these rights, regardless of race, color, sex, religion, and national or social origin.

— Based on the United Nations Declaration of the Rights of the Child, 1959, full text at www.kidsrights.org/UNDeclaration.htm.

4. Next, ask students to discuss and record what changes they would make in either document (5 minutes).

5. Ask the reporters to read aloud to the class their group's responses for each category (5 minutes).

Wrap-up: For personal reflection, ask students to decide which three rights from the United Nations Declaration they would keep if they had to eliminate all but three, and to explain in their journals why these are the most important to them (5–10 minutes).

Note: This personal reflection could be a group activity. Ask students to cut out each of the rights in the United Nations Declaration and arrange them with the most important right at the top and least important at the bottom. The value of this exercise is in the discussion among group members in the process of reaching consensus.

"I have a right ... I have responsibility"

This is a good time to use the song "I Have a Right" (page 153), which includes the major ideas of the United Nations Declaration of the Rights of the Child. The song's lyrics may also be used as a poem. In learning and singing or reciting the lyrics of the song, students absorb the ideas about children's rights in another way.

Materials: copies of the song "I Have a Right," recording material for each student (journal, notebook), newspapers, magazines, copies of Principles of the United Nations Declaration of the Rights of the Child

Time: 60 to 80 minutes

Procedure:

1. Give each student a copy of the song "I Have a Right."

2. As a class, sing or recite the song, perhaps assigning each verse to a different group (10–15 minutes, or more, depending on how you choose to work with the song; if instruments are available, for example, rhythm accompaniment is easily incorporated).

3. As a class or in small groups, have students determine the correspondence between the lines of the song and the rights listed in the United Nations Declaration of the Rights of the Child (5 minutes).

4. As a class, brainstorm examples of rights that belong to everyone class, as members of a family, group, or nation. Record these on a board (5 minutes).

5. Explain that rights come with responsibilities, and offer examples. If, for example, we

have a right to personal property, then we have a responsibility not to steal the property of others or take things without asking. If we have a right to feel safe, we have a responsibility to avoid behavior that threatens the safety of others (e.g., bullying, teasing, name-calling, or intimidating).

6. Have students, working individually, fold a piece of paper vertically to produce two columns. Ask them to title the left column "This is a right that I have" and to record rights that they believe they have in that column. Have them title the right column "This is a responsibility that goes with my right," and opposite each right listed, record a corresponding responsibility (10-15 minutes).

7. Ask students to reconvene in their groups to share their lists; they can add to their personal lists as ideas are stimulated by others (3–5 minutes).

8. Have each group search newspapers and magazines for stories that show an abuse or violation of one or more of the rights listed in the United Nations Declaration, and identify which right was violated. Have them summarize and share this information with the class (15–20 minutes).

Note: This assignment could be homework and the search expanded to include the library, television programs, or the Internet. Each student's results could then be shared with the class, perhaps through a bulletin board, an oral presentation or a handout, or in the form of a press release.

Anna Payne-Krzyzanowski

I Have a Right

Music and lyrics by Alanda Greene

Wrap-up: For personal reflection, ask students to describe in their journals an occasion when they personally have not respected the rights of someone else. What was the outcome? How could they have acted differently? (3–5 minutes).

Extension Hold a circle discussion, offering students a chance to tell of a time when they personally experienced a violation of their rights and how they felt about it. When exploring this topic, ask students to focus on the event and action and avoid naming particular persons. Remind students that speaking is voluntary but everyone has the right to a turn; that they must listen to each speaker, speak one at a time, keep what's said in the circle within the circle, and avoid distractions, put-downs, gossip, and probing of comments made.

Note: If you have students in your class who have suffered abuse, this discussion may not be appropriate (10–15 minutes).

Earth Rights

Students have now examined the United Nations Declaration of the Rights of the Child and have explored thoughts and feelings about rights and responsibilities. This examination provides a context from which to consider human rights and responsibilities in relation to the Earth.

Note: This activity presupposes that students are familiar with role-play (i.e., use of space, focus on task, sustaining a role). Before this activity, you could review these skills.

Time: 60 to 90 minutes

Materials: posted Declaration, paper, pencils, felt pens

Procedure:

1. Ask students to work in pairs and explain that each pair is to assume the role of "ambassadors" or representatives of some element of the biosphere other than humans. They could represent water (or rivers, or lakes, or oceans); animals (birds, mammals, insects, reptiles, or a specific creature); trees, grasses, flowers, cacti, mountains, wind, air.

2. Ask each pair of students to develop a list of what they consider to be the rights of the element, plant, or creature they represent. (As examples, water might have the right to be clean and unpolluted, an animal might have the right to wilderness or a habitat.)

3. After a few minutes of discussion, ask each pair of ambassadors to meet with another pair and state their position; that is, introduce themselves and tell the other pair of one right that they feel should be protected, and why. (The idea is to share their ideas, not debate them.) When both pairs have exchanged ideas, ask them to separate and move on to meet different pairs. Continue until all pairs have met (8-10 minutes).

4. Have students work again in their groups (or as a class), to brainstorm environmental problems and what Earth Rights they might violate. (As an example, air pollution might contravene the Earth's right to a clean atmosphere.) Have students analyze their lists to determine the ten most important rights that the Earth might have. This becomes the group's "Declaration of Earth Rights" (10–15 minutes).

Note: During this process, direct students' attention to the possibility that abuses of the Earth could lead to the creation of a universal document like the one they are developing, just as abuses of children led to the formation of the United Nations Declaration of the Rights of the Child. As such, students need to focus on the most important rights.

5. Ask each group to share its declaration with the class. Then offer students the opportunity to revise their choices, either in their groups or as a class. The final selection of ten rights can then be recorded on a large sheet of paper and posted in the classroom as the entire class's "Declaration of Earth Rights" (10 minutes). Alternatively, each student could select one of the Earth Rights to use as the theme for a poster, and all of the posters could be displayed by theme.

Wrap-up: For personal reflection, ask each student which of the Earth Rights they think the Earth would feel are being most abused. Have them explain in their journals what responsibility they personally have in relation to the Earth (5 minutes).

Alanda Greene is the author of Rights to Responsibility: Multiple Approaches to Developing Character and Community *(Zephyr Press, 1997). Now retired from teaching, she lives in Crawford Bay, British Columbia.*

Anna Payne-Krzyzanowski

Where Do You Stand?

An activity that encourages open-mindedness and demonstrates the wide range of views on any controversial topic

by Alanda Greene

Subject areas: language arts, social studies, environmental studies

Key concepts: Thoughtful decision making requires being open to other points of view and adjusting one's position when new information is acquired

Skills: listening, speaking, evaluating, decision making

Location: large open space

Time: 10-15 minutes per scenario below

Materials: masking tape or string

Most of us grew up with considerable exposure to television and movie screens that repeatedly offered us models of the strong individual who always knew right from wrong, defended the good and punished the bad, and never wavered in knowing which was which. Such models supported a common human tendency to divide the world into opposing camps: believers and infidels, enlightened and ignorant, righteous and heathen, friend and enemy, worthy and unworthy. There's a sense of security in knowing what's right, and integrity in taking a stand for it. But the black and white world of old westerns and war movies does not offer effective strategies for meeting the challenges of a complex real world. Polarized thinking only exaggerates divisions between people, supporting conflict, exclusion, and hatred. Just consider how those bad guys were treated, and their treatment justified, by the good guy heroes.

Situations in which there is no clear right or wrong are far more common in life than those in which a simple yes or no will serve; yet students have little opportunity to explore this in school. Discussions and debates tend instead to give practice in choosing a position and defending it all the way to victory or defeat. How can this for-or-against attitude encourage students to be flexible and to listen to and respond to the ideas and wisdom of others? The skills of the peacemaker, consensus builder,

> *The skills of the peacemaker, consensus builder, mediator, and problem solver are the ones most needed in today's world.*

The real world is never this black and white: polarized thinking exaggerates divisions between people.

Alanda Greene

mediator, and problem solver are the ones most needed in today's world. These skills include the ability to see many possibilities, to be flexible, and to include others. If we value these skills, we must give young people opportunities to learn them.

The activity Where Do You Stand? allows students to explore the gray areas that lie between black and white polar opposites of an issue. It asks each person to find a place on the continuum between absolute agreement with a position and absolute disagreement. While everyone must take a position, the activity does not ask participants to defend territory or try to convince others that they are right. Rather, its salient feature is recognition of the knowledge, opinions, attitudes, and values supporting various positions. This emerges as people discuss their current position and the reasons they chose it.

Students whose stands are based on poor information or reasoning are not considered wishy-washy if they change their positions after listening to others; rather, they are encouraged to recognize that this is what responsible, open-minded, thoughtful, learning people do as they acquire more information. Thus, the activity encourages an open mind and a willingness to change as a result of learning and listening. The activity can be used at many levels, from primary to secondary, and requires involvement from everyone in the group. Even though some participants may not express an idea, they must choose a place to stand. Because at any given moment the range of opinions on an issue is visible, students can develop an appreciation for the spectrum of possible views.

Where Do You Stand? shows students that many issues are complex, that there are no easy answers, and that black and white thinking does not reflect the complexities inherent in many of the problems facing us. Learning to be flexible, open, and responsive is what this activity is designed for, and it does not depend on students' having any special expertise on an issue. Used at the beginning of a unit, it may stimulate further research, writing, and discussion. Repeated at the end of a unit, it can assess what the students have learned over a period

Gail Littlejohn

of time and how their views have changed as a result of their learning.

Procedure:

1. In a space large enough to accommodate the group, designate one end as "Totally Agree" and the other as "Totally Disagree." Connect these opposite poles by marking a line on the floor with masking tape or string to represent the continuum of positions that lies between them.

2. Read an issue scenario aloud (see examples below), perhaps twice if needed.

3. Ask students to stand at one end or anywhere along the tape or string to reflect their position or opinion on the issue.

4. Once everyone is in place, ask each student in turn to explain why he/she decided to stand in that place. Encourage students to respond to opinions, reasoning, or ideas expressed by others but do not allow attacking of another student's choice. Explain that they are free to adjust their positions when they hear ideas they had not previously considered.

Sample issue scenarios

These issue scenarios are summaries of actual situations. Once students are familiar with this activity, they can develop their own scenarios based on issues that interest them or on current controversies reported in the media.

Wolves and cattle

Wolves are natural inhabitants of Yellowstone National Park in Montana and Wyoming, but human predation killed off all wolves in the region in the 1900s. After many years of hard work, environmental groups have convinced the government to release a group of wolves into the park to re-establish a wolf population.

Sara, who works for Wolves in the Wild, says that wolves must return to these wild areas because they are an important part of the ecosystem and will help to restore the natural population balance of many wildlife species. "We destroyed these animals in what was their natural habitat. It's only right that we return them to it. It isn't the same country without the wolves."

Hank is a rancher who points out that wolves don't know about park boundaries and there's no way to protect his cattle from them. "They're as happy to bring down a heifer as they are to kill a whitetail. I shouldn't have to have my cattle's lives threatened. This is now, not 40 years ago: the wolves are gone; let them stay away. I have to make a living."

Question: Where do you stand on the question of introducing wolves back into the park (Sara's position)?

Logging the frontier forests

A major international study recently rcvcalcd that only about one-fifth of the world's wild forests, called frontier forests, remain on the planet. The study determined that all the frontier forests have been eliminated in Africa and the Middle East, and nearly all are gone from Europe. In the temperate climate zone, which includes Canada and the continental United States, about three percent of the frontier forests remain.

Carla, who works with an environmental group in the Pacific Northwest, wants all logging in these forests to stop. The group says that these wild natural forests need protection because they are home to many species of plants and animals that can live only in these environments. Carla maintains, "So many forests have been destroyed. We want to keep what remains, not remove it. Too much has already gone."

Ali works for a logging company that plans to clear-cut some areas of a frontier forest in the coming months. She claims that the best timber is located in these forests and that loggers have a right to take some of it. "Our company is just as entitled to use these forests as are other people and animals. We should be able to take a share of this timber. We need to make a living."

Question: Where do you stand on stopping the logging of this frontier forest (Carla's view)?

Whales and jobs

In the coastal waters of Mexico there is a small bay, isolated and protected. For as long as anyone remembers, gray whales have gone there when it is time to give

Gail Littlejohn

birth. The warm, sheltered bay is an ideal place for young calves and their mothers to rest until they are strong enough to return to the open waters of the Pacific Ocean. Without such a place of safety, many of the newborn calves would likely die in the first weeks of life.

A large company has plans to build a factory in the bay that will extract salt from ocean water. This will drive the whales away. A group of people has organized to protest the building of the factory, saying that the whales have a right to this bay where they can safely have their calves. Others want the factory to be built because it will provide jobs and bring money to the region. The area is quite poor and many families from the nearby village would find employment in the factory.

Question: Where do you stand on building a salt factory in this bay?

Fish now or later?

Allan has made a living for himself and his family for the last 20 years by salmon fishing on the west coast. Anticipating greater expenses as his three children enter high school, he recently purchased a larger fishing boat. The payments on the boat are high, but with it Allan can bring in more salmon.

Allan's neighbor Doug is a government marine scientist who has been studying salmon populations for the past ten years. He supports a large reduction in the number of salmon allowed to be caught each year. He says, "Salmon stocks once had huge populations, but every year fewer and fewer are returning to spawn in rivers. Already, 142 salmon stocks are extinct and 624 salmon stocks are in danger of extinction. It is urgent that fishing be cut back."

"I can't cut back," replies Allan. "I have to make payments on my boat and I have a family to support. Keep the rivers in better shape so the salmon that return and spawn will have a higher number of offspring that survive. Don't make me and my family suffer."

Doug replies by saying, "If we don't act now, there won't be any fish left in a few years, and no one will have a job in the salmon industry. Look what happened to the cod stocks on the east coast."

"There are still lots of fish out there," answers Allan, "and I expect to be able to catch my fair share. How else can I pay for this boat and earn a living?"

Question: Where do you stand on not cutting back on salmon fishing (Allan's position)?

Alanda Greene is the author of Rights to Responsibility: Multiple Approaches to Developing Character and Community *(Zephyr Press, 1997). Now retired from teaching, she lives in Crawford Bay, British Columbia.*

Superheroes:
From Fiction to Reality

*Children's natural fascination with heroes can be channeled
toward values and actions needed to solve global problems*

by Ron Ballentine, Al Finlayson, and Sharon Laivenieks

Subject areas: language arts, visual arts, drama, social studies, science and technology

Key concepts: adaptation, biodiversity, compromise, conflict resolution, environmental protection, global perspective, heroes, interdependence

Skills: problem solving, goal setting, decision making, inquiry/research, communication skills

Location: indoors

Time: 4-6 weeks, or up to 1 year

Materials: markers, tempera paints (to color models), tissue paper (for stuffing), materials for papier-mâché (or drawing paper)

Many teachers are familiar with the phenomenon of students who resist reading in school but are nevertheless fascinated by comic books. What is it about the comics that appeals to these kids? The stories present a wide variety of conflicts, characters, and creatures — but one feature appears common to all: in replaying the age-old battle between good and evil, comic books serve up an abundance of larger-than-life heroes. From Superman to Batman, from Spiderman to the X-Men (three of whom are women), these modern superheroes are usually athletic, good-looking, and — most important — in possession of special powers to defend values that would better our world. As educators we hope that our students,

too, will come to hold values that lead them to take action to improve the world. Education for a global perspective is one means of encouraging this.

In its simplest terms, global education seeks to help students to see the big picture, to look beyond national interests to the global community. It encourages them to regard themselves and others as "crew members," dependent on one another and on the limited resources of "Space Station Earth." This unit on superheroes may be one way that we can link this perspective with students' ready admiration of comic book superheroes. It places current issues at the heart of learning by asking students to develop a team of superheroes for a story about non-violent resolution of a major global problem. In considering how heroism is defined, students are exposed to positive role models and come to realize what ordinary individuals and small groups can do to improve the world. It has the potential to strengthen students' development as responsible, action-oriented global citizens who care enough and know enough to be able to do at least one thing to improve the planet. Perhaps, years from now, you might even recognize the name of a new global hero.

Preparation:

One of the aims of this unit is to motivate students to improve their reading and writing, their creative thinking, and their ability to work collaboratively with others. Before starting, some teachers may find it helpful to lay a foundation for creative thinking and problem solving using exercises that promote divergent thinking in a wide variety of situations.

Sharon Laivenicks

Similarly, if one of the primary goals is to develop the social skills necessary for successful collaboration, you might spend time on self-esteem and cooperative group exercises and experiences. (See suggested texts in Resources, page 162)

Procedure:

1. Begin by reviewing what the students already know about heroes, and generate a list of the common characteristics of a hero (i.e., is admired, works for the common good, cares for others, solves problems).

   Note: Rovin's *Encyclopedia of Superheroes* (see Resources page 162) provides lists of characteristics common to superheroes.

2. Have students brainstorm a list of global heroes, past and present. The choice of persons does not matter as much as students' recognition that such people are real heroes who have made a difference. They could include individuals from a variety of backgrounds (e.g., science, medicine, the arts, sports, and politics) as well as "ordinary" people whose accomplishments make them a role model for others; for example:

   • Rachel Carson for her groundbreaking work in drawing attention to threats to the environment

   • Nelson Mandela or Martin Luther King for fighting racism

   • Mahatma Gandhi for championing the rights of the oppressed through non-violent means

   • Terry Fox for his contribution to cancer research

   • Marshall McLuhan for his vision of the "global village"

   • David Suzuki for his championship of environmentalism

Sharon Laivenicks

Sharon Laivenicks

Others to consider are the "eco-heroes" selected annually for the Goldman Environmental Prizes, many of whom are ordinary citizens who have been stirred to action by environmental problems in their midst.

3. Have students, individually or in small groups, research the life and contribution of one of these global heroes. In addition to looking at the person's accomplishments, students may consider why their subject qualifies as a hero and examine the values and vision underlying the individual's actions. As a way to emphasize the hero in all of us, you might provide a chart on which students compare their own values, characteristics, and accomplishments with those of people regarded as global heroes (or at least national heroes).

   Note: To reduce the time for brainstorming and subsequent research, teachers could collect information about individual global heroes (such as those mentioned above) in folders that students can share or work on collaboratively.

4. To introduce the concept of superheroes, have students bring their comic books to read and exchange. Then have the class generate a list of comic book superheroes and repeat the process (from step 1, above) of looking for common features (i.e., have extraordinary mental or physical powers and weapons, are not selfish or vindictive). Students might also look at myths and legends of the past to learn that superheroes, such as Hercules of ancient Greece or Robin Hood of the Middle Ages, fulfilled needs that could not be met by other means.

   Note: Rovin's *Encyclopedia of Superheroes* provides excellent links to myths and legends.

5. Have the students examine their list of superheroes to determine how many use violence to solve their problems. They will likely find that most use violence despite their good intent. Discuss alternative methods of conflict resolution and extend the discussion to

superheroes on the list. How might a super-hero solve problems without resorting to violence? Stress that the real-life heroes about whom they have learned often do not use violence.

6. Ask students to list the big problems that are facing planet Earth. Sort these problems into such categories as political, economic, social, and environmental.

7. Divide the class into groups and have each group select one category of global problem and one problem within that category.

8. Ask each group to create a team of global superheroes who solve the problem using their own talents and skills and without using violence. (See example, page 162) Have students complete one Global Superhero Worksheet to describe the characteristics and qualities of each of their superheroes.

   Note: Students may work individually to create their own superheroes; however, working in cooperative groups reinforces the idea of interdependence.

9. Once they have established characters and conflict, ask students to develop a plotline that shows the superheroes in action. It is important to remind students that the real heroes who succeed in improving the world do not see issues as simply black and white or good and evil. Instead, they view complex issues from various perspectives and practice the art of compromise. They also rely heavily on the support and hard work of others. You could guide students to understand that anyone can embrace these characteristics and work toward the good of their community, locally, or globally.

   Note: In story writing, students might be more responsive if given the freedom to use such comic book conventions as mutancy and superhuman powers. You could guide them to combine these components into a scenario involving, for instance, an environmental problem (e.g., toxic waste) and a mutation that strengthens an existing positive power (e.g., exceptional linguistic intelligence transformed into telepathy). Since an essential component of this exercise is to promote positive and non-violent solutions to problems, students should be guided away from powers or scenarios involving destruction of life. This may be an enormous challenge because even students with experience in conflict resolution find it difficult to avoid the pervasive influence of violence in comic books, television,

---

Global Superhero Worksheet

Fill in information about each Global Superhero.

Age: _____

Gender: _____

Culture: _____

Values: _____

_____

_____

Powers: _____

_____

_____

Other characteristics: _____

_____

_____

_____

Select your Superhero's most important value and draw the symbol that you think best represents it.

My Superhero's most important value is:

_____

The symbol for this value is:

Design your superhero's costume: _____

_____

_____

_____

Circle the best colors for your Superhero's costume. Make sure the colors are representative of your Superhero's symbol, name, values, powers, and other characteristics.

Traditional Color Symbolism

purple	royalty, reverence, honor
red	liberty, love, life, protection
white	strength, purity, innocence, immortality
blue	truth, protection, strength, holiness
yellow	sacredness, life, sun, truth, family
green	abundance, happiness, good fortune, growth
black	strength, magic, death, fear, sorcery
brown	pleasure, earthiness, humility

Example of a Team of Global Superheroes

In creating a team of global superheroes to present to students as an example, we wanted to break with traditional stereotypes and create characters who depend mainly on their wits and stamina rather than on violence, supernatural powers, and wondrous technologies. To stress interdependence and diversity among people, we came up with the idea of an interdependent team of superheroes who would represent not only the power of collaborative problem solving but also our multi-age, multiracial, and multicultural global community. These heroes would champion tolerance and equity, encourage others to examine their values, and empower others with the confidence to improve their lives. We decided on a team of four, two male and two female, who possess the critical skills needed to resolve world problems. Here is our example team:

- Annet is a young Afro-American girl who is a genius at computers, math, and telecommunications, and has expertise in environment-friendly technologies.

- Guya is a Thai man, a systems thinker, philosopher, and environmental scientist who understands the workings of the forces of nature.

- Liv is a Swedish woman who is an expert in conflict resolution and gains spiritual power from meditation and the martial arts, but uses that power to redirect aggression into positive action and to promote personal and planetary well-being.

- Teyoninhokarawen (*trans.* he who speaks clearly) is an elderly aboriginal storyteller with extraordinary telepathic skills, a blind artist well versed in all of the fine arts, a musician and composer skilled in communications media.

Tom Goldsmith

movies, and electronic games. Further discussion and practice of conflict resolution through role-playing and peer mediation may open students' imaginations to other means by which their created heroes can solve problems.

10. When the superheroes and their stories are complete, students could design and create life-sized three-dimensional models of their superheroes.

Wrap-up: Have students present their superheroes and stories to the class.

Extension: Teachers might consider proposing the scenario of a global summit meeting in which the superheroes are invited to address a current crisis.

Ron Ballentine is Coordinator of Science and Technology and Environmental Education with the Halton District School Board in Burlington, Ontario. Al Finlayson teaches at Oakville Trafalgar High School in Oakville, Ontario. Sharon Laivenieks teaches at Central Public School in Burlington, Ontario.

RESOURCES

Creative and divergent thinking

Bellanca, James, and Robin Fogarty. *Teach Them Thinking.* Skylight Publishing, 1986.

Gardner, Martin. *Aha! Insight.* Scientific American with Freeman and Co., 1978.

Von Oech, Roger. *A Kick in the Seat of the Pants.* Harper & Row, 1986.

Von Oech, Roger. *A Whack in the Side of the Head.* Warner Books, 1990.

Cooperative teamwork

Bennett, Barrie, Carol Rolheiser-Bennett, and Laurie Stevagn. *Cooperative Learning: Where Heart Meets Mind.* Educational Connections, 1991.

Heroic lives

Boulton, Marsha. *Just a Minute.* Little, Brown & Co., 1994.

Merritt, Susan E. *Her Story.* Vanwell Publishing, 1993.

Nader, Ralph, et al. *Canada Firsts.* McClelland & Stewart, 1992.

Rovin, J. *Encyclopedia of Superheroes.* Facts on File Publications, 1985.

Wallace, Aubrey. *Eco-Heroes.* Mercury House, 1993.

Theme Days: A Cause for Celebration

As an antidote to commercial holidays, theme days shift the emphasis from consumerism to relationship-building and global citizenship

by Sara Coumantarakis

Subject areas: interdisciplinary (social studies, science, language arts, art, drama)
Key concepts: responsible global citizenship
Skills: critical and creative thinking
Location: indoors

The unsold Christmas goods disappear and the glittering decorations come down. The hearts go up in preparation for Valentine's Day. Easter is right around the corner. Retailers are ready for the onslaught of shoppers encouraged by a barrage of advertisements that punch home the message to "buy, buy, buy." It seems there are few celebrations or public holidays that have not been turned into major merchandising events offering shallow, short-lived satisfaction at a high cost. Teachers often witness the after-effects of this rampant consumerism: overwrought students, struggles over possessions brought to school, and the teasing of those whose purchasing power or image does not measure up to what is "cool." As we fall prey to the merchandisers' injunctions to consume, the Earth's resources are depleted and ecosystems disrupted, endangering future generations' ability to meet even basic needs.

One way to distance the classroom from commercial

Tom Goldsmith

holidays is by celebrating special days that provide opportunities to learn about one another and the Earth. The following alternative celebrations and activities shift the emphasis to helping others and caring for the Earth. Many of the suggested activities are discussion-oriented and are intended to serve as starting points; teachers are encouraged to extend these ideas using strategies that stress active, participatory learning with opportunities for action. Role-play, simulations, drama, debate, sculpture, and collage will help students to think critically and creatively about global issues and to synthesize information before determining avenues for action as global citizens.

October 16: World Food Day

In many parts of the United States and Canada, October signals the end of harvesting: granaries are full, farmers markets are burgeoning with vegetables, and grain dust in the atmosphere creates stupendous sunsets. We know that Thanksgiving is right around the corner, a day to be thankful for the abundance of harvests and to enjoy a feast with family and friends. For families in other parts of the world, however, the reality may be quite different: nearly 800 million people today are chronically undernourished and approximately 200 million children under the age of five suffer acute or chronic symptoms of malnutrition. Children born of malnourished mothers have low birth weights and stunted growth and are robbed of the energy they need to develop to their highest potential. At the same time, obesity from overeating threatens the health of millions of people worldwide and incidence of its related illnesses of diabetes and heart disease continues to increase. World Food Day on October 16th provides an opportunity to assess our own eating habits and to think about our role as global citizens in assuring adequate food for all. World Food Day is celebrated in more than 150 countries around the world to encourage people to take action against hunger.

Activities

- Play the Cookie Game to demonstrate that, although enough food is produced worldwide to provide adequate nutrition for all, many do not have enough to eat. Divide the class into four groups and ask one person from each group to collect cookies for their group. Group 1 receives a plate heaped with 40 cookies; groups 2, 3, and 4 receive plates with 3 cookies per plate (to reflect the fact that 20 percent of the world's people use about 80 percent of the world's resources). Record students' reactions to this situation and discuss how students in each group felt. Ask them to propose solutions to this exercise that will ensure a peaceful classroom as an end result. Collect the cookies and distribute them equitably.

- Invite a guest speaker from a local food bank to speak about food issues in your community. Create a donation box and invite students to bring non-perishable items to be delivered to the food bank prior to Thanksgiving and Christmas.

- Help students discuss food security issues — fair trade, agribusiness, poverty, famine, climatic disasters, genetic modification — through such lessons as "A World in Jeopardy," accessible online at <www.feedingminds.org> or <www.oxfam.ca/campaigns/worldFoodDay.htm>.

November 11: Remembrance Day

Each November on the date that World War I ended, we pause to remember the men and women who have fought in the service of their country as well as those who have died on peacekeeping duty. Each person at Remembrance Day services no doubt longs for a more peaceful world; yet humanity appears to be moving in the opposite direction. The United Nations' *Human Development Report 2000* stated that $780 billion was spent that year on the world's militaries. The military costs of present conflicts are yet to be tabulated, but each day's newspapers report the incalculable personal costs to civilians, soldiers, and soldiers' families.

Former Nobel Peace Prize laureates created Manifesto 2000 to initiate the United Nations "Decade for a Culture of Peace and Non-Violence for the Children of

the World." The authors of Manifesto 2000 concluded that it is up to individuals to transform our present culture of violence into one of peace, that we cannot afford to wait for governments to take this responsibility. In six simple statements, the manifesto presents a complex blueprint for living:

1. *Respect all life:* Respect the life and dignity of each human being without discrimination or prejudice.

2. *Reject violence:* Practice active non-violence, rejecting violence in all its forms: physical, sexual, psychological, economical, and social, in particular toward the most deprived and vulnerable such as children and adolescents.

3. *Share with others:* Share my time and material resources in a spirit of generosity to put an end to exclusion, injustice, and political and economic oppression.

4. *Listen to understand:* Defend freedom of expression and cultural diversity, giving preference always to dialog and listening without engaging in fanaticism, defamation, and the rejection of others.

5. *Preserve the planet:* Promote consumer behavior that is responsible and development practices that respect all forms of life and preserve the planet.

6. *Rediscover solidarity:* Contribute to the development of my community, with the full participation of women and respect for democratic principles, in order to create together new forms of solidarity.

Activities

- Join more than 75 million people who have signed Manifesto 2000 on the UNESCO website <www.unesco.org/manifesto2000>. Ask the class to brainstorm practical ways to take action on these goals. What can we do to preserve the planet? How can we share with others? Create posters to share your ideas with other classes in your school. For mural examples, visit <www.change-forchildren.org/paintingpeace>.

- Talk about what it means to practice active non-violence in situations familiar to students, such as when a classmate is bullying or teasing them. Explain that when a person becomes angry, the body responds quickly: blood leaves the brain and rushes to the large muscles to prepare for "flight or fight," the heart rate doubles, peripheral vision lessens, hearing may be inhibited by a pounding in the ears, and breathing becomes shallow. Hormones are released that remain in the body for up to 90 minutes. One of the most effective means of reversing these physical responses and deterring angry, impulsive action is to practice deep breathing until you are once again in full control of your behavior. Have students practice this: Inhale slowly through the nose, paying attention to the breath and mentally following its path down into the lungs. Drop the shoulders down and hold the breath for as long as possible. Exhale slowly through the mouth, pushing as much air out as possible. Repeat.

December 10: Human Rights Day

Human Rights Day is celebrated each December 10 to draw attention to the United Nations Universal Declaration of Human Rights, a document considered to have such universal worth that it has been adopted by most of the world's nations. The Declaration arose from the longing for peace after the World War II. However, the rights it describes — to adequate food, health care, work, education, freedom of expression, democratic process, and to be free from torture and slavery — have not been realized by many of the world's six billion people. Human Rights Day invites students to think about their human rights and the responsibilities that each right brings.

Activities

- Find the full United Nations Universal Declaration of Human Rights on-line at <www.un.org>. Ask the students to create a human rights mural to illustrate an article that is important to them. Display the mural in a public place to help others learn about human rights.

- Form a group that promotes human rights, or join an existing one such as Amnesty International (online at <www.amnesty.org>), Human Rights Watch (on-line at <www.hrw.org>), the Canadian Coalition for the Rights of the Child (online at <www.rightsofchildren.ca>), or Free the Children (on-line at <www.freethechildren.org>).

- Read students Article 1 of the Universal Declaration, which states, "All human beings are born equal in dignity and rights … and should act toward one another in a spirit of brotherhood." Suggest that students celebrate Human Rights Day by sharing food from their cultural backgrounds. Students can attach a note describing the significance of their food to them and their family.

January 15: celebrating heroes

January 15 is the birthday of Martin Luther King Jr. This activity helps students recognize the role that a modern hero can play to make a difference in the world.

Activity

1. Ask students to brainstorm their heroes and identify the personal qualities or achievements of each. Then have them compose a definition of a hero based on the qualities these people have in common. Compare this to the dictionary definition of a hero as someone admired for exceptional achievements and qualities or who shows great courage. Discuss as a class which of the students' heroes has been courageous.

2. Relate highlights in the life of Martin Luther King Jr. from this summary (adapted from Jean Darby, *Martin Luther King Jr.*):

   Martin Luther King Jr. was born January 15, 1929. As a boy, he played with two boys who lived down the street and whose father ran a store. But when Martin was old enough to start school, he was sent to a school where all the children were black, while his two white friends were sent to an all-white school. His friends were told by their parents that they couldn't play with Martin any more. When Martin's parents tried to explain why the community was segregated [separate facilities and services determined by skin color], he knew this was wrong. He became a minister like his father and began to work toward his dream — that all people would respect and help one another, regardless of their differences.

   As a college student, Martin got a job in Connecticut where there were no laws denying blacks the same privileges as whites. He got to know white people. He heard about the struggle of Gandhi to help India obtain independence from England and, studying Gandhi's methods of peaceful resistance [using peaceful methods to change things such as fasts, boycotts, strikes, disobeying laws seen to be unjust and marches], he began to see a method to work against segregation. Martin Luther King Jr. was only 39 years old when he was shot by a white man. But by that time, he had worked to enact laws that gave black people the right to vote and that made it illegal to impose segregation or to refuse to hire or rent a house to someone because of the color of their skin. In 1964, he received the Nobel Prize for Peace. He was truly a person who made a difference in the world.

3. Using Martin Luther King Jr. as an example, have students add to their lists of heroes. Consider the following:

   - Rosa Parks, a black woman, was arrested for refusing to give up her seat on a bus to a white person. The ensuing court case brought the legality of segregation before the courts.

- Mother Teresa sheltered, fed, and cared for people who were dying on the streets of Calcutta.

- Florence Nightingale took a group of women to the battlefront of the Crimean War to nurse wounded soldiers. After the war, she established a school to provide proper training for nurses and raised nursing to a respected profession.

- Emily Howard Stowe was the first female doctor in Canada.

- Louis Riel, although hanged as a traitor, has always been recognized as a hero by the Métis people for his leadership of their nation in the face of Canada's western expansion.

- Emily Murphy, the first woman magistrate in the British Empire, campaigned for equal rights for women; she and four other women initiated a successful legal appeal, known as the Persons Case, to have women recognized as "persons" within Canadian law, thereby giving women the right to be appointed to the Senate.

- Susan B. Anthony was a leader in the anti-slavery and women's rights movements in the United States.

- Terry Fox, having lost a leg to cancer, set out to run across Canada to raise money for cancer research. He died before completing his run; however, fundraising for cancer research continues, as many communities host Terry Fox runs. (See <www.terryfoxrun.org>.)

4. Discuss the traits that helped these people to make extraordinary accomplishments. Does everyone have the potential to be a hero? What kind of hero would your students like to be?

February 14: Helping others

In the fun of exchanging cards and enjoying candy, the original significance of Valentine's Day is often forgotten. Have students research the life of the Roman doctor who became St. Valentine, or read this excerpt (from Robert Sabuda, *Saint Valentine*):

Valentine, a physician, lived in Rome and worked in a poor area of the city. He mixed his own medicines, treated his patients with kindness, and would accept for payment only what a patient could offer. Valentine's reputation as a healer spread and one night he was visited by a man who worked as a prison guard. He brought his blind daughter for healing. Valentine began weekly treatments with an ointment he prepared.

At that time, most Romans worshipped many gods, but Valentine belonged to a small group of Christians who were often persecuted for their beliefs. One day there was an uprising in the city and the Christians were blamed for it. Valentine's office was raided, and he was arrested and jailed in the prison where his patient's father was a guard. Valentine wrote a note for the guard to take home to his daughter. When the guard read it to his daughter that night, it said, "from your Valentine." According to the story handed down, the child regained her sight at that moment. Valentine was executed on February 14, 270.

Activities

- Review the reason for the imprisonment of Valentine and ask students if people are jailed today for their beliefs. Where does this happen? Students could seek information from human rights organizations such as Human Rights Watch (<www.hrw.org>) or Amnesty International (<www.amnesty.org>).

- Ask students to search for advertisements of products or services to celebrate Valentine's Day in newspapers published in the days before February 14. Have them tabulate how many column inches of space are given to these ads. Discuss whether our current practice is in keeping with the original meaning of Valentine's life (i.e., helping others).

- Discuss the slogan "Think globally; act locally," which encourages us to consider how our actions affect people in other parts of the world. Ask the class to brainstorm ways to help others, not only people close to us but also those in other countries. Ask each student to cut out a valentine heart and write one idea for helping others on each side of it. Place a fallen branch from a tree in a large pot (or provide a living indoor plant with lots of branches) for students to decorate with the valentines.

- The "Valentine Tree Project Kit" developed by Save the Children Canada (see references) offers additional ideas for drawing children closer to the original intent of Valentine's Day.

March 8: International Women's Day

At the 1995 United Nations World Conference on Women in Beijing, China, 189 governments pledged to improve the lives of women and girls (according to Human Rights Watch <www.hrw.org>). Yet the plight of women around the world has not improved:

- In Russia, it is estimated that 12,000 women die each year as a result of domestic violence.

- In Pakistan, upward of 80 percent of women are victims of domestic violence.

- In South Africa, there were 49,280 reported sexual assaults in 1998.

- Peru's National Police received 28,000 reports of domestic abuse in 1998.

- In Jordan each year, one-third of the country's homicides are those in which women are killed by family members in the name of honor.

- In the United States, the Center for Disease Control reported that at least 1.8 million women are assaulted every year by their husbands, partners, or boyfriends.

- An estimated 135 million of the world's girls and women have undergone genital mutilation (<www.amnesty.org>).

Activity

1. Ask students if they would sooner be born a boy or girl. After hearing the reasons for their choice, discuss why it is much safer to be born a boy in many parts of the world.

2. The United Nations Conference on Women created a Plan of Action. Read the following statistics (Source: CIDA, *Under the Same Sun*, Spring 1995):

   - There are more men than women in the world, especially in Asia and the Pacific region where men outnumber women by 73 million. The reason lies in the treatment of girl babies: female infanticide is common, and girls receive inferior health care and nutrition.

   - In Africa and Asia, women work an average of 13 hours a week more than men.

   - Women make up 60 percent of the world's 960 million illiterate people.

   - Each minute of every day, a woman dies from complications related to pregnancy or childbirth. One-fourth of these deaths are among teenagers.

   - Half of the world's food supply is cultivated by women but they rarely own the land they cultivate.

   - In 1990, men headed 95 percent of the world's countries, major corporations, and international organizations.

   - Women in many countries are denied the right to own land, inherit property, or establish credit.

3. Have the class create a Plan of Action for girls and women. List the changes needed in families, communities, schools, law, and government that might result in equality between males and females.

4. Have students identify which parts of their Plan of Action they can influence as individuals or as a group.

April 22: Earth Day

Earth Day is an opportunity to celebrate the beauty and bounty of the Earth and to take stock of how well we are doing as caretakers of its resources.

Activities

- Have students think of some familiar advertisements and work in small groups to adapt one as a promotion for the Earth. Ask them to imagine that they are trying to sell the Earth to someone who thinks it might not be a good investment. What are its selling points? What techniques can they use in their ad to make the Earth very appealing? Will they have to ignore some of the things they know about the Earth if they are going to convince the buyer? Have each group present their ad to the class.

- Ask the students to brainstorm habits and practices we might need to change so that the Earth will be in the same or better condition for students' grandchildren. (Many aboriginal peoples believe that when making a decision it is necessary to consider its effect on the seventh generation.) Ask students to consider what behavior can stay the same. What must stop? What things can each student do? What can the class do? What can each student's family do? What can the government do? Some areas to consider are energy and water use, transportation, pollution and waste reduction, consumerism, and protection of endangered species. Have students commit to one activity as an individual and one as a class until Environment Week in June. Decide how you will track your progress and encourage one another's success.

- Consider non-human inhabitants of Earth. The number of African lions, for example, has decreased by 90 percent since 1980, leaving about 23,000 alive today. The tiger is also endangered, its population in the wild estimated at fewer that 8,000 in 2003. Ask students to research endangered species to discover reasons why many large mammals are threatened with extinction.

May: celebrating heritage

The month of May offers opportunities for students to explore and share their cultural heritage. In Canada, Citizenship Day (the Friday before Victoria Day) is a good time to celebrate diversity as a people with roots in other countries. In both Canada and the United States, Mother's Day (the second Sunday of May) presents an opportunity to discuss and compare families around the world and to construct a family tree.

Activities

- Pin a large world map to the wall. Have each student use a green-headed pin to mark the spot where they were born. Have students use red-headed pins to mark the spots where their parents were born, blue-headed pins to mark the spots where their grandparents were born, and white-headed pins to mark the spots where their great-grandparents were born. Ask if anybody can go back any further. If so, use black-headed pins to mark these birthplaces. Invite parents to participate by sending a letter home asking them to provide: 1) the birthplaces of their parents, grandparents, great grandparents, and great great grandparents; and 2) one game, recipe, tradition, song, or story that has been handed down in their family, and the name of the country in which it originated.

- Plan a celebration for Citizenship Day to recognize the gifts and talents that people have brought to North America from all over the world. Invite students to present a game, recipe, tradition, song, or story from their culture. Culminate your celebration by sharing special foods. (See, for example, Unicef's book *The Little Cooks*).

Sara Coumantarakis coordinates Alberta Learning's Teacher Exchange Program for Learning Network in Edmonton. She has been involved with the Alberta Teachers' Association Global Education Project and Safe and Caring Schools Project, as well as Learning Network's Global Education Program.

REFERENCES

Canadian International Development Agency. "The Two Halves," *Under the Same Sun* (Spring 1995). Theme issue published by Youth Editions, P.O. Box 1310, Postal Station B, Hull, QC J8X 3Y1.

Canadian Save the Children Fund. "The Valentine Tree Kit". Available free from Canadian Save the Children Fund, 4141 Yonge Street, Suite 300, Toronto, ON M2P 2A8, 416–221–5501 or fax 221–8214.

Darby, Jean. *Martin Luther King Jr.* Lerner Publications Company, 1990.

Parry, Caroline. *Let's Celebrate! Canada's Special Days.* Kids Can Press, 1987.

Sabuda, Robert. *Saint Valentine.* Atheneum, 1992.

Making Interdisciplinary Connections

Heartland All Species Project

Rivers and the Arts

An interdisciplinary inquiry through the arts

by Francine Morin, Ann Stinner, and Elizabeth Coffman

Subject areas: music, drama, art
Key concepts: rivers, interdisciplinary inquiry
Location: indoors and outdoors
Time: 4 to 6 weeks

Since the 1960s, teachers have become increasingly aware that learners use many modes or languages of thinking — and that the arts are critical dimensions of a complete education. The very existence of the fine and performing arts is indicative of the fact that not all meanings can be adequately constructed or expressed linguistically and mathematically. Each of the arts represents a unique way of knowing and, collectively, the arts offer unlimited resources for enriching curriculum, providing a variety of sensory experiences and alternate learning opportunities for students with different backgrounds, learning styles, and intelligences. As sophisticated forms of play, artistic processes are particularly important for enabling middle years students to tell their own stories and respond to the stories of others.

During an innovative approach to study in the arts at the University of Manitoba,[1] teachers examined the potential of the arts as modes of learning through which middle years students could broaden their knowledge in an integrated environmental study. A focus on rivers — an inherently fascinating theme for learners of all ages — provided a rich opportunity for participants to grow as environmentalists, to struggle with the process of expressing ideas through

Francine Morin

the diverse languages of the arts, and to translate that experience to their middle years classrooms. This article presents guidelines that could be considered by teachers planning similar interdisciplinary studies in their own classrooms.

Selecting a theme

The key to developing any successful interdisciplinary inquiry is the selection of a theme that will engage students and offer opportunities for in-depth study. Ideally, the theme is one that has local relevance and immediacy but is broad enough to allow for multifaceted inquiry. A west coast teacher might choose the Pacific rainforest, while one from the east might choose ocean life. In Manitoba, teachers selected rivers as a theme because of the importance of rivers not only in this region but in the lives of all people, past and present, around the world. The theme connects naturally to most science and social studies curricula for Grades 5 to 8, allowing teachers and students to consider many of the universal ideas that engage us as human beings: continuity and change, creation and destruction, connections and divisions, sustainability and waste.

Brainstorming and webbing

To explore the potential wealth of content and experience related to the rivers theme, teachers who have general expertise in all core subjects can begin by meeting with the arts specialists in their schools for a brainstorming and webbing session. The aim is to develop a web with branches of ideas from all curriculum areas (i.e., science, social studies, mathematics, languages, music, art, drama, movement, and technology) stemming from the main theme. For instance, one branch might represent the basic science of river ecology (insects, tree and plant life, animals, fish), river environments (water flow, flooding, riverbanks, pollution), and river geology (soil, clay,

Francine Morin

What is Interdisciplinary Inquiry?

Interdisciplinary inquiry is a way of integrating curriculum that is still a relatively new phenomenon in classrooms. In essence, it involves the integration of ideas about how the world works (content disciplines) with a variety of ways to represent how we see and make sense of our world (process disciplines). Ininterdisciplinary inquiry:

- The integrated nature of intelligence becomes the model for teaching and learning.

- The disciplines are connected through a broad theme.

- The disciplines are used as tools for learning, to provide different perspectives and answers to questions.

- Teachers and students are co-learners and collaborate in the planning of curriculum.

- There is an emphasis on exploring the interests and questions of students through authentic, exciting, meaningful events that acknowledge and extend their experiences.

- There is an emphasis on using all of the sign systems — art, music, language, drama, movement — for making and communicating meaning.

- There is an emphasis on the social nature of learning: cooperative work, student networking, developing communities of learners.

rocks). Further consultation with colleagues in related subjects, including science specialists, will help to ensure that the theme is explored as fully as possible in each discipline. This exercise will result in several possibilities for large group study as well as a variety of subthemes for individual research.

Gathering resources

In preparation for an interdisciplinary inquiry on rivers, teachers and their partners in the arts will need to collect resources, both print (e.g., textbooks, magazines, pamphlets, fiction) and nonprint (e.g., objects and artifacts, films, community sites, maps, photographs), that will motivate and interest students in the theme. Library, community, and Internet searches can lead to diverse materials about rivers. Rivers have inspired a wide range of art, from novels, films, songs, and symphonies, to installations and performance pieces, many of which are appropriate for use in a middle years classroom. Clusters of river resources to be gathered might include such materials as:

- fiction (e.g., Gary Paulsen, *The River*)

- poetry (e.g., Carl Sandburg, "Prairie Waters By Night")

- legends (e.g., Nigeria's "Faran and the River Spirit")

- nonfiction (e.g., Maryjo Koch, *Pond Lake River Sea*)

- songs (e.g., Linda Steen Spevacek, "Reflections")

- instrumental works (e.g., Toru Takemitsu, "Riverrun for Piano and Orchestra")

- choral works (e.g., Murray Schaeffer, "Miniwanka")

- visuals (e.g., M.A. Suzor-Côté, "Sunset on the Nicolet River")

- newspaper articles (e.g., Jake MacDonald, "Rivers Are the Life of Real, Book Worlds")

Inviting questions

An interdisciplinary inquiry approach to teaching and learning begins not with curriculum objectives and a set lesson plan, but rather with students' own questions and interests. The study of rivers could be launched by inviting students to share their knowledge and questions about rivers. The outcome will be a barrage of questions that can be categorized conceptually and used as the focus for small group research on various subthemes. To illustrate, one group might pursue a line of science questions, such as:

- What is the chemical content of a river?

- How is aquatic life in the river different from aquatic life in the ocean?

- How is water treated for human consumption?

- Why doesn't a river empty a lake?

- What wildlife species are supported by rivers?

- What constitutes a healthy river?

- How can a polluted river be cleansed?

Throughout the study, members of each interest group investigate their questions together, gather additional resources on their own, and collaborate in using the arts as modes of inquiry, expression, and sharing of their learning.

Designing learning experiences

After students' questions and subquestions are defined, teachers can begin to construct a series of activities and lessons to help students explore those questions through the arts. Most young adolescents have had exposure to the arts in their early years but have rarely been encouraged to use their skills as modes of learning in other subjects. Therefore, initial learning experiences need to give students the opportunity to discover that each art form provides a unique lens for considering the theme of rivers. Visual arts, for instance, offer the chance to record information and communicate ideas and feelings through line, shape and form, and color and texture. The mediums of sound and movement encourage students to think musically and kinesthetically, using such building blocks as melody, harmony, weight, time, and flow, and such processes as performing, composing, and listening. Drama, on the other hand, offers a social and interactive medium, encompassing vehicles such as improvisation and characterization for responding to the rivers theme.

Francine Morin

Exploratory river walk

A good way to begin exploring the river from the perspectives of drama, visual art, music, and movement is to take students for a walk along the banks of a nearby river. In addition to receiving safety instructions, students will need to be equipped with:

- materials for painting, sketching, and writing
- equipment for sound and visual recording
- bags and containers for collecting found objects.

The following are suggestions for ways in which students can experience the river walk through each of the four art forms.

Drama

In its most basic form, drama is a story enacted. Anyone who lives near a river probably has a story to tell about it. The simplest introduction to drama would be to have students tell their river stories to each other. They could then use almost any dramatic form to dramatize their own stories or a combination of stories, working either individually or collectively. Middle years students are very capable of developing their own scripts for a dramatized readers' theater, for example, or of transforming their written stories into pantomime.

What might be more elusive for students is seeing the dramatic possibilities in the character of the river itself. If

the river can be given human qualities, its characteristics become much more evident. A student performing as a river can express the peaceful nature of a slow meandering summer river, for instance, or the dangerous flood potential of early spring's swollen currents. Have students consider how the river speaks, moves, and interacts. Students representing trees, birds, fish, or other life forms along the river can also deliver particular points of view about a river. Characterization can be developed through dramatic monologs or in group work. Remind students that many legends and stories about rivers give voice to the plants and animals who live by them; such narratives could be used as a basis for students' dramatic explorations.

Visual arts

For the visual arts, students can be instructed to sit on the riverbank and record in their logs or journals both visual and verbal notes on what they see. For example, they could start with a roughly sketched map showing the main physical features of the riverbank near them. They might also try drawing a panoramic view of the river, indicating features that would be of interest to different observers, such as a geologist, meteorologist, ecologist, or artist. Then, focusing on a very small area, such as a 30 by 30 centimeter section (one square foot) of riverbank, students can make drawings in which they include everything they can see, both living and nonliving. Sketches could also selectively focus on particular artistic elements seen along the riverbank: lines, shapes, or textures, for example. The movement or color of the water itself could also be a subject for note taking. A further challenge might be to capture visually intangible characteristics of the river such as its peacefulness or its power. Students should also be encouraged to explore other parts of the riverbank, documenting similarities and differences in terrain and vegetation, supplementing their note taking with photographs or videotapes, and collecting found materials that could be viewed more closely under a microscope or could offer a starting point for subsequent artwork.

Sound and movement

To gather sounds and kinesthetic images, students might first be instructed to explore the banks of the river as quietly as possible, concentrating on minute noises and movements that are present all the time but which we rarely perceive. Total awareness of all sounds and movement is important, as are densities, weights, and thicknesses. Encourage students to make sound and movement maps of their journeys so that these elements can be reconstructed later. Students might also list or chart sounds and movements, or make sound or video recordings. As they note sounds and movements, instruct them to create representative symbols for them, thinking carefully about how they could visually depict variations in density and time.

To get the most out of the river walk, students can also collect materials that can be used to make sounds: stones, for instance, or twigs that can be scraped against bark, or a branch of dry leaves that can be shaken. To find objects that evoke ideas for movement sequences, students should be on the lookout for materials that might be incorporated into a dance. Tell them that such soundless objects as mist, clouds, or the sun can be interpreted in sound according to their observed qualities. The same notion holds for motionless objects that have the potential to be interpreted kinesthetically. Even the textures of touch, sound, and movement can be compared and represented (e.g., the feel of rough bark or a smooth leaf can be represented in sound or movement). It is also likely that the sights, smells, and textures of the river environment will suggest words or phrases that can be recorded for future work. Even onomatopoeic text (words that imitate the sounds they represent) might come to mind as events and objects are encountered enroute.

Francine Morin

Teachers can expect a range of responses to these assigned tasks, such as detailed drawings, color and movement sketches of water, sound mapping, movement charts, closeup studies of the habitat, photographs, written notes, word pictures, rubbings of bark, leaves and rocks, water and soil samples, driftwood, feathers, and stones. Using their sharpened senses, students will have employed several symbol systems to record information about the riverbank as well as their impressions and feelings about the river. This multisensory experience and gathering of motifs will later serve as the point of departure for works of art to be created by students. Beginning in this fashion allows teachers to demonstrate not only what the arts are about, but what any authentic inquiry is about: the growth of community,

the personal nature of learning, and the importance of students' voices in the classroom.

Community arts

As a further resource for exploring the theme of rivers through the arts, consider inviting local artists from diverse disciplines to share their interpretations of the river theme. Alternatively, students might attend a local community art exhibition, theater or musical performance. At about the midpoint of our rivers study in Manitoba, for example, we toured an art exhibition titled "A River Runs Through It." A guided tour by the curator gave participants insight into historical and contemporary concepts of rivers and their importance in North American life, while the artworks served as points of departure for sound, movement, and drama pieces created later by participants. For example, a painting featuring figures on a riverbank inspired an improvisational role-play based on a careful viewing of the figures' clothing and body language.

When visiting a gallery, students should first have the opportunity to tour an exhibit on their own, responding to the art on a personal level. They might be asked to create a chart to record titles of works and names of artists, as well as words or sketches that capture the esthetic qualities of the works (e.g., spirit, flow, movement, energy, emotions). Students might also make notes of personal experiences, songs, stories, poems, or other ideas evoked by the works of art. Having had this opportunity to form their own responses to the art, students will then be prepared for a more formal guided tour of the exhibit by the gallery staff.

Tracking and sharing learning

Assessment in an interdisciplinary inquiry needs to be open-ended, student-directed, and multifaceted. One way of ensuring this is to have students track their learning by means of a portfolio in which they gather and display what they come to know about rivers and the arts. The contents could include:

- presentation of their responses to questions about rivers (e.g., reports, concept maps, journal entries, semantic webs)

- records of and reflections of learning experiences (e.g., What did we learn? What new questions do we have? What experiences were most helpful? What did we do well? What could we improve? What do we do next?)
- responses and reactions to print and nonprint resources about rivers (e.g., book reports, listening log entries)
- incomplete and finished creative works (e.g., drawings, songs, photographs, dramatic sketches, video productions, soundscapes, sculptures).

Because self-assessment encourages reflection and gives students greater ownership of their learning, a collaborative approach is more meaningful than assessment by the teacher alone. One strategy for involving students is to draft a rubric for grading portfolios to identify specific criteria to be met. This draft can be presented to students for their input and later revised to reflect what they value. To receive a top grade, students might negotiate that these sample criteria be met:

- An open and thorough exploration of river questions is included.
- Understanding of rivers is presented effectively through all art forms.
- A high level of learning is demonstrated.
- A minimum of three print and three nonprint resources have been used.

Displaying students' efforts

An exhibition of finished artworks and performances can take place at the end of the unit. Teachers and students will be astounded at the quality and variety of the collective work from a study such as this. Students will have developed ideas both individually and collaboratively, producing finished pieces representing many perspectives on the river. Some may express ideas about environmental issues through collages, murals, sculptures, dramatizations, and original raps, songs, or poems. A performance piece might present the life of a river through movement against an impressionistically painted backdrop and sound carpet. Another group might recast an aboriginal legend about a river, featuring actors wearing animal masks, performed in front of a dramatic river mural. Still other students might choose to focus on the historical relationship between rivers and human habitation, creating visual or sound interpretations of, for instance, ancient Egypt's reliance on the Nile, or the growth of native and European settlements in a local river valley. Finally, many students will create individual works — songs, paintings, wall-hangings, dramatic monologs, instrumental works — that express personal ideas and feelings associated with the rivers in their lives.

Through our work with teachers and students, we have seen that an interdisciplinary inquiry through the arts can be a powerful avenue to exploring environmental themes such as "Rivers." The cross-curricular connections forged in such an inquiry can lead students far beyond basic science, to literary classics, music, dance, politics, history, and mythology. Just as important, the opportunity to work in a variety of symbol systems — such as drawing, gesture, and music — rather than merely words and numbers, stimulates intellectual and aesthetic growth, brings new perspectives, and gives students an exhilarating sense of their own creative potential.

Francine Morin is a professor of music, movement, and arts education. Ann Stinner has recently retired as an instructor of art education. Elizabeth Coffman is an instructor of art and drama education at the Faculty of Education, University of Manitoba, in Winnipeg.

Note

1 The Faculty of Education summer institute "Teaching the Middle Years Through the Arts" was funded by the Summer Session 1996 Innovation Fund, Continuing Education Division, University of Manitoba.

SUGGESTIONS FOR FURTHER READING

Boomer, G., N. Lester, C. Onore, and J. Cook, eds. *Negotiating the Curriculum: Educating for the 21st Century.* Falmer Press, 1992.

Drake, S.M. *Creating Integrated Curriculum.* Corwin Press, 1998.

Jacobs, H.H., ed. *Interdisciplinary Curriculum: Design and Implementation.* Association for Supervision and Curriculum Development, 1989.

Leland, C.H., and J.C. Harste. "Multiple Ways of Knowing: Curriculum in a New Key." *Language Arts,* vol. 71, no. 5, 1994, pp. 337–45.

Martinello, M.L., and G.E. Cook. *Interdisciplinary Inquiry in Teaching and Learning,* 2nd ed. Merrill / Prentice Hall, 2000.

Pate, P.E., E.R. Homestead, and K.L. McGinnis. *Making Integrated Curriculum Work.* Teachers College Press, 1997.

Wood, K.E. *Interdisciplinary Instruction: A Practical Guide for Elementary and Middle School Teachers,* 2nd ed. Merrill / Prentice Hall, 2001.

A Mohawk Vision of Bioregional Education

The Ahkwesahsne Science and Math Project is a holistic bioregional curriculum designed to help students learn to walk in two worlds

by Mary Henderson and Margie Skidders

Subject areas: mathematics, science

Key concepts: sense of place, symbols, bioregional curriculum, cross-cultural awareness

In 1990, Health and Welfare Canada wondered why, after all its efforts to recruit aboriginal young people to the health professions, there were still so few entering these professions.[1] The aboriginal health professions program at the University of Toronto helped to clarify the matter: most of the applicants did not have high school math and science; and when faced with the prospect of making up so many courses, aboriginal students chose not to pursue health careers at university. The educational level of native people in Canada has been and remains abysmally low. Statistics from the late 1980s showed that more than 40 percent of aboriginal people had never reached high school, as opposed to 20 percent of non-aboriginal Canadians. University degrees were held by two percent of aboriginal people as compared with eight percent of non-aboriginal Canadians.[2] Almost 20 years later, these percentages have doubled, but the gap has not closed; and while statistics reflect higher numbers of aboriginal health professionals, native people are still underrepresented in the health sciences.

In 1990, seeking a means of reversing this trend, the University of Toronto looked for a partner community in which to develop and pilot a science and math

Learning to construct a debris hut, a simple but effective survival shelter.

curriculum for aboriginal students. They found their ideal partner in the sovereign territory of Ahkwesahsne (ah-kweh-zah-snee, "the land where the partridge drums"), a Kanienkehaka (gan-yong-geh-hah-gah, "the people of the flint") or Mohawk community that sits astride Ontario, Québec, and upstate New York. Like aboriginal governments throughout North America, Ahkwesahsne was at a crossroad, seeking to regain control of its children's education and facing the fact that non-native concepts of what and how children learn in school had not worked for Mohawk students. Of the several hundred Ahkwesahsne students registered in the local high school in nearby Cornwall, Ontario, not one was enrolled in advanced science or math at the senior level. A little research showed that students' problems did not begin at the high school level, however; they began much earlier, in the clash of native and non-native worldviews that becomes most obvious with the formal introduction of science in Grade 7.

An Ahkwesahsne curriculum

A curriculum team was gathered to develop from scratch a Grade 7 and Grade 8 curriculum specific to the pedagogical and cultural needs of Ahkwesahsne. The team members began the ten-year project by turning to the community. They asked biologists and other health and science professionals within the community to reflect on their experiences. How had they managed to get through the education system? What would they change? What was important for Mohawk students to know? In addition to this group of scientists, the community's Elders, Chiefs, Clan Mothers,

Faithkeepers, teachers, and parents were also asked to reflect on their experience of science in school and on what they wanted for their children and grandchildren.

It became clear that many community members had found science education lacking practical application in their everyday lives. Their reflections echoed a much older story in which some English gentlemen offer to take young Iroquoian men and give them the best education of the times. Red Jacket, a noted speaker, eloquently tells the Englishmen that the young Iroquoian men they had "educated" previously were of no value to their community on their return: they could not read the signs of the land and therefore they could not hunt; they did not know their language and therefore could not recite speeches in ceremonies or give thanks to the Creator; most of all, they did not know their duties and responsibilities to their family, to their clan and community, and to the land. Like the young "educated" Iroquoian men, many young people in Ahkwesahsne did not have a place to learn the teachings of their own culture. "Western schooling, especially science, separates education from living," Brenda LaFrance, a pivotal person in the project, summarized. "The experience alienates us from our surroundings and therefore our culture." Ironically, the assimilation policies of the school system — now so interested in aboriginal peoples' lack of educational achievement — had been one of the most potent forces in extinguishing traditional knowledge and self-esteem.

What to include?

In designing the new curriculum, the team wanted to increase the number of aboriginal students in post-secondary education. But, more than that, they wanted to prepare Ahkwesahsne students to walk in two worlds — to have a strong sense of who they are as Kanienkehaka

> *Our people need to know who they are and be aware of the power and wisdom our tradition holds ... We need ... curriculum based in our ways, that starts with our values and teachings.*

Mary Henderson

Conducting water quality tests on the St. Lawrence River

Kahnastatsi Geraldine Jacobs

Learning from an Elder about fire safety inside a tipi.

and at the same time to learn to function within the dominant society in off-reserve schools, universities, and professional communities. LaFrance noted that:

Without knowing who we are, we are adrift.... Our people need to know who they are and be aware of the power and wisdom our tradition holds.... We need curriculum based in our ways, that starts with our values and teachings.

Equally important, she wanted the students to appreciate how Mohawk ways can help solve modern problems. That meant teaching students to understand and practice the "good mind" — the right relationship with Land and Creation, Self, Creator, and Others.

To learn in the Mohawk way

The most influential part of the curriculum design process was sifting the ideas gathered at community meetings. From the long list of ideas contributed by Elders, Chiefs, Clan Mothers, Faithkeepers, professionals, parents and teachers, the curriculum team arrived at four major recommendations:

Symbols: Mohawk history is entirely immersed in symbols, so students must be able to use metaphor fluently; they must have symbolic literacy, the basis for the oral tradition, as well as written literacy. For example, students must understand the deep symbolism of the creation story, the tree of peace, wampum, the condolence cane, animals and birds, dreams, and metaphors that are used in everything from everyday decision making to treaty making.

Place: Education must be less general and more precise, and thus reflect and support our traditional teachings. Some community members noted: "When our students go to school they learn about trees, but when they come out and you ask them, What kind of tree is that, and what is its medicine?, they don't know." Students must know the natural world around them if they are to fulfill their responsibilities to it. Units must involve tasks that support and reflect Mohawk culture and customs, lessons that teach the roles and responsibilities that will sustain the web of life in this community and in the broader global community.

Two Worlds: Students must earn to live in two worlds, native and non-native. Students must learn how to make decisions about how they will make their path within both the dominant society and their own communities. They must have words, images, and opportunities to talk about this challenge. For example, students need to be exposed to aboriginal ways of knowing — dreams, visions, prophecies, and teachings from the land — as well as to scientific understanding. Not only must we recognize the differences between the two cultures, but we must also recognize ourselves and who we truly are.

Living with Contradictions: Many things that seem to contradict — such as science and aboriginal beliefs — can find ways to live together. We need to ease the conflict between aboriginal and dominant societies so that, instead of feeling forced to choose one worldview or the other, students can choose both and decide when to use each. We need to recognize that we can live with ambiguity, that students can choose a science or environmental career and still retain traditional teachings.

It became apparent that to teach about the Earth in a traditional aboriginal way, exploring all aspects of our relationship with the Earth and cosmos, the curriculum would need to integrate many school disciplines: stories (language arts), history, culture, studies of the land and economy (social studies), and art as well as math and science. The Thanksgiving Address, a traditional greeting used to open and close gatherings, was chosen as the organizing principle for the curriculum. The Thanksgiving Address has 12 to 14 sections in which thanks are given to everything in the universe, beginning with Mother Earth and then moving

Students prepare for a nature scavenger hunt in which they must find such items as porcupine quills, maple leaves, deer scat, and chewed branches (indicating the presence of certain animals).

During annual camping trips near Lake Placid, New York, students search for herbs and medicinal plants, such as golden thread (Coptis groenlandica), which are used to make teas back in the cabins.

through plants, animals, and waters and then on to the sun, the moon, and the stars, the Four Sacred Beings, and finally, the Creator. For each part of the address, the team brainstormed the components of a unit.

The discussions were heated. Some argued that information from the veiled medicine societies could not be shared, that we needed to respect the fact that it is secret and deemed powerful enough to be dangerous. Others pointed out that facemasks formerly forbidden to be viewed by anyone but members of medicine societies are now publicly displayed on the covers of books, and that plenty of dangerous and inappropriate materials are available to students already. The final consensus was that the team must look for ways to share information with students that would pique their interest and capture their imaginations and pride, yet withhold knowledge that was too powerful for them to handle. This would also help protect our inherent cultural rights. At the same time, the team tried to create opportunities for young people to find mentors in the community from whom they might get more information if they wished. Students would be taught that their culture is rich and complex, and that they can choose to learn more when they are ready for the responsibility that comes with that knowledge.

Elders were clear that education needed to be specific to the Ahkwesahsne watershed: "All that feeds into our lands must be known by our children so that they can care for and protect what is left." So the curriculum stresses knowledge of the local ecosystem. In the Trees unit, for example, students learn the Mohawk and English names of 18 trees in the area. In the Animals and Birds unit, they learn 50 local birds as well as the tracks and habits of all local mammals. Units also address the local issues that threaten the ecosystem. Students evaluate the practices of two factories in the area, as well as gas stations, sewage treatment, and waste practices. (See the summary of the units, page 178.)

Sources, values, and links

One source of information that we mine heavily is creation stories that tell us who we are and define our relationship with the Earth and other creatures. We look at stories from many cultures, including scientific and biblical stories, in order to understand how the relationships modeled in them are reflected in the daily life of the societies they influence. Understanding the scientific creation story clarifies some of the fundamental differences between the Mohawk and non-aboriginal worlds; it also gives students the tools to function in the scientific milieu, even if they do not hold to the scientific assumptions in other aspects of their lives. In this way, those who do not necessarily subscribe to scientific assumptions about the world can contribute to the scientific world. In fact, they are the individuals who can push hardest at the edges of what we know or think we know.

Most of the units contain a section entitled "How are we dependent?" through which students explore our

The curriculum stresses knowledge of the local ecosystem. In the Trees unit, for example, students learn the Mohawk and English names of 18 trees in the area. In the Animals and Birds unit, they learn 50 local birds as well as the tracks and habits of all local mammals.

logging practices; in the Earth unit, they study the effect of local solid waste facilities. Each of these issues challenges them to consider the relationship of humans with creation and raises the question, What is our responsibility?

One of the things that we have had to fight is the fear of difference. At first some of the teachers said, "Aren't we really all the same? Why can't we talk about our similarities, which are much greater than our differences?" We have found that, while it is much less comfortable to talk about our differences, it is essential. For

current relationship with each part of creation. For example, in the Water unit, students assess the impact of the St. Lawrence Seaway on local waters; in the Trees unit, they assess local

Mary Henderson

too long, aboriginal students have been told that they are the same, yet they have felt different. Throughout the curriculum, then, we emphasize the fact that difference is essential. Within the Ways of Knowing unit, for example, students explore the differences in where and how people acquire knowledge. We consider how what we know is influenced by our language, experiences, dreams, and visions, as well as by where we go for help — whether to friends, relatives, books, science, or the natural world. We acknowledge that the sources of our knowledge can make us different from one another — and give us more to share.

Sharing our success

From the beginning, the curriculum was designed to meet the unique environmental and cultural circumstances of Ahkwesahsne. However, the curriculum team has received calls from aboriginal communities throughout Canada and the United States who are interested in this place-specific, culture-specific model. Many say that, for too long, aboriginal education has involved generic "Indian" curriculum that is not respectful of or factual about any Nation. They are willing to replace the parts of our curriculum that are specific to Ahkwesahsne with the knowledge that is particular to their people and their place. The curriculum project also continues to gather

interest from teachers in non-aboriginal and mixed schools who realize that current resources on aboriginal peoples tend to dwell on pre-contact and rarely allow students to explore a subject or issue from a current aboriginal perspective.

It is our belief that the Ahkwesahsne Science and Math Project represents a curriculum model and process that can be used around the world in both aboriginal and non-aboriginal communities. It is a model that strives for excellent education for all people, preparing students to bring a diversity of perspectives to the challenges that we will all face in the 21st century.

Mary Henderson was a member of the Ahkwesahsne Science and Math Pilot Project curriculum team and now lives in Pemberton, British Columbia. Margie Skidders taught the curriculum for five years. Currently a Principal for the New York State Board of Cooperative Educational Services, she is in charge of Special Education Programs in three schools in northern New York.

Notes

1 Health and Welfare Canada figures for 1988 indicate 16 Aboriginal physicians, 4 dentists, 1 physical therapist, and 400 nurses in Canada.

2 Indian and Northern Affairs Canada statistics, 1996.

Two Rivers Project

A framework for using local environmental issues as the integrating context for interdisciplinary and cross-curricular studies in Grade 7

by Loris Chen

Subject areas: science, language arts, mathematics, social studies

Key concepts: vertical integration of curriculum, biodiversity, sustainability

Skills: observation, analysis, evaluation, critical thinking

Location: indoors and outdoors

Time: up to one year

Each October, loaded down with wading boots, seining nets, buckets, chemical test kits, and maps, seventh grade students of the North Arlington Middle School leave the concrete pavement of their urban world for the leaf-littered forest floor of the Scherman-Hoffman Sanctuaries surrounding the headwaters of the Passaic River. It is the start of a journey that covers 12,000 years of natural and human history, from the origins of the river to the current environmental issues associated with water and land use in the Passaic-Hackensack watershed of New Jersey.

More than a watershed and river monitoring project, the Two Rivers project involves a team of four teachers who use the environment as an integrating context for interdisciplinary and cross-curricular studies. Each teacher is responsible for instruction in one of four core subject areas: science, reading, math, or social studies. However, the subject curricula differ from traditional curricula, in that they identify skills and knowledge common to all subject areas, and coordinate skill development and knowledge acquisition across the curriculum using thematic units that are based primarily on the environment. For example, to learn the skill of interpreting information on a topographic map, students construct physical relief maps and draw topographic maps in science class

Loris Chen

from measurements, use topographic maps in social studies class to answer geographic questions, draw topographic maps at various scales in math class using ratio analysis, and explain how topography affects the events in a story in reading class. The skill is later applied to solving environmental problems associated with development in a reservoir watershed.

The curriculum

All four teachers collaborate in selecting themes for the integrated units, but ultimately it is the state core curriculum standards that drive the content. Since the reading and math standards are oriented more toward process and skill development, the content of the theme units is determined primarily by the science and social studies standards.

The seventh grade science curriculum includes four main areas of investigation: ecology, life science, Earth science, and space exploration. Each unit focuses on specific scientific principles and includes applications of knowledge acquired in previous units. The themes of biodiversity and sustainability run throughout: biodiversity studies cover 3.5 billion years of life on Earth, and the culminating activity is the construction of a model sustainable community for colonization of Mars. Because of the concentration of environmental themes in science, the science curriculum tends to frame the integrated units and lessons.

The seventh grade social studies curriculum is geography: how human activity affects the Earth and how the physical Earth affects and influences human activity. This includes analyses of human/environment interactions at local, regional, national, and international scales. Trade economics and the distribution and use of resources are broad topic areas that span the globe.

Lessons about water, land use, and sustainability flow between science and social studies. For example, in social studies, students map water resources and read about and sketch the water cycle. In science, they conduct experiments and construct models that demonstrate scientific principles of the water cycle and water pollution. The double exposure reinforces the concepts and raises students' awareness. Students themselves find it easier to retain information that crosses curricular areas and involves hands-on activities.

While most of the factual information is transmitted in social studies and science, an important analytical component occurs in the math class. During a field trip to the Scherman-Hoffman Sanctuaries, for instance, students take measurements of the Passaic River. These calculations are used in math class to estimate flow rates and volume, and in science class to predict the effect of various contaminants that could enter the river. In science, students role-play various freshwater macroinvertebrates whose populations change as soil that is eroding from a clearcut forest lowers the dissolved oxygen content in the stream. Students take the census data from this simulation to math class where they are converted into a graphic representation of what is happening to the macroinvertebrate diversity. Analysis of the same census data helps students later to interpret macroinvertebrate profiles from selected sites along the Passaic River and its tributaries. Students become adept at locating the census sites by combining their knowledge of the effects of land use on water quality, and the relationship between water quality and biodiversity.

Loris Chen

In a unit on farmland preservation, students learn about the practices and economics of sustainable agriculture.

birds and migratory waterfowl who depend on it for both nesting and resting. Students hotly debate a proposed mall development in the meadowlands from personal, economic, and environmental perspectives. The Delaware Bay region of New Jersey hosts a massive horseshoe crab and shorebird migration each May because of its unique location along the Atlantic flyway. As the culmination of a one-day migration theme, students develop a plan for horseshoe crab harvesting.

With 450 species of birds recorded each year, New Jersey is second only to Alaska in avian biodiversity. The development of the New Jersey highlands has become a controversial environmental and political issue because the highland forests are important habitat for neotropical migratory birds as well as the source of drinking water for two million New Jersey residents. Discussion of land development in the highlands includes lessons in both biodiversity and watershed management. Chronic water shortages attributable to demand and cyclic drought are brought down to the personal level through a water-use journal and family water-rationing plan.

The preservation of farmland and open space is an important New Jersey environmental issue, which became a hot political topic in 1998. Students prepared for a debate on the pros and cons of public funding for land acquisition by mapping population density and land use, graphing agricultural production, studying the economics of New Jersey agriculture, and analyzing population trends.

Some units of study involve only two core curricular areas, while others include all four. Activities may extend for the duration of a marking period or conclude in one day. For example, activities related to horseshoe crabs and shorebird migrations begin in science with a video about the Delaware Bay. The next day, students read a story about a golden plover in reading class; map migration routes of four species of shorebirds in social studies; calculate weight gains, losses, and flight distances in math class; and simulate migration in science class. Since each subject area lesson is a stand-alone, it doesn't matter in which order the students do them. However, by doing all four in the same day, students develop sufficient awareness of the topic to write

Without a strong commitment from each teacher to maintain and develop thematic activities and units, we would easily have slid back into traditional subject area teaching.

Cross-curricular thematic units

Several units have been developed to maximize the integration of the subject areas. Each explores a theme linked to local or state environmental issues, all of which have international implications because of the geography of the Hackensack Meadowlands region and of New Jersey. The region is part of the New York–New Jersey Harbor Bight, an important international port that requires periodic dredging to accommodate large ships. Students analyze both the economic and the environmental costs and benefits of dredging. The Hackensack Meadowlands are an extensive wetland habitat for shore-

persuasive letters in writing class about proposed legislation on horseshoe crab harvesting. In their letters, they must consider not only environmental but also economic consequences or benefits of limiting the harvest.

Many outside educational resources have enhanced the integrated units. For instance, non-formal environmental educators lead field trips and visit classrooms, bringing additional perspectives. The students also participate in projects that provide opportunities to network with other schools, both in New Jersey and further afield. These include a network of schools along the Passaic River organized by the New Jersey Audubon Society for research and communication; a similar network organized the Hackensack Meadowlands Development Commission Environment Center, using interactive television to bring students together; and an international partnership directed by the Education Development Center that pairs schools in New Jersey with schools in Costa Rica for research projects that use the Internet for communication.

Planning and funding

The core team of teachers meets regularly to plan units, activities, and events, and to track students' academic achievement and social development. Ideally, these meetings occur daily during a common planning period. In many years, however, unsynchronized schedules have made planning much more challenging, requiring telephone calls, e-mail, and summer meetings. Without a strong commitment from each teacher to maintain and develop thematic activities and units, we would easily have slid back into traditional subject area teaching.

Some activities require financial assistance, for which planning begins a year in advance. As a team, the four teachers discuss the needs for the following year and the resources required. Some items are budgetary and funded through the school tax levy. For those that require grant money, the Internet has been a great place to research funding opportunities. Grant proposals have been both collaborative and individual efforts, depending on the particular activity to be funded. In general, all team members contribute ideas and suggestions, but the proposals are written by the science teacher simply because there is more money available for science and technology projects. An important follow-up to activities is an environmental

Loris Chen

Collecting leaves to learn about biodiversity in New Jersey's highland forests.

Where We Found Support

Local government: The local town council cooperated in grant programs by offering in-kind services and co-authoring grant proposals. One project undertaken jointly was the planting of vegetation to stabilize the bank of the Passaic River.

Regional agencies: The Hackensack Meadowlands Development Commission is a semi-autonomous agency. One project undertaken jointly was a butterfly garden along the North Arlington Scenic Overlook Path.

State agencies: The New Jersey Department of Environmental Protection awarded a grant to develop a watershed education community action project on the Passaic River. The grant provided a computer, software, and water monitoring equipment for a study of the watershed using geographic information systems.

Federal agencies: The U.S. Environmental Protection Agency provided funding to train teachers to conduct the river monitoring and watershed education lessons. The agency also administered the student awards program. The U.S. Department of Agriculture Soil Conservation District grant program supported projects to prevent riverbank soil erosion. Our students also took part in the essay competition and, over the years, have won local and state recognition.

Professional societies: The Alliance for New Jersey Environmental Education (ANJEE) provided a networking framework. Through ANJEE, partnerships were forged with the New Jersey Audubon Society and its affiliated nature centers. Training provided by the New Jersey Geographic Alliance gave us access to grants from the National Geographic Education Foundation. The Geological Association of New Jersey was an invaluable resource for teacher training and field trip planning for the geology unit. Additional funding came from the New Jersey Agricultural Society, along with teacher training and field trip planning advice. The New Jersey Education Association provided financial support and the opportunity to participate in a documentary on environmental education projects. Recognition and the opportunity to share lessons came through the A+ for Kids Teacher Network. Professional journals, newsletters, and websites usually list teachers' workshop and grant opportunities.

awards program that not only recognizes students' achievement but also generates publicity that can in turn be used to obtain new funding. Often, success breeds success. One well-executed grant proposal that garners attention can be a springboard to more grants.

Vertical integration and extracurricular connections

While the environment is a focus in the seventh grade at North Arlington Middle School, it is a theme that spans the school's three levels from Grade 6 to Grade 8. The sixth grade curriculum includes a year-long investigation of scientific methods, tools of the scientist, and connections between environment and personal health, such as the effects of exposure to ultraviolet radiation and the relationship between air quality and respiratory disorders. This is followed, near the end of the school year, by an intensive three-day environmental field trip to a highland nature center. Cross-curricular activities during the field trip set the stage for more intensive investigations in Grade 7.

Eighth grade students continue their environmental studies through investigations of global climate change and oceanography. The seventh grade study of horseshoe crabs and migratory birds sets the stage for a cross-curricular eighth grade study of oceans and climates. The unit includes a field trip to Sandy Hook, New Jersey, for marine studies on the beach with naturalist educators.

Having been exposed to environmental education in class, many students join the school's ecology club, an active organization that challenges them to undertake and complete real environmental monitoring or improvement projects. Students have monitored water quality in the Passaic and Hackensack rivers, cataloged biodiversity in the meadowlands, designed and implemented habitat enhancements in both watersheds, and

Loris Chen

Students discover the relationship between pressure and temperature in the atmosphere. Their data was later graphed and analyzed in math class.

Loris Chen

Students visit a mine to learn about the geology of New Jersey and the environmental impact of mining.

developed lessons for younger students.

Fifth grade students are introduced to the middle school through the Schuyler Avenue Butterfly Garden project, located on an abandoned landfill behind a firehouse. Students in the North Arlington Middle School Ecology Club have developed and taught lessons to fifth grade students about soil testing, butterfly garden design, and butterfly life cycles. Preparation of the lot was an eye-opener for students because the fill was loaded with debris, bottles, and waste rock from the construction of the New York City subway system. Students became historical and environmental detectives as they sleuthed for clues about the origin of the fill materials. Senior citizen mentors were a great resource.

Conclusions and outlook

Vertical integration of environmental education provides students with continuous experiences that build on one another. Each year students participate in new activities that have links to what they have done previously. The result is reiteration without repetition. Horizontal integration of environmental themes during the seventh grade helps focus students' attention during a year when many adolescents become easily distracted. The observed results are that students are more engaged in learning. They tend to participate more in class and are enthusiastic about homework assignments that involve backyard research.

Using the environment as an integrating context for learning also benefits the community. Many students who are now in high school have chosen environmental action projects for their community service component. The butterfly gardens are attractive enhancements to a highly urbanized region. The river monitoring project has spawned both riverbank cleanups and a new project that will stabilize a section of the riverbank to improve habitat for fish.

Loris Chen teaches science at the Dwight D. Eisenhower Middle School in Wyckoff, New Jersey. She led the development of this program while teaching at North Arlington Middle School in North Arlington, New Jersey, with colleagues Annette Boyd, Diane Sereika, and Leanne Fisher.

Planning and Implementing an Integrated Curriculum

Integrated units take time to plan, implement, expand and stabilize. It may take three to five years for the curriculum to mature from startup to dynamic units that adjust to take advantage of changing opportunities. The following timeline of the Two Rivers project may be helpful in planning your own program.

Year 1: Planning

- Identify and organize a team of teachers who will develop the integrated curriculum. The team should meet specifically for the purpose of planning the unit or lesson. This can be done during the summer as a workshop, during the school year once a week after school, or during regular team planning periods.

- Using curriculum mapping techniques, identify areas of skill or content overlap that already exist in the subject areas.

- Using examples from textbooks or other content materials, connect the standard examples to local, state/province, or regional examples. In other words, answer the question: How can we use our local environment to teach the content or skills?

- Select one topic to develop into a unit for the first year of implementation. Ask the questions: What topic will we use as the focus? Why should this unit replace, or integrate into, an existing unit? When during the school year would this unit work best? Who will teach each piece of the unit? Where in the community, state/province, or region can we visit to make observations? How will this project be funded? Are outside resources needed?

- After answering the above questions, begin writing the lessons, developing funding proposals, and seeking community partnerships. This first stage of the timeline will take a full school year to complete.

Two Rivers Project example

We decided to use our school's location on the Passaic River and Hackensack Meadowlands as a starting point. A local councilwoman helped us contact the Passaic River Coalition, and the town's mayor helped us forge a partnership with the Hackensack Meadowlands

Development Commission. Through the New Jersey Alliance for Environmental Education, we developed partnerships with the New Jersey Audubon Society and the New Jersey Department of Environmental Protection. All of the partners were in the early stages of developing watershed education materials and were eager to have us as a partner. The Hackensack Meadowlands Development Commission Environmental Education Center personnel assisted us in applying for a grant to fund a community environmental improvement project. The grant required a community partnership consisting of a school, local government, and a local environmental organization.

Year 2: Implementation

- Keep a diary or log of the project. Record reflections, observations, evaluations of lessons. Take photographs and include them in the project record. Keep a record of any changes that need to be made. This is the time to identify what works and what doesn't.

- Continue to meet on a regular basis with team members to refine the program and develop new projects. Constantly assess students' achievement and monitor progress.

- If the project is funded by one or more grants, keep a careful record of expenditures. Use the project log to augment reporting to the funding agencies.

- Begin the next cycle of grant applications if the program funds are needed external to the school district budget.

- Continue the development of integrated lessons.

Two Rivers Project example

After developing watershed lesson plans, we added geology lessons based on the local conditions of Mesozoic volcanism associated with the breakup of Pangaea, copper deposits from magma intrusions, and disturbances caused by Holocene glaciation. By expanding the geology study to the entire Passaic-Hackensack river basin, we were able to link historic land use in the New Jersey highlands to current land management decisions that could affect the drinking water of two million northern New Jersey residents.

Iron mining in the early 1800s had led to deforestation of the highlands. When iron mining was abandoned in New Jersey with the discovery of richer deposits in the Great Lakes region, the land was allowed to return to forest. At the same time, Newark brewers were interested in obtaining pure clean water for their products. By buying up land and creating a reservoir system, the companies ensured a reliable supply of clean water surrounded by undeveloped forestland. Population growth, expansion, and development have placed pressure on these resources, leading to lessons that allowed students to debate public policy issues.

Year 3: Expansion

- Add a new activity or unit in the third year.

- Apply for recognition for student projects (e.g., the U.S. Environmental Protection Agency Environmental Youth Awards).

- Continue writing grant applications.

Two Rivers Project example

Farmland preservation gained attention when New Jersey voters were asked to fund the program through a tax referendum. Working with the New Jersey Agricultural Society, we obtained grants for students to observe sustainable agricultural practices. We also used the farmland preservation act as the basis for developing a set of geography study skills lessons that were published by Global Learning, Inc. for dissemination in New Jersey. In the same year, the meadowlands enhancement project that our students had implemented the year before was honored with a national Presidential Environmental Youth Award.

Years 4 and 5: Stability

- By the fourth or fifth year, the process of reflection, refinement, and financing should be established, and the program should reach stability.

Environmental Laws:
A Matter of Debate

In this integrated unit, Grade 6 students get firsthand experience of legislative processes by writing and debating environmental protection laws

by Ruth Ann DePitera, Joe Rossow, and Gretchen Lange

Subject areas: language arts, social studies, science
Key concepts: ecosystems, multiple perspectives, legislation
Skills: debate, research, legal and legislative writing
Location: indoors
Time: 1 month

Dressed in wool plaid shirt and baggy jeans, Trianni stands before lobbyists and lawmakers on the floor of the Minnesota House of Representatives to plead for the job that pays her bills. A divorced mother of four, she is a logger in the forests of northern Minnesota. On this cold December day, Trianni argues her case:

> I love my job. I never want to stop being a logger. I can tell you that I stand for a lot of people who are in the same position I am in. Our companies will have to start firing us if our amendments do not pass because they will not have enough money to pay us. This will leave a lot of people jobless. We have a very reasonable compromise. If we can be allowed to cut no more than 15 percent of forest land per year, we will cut and take away all of the diseased trees. This will keep the surrounding trees healthy. Think about this compromise and the position we are in before you give your answer.

Nearby sits Mike, who has cerebral palsy. He is a lobbyist for the snowmobile industry, but he is also concerned

Joe Rossow

about the accessibility of parks to disabled people, particularly parks such as the wilderness areas that the camper sitting to his right wants to protect. Dressed neatly in a blue sports coat and tie, Mike looks skeptically at Becky, who is wearing her fishing vest and shorts on the House floor.

Trianni, Mike, and Becky are 3 among 75 citizens who on this day are debating an amendment to a logging bill. A closer look at their faces, however, reveals that these are not the worldly-wise characters they so convincingly portray. Trianni's round, sweet face gives away her true identity as a sixth grader at a Minneapolis elementary school. Mike, a classmate, does have cerebral palsy, but he is just beginning to show facial hair. Becky's youthful voice is raspy with the excitement of the day. These students have spent the last two months negotiating the churning waters of environmental policy through a multidisciplinary English, social studies, and environmental science unit focused on the use of state forestland. They are on the floor of the House to argue their carefully researched and prepared points of view in the way that all policymakers do — in full view of the public.

This House debate is the culmination of one of eight integrated units in the Grade 6 curriculum at Dowling Urban Environmental Learning Center, an elementary school situated on 9 parklike hectares (22 acres) on a bluff overlooking the Mississippi River in Minneapolis. Begun as a school for students with disabilities, Dowling opened its doors to all students in 1988 and adopted a focus on the environment as a context for integrating curriculum in a meaningful way.

In the primary grades, Dowling students learn about habitats, the community environment, and the ecology of river, pond, and lake environments. In Grades 4 to 6, they build on these basics through an integrated curriculum organized around thematic units. All of the themes incorporate writing, reading, social studies, and science, and most have an environmental focus. As an example of this integrated teaching, the law unit combines environmental science with writing, research, and debate on an environmental issue and hands-on experience of legislative processes. Instead of learning forest management in one class, studying how laws are created in another, and reading literature on forests in a third, the Grade 6 students discover how all of these issues intersect in the process of creating public policy.

The topics for the law unit differ from year to year and are often derived from news articles reporting on a current controversy. For instance, in this case, it was whether to open the Boundary Waters in northern Minnesota to motorized crafts and to provide accessibility for disabled people. We knew the topic would invite many different points of view, but we wanted to focus on a locale closer to home and more familiar to students. Therefore, we shifted the debate to motor use and accessibility for disabled people in Minnesota forests.

Developing positions and selecting roles

We begin each law unit by reviewing environmental concepts that students will need to apply in the debate — in this case, those associated with forest habitats and ecosystems. Working in teams, the students then study and present the potential environmental impacts of the policy changes under discussion. Armed with this background study, they write a pro/con sheet, listing reasons for supporting one side or the other. Often these reflect a single viewpoint that must be broadened by introducing economic and social factors that students have not considered. To do this, students brainstorm the various interest groups or individuals who might have a stake in the debate. In our forest-use unit, for example, these included such people as loggers, snowmobilers, hunters, campers, and conservationists.

Each student chooses one of these roles and creates a

Joe Rossow

Most students had dressed for their role, every student had a voice and a vote, and the session was complete with a Speaker of the House and plenty of yeas and nays and gavel pounding.

character whose point of view they will present at the capital. These politically charged characters are developed using a webbing technique called character mapping, in which students decide on their character's vital statistics, hobbies, families, jobs, and opinions about the issues under discussion. When the map is complete, students write an in-character autobiography and finalize their perspectives by writing a position paper from their character's point of view.

Formulating the bill

In the next phase of the unit, students are introduced to the Constitution with particular emphasis on the process of making laws. In small groups, students brainstorm ideas about the contents of a law pertaining to the issue at hand. Then a team of students gathers these ideas, combines those that are similar, and formulates a legislative bill. The bill is divided into four major sections: definitions, the elements of the law, the consequences of breaking the law, and how to pay for implementation and enforcement of the law. The definition section is extremely important because it establishes the exact parameters of the law. It is a tool that creates precision and promotes discussion about the potential problems of ambiguity. For example, the authors of the forest-use bill offered the following definitions:

"'Natural areas' means any ground that is not disturbed by human use, with the exception of walking, hiking, or skiing trails. 'Campgrounds' or 'campsites' means an area intentionally cleared for human use."

Students then addressed the following elements in their law: campsite requirements, including accessibility; hunting restrictions; timber removal; and motor use. The consequence section included fines and confiscation of property. The financing of the bill would be through fees and fines that were collected.

At this point in the process our bill is sent to the office of a member of our House of Representatives who has sponsored and assisted our students in this project for more than a decade. There, it is drafted into official bill form and translated into political and legal language. When it is returned to our class, students study the bill from the point of view of their fictional characters, and respond by either supporting it or proposing changes as written amendments. Like the original bill, these amendments are forwarded to the legislature and put into legal and political language and format. Once the bill and amendments have been revised and sent back to the students, the role-playing and debate begin in earnest in a mock legislative session at the Capitol.

Debating amendments

As the snow was flying in December, the student legislators climbed the icy steps at the Capitol to debate their forest-use bill. Acting as legislators, they began by introducing their pro-conservation Forest Preservation Bill. Then, one by one, the students were allowed time to present the amendments they had written from their characters' points of view. Following each presentation, the floor was open for debate. Using all of the proper House rituals, the legislators argued their positions with expertise and emotion, so immersed in the activity that they were unfazed by the challenge of public speaking using microphones. Most students had dressed for their role, every student had a voice and a vote, and the session was complete with a Speaker of the House and plenty of yeas and nays and gavel pounding. After much discussion and argument, many well-devised amendments were adopted, and others were rejected. But all of the amendments piqued interesting debate and many witty and thoughtful comments. At the end, the students voted and passed into law a new and amended Forest Preservation Bill.

The environmental law unit is an example of the sort of engaging, hands-on learning that is possible when teachers work together as a team to integrate disciplines in a meaningful way. Using the environment as the context for our integrated curriculum enables us to broaden students' understanding of the complexity of environmental issues, while at the same time infusing elements of action and citizenship into traditional subject content. Just as important, it makes teaching and learning more fun for all of us.

Ruth Ann DePitera and Gretchen Lange, now retired, formerly taught Grade 6 at Dowling Urban Environmental Learning Center in Minneapolis, Minnesota. Joe Rossow teaches Grades 4 and 5 at the school.

STREAMS: Integrated Curriculum

Through hands-on learning, STREAMS students have tackled major environmental problems in their county, have earned numerous awards for their efforts, and have become leaders in community improvement

by Frederic R. Wilson

Subject Area: science, social studies, language arts, math

Key Concepts: watersheds, wetlands, renewable and non-renewable resources, environmental health, ecosystem interactions, endangered species

Skills: water quality testing, data analysis, inquiry, problem solving, communicating, critical thinking

Location: indoors and outdoors

Time: 75+ hours

In 1995, the Borough of Huntingdon in southcentral Pennsylvania was granted a quarter of a million dollars to correct a sewage leak that was polluting a local stream. The grant was welcome news for the community. But for a certain group of persistent sixth graders, who had uncovered, investigated, and reported the problem, it was more than good news: it was proof that young people can make a tangible difference in the world.

For the past 13 years, students at Huntingdon Area Middle School have been learning about watershed ecology in an integrated interdisciplinary program called Science Teams in Rural Environments for Aquatic Management Studies (STREAMS). They then go a step further and apply their knowledge to resolving local environmental problems. STREAMS integrates environmental topics into hands-on learning in social studies, science, mathematics, and language arts. Every Grade 6 student participates in the core of the program, which is conducted over 75 hours at the beginning of each school year. Thereafter, any student in Grades 6 through 8 who wants to pursue further voluntary independent study or environmental projects can

do so by joining a student-organized environment club. Since the program's inception, students have tackled major environmental problems in the county, have earned numerous awards for their efforts, and have become leaders in community improvement.

STREAMS originated with teachers' observations that the traditional curriculum was disconnected from the real world of the young people in this rural community, and that students are more engaged in activities that take place outdoors, have a direct impact on their families and community, and give them some control of their educational experience. Developed by social studies teacher Frederic Wilson and science teacher Timothy Julian, STREAMS was implemented as a voluntary program during study hall periods but soon became part of the Grade 6 curriculum, fully aligned with state academic standards. Instrumental to its success have been the cooperation of the community and a team teaching approach that maximizes the potential of using the environment as the context for learning. The key factor, however, has been the students themselves, whose enthusiasm has been a catalyst in raising environmental awareness among adults of the community.

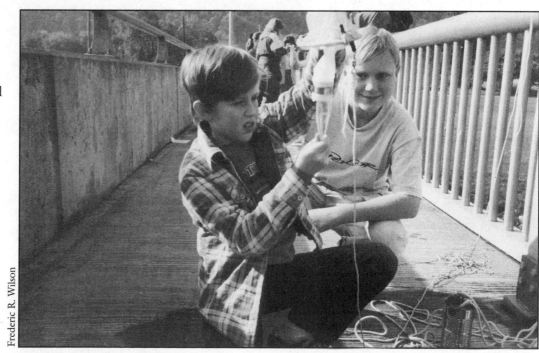

Frederic R. Wilson

Collecting plankton samples.

STREAMS curriculum

The main topics of the curriculum were developed during the first three years, but modifications are made annually to provide students with new field study experiences and to integrate supplementary content. Through experimentation and fieldwork, STREAMS students study stormwater runoff, erosion, sedimentation, nutrient enrichment, wetlands, groundwater, and the effects on waterways of acidity and household pollutants. One important aspect of the program is the study of a local stream from its headwater to its mouth. Students monitor the quality of the water, conduct limnological tests, and learn about local water treatment facilities. On completing the program, they understand the ecological interactions in a watershed, factors that have a negative impact on it, and how to collect, analyze, and interpret data to formulate solutions to problems.

All four teachers in the Grade 6 teaching team get their hands wet in the outdoor field studies, but each also contributes specialized expertise in a particular subject area.

Language Arts: The language arts teacher prepares students for STREAMS activities by introducing the vocabulary they will need, works with students on STREAMS writing assignments, and assists in grading other subject papers written under STREAMS.

Math: The math instructor gathers and crunches environmental data collected by students in field studies and collaborates with colleagues to teach students how to interpret statistics, construct charts and graphs, and use word processing and database programs for the completion of their projects. He also uses the environmental data in problem-solving activities and in teaching fractions, percentage, median, and mode.

Science: The science teacher integrates the theme "pathways of water," which is designed to help students understand the properties of water and the physical features of streams (e.g., flood plains, meanders, and levees), groundwater, lakes, and glaciers. Students investigate

processes for purifying drinking water and treating wastewater, conduct limnology tests, examine plankton, compare fresh and salt water, and participate in such follow-up activities as constructing a three-dimensional map of a river and using computer programs to chart, graph, and analyze their limnological data.

Social Studies: The social studies teacher guides students to address environmental issues as social issues by evaluating the effects on water resources of such land uses as residential development, agriculture, and mining. Topics include the impact of stormwater runoff and acidity, types of water pollution, the effects of household products on water quality, the functions and benefits of wetlands, and best management practices. Students share their discoveries with appropriate authorities and write letters expressing their concerns. As environment club advisor, the social studies teacher provides students with the opportunity to work year-round in voluntary environmental learning activities and community service projects.

Frederic R. Wilson

Full swing in the swale: students and community partners constructing a channel to divert stormwater from residents' basements.

On a typical STREAMS day, all the subject-specific curricula are integrated around the same topic. For example, when students are learning about the water cycle, the social studies instructor teaches what a water cycle is and takes students outdoors for an activity in which they become a water molecule, tracing their way through groundwater, plants, clouds, oceans, animals, etc. In math, students use the data from the water molecule activity to total and graph the number of times they were a molecule in groundwater, seawater, etc. The language arts teacher has the students write a creative story of their journey as a water molecule, undergoing phase changes as a solid, liquid, and gas as they travel through the water cycle. The science teacher has students draw a diagram of the water cycle and then create a model that is placed outdoors for several days so they can observe how water moves in a cycle. On another day, students in science make and introduce food coloring into a groundwater model to observe the pathways of pollutants. In social studies, they learn various causes of groundwater contamination and analyze the means and costs of eliminating it.

As with any integrated program that includes field studies, STREAMS requires organization, funding, and careful scheduling. An early challenge was to convince community leaders to involve students in local problems, but students easily earned the cooperation of community members and parent volunteers as they proved themselves capable of designing relevant projects and doing accurate fieldwork. Small grants helped meet initial unding needs, but today the program is completely funded by the school district; the cost of implementing and maintaining it has been minimal because field studies are conducted close to the school and the water-monitoring equipment required is inexpensive. With staff and administrative support, time is provided for extra learning and projects by using study hall periods, altering students' schedules, and allowing students to continue activities after school. In addition, a block schedule enables team teachers to carry out multiple field studies on a single day. One of the field days, for instance, has students visiting both the local wastewater treatment plant and the water filtration plant, and conducting limnology activities at a river. The students — more than 100 of them — are divided into three groups, and one bus is used to transport them in rotation until all have participated in the three events. On another day, one group of students examines a local stream from the headwater to the mouth, while another group conducts watershed assessment activities.

The ecological knowledge that students gain from the STREAMS program is put to use throughout the year in voluntary studies and community action projects organized through the student-run environment club. A majority of students — approximately 70 percent — elect to participate in these extra activities, which include environmental research, survey analyses, watershed assessments, microbiology studies, presentations at conferences or civic organizations, letter writing, and community service projects. Parent volunteers and educational partners — for example, college and conservation district personnel — assist with extra academic projects off-campus.

Applying environmental literacy

The most noticeable environmental impact of students' work is that, after years of talk, the county is tackling its

Because lessons in one subject area are revisited and reinforced by activities in others, students are better able to comprehend, retain, and assimilate concepts.

Frederic R. Wilson

Student volunteers test the biodegradability of plastics.

number one environmental issue: stormwater runoff. The impetus for action came when students' water-quality tests showed high levels of bacteria in a local stream called Muddy Run. Having learned about pollution associated with stormwater runoff, the students traced the problem to the town's sewer system, where crumbling pipes overloaded with stormwater were leaking raw sewage into the stream. Mounting a massive three-year letter-writing campaign, the students informed the public, and urged state and local agencies to correct the problem. The state grant of $250,000 to repair the sewer system came as a direct result of this hard work. More than five kilometers (three miles) of broken sewer lines were replaced.

Next, students turned their attention to constructing a wetland on school property that would help reduce stormwater runoff in the upper Muddy Run watershed. They wrote letters, made presentations to authorities, and helped to design, pay for, construct, and landscape the wetland, which was completed in September 1996.

In the past few years, they have tackled another long-standing problem caused by stormwater runoff: the flooding of homes in residential areas. To stop basement flooding and reduce erosion of the Muddy Run stream, the students worked with local partners to construct a swale and stabilize the stream bank. Excavation of the swale channel — 168 meters (550 feet) long, 11 meters (35 feet) wide, and 0.6 meters (2 feet) deep at the center — was completed in 1998. Planting a riparian buffer zone of large trees and understory shrubs to stabilize the swale completed the project. State funding for the project was obtained through a grant proposal co-authored by students. Other student projects have included:

- raising funds to purchase and plant more than 100 municipal street trees that were given free to homeowners
- completing watershed assessments for the Pennsylvania Department of Environmental Protection as part of the department's goal to assess more than 133,600 kilometers (83,000 miles) of streams by the year 2006
- completing streambank restoration projects
- creating and delivering an informational flyer to 400 residences in the Muddy Run watershed to

educate the public about land management practices that could help prevent stormwater runoff

- creating and disseminating a booklet listing the effects of 30 types of household pollutants and their environmentally safer alternatives

- initiating a school recycling program, which was later expanded to include the high school

- collecting water-quality data for use in a county-wide monitoring program

- presenting students' environmental work and findings to local service clubs, and at state and regional conferences

- raising funds for county projects to eliminate stormwater runoff problems

- educating the public by writing articles and educational advertisements dealing with environmental issues for the local newspaper

- establishing a tree honorarium program to recognize citizens who have made significant contributions to improve the quality of life in Huntingdon

By taking an active role and speaking constructively, students have also served the community in a less tangible but perhaps more important way: they have set examples of environmental stewardship and citizenship to demonstrate that genuine partnerships between youth and adults can bring great benefit to their communities. Student Heather Mentzer summarized the significance of becoming involved in community projects: "I've realized that, when students have the courage to speak and act with knowledge, adults will listen, and that not only adults have power to change things but students also have that power."

Academic impact

STREAMS dramatically affects how students learn and how instructors teach. By using the environment as the integrating context for their curricula, the team teachers have been able to provide more differentiated instruction and multiple-intelligence learning opportunities that enable students to understand the interconnections of content, links that are too often missed in traditional subject-specific teaching. Because lessons in one subject area are revisited and reinforced by activities in others, students are better able to comprehend, retain, and assimilate concepts. This combination of relevant hands-on learning and consistency across disciplines creates enthusiastically engaged learners, reduces discipline problems, reaches students with different learning styles, and significantly increases learning.

Two to five months after the STREAMS program, students are given multiple unannounced post-tests that assess their ecological knowledge and ability to interpret and analyze data. Some post-tests are constructed to be similar to national norm tests and the Pennsylvania State System Assessment tests for science, environment, and ecology, emphasizing vocabulary, comprehension, and analysis. Since 1992, students have demonstrated a high level of mastery and the average on these tests has been above 76 percent, whereas pre-test averages were in the 30 percent range. The educational benefit of using an integrated, interdisciplinary methodology is so significant that the program has been expanded to incorporate studies of other ecosystems and biomes, as well as agriculture. The school district now has a K–12 environment and ecology curriculum.

Providing students with a stimulating integrated environmental education that involves community action projects is a challenging but enjoyable reality at Huntingdon Area Middle School. "It is this type of academic endeavor that will help schools meet national standards in math and science," said school principal Jill Adams. "All it takes is a change in teaching approach, cooperative collaboration, and a willingness to make it happen."

Frederic R. Wilson teaches social studies at Huntingdon Middle School in Huntingdon, Pennsylvania, and is a workshop leader and consultant in environmental education.

Growing an Integrated Unit — Organically!

Food can unlock the rich potential of students to direct their own learning and to develop and act on new perspectives

by Dianne Clipsham and Letitia Charbonneau

Subject areas: geography, language arts, visual arts, health and science

Key concepts: integrated learning, process-mindedness, problem solving, global awareness

Skills: research skills

Location: indoors and outdoors

Time: 2-3 months

Materials: research tools

hat would an integrated thematic unit incorporating the goals and methods of global education look like? This was the question that two teacher-librarians (one middle school, one secondary) and one middle school French immersion teacher set out to explore as we planned the launch of a Grade 8 food unit on World Food Day (October 16) in 1993. We knew that the topic of food would rank high in interest among 13-year-olds; and we realized that having students investigate issues raised by the choices they make about the food they eat would offer us many opportunities for integrating traditional subjects (i.e., geography, language arts, visual arts, health, and science) with the goals of global education (development, peace and social justice, environment, and human rights).

We wanted the unit to help students develop both their research abilities and their initiative. We therefore tried to replace the traditional teacher-driven approach with a more democratic student-driven approach, using techniques of cooperative learning and peer teaching, and giving students the information they needed to begin their quest for answers to problems that they themselves identified. Whereas, formerly, the availability of resources might have determined the content of the unit, this time decisions about the problems to investigate were made by the students, and resources were then found to explore those issues more fully. Risky? For sure. But, with three teaching partners, two of whom had previous experience with these students, we thought we

could involve them and inspire them to action, as well as present opportunities for learning.

In planning the unit, we took very seriously the goal of process-mindedness, as expounded by Selby and Pike in *Global Teacher, Global Learner*, that "students should learn that learning and personal development are continuous journeys with no fixed or final destination."[1] The unit included three stages: developing awareness, providing opportunities for analysis, and lending support for action.[2] These stages were integrated into a process intended to develop creative problem-solving abilities with emphasis on divergent and convergent thinking skills (see diagram below).

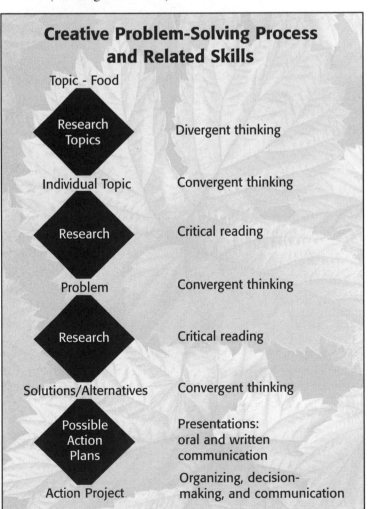

Creative Problem-Solving Process and Related Skills

Topic - Food	
Research Topics	Divergent thinking
Individual Topic	Convergent thinking
Research	Critical reading
Problem	Convergent thinking
Research	Critical reading
Solutions/Alternatives	Convergent thinking
Possible Action Plans	Presentations: oral and written communication
Action Project	Organizing, decision-making, and communication

Making Interdisciplinary Connections

Awareness

Students began the unit on World Food Day by playing a simulation game called Playing Fair? The Rules of World Hunger,[3] which sets out to dispel some of the myths about food shortages and to identify the causes of hunger. In playing the game, students learned that the main cause of hunger is not insufficient food, natural disaster, laziness, overpopulation, or ignorance of modern agricultural methods, but, rather, poverty. Students' interest was further stimulated by a series of spelling dictations from *The Supermarket Tour*[4] that related to the low nutritional value of popular breakfast cereals. Students also explored statistics related to food production and distribution using the MacWorld atlas and database on CD-ROM.

The theme of food was then introduced as a focus of a research project. Students brainstormed possible topics, first individually and then in small groups. Together we made a web of all their ideas, from which they selected their research topics (see diagram below). In previous research projects, students had been expected to formulate a fairly specific problem before beginning their research. This time, they had only very broad topics, and they worked closely with the teacher-librarian in the school resource center to focus and refine them.

The research component was integral to the process. In the first stage, the middle school teacher-librarian began by building on skills that students had previously acquired while researching the theme of water. After cautioning them that this kind of research can be frustrating and that they would "need a high level of tolerance for uncertainty," she introduced them to a wide variety of current materials from government and non-government agencies and provided a learning log to guide their research. The students were responsible for contacting local, national, and international agencies by telephone (in the library office) or the school fax

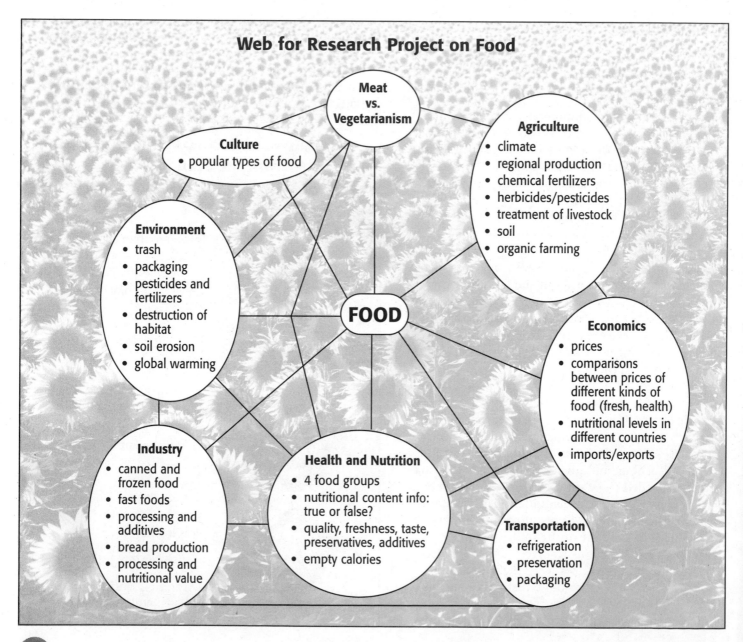

Web for Research Project on Food

Meat vs. Vegetarianism

Culture
- popular types of food

Agriculture
- climate
- regional production
- chemical fertilizers
- herbicides/pesticides
- treatment of livestock
- soil
- organic farming

Environment
- trash
- packaging
- pesticides and fertilizers
- destruction of habitat
- soil erosion
- global warming

FOOD

Economics
- prices
- comparisons between prices of different kinds of food (fresh, health)
- nutritional levels in different countries
- imports/exports

Industry
- canned and frozen food
- fast foods
- processing and additives
- bread production
- processing and nutritional value

Health and Nutrition
- 4 food groups
- nutritional content info: true or false?
- quality, freshness, taste, preservatives, additives
- empty calories

Transportation
- refrigeration
- preservation
- packaging

machine to set up interviews or add to their materials. At the end of the first research component, students formulated a problem statement based on the information they had collected. (See "Sample problem statements," below.)

Analysis

Having formulated their problem statements, students then moved from the awareness stage to the analysis stage. At this point, the unit became more student-driven and the classroom teacher became much more a facilitator and co-learner. Students who had similar areas of interest were placed together in groups, and within their groups they pooled information and became experts in that area.

The six groups covered a wide range of topics and issues, from nutrition and vegetarianism to food processing, agricultural practices, and food distribution. We wondered, however, whether their research would lead them to see the displays in the local food store with new eyes. We decided to take a supermarket tour in order to find out. For the tour, the groups were jigsawed, so that every tour group had one member from each of the expert groups. Students were given a questionnaire (see "Example of Supermarket Tour Questionnaire," right) and were expected to gather information at each of several defined stations in the store. In addition, at each station on the tour, the individual "experts" were responsible for sharing relevant information they had acquired, thus putting their research into context.

As a follow-up to the supermarket tour, students saw the video *The Hand That Feeds the World*.[5] While its focus is gender roles in food production and distribution, the film is also a very accessible introduction to the notion of food as a commodity. It provides a brief overview of the historical progression leading to the debt crisis that has forced many developing countries into maintaining cash crop

economies that reduce self-reliance and create a dependency on expensive imported products. The video helped students put the information they had gathered on the supermarket tour into a more global context. Discussion and analysis following the tour helped to prepare students for the second stage of research, which was to identify solutions to their problem.

The next step in the research process was a visit to the Merivale High School library where the teacher-librarian and her "peer researchers" introduced the Grade 8 students to resources within and beyond the school walls. The students learned how to locate and evaluate sources from a variety of media, from newspapers and magazines on CD-ROM to the Internet. Aware of one another's research problems, students began to share information and many came to realize that numerous food issues are closely connected. For example, students studying the economic impact of chemical pesticides and fertilizers came across information related to the impact of these products on human health, which they passed on to students working on health and nutrition. Students working on the health effects of meat consumption found

---

Example of Supermarket Tour Questionnaire

Station 1: Fresh Produce

1. *(Space left for point form notes on experts' information)*
2. Identify seven countries and their products.
3. In what country do the majority of products originate?
4. Is it always possible to identify the country of origin? Why or why not?
5. Can you find a product that seems to be Canadian/American but is actually from another country? What do you think causes this confusion?
6. What is used to preserve the mandarin oranges? Can you find other examples of how fresh produce is preserved?

Sample Problem Statements

- Chemical fertilizers and pesticides can affect our health. What are the alternatives?

- Why are independent farmers' revenues decreasing? Who benefits?

- Raising cattle creates environmental problems. What can people do to eat less meat but still get the protein they need?

- Food packaging is a problem for the environment and increases the cost to buyers. How can food be transported and preserved without so much packaging?

- Many countries need food relief so that people will not suffer from hunger. What are the good and bad aspects of food aid? What needs to happen so that food relief is no longer needed?

- Eating disorders can damage your health. What causes these disorders and how can young people be helped to overcome them?

- Some animals suffer because of the way they are raised. What are some of the ways this could be avoided?

information on the environmental costs of raising beef, which they passed on to students working on the environmental impact of agriculture. Many students also began to discover that what is happening in developing countries is also happening at home (e.g., the impact of agribusiness on individual farm incomes, requiring farmers to work at other jobs). Our hopes began to materialize at this point, as students became enthusiastic learners.

Presentation

Students presented their information orally to their jigsawed groups and handed in written reports in which they were required to give background information on their problem and justify the solution(s) they had identified. Their imagination and originality made it a pleasure to evaluate their work. Games, videos, articles, posters, and pamphlets were only some of the forms their reports took. The high quality and depth of the reports reflected well-honed research and thinking skills, and convinced us that the students had been able to integrate, analyze, and evaluate a tremendous amount of information.

Action Planning Guide

Developing a Strategy

1. Identify key people to work with on the issue: who has power? who has responsibility? who is affected?
2. Determine obstacles to accomplishing your goal as well as the resources available to overcome them.
3. Consider ways to build support in class, school, and the community.
4. Outline a plan and a timeline; identify tasks and roles (who will do what when?)

Organizing

These organizing principles may help guide you in your action project:

1. Dialog: be willing to listen to other viewpoints and to change positions.
2. Support: work as a team; build support within your group and in the community; think of the people, not only of the tasks; get advice and help.
3. Leadership: be a facilitator rather than a director; share leadership rather than taking control; listen, encourage, help, and show appreciation.
4. Appropriate action: don't make assumptions about what others want or need; be realistic; try to fit in with others' efforts; keep others informed.
5. Persistence: be ready to take risks, learn from mistakes, and be flexible; don't give up!
6. The means are the ends: the way you go about creating something will reflect on what you create; respect others rather than antagonize them.

Action

Following their presentations, students, now aware of the problems and solutions identified by their class, started formulating plans for an action project. Examples of actions toward solutions included:

- participation in World Vision's 30 Hour Famine
- persuading the student council to "purchase" four hectares (ten acres) of rainforest through the World Wildlife Fund
- increased participation in the school's Trashless Thursdays program
- planning for a video on eating disorders
- creating a game for younger students that integrated all of the food issues we had explored

The students were provided with a guide to planning action projects (see "Action Planning Guide" sidebar), but the outcome of these projects was very much left to students' initiative and persistence. Not all students were able to follow through because of logistics and time constraints; however, all of them benefited from planning together. This phase of the unit was crucial, for how could students think that their work or the problem they researched was significant if it ended with a report gathering dust on the teacher's desk? Their experience in this area demonstrated that change occurs in many small ways and that, individually and collectively, they could make a difference.

Evaluation

In such a process-oriented unit, skills development was much more the focus of evaluation than was content. Since the French immersion teacher was responsible for teaching science, geography, language, and visual arts, aspects of each activity and product were identified as pertaining to at least one of these subjects for summative evaluation, making it a truly interdisciplinary unit. Formative evaluation was an important part of the process, helping both to guide the development of the unit step by step, and to make students accountable for their use of class time and for deadlines. (See "Evaluation criteria," next page.) Peer evaluation was used a great deal to assess group work and presentations, and provided a means for making students accountable to one another.

The unit in retrospect

The success of this unit depended in large part on the presence and programs of teacher-librarians in both the middle school and high school settings. All three of us worked together to guide and nurture each student's independent thought and action. To succeed, we had to give up the time-honored teacher's role as the fount of all knowledge.

Nevertheless, we had to be aware of the concerns students would have as they became more conscious of food issues, and we had to become informed on these issues ourselves so that we could offer guidance. In the process, our own biases undoubtedly appeared. The students forced us to "walk our talk"; Letitia, for example, could not appear with a fast-food burger in her classroom again!

Experiences and explorations were planned to raise questions about food issues, but students were quick to form their own opinions. For example, the fact that cheese produced locally is priced higher than the corporate brand taught them about economies of scale — and many students saw the value of supporting local products even at a higher price. Similarly, they knew from previous research that pesticides are an environmental problem — but the fact that they are also a health problem convinced students of the value of organic produce. Parents, no doubt, were educated as well.

The students' enthusiasm and eagerness to influence change was astonishing to us. The three months we spent on the theme was not long enough and some students carried on throughout the year. Here are some of their comments:

"This project has really made me careful about what I put in my mouth."

"I had never thought that what I was eating made any difference to somebody else in another part of the world."

"I wish all our units had action projects. That was the part I felt the best about."

Partners developing an integrated global unit have to be willing to take risks and they must commit to working together in a more democratic, organic way of teaching than ever before. The integrated approach might seem time-consuming, and certainly involves much coordination and effort on everyone's part; but the results — such as seeing students making connections between global issues, and linking these to their own lives — are definitely worth it. And we really have no choice, for, as Thomas Berry has said, "What is clear is that the Earth is mandating that the human community assume a responsibility never assigned to any previous generation."[6]

Letitia Charbonneau teaches Primary Core French at A. Lorne Cassidy Elementary School in Stittsville, Ontario. Dianne Clipsham is a global education and school library consultant in Ottawa, Ontario. Both are founding members of the Ottawa Global Education Network <www.global-ed.org>. Gayle Brush, the third partner in the development and implementation of this unit, teaches at Henry Munro Middle School in Gloucester, Ontario.

Evaluation Criteria

For a research project:

Throughout the project, the student:

- identifies appropriate sources of information
- uses a variety of different and current sources of information
- takes clear point form notes
- distinguishes between fact and opinion
- detects and describes author's bias
- identifies main points and secondary detail
- collects sufficient information to support main topic
- formulates relevant research questions
- organizes research notes
- effectively uses supporting visual information (graphs, tables, maps, diagrams)
- prepares and edits a draft of final report
- respects timelines
- uses quotations and footnotes correctly
- prepares a complete bibliography
- clearly identifies, describes, and explains the problem and solution(s) related to his/her topic

For group work:

Here are some criteria that can be used for peer- or self-evaluation of students' participation while working in groups.

Throughout group work, the student:

- participates effectively in group discussions
- contributes to group effort with relevant information and ideas
- respects the group's timelines
- helps others by sharing relevant information
- listens to and respects others' ideas
- demonstrates initiative and/or leadership
- performs as an effective "expert" during the supermarket tour
- gives an effective oral presentation with supporting visual information
- contributes to the group's action plan
- participates in undertaking the group's action plan

Separate evaluation forms could be developed for the last four group activities with more specific criteria.

Notes:

1 Graham Pike and David Selby. *Global Teacher, Global Learner*. Hodder & Stoughton, 1988, p. 35.

2 For this approach, we credit the work of Janice Brown: see *The Leaven Project for Social Justice*. One World Research and Education Network. P.O. Box 381, Belleville, ON K8N 5A5, 613–478–5110, <www.owren.org>.

3 "Playing Fair? The Rules of World Hunger," World Vision Canada, 1990, <www.worldvision.ca>.

4 Philip White. *The Supermarket Tour*. Ontario Public Interest Research Group, 1990, p. 23. See revised 2002 edition listed in "Resources, Teachers Recommend," below.

5 Canadian World Food Day Association. *The Hand That Feeds the World*. Out of print. Excellent current information is available from <www.oxfam.ca/campaigns/WorldFoodDay.htm>.

6 Thomas Berry. *The Dream of the Earth*. Sierra Club Books, 1990.

RESOURCES

Students Recommend:

Additive Alert: What Have They Done to Our Food? Pollution Probe, 1994 625 Church Street, Suite 402, Toronto, ON M4Y 2G1, 416–926–1907, <www.pollutionprobe.org>.

Myers, Norman. *GAIA: An Atlas of Planet Management*. Doubleday, 1993.

Teachers Recommend:

Ballin, Amy, Jeffrey Benson, and Lucie Burt. *Trash Conflicts*. Educators for Social Responsibility, 1993. 23 Garden Street, Cambridge, MA 02138, 617–492–1764, <www.esrnational.org>.

Berry, Thomas. *The Dream of the Earth*. Sierra Club, 1990.

Burgess, Teri. "Economics For All" teacher's kit Oxfam Canada, 2000 (downloadable at <www.oxfam.ca>).

Global Education Network. "Chocolate: A Fair Trade and Human Rights Unit, Grades 6-10, 2003." Downloadable at <www.global-ed.org/cu-chocolate.pdf>.

Lee, Stella, Caroline Liffman, and Cindy McCulligh. *The Supermarket Tour*. Ontario Public Interest Research Group, 2002. Downloadable at <http://pirg.uwaterloo.ca/download/docs/TheSupermarketTour.pdf>; printed copies from OPIRG McMaster, 905–525–9140 ext. 27289.

Ontario School Library Association. "Information Studies: Kindergarten to Grade 12," 1998–99 <www.accessola.com/action/positions/info_studies>.

Oxfam Canada. "Putting Food on the Global Table" teacher's kit, 2000. Downloadable at <www.oxfam.ca>.

Pike, Graham, and David Selby. *Global Teacher, Global Learner*. Hodder & Stoughton, 1988.

Maps Tell Stories: Folklore and Geography

An interdisciplinary activity that uses geography, measurement, Earth science and folklore to explain landforms

by Brian "Fox" Ellis

Subject areas: social studies, language arts

Key concepts: relationships between mythology and geology, science and folklore.

Skills: map reading, map making, and creative writing

Location: indoors

Time: 2-3 hours for all 3 activities

Materials: see activities below

Throughout the world people tell stories of how things came to be. Mysterious mountains, unusually deep canyons, and precipitous cliffs are pregnant with stories of adventure, failure, and triumph. The Dine, or Navajo, say that the landscape stalks us with stories. These stories remind us of our place in the world; that cliff or this boulder reminds us of our relationship with others, of the right way to walk in this world. The Aborigines of the Australian Outback use stories as maps to help them find their way in that bleak landscape. The stories are told at a walking pace as they cross the land. As features of the landscape come into view, travelers are reminded of the next chapter in the story; and, as the story unfolds, they are reminded of which way to turn to get to the next watering hole, the next village, or wherever the chosen story leads.

These stories can be powerful tools for teachers who want to bring geography to life. Although they are considered fiction or folklore, many of them contain scientifically accurate interpretations of geological processes. Case in point: in many aboriginal versions of the creation of Turtle Island, or North America, the continent is shaped like a turtle and it is swimming in the ocean. It takes very little imagination to see Florida and Baja California as hind legs and Mexico as a tail; Alaska and Nova Scotia are peninsulas, or front legs, and Greenland is the head. The fact is that North America is moving like a turtle, slowly drifting five to eight centimeters (two to three inches) per year. Another example: in a Hawaiian creation story, the Earth Goddess belches fire and gives birth to Pele, the Goddess of the Volcano. Indeed, the Hawaiian Islands are volcanic eruptions from the Earth's underwater crust. These stories can make flat maps multidimensional, adding drama and suspense to the study of geography and geology. Such stories also add multicultural dimensions to the teaching of

Tom Goldsmith

geography. This is especially pertinent if you are teaching an ethnically diverse class and can include stories from students' cultures to enhance the teaching of content.

Reading the landscape

Begin the unit with a brief discussion of common landforms and how they are made. The following lists, while in no way complete, will serve as an introduction.

Types of landforms: hills, volcanoes, mountains, valleys, plateaus, rivers, plains, bays, canyons, islands

Causes: erosion, wind, water, plate tectonics, glacial carving, moraines, faults, earthquakes

Also introduce map vocabulary such as "elevation," "latitude," and "longitude," as well as color-coded keys. To make these ideas graphic and to give kinesthetic learners a hands-on opportunity to create topographical maps, invite the class to do one or both of the following activities.

Knuckle mountain

Goals:

• to gain a hands-on understanding of topographical maps

• to learn basic cartography skills

• to improve visual-spatial thinking ability.

Time: 25-30 minutes

Materials: paper and pencil, a water-soluble pen for drawing knuckles

Procedure:

1. Demonstrate for students by balling one hand into a fist and laying it flat on a table or desk. Next, draw concentric circles on your knuckles,

Tom Goldsmith

moving down in elevation approximately one centimeter (one-half inch) with each circle. The first circle will be a small irregular oval around the tallest knuckle. Moving down about one centimeter, draw a second oval that includes two or three knuckles. Draw a third, fourth, and fifth oval, each time moving one centimeter lower on the topography of your fist. You will notice that steep places have lines closer together, less steep places have lines farther apart, the gaps between fingers are inverted Vs, and, if you have bony hands or large blood veins, you will see little Us on the back of your hand.

2. After drawing the lines on your fist, flatten your hand on the table and you will see a two-dimensional topographical map that approximates the three-dimensional Knuckle Mountain. Demonstrate this for the students and then draw your topographical map on the chalkboard or overhead projector.

3. Discuss water drainage, elevation changes, and how the proximity of lines relates to steepness, thereby capturing three dimensions on a flat page.

4. Ask students to draw lines on their fists, flatten their hands, and then copy the topographical map of their Knuckle Mountain on a piece of paper.

5. Have students color code their maps and make a key to explain the colors. To further their understanding of three-dimensional thinking, students could also draw a mural of Knuckle Mountain based on the reading of their topographical maps. What would this mountain look like from the south? from the northeast?

Underwater mountains

Students can perform this activity individually or in small groups of two to four students. The advantages of group work are that students ensure each other's accuracy and you need fewer sets of materials.

Goals:

• to gain a hands-on understanding of topographical maps

• to learn basic cartography skills

• to improve visual-spatial thinking ability

Time: 25-30 minutes

Materials: small pointed rocks with a diameter and height of 10–15 centimeters (4–6 inches) water a large flat-bottomed bowl with straight sides deep enough to submerge the stones, paper and pencil

Procedure:

1. Instruct students to measure carefully the depth of the bowl and draw notches every one centimeter (one-half inch) on the inside of it.

2. Ask them to place one pointed rock in the bottom of the bowl and then pour one centimeter of water into the bowl. Have each group of students draw the shape of their stone at the water line.

3. Ask the students to add water to raise the water line to the next one-centimeter increment, and then draw the shape of the stone at the new water line on the same map they began in the previous step.

4. Repeat this process until only a small tip of the rock protrudes from the water. The maps will be a series of concentric circles.

5. Have students color code their topographical maps and make a key to explain the colors.

6. As a test of the efficacy of their maps, have each group or student trade maps with another who used a different stone. Using only the map, have them draw the stone it depicts. When everyone is finished, place the stones on a central table. Ask students to try to match their own drawings and their partners' maps with the correct stone.

Extension: Each group or student now has a topographical map of their rock. This could be a springboard for discussions of scale, volcanoes as underwater mountains, altitudes above and below sea level, ways in which actual mountain maps and seafloor maps are drawn, and the reading of real topographical maps.

Telling and writing landform stories

Time: 1-2 hours

Materials: class set of topographical maps, collections of mythology

Once students have a basic understanding of topographical maps and landforms, introduce landform stories from various cultures. Discuss, for example, Paul Bunyan, Pele the Fire Goddess, Turtle Island, Sleeping Bear Dunes, Devil's Tower, and other landform stories they may know. (See Recommended Reading) Tell the story of "The Twin Sisters," "Coyote Dances with the Stars," "Grandma Turtle," or one of your favorite landform stories. After telling the story discuss the facts and the fiction within the story. Which parts are scientifically accurate? Which are fictional? What could we learn from this story about the creation of landforms? What could we learn from the culture depicted in the story?

Pass out detailed topographical maps of your region, country, or the world. Challenge students to choose an actual landform on the map, such as a river valley or mountain, and draw a picture of it based on their translation of the two-dimensional map representation into a three-dimensional landform. Ask them to hypothesize about the geological processes that created this landform as they draw. They could also begin to daydream about stories in which they would explain this formation.

Using the Prior Knowledge Quiz below, challenge students to brainstorm the details of their creation myth. You may want to begin with the questions about setting and then ask the questions about characters. Ask students to close their eyes and, using their answers to the questions as the raw materials, daydream a vivid, virtual-reality version of their story. Tell them to make it up as they go along, as if they are watching a movie inside their head. When they open their eyes, ask them to turn to a partner and take turns telling their stories. Writing is always clearer and more succinct if students first tell it and then write it.

After students have a rough draft of their stories, assist them in researching the scientific facts about their landforms, focusing on the geological processes that actually shaped their piece of the Earth. As an incentive, offer bonus points for weaving this scientific information into their story as they rewrite their creation myths.

When the stories are finished, each student could create a topographical map of their landform as well as a mural of their story with the canyon, mountain, or island in the background. These could be bound together as a classroom collection of short stories or mounted on a bulletin board. Students could also recite or perform their stories for their class.

The Prior Knowledge Quiz

Every story needs three main ingredients: characters, setting, and plot. The following questions will help your students to gather their thoughts and collect the information they need to bring their stories to life. I use these questions to help students write a wide range of stories, from ecological adventures to historical fiction, ghost stories to fables.

Warn students that the questions will be asked at a rapid-fire pace and you do not expect them to answer all of them. (It's a good idea to repeat the most important questions two or three times to be sure they are answered.) Many of the questions can be answered in one or two words and some will need a brief phrase or two, but complete sentences are not needed at this point. For questions they cannot answer, ask students to make up an answer or do a little research to find the correct answer. Together, these answers will become the raw materials for building their stories.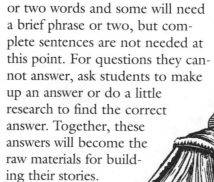

Characters: The big character question is who is in the story? Answer each of these questions for all of the characters: What are their names? What do they look like? What kind of clothes do they wear? What color of skin, hair, and eyes do they have? Are there any scars, deformities, or unusual characteristics? You can tell a lot about people by what they look like, but don't stop there. How do they talk? What do they talk about? What tone of voice? You can tell a lot about people by what they say and how they say it. Take a minute and imagine a dialog between two characters: what do they talk about? What do they do? What kind of job do they have? What do they do for fun? What do they eat? What kinds of games do they play? What kinds of songs do they sing? Don't say they are nice or evil: show this through their behavior; you can tell a lot about people by what they do and how they do it.

Setting: The big setting questions are where and when does the story take place? What country, what city? What kind of environment? What plants and animals live there? What type of weather do they have? If they are traveling, where are they coming from and going to? What does the landscape look like? Are there any mountains, rivers, hills, or valleys? How does the landscape change? What does their home look like? Of what is it made? What time of day is it? What time of year? What time in history? Don't just say it was ten o'clock on a winter morning: show this in the details. How do you know what season or time of day it is? Use all of your senses: What do you smell? hear? feel? Is it moist or dry? cold or hot? What is the emotional feeling of the place? Do the characters feel safe? Is it tense? scary? relaxed? How does this feeling change as the story changes?

Plot: The big plot question is what happens? The little question is: and then what happens? and then what happens? and then what happens? What problems do people face in this environment? What problems do people have with the weather, storms, droughts, floods, or blizzards? What problems do people have with the plants, animals, or insects? What are the universal problems that people have always had, such as loneliness, jealousy, head-over-heels love, rage, rudeness, birth, death, separation? Make a list of possible problems. Next to each problem make a short list of possible solutions. If you were that person in that situation, what would you try to do to solve the problem? What do you learn from this experience? How does your character change because of this success or failure? How does this problem and its solution help to shape the landscape?

Make an outline of your plot. What happens first? Where is a good place to start? And then what happens? What problem do your characters face? How do they respond? Maybe they try but fail the first time. What happens next? How do they succeed? How does your story end?

Brian "Fox" Ellis is a storyteller and naturalist who performs at schools and conferences throughout North America. He is the author of Learning from the Land: Teaching Ecology Through Stories and Activities. *He lives in Peoria, Illinois.*

RECOMMENDED READING

Baylor, Byrd. *The Way to Make Perfect Mountains.* ill. Leonard F. Chana. Cinco Puntos Press, 1997. ISBN 0-938317-26-11997; 62 pp.

Beautifully erasing boundaries between science and mythology, Byrd Baylor uses finely crafted poetry to illuminate the mountains of the southwest desert. With an emphasis on magic and mystery, she retells aboriginal legends of sacred mountains that she has collected from her neighbors and literary sources. The unique stippling method of the illustrator could be used to teach the students a new form of landscape illustration.

Bruchac, Joseph. *Between Earth and Sky: Legends of Native American Sacred Places.* ill. Thomas Locker. Harcourt, 1996. ISBN 0-15-200042-9; 32 pp.

Featuring such famous North American landmarks as the Grand Canyon and Niagara Falls, Bruchac briefly retells the aboriginal legends of several unique geological formations. Locker's glorious oil paintings are reminiscent of the Hudson River School of Art, which celebrated the wild landscapes of America at the turn of the century. These brief retellings could easily be researched and elaborated into dramatic performance material or rewritten as myths that have an emphasis on science.

Craighead George, Jean. *Dear Katie, The Volcano is a Girl.* ill. Daniel Powers Hyperion Books, 1998. ISBN 0-7868-0314-2; 32 pp.

This is the perfect example of mythology-meets-science in a beautifully illustrated children's book. Through a fictional dialog between a scientific grandmother and a little girl who believes in the mythology of Pele, the Fire Goddess of Hawaii, the reader sees the validity of both points of view. The illustrator even went so far as to include a mystical goddess prompting the scientific schematic drawings of how volcanoes are made.

Wargin, Kathy-jo. *The Legend of Sleeping Bear.* ill. Gijsbert van Frankenhuyzen. Sleeping Bear Press, 1998. ISBN 1-886947-35-X; 42 pp.

Gail Littlejohn

A forest fire in Wisconsin forces a mother bear and her two cubs to swim across Lake Michigan. The cubs do not make it, leaving the mother to grieve on the Michigan shore, forming Sleeping Bear Dunes. The cubs become North and South Manitou Islands. The illustrator earns extra points for scientific accuracy in his realistic renderings of the plant and animal life. He even included a map in the end papers. This Ojibwa story is well told, if a bit flowery. It could be a stronger example of a landscape story with just a sentence or two about the sand deposition from glacial times in the formation of these islands and sand dunes.

Rossman, Douglas A. *Where Legends Live: A Pictorial Guide to Cherokee Mythic Places.* ill. Nancy-Lou Patterson. Cherokee Publications, 1998. ISBN 0-935741-10-0; 48 pp.

With black and white photos, extensive site descriptions, and a keyed map, this is the ultimate field guide to the mythic places of the Cherokee homeland. The author gives only a brief synopsis of each story, but recommends James Mooney's *Myths of the Cherokee* for a more complete version. If every region of the country had a book like this, we would have a much richer relationship with the mythos of our home and a much deeper sense of place.

Environmental History: If Trees Could Talk

Interdisciplinary projects that invite original research and a deeper understanding of human relationships to land

by **Marsha Alibrandi, Lucy Laffitte, Cheryl Oakes, and Steven Anderson**

Subject areas: social studies

Key concepts: cultural landscape, historic trees, place names, paleobotany, paleoclimatology, dendrochronology

Skills: mapping, data collection, trends analysis, nterviewing, critical thinking

Location: indoors and outdoors

Time: 2 days to one 1 semester

Materials: Internet, software, see also individual activities

On the last day of school in 1998, just as the final busload of students was leaving, bulldozers were already clearing the site for the expansion of Ligon Middle School in Raleigh, North Carolina. The buzz of chainsaws drew two teachers to their classroom windows. Below, the oak trees that had guarded the school's front entrance were being cut down. Heartsick at seeing historic trees felled, the teachers rushed out to the tree crew and asked them to set aside cross-sections of the trees. The crew salvaged two huge heavy slabs, 1 meter (3 feet) across and 10 centimeters (4 inches) thick, and helped the teachers to carry them inside the building for safekeeping. Silent witnesses to history, these giant cross-sections sent a message that was loud and clear: there is a story here that needs to be told. Since then, the salvaged tree sections have become an insistent link to the past, leading the teachers and their students to embark on an interdisciplinary environmental history project that has transformed the school community and inspired a deep appreciation of its unique history.

Tim Grant

Students have recorded oral histories of the school's African-American alumni, mapped historical architecture in town, generated Geographic Information System maps of Civil Rights era segregation, used CITYgreen software[1] to document tree locations and growth, and presented their research at school and community events and in newspaper articles, journals, and books. Through school and community partnerships, the school is now a site on the city's Millennium Trail — literally, on the map — and a model of interdisciplinary curriculum. One of the cross-sections of the tree, now preserved, is being mounted in a permanent museum-quality exhibit as a timeline for the school's riveting history as the city's premier African-American high school before and during the Civil Rights era.[2]

Environmental history is everywhere

Environmental history is everywhere, in every schoolyard, every neighborhood, and every community. Defined as "the history of human interaction with the natural world,"[3] it can be seen in the patterns of stone walls, in the placement of roads and bridges, in the materials of buildings, in the artifacts of prehistoric settlements, and in the changing patterns of land use over time. Our parks, plantings, farms, places of worship, hunting grounds, cemeteries — all are evidence of human needs and cultural preferences that have modified, and been modified by, the natural landscape. Literally "hands-on history," environmental history combines investigations of the natural environment with studies of material culture in order to create a deeper understanding of human relationships with land. It can range from a study of the history of logging or mining in a region to investigations of land use, urban development, and subsistence agriculture through time.

Environmental history can be critical to understanding some present-day environmental problems. For example, in a 1980s court case, investigation of the history of an industrial site helped to unlock the mystery of high cancer rates, including the leukemia deaths of eight children, in a Massachusetts community.[4] In that case, environmental history revealed the mortifying toll that human-environment interactions can take: a community's groundwater supply had been contaminated with chemicals used by successive tenants of a streamside property, from 19th century tanners to 20th century chemical manufacturers.

Because environmental history concerns itself with the interaction between humans and the landscape over time, it has the potential to put environmental studies into a wider and, at the same time, more personal context. We dwell in landscapes that are rapidly being altered by human activities. Any group of 13-year-olds can tell of changes in their own neighborhood during their short lives. Environmental history adds this chronological aspect to environmental studies, combining students' natural curiosity about their environment with the study of local history and culture. By investigating how their own landscapes and communities have changed over time, they can begin to understand the cultural, economic, and political influences behind these changes and to think about the imprint that they themselves might leave on the land.

Environmental history in the curriculum

Depending on the scope and breadth of your curriculum, environmental history can fit into subject areas beyond traditional environmental studies and science and into geography, history, and social studies.

In history and environmental studies, students can

By investigating how their own landscapes and communities have changed over time, students can begin to understand the cultural, economic, and political influences behind these changes and to think about the imprint that they themselves might leave on the land.

Forest History Society

Old photos are a starting point for environmental history: above, clearing land for a Pennsylvania homesteader's cabin; below, forest turned into a mountain of railroad ties.

correlate landmarks in environmental history with human timelines to discover connections between socio-political and environmental changes. The past 400 years in the history of North America's forests provide a classic example of the inter-relationship of ecology and human history. In general, forests along the east coast were harvested during early settlement, overcut during the industrial age, left to regenerate during the World Wars, and protected in the post-war and contemporary eras. The story west of the Great Lakes skipped the settlement harvesting and began with the industrial age. The history of the condition of North America's forests therefore reflects patterns of settlement, economic conditions, technological change, political events, and changes in North American attitudes toward the natural environment. Such case-study environmental history modules can help students begin to develop the perspectives necessary for making decisions about the future of the landscapes they themselves will inhabit.

In Earth science, environmental history can introduce students to new areas of research such as paleobotany, paleoclimatology, dendrochronology, and glaciology, encouraging students to understand how knowledge of the Earth's past helps to inform our understanding of environmental issues such as climate change. For example, using core samples from glaciers and lakes that contain preserved pollen, ash, and even trapped gases, scientists are creating multilayered snapshots of past climate and ecology in specific regions. As a mosaic of regional studies develops, students can analyze grander patterns, such as atmospheric conditions over time, and thus discern the role of human activities in environmental change. Trends in concentrations of atmospheric carbon dioxide, for instance, illustrate the impact of our use of fossil fuels over the past hundred years. This knowledge is in turn guiding the development of alternative and more energy-efficient technologies.

Geography, because it encompasses both culture and landscape, has a natural connection to environmental history. By researching historic maps — accessible through digital archives such as those at the Library of Congress website — students can gain an understanding of settlement and land-use patterns and the historic locations of natural resources. By determining the original habitats of indigenous species in their region, students can learn about previous ecological conditions and investigate how and why these conditions have changed over time.

Environmental history projects can also include investigations of natural features, such as trees, that are closely linked to the culture and history of the people who planted or protected them. Consider that people plant trees for many reasons: for beautification; for protection from wind and sun; as sources of food, fuel, paper, and building materials; as living memorials of people and events. The placement of trees and parks in urban landscapes and the protection of large tracts for regional or national parks or historic preserves represent the actions and attitudes of humans toward the environment, both past and present.

Many older trees, by their species, are indicators of past ecological conditions and/or human values. Some are evidence of past social customs, such as the bridal trees — trees planted in pairs on the front lawns of colonial homesteads — that can still be seen in preserved North American landscapes. Many individual trees have interesting histories of their own and some are even documented, both in local histories and in national databases of "big" and "significant" trees. In Amherst, Massachusetts, students developed a tree inventory around the city's 17th-century common. By correlating this with an inventory of historic houses and bird's-eye views of Amherst from earlier days, it was possible to construct a picture of the town through various periods in its history.

Getting started

How can teachers and students go about reconstructing the successive layers of their own region's environmental history? Land titles, historic accounts of towns and counties, old photographs, paintings, and bird's-eye drawings from the 1800s can all provide starting points

Tim Grant

Our parks, plantings, farms, places of worship, hunting grounds, cemeteries ó all are evidence of human needs and cultural preferences that have modified, and been modified by, the natural landscape.

for environmental history investigations. Consider the following:

- Collect historic maps of the county or region. Check to see whether a series of maps from different periods already exists in a community archive, museum, or planning office. Otherwise a scavenger hunt of the maps available from various resource agencies should help students to construct a timeline.

- Visit local archives to view current and historic tax maps and assessment rolls. Have students find out the age of their own houses or other significant buildings, and the names of previous residents.

- Locate abandoned mines or mills on maps using toponymy (the study of place names) as a clue. A town named Millcroft may no longer have a mill, but its name tells a story that can become the basis for further research.

- Take a walk to local historic districts, commons areas, historic landmarks, parks, and cemeteries, and locate these on maps. If students have cameras, they can photograph interesting features of these sites and begin to develop a photo archive.

- Search the Internet for bird's-eye views of the town. Many such drawings were lithographed in the 1800s.

- Gather the oral history of the community by interviewing long-time residents, especially those whose livelihoods are closely linked with natural resources, such as hunters, loggers, fishers, farmers, and builders. Aboriginal communities may be willing to share some of their oral histories or traditional knowledge about your area.

- Invite a title searcher to speak to the class about local land use history to help students begin to develop a time-layered understanding of places and the people who have lived in them.

- Initiate learning about material culture by visiting a local historical museum. Give students an assignment to draw an object from the past, of which they do not know the origin or purpose. Have them research these items through antique inventories or journals as a starting point for understanding life in different eras.

Environmental history is an exciting new area that will grow ever more complex through our students' lifetimes. Because the field is young, it offers middle school students an opportunity to conduct original research in their own social and natural environments — to expand their personal landscapes, to discover their neighborhoods and communities, to understand the forces behind past and present changes. By analyzing their surroundings in this way, students can begin to develop the perspectives necessary for making thoughtful decisions about what these landscapes will become in the future.

Arboreal archives

Skills: mapping, data collection, analyzing trends

Location: indoors and outdoors

Time: 2 days and up

Materials: copies of map or aerial photo of schoolyard, tags, measuring tape, line level, pencils, paper or notebooks, camera.

Many students participate in planting trees in the schoolyard, but often their efforts are not documented beyond the photos taken to capture the excitement of planting day. Maintaining long-term records of schoolyard trees helps to build an appreciation for the importance of these organisms, both as living symbols of the school's history and as part of the changing ecology of the schoolyard. By systematically recording observations of factors such as tree growth, canopy, shade cover, the presence or absence of companion species of birds and insects, and even diseases, students can begin to understand progressive ecological relationships. Are migratory

Tim Grant

species nesting in the trees year after year? Are there invasive species or diseases affecting the trees' health that were not present in the past? When students return to the schoolyard in 10, 20, or 30 years, how will the trees have changed? With attention to these micro-ecosystems, students can begin to develop a detailed understanding of the complexity of factors affecting even schoolyard environments.

Beyond their ecological role, schoolyard trees also have enormous esthetic, cultural, and historical value. The spindly sapling planted today will become, for tomorrow's students, a leafy haven under which to meet friends, a place to hang a handmade birdfeeder, a durable companion to lean on, an inspiration for art, poetry, and songwriting. The tree itself will also have stories to tell: of the big storm that split a branch, of the careless mower that gouged the bark, of the day the school bus backed up too far. By keeping records of these events, and reading the records kept by previous students, students can begin to appreciate the relationship that develops between humans and their natural and cultural landscapes, and to see themselves as part of the continuum of the school's and community's history.

As a first step in documenting schoolyard trees, students should conduct a survey to gather as much information as possible about the number, size, species, location, and condition of the trees, as well as their value to the school and community. This information can become the basis of a database and archive that will grow and develop as new observations are recorded in successive years. The school librarian may be able to guide students and teachers in archival techniques and

Sample Tree Survey				
Tree #	Species	Girth	Human interactions	Value to school
11	White cedar	28 cm (11 in.)	planted, pruned, mulched	Planted for appearance. Winter birds roost in branches. Kindergarten hangs handmade birdfeeders on it.
12	Sugar maple	49 cm (19 in.)	soil compaction around roots	Provides needed shade in play ground. Robins nest in branches. Fall leaves beautify the schoolyard and are used in art projects.
13	White oak	76 cm (30 in.)	barbed wire buried in bark, mower scars at the base	Magnificent oak, probably planted by first family to build a home on this site. Important history is embedded in the tree.

206

procedures, and set aside a shelf in the library along with other school archival information. This would likely include the original blueprints for the building, and perhaps photos that could help in identifying the locations and planting dates of schoolyard trees.

The design of forms for systematic collection, recording, and presenting of archival information is a study in itself. It can foster organizational and systems skills that will help students in any subject area. (A simple example is shown on page 206.) Having students work in groups to complete the tree surveys will likely yield uneven data that will need to be shared, reviewed, and revised. This not only gives practice in the process of conducting original research, but also results in a collaborative team product.

Tree survey procedure:

1. Obtain a map of the schoolyard, preferably an aerial photograph. This might be obtainable from the physical plant office of the school board or via the Internet. Number every tree on the map and make distribute copies of the map to the class.

2. In the schoolyard, have students locate every numbered tree and tag each tree with the number assigned to it on the map.

3. Have students draw in trees that have been planted since the map or photograph was made, and cross out any trees that have been removed.

4. Using a measuring tape and a line level, have students measure and record the circumference of each tree at 1.3 meters (4.5 feet) from the ground.

5. Ask students to observe and record any evidence of human activity that has affected the shape or condition of each tree.

6. Back in the classroom, have students create a list of the trees. On the list, ask students to note the value of each tree to the school in economic, esthetic, and ecological terms.

7. Have students design a permanent exhibit and an archive to present the information they have collected, and find a place to store it so that other students can carry on their observations over time.

Tim Grant

A school tree ordinance

An ordinance is a formal document that expresses community values by establishing rules related to a matter of

public interest or public lands. One way to raise awareness of the value of the school's trees, and the need to plant and preserve them, is to have students work together to draft a school tree ordinance. Ideally, an ordinance will have three main sections:

- *Findings:* states evidence that forms the rationale for the guidelines laid down by the ordinance; in a school tree ordinance, this section could include significant findings from students' tree surveys (e.g., numbers of trees), the various ecological services performed by the trees, and the values that humans place on the trees.

- *Purposes:* states the purposes of the ordinance; for a school tree ordinance, these might include implementing a tree-planting program, establishing guidelines for maintenance, or educating students and community about the importance of schoolyard trees and the urban forest in general.

- *General Authority:* states who is responsible for the actions and activities to implement and enforce the ordinance.

If it is to be implemented, a school tree ordinance requires the input and support of the entire school community. One group of students might do the groundwork by drafting sections and circulating them to the administration, students, and staff to elicit further ideas. To fire enthusiasm, the group could make an initial presentation to the school community in which they highlight findings from their tree survey, complete with maps of the schoolyard and descriptions of the values of the significant trees. Ensure that you have the support of school administration and maintenance personnel by including them in all planning sessions.

As an aid in drafting their own ordinance, have students investigate whether the local municipality has a tree ordinance that could serve as a model. Otherwise, have students read the excerpt from the tree ordinance established by the U.S. Congress in the 1978 *Cooperative Forestry Assistance Act* (see page 209). The Tree Ordinance Brief (see page 208) is a sample outline that students could use as a guideline in formulating the school ordinance.

Tree Ordinance Brief

Findings

Because

- the schoolyard is home to ___ trees
- the schoolyard is shaded by trees __% [use map to estimate]
- the trees provide _____
- the trees aid _____
- the trees promote _____
- the trees enhance _____
- the trees improve _____
- the trees strengthen _____
- the schoolyard trees keep several tons of CO_2 out of the atmosphere, a schoolyard tree ordinance is in order.

Purposes

The purposes of this ordinance are to

- improve _____
- encourage _____
- provide _____
- implement _____

General Authority

The school principal is authorized to

- protect existing trees,
- raise money to finance tree protection by _____
- have mulch spread by _____
- have limbs and branches trimmed by _____
- have new trees planted every _____
- raise money to purchase new trees by _____
- have a landscape plan drawn up by _____
- ensure tree planting is supervised by _____
- ensure that care and maintenance of the new trees is carried out by _____

RESOURCES FOR ENVIRONMENTAL HISTORY PROJECTS

On-line curricula

<www.lib.duke.edu/forest/curriculum/> *If Trees Could Talk*. curriculum by The Forest History Society, Durham, North Carolina.

<www.ncsu.edu/ligon/about/ history/intro.htm> The Ligon History Project, an environmental history project in a North Carolina middle school.

<www.nhc.rtp.nc.us/tserve/nattrans/nattrans.htm> Nature Transformed, an environmental history curriculum.

<www.nationalgeographic.com/xpeditions/lessons/06/g912/ cultural.html> A cultural landscape lesson plan from *National Geographic*.

<www.runet.edu/~wkovarik/hist1/timeline.new.html> Environmental History Timeline.

<www.iisd.org/rio+5/timeline/sdtimeline.htm>.

<www.geocities.com/RainForest/3621/HIST.HTM> Sustainable Development Timeline. Environmental Conflict in History.

Historical maps and bird's-eye views

Antique maps and on-line galleries; also images of maps are for sale. <www.georgeglazer.com> and <www.portsmouthbookshop.com/ world_index.htm>.

Bird's eye views of Canadian cities. <www.ssc.uwo.ca/assoc/acml/ views.html>.

Pre-fire bird's-eye views of Chicago, 1820–71. <www.chicagohs.org/fire/prefire/views.html>.

U.S. Library of Congress Map Collection, 1500–2003 (includes some Canadian regions): <http://memory.loc.gov/ammem/gmdhtml/ gmdhome.html>.

Public Archives of Canada. *Bird's-Eye Views of Canadian Cites: An Exhibition of Panoramic Maps (1865-1905), July to November 1976.* Public Archives of Canada, 1976.

Reps, John W. *Views and Viewmakers of Urban America: Lithographs of Towns and Cities in the United States and Canada, Notes on the Artists and Publishers, and a Union Catalog of their Work, 1825-1925.* University of Missouri Press, 1984. A comprehensive discussion and listing of panoramic maps of North American towns.

Champion and historic trees

Big trees of British Columbia. <srmwww.gov.bc.ca/cdc/trees>.

American Forests National Register of Big Trees. <www.americanforests.org/resources/bigtrees/>.

The Historic Trees Project (U.S.). <home.earthlink.net/~jeffkrueger/histtree.html>.

Champion Tree Project International. <www.championtreeproject.org>.

Archiving photographs

The creation of a digital photo archive can be facilitated by using an on-line photo service such as Photoworks or Shutterfly. Whether using a digital or conventional film camera, you can receive prints, order images on disk or CD, and store images on-line for no extra charge. The on-line archive service is an excellent depository for a budding collection. The Ligon History project used the service for retrieving and storing images.

Gail Littlejohn

Natural and cultural history converge at the 150-year-old Red Cloud Cemetery in Ontario. Planted red pines were cut down in the 1990s after botanists recognized the site as a rare and restorable remnant of tallgrass prairie.

Cooperative Forestry Assistance Act of 1978   Sections 9(a)–(c)

Findings

9. (a) The Congress finds that:

1. the health of forests in urban areas and communities, including cities, their suburbs and towns, in the United States is on the decline;

2. forest lands, shade trees and open spaces in urban areas and communities improve the quality of life for residents;

3. forest lands and associated natural resources enhance the economic value of residential and commercial property in urban and community settings;

4. urban trees are 15 times more effective than forest trees at reducing the build up of carbon dioxide and aid in promoting energy conservation through mitigation of the heat island effect in urban areas;

5. tree plantings and ground covers ... in urban areas and communities can aid in reducing carbon dioxide emission, mitigating heat island effects and reducing energy consumption, thus contributing to efforts to reduce global warming trends;

6. efforts to encourage tree plantings and protect existing open spaces in urban areas and communities can contribute to social well-being and promote a sense of community in these areas;

7. strengthened research, education, technical assistance and public information and participation in tree planting and maintenance programs for trees and complementary ground covers for urban and communities forests are needed to provide for the protection and expansion of tree cover and open space in urban areas and communities.

Purposes

(b) The purposes of this section are to:

1. improve understanding of the benefits of preserving existing tree cover in urban areas and communities;

2. encourage owners of private residences and commercial properties to maintain trees and expand forest cover on their properties;

3. provide education programs and technical assistance to State and local organizations in maintaining forested lands and individual trees in urban and community settings;

4. implement a tree planting program to complement urban and community tree maintenance and open space programs and to reduce carbon dioxide emissions, conserve energy, and improve air quality in addition to providing other environmental benefits.

General Authority

(c) The Secretary is authorized to provide financial, technical and related assistance to State foresters for the purpose of encouraging States to provide information and technical assistance to State foresters or equivalent State officials for he purpose of encouraging States to provide information and technical assistance to units of local government and others that will encourage cooperative efforts to plan urban forestry programs and to plant, protect and maintain, and utilize wood from, trees in open spaces, greenbelts, roadside screens, parks, woodlands, curb areas and residential developments in urban areas. The Secretary is also authorized to cooperate directly with units of local government and others in implementing this section whenever the Secretary and the affected State forester or equivalent State official agree that direct cooperation would better achieve the purposes of this section.

Forest History Society

Marsha Alibrandi is associate professor of teacher education at North Carolina State University. Lucy Laffitte is an environmental educator. Cheryl Oakes is an archivist at the Forest History Society in Durham, North Carolina. Steven Anderson is president of the Forest History Society in Durham, North Carolina.

The Tree Survey and School Tree Ordinance activities are adapted from Durham, North Carolina, Forest History Society, "Trees in Your Own Backyard" in If Trees Could Talk: A Curriculum in Environmental History *(<www.lib.duke.edu/forest/curriculum/>).*

Notes

1 CITYgreen software is an extension of ArcView, a Geographic Information System (GIS) software produced by the Environmental Systems Research Institute and commonly used in educational settings. If students are already using ArcView to create GIS maps of the schoolyard, CITYgreen will help them to frame their data collection and create an ongoing environmental history archive. Users can represent trees on GIS maps, input photos and data on specific trees, maintain data on soil and other conditions, and project the growth of trees into the future. CITYgreen is available from American Forests at <www.americanforests.org>.

2 A description of the Ligon History Project and many of its subsequent developments can be found on-line at <www.ncsu.edu/ligon/about/history/intro.htm>.

3 Definition by the American Society for Environmental History, publishers of the international journal *Environmental History*.

4 The case was documented in Jonathan Harr's book *A Civil Action*, Random House, 1995, and also made into a film.

Paradise Lost:
How Do We Define Progress?

Learning about the past helps students adjust their sights on the future

by Brian Loggie and Jim Petrie

Subject areas: social studies, language arts, science

Key concepts: progress, sustainable development, perspective

Skills: analyzing trends, constructing interviews, evaluating oral history, critical thinking

Location: indoors

Time: 1 hour a day for 1 week

Materials: paper, pencils, tape recorder (optional)

Are solutions to present problems to be found in the past? What was really so good about the "good old days"? What was life like before computer games, three-wheelers, and fast-food burgers? Does progress equate with change? What criteria might we use to measure progress? These are big questions and ones that students should address — but how does one have students explore these rather abstract concerns? What framework may be used to explore these questions so that discussion is not simply a matter of uninformed opinion?

Isaac Erb Collection, Provincial Archives of New Brunswick

The Grade 6 class at Napan Elementary School near Miramichi, New Brunswick, decided that a case study — which would have them compare the local environment in their grandparents' day with that of the present — would allow them to measure the cost of progress in one area. While the findings of this particular study are unique to the Miramichi region, the process is generic and may be adopted by classes elsewhere. The process in this instance is central to learning:

- It requires that students establish a set of criteria on which to base their judgment.
- It outlines a strategy for collecting the required data so as better to ensure its validity.
- It helps students understand the variety of competing perspectives that may exist on any given issue, and to understand how perspective shapes our position.
- It encourages analytical and systems thinking by noting the interplay of social, environmental, and economic forces at work in a community.
- It encourages students to act on the knowledge they acquire by undertaking projects to address perceived problems in the local environment.

Organizing the data

In order to engage students in a consideration of the wider issue of progress, one may begin by having them consider whether the introduction of some piece of technology is good or bad.

1. Have students select one example of modern technology (i.e., automobile, com-puter, all-terrain vehicle, cell phone).

2. Ask students whether the introduction of this technology was good or bad.

3. Following the students' responses, introduce the PMI model for bringing order into such discussions. Ask students to divide a piece of paper into three columns labeled "Positive," "Minus," and "Interesting." Indicate that

Samplings from the Miramchi

Having interviewed their grandparents and other seniors in their community about life along the rivers and the bay of the Miramichi region, Napan students found that their elders remembered an era when things were certainly cleaner and safer.

Grandparents recalled days when the rivers were teaming with salmon, trout, smelt, gasperaux, and tommycod. Locals used small fish, fish eyes, and worms for bait, and there were no regulations about nets or seasons. Fish were more plentiful, larger, and healthier.

Composting was done as a matter of course. Fish guts, fish heads, and seaweed were used to fertilize gardens.

No chemicals were leaching from the farmers' fields into nearby streams.

People didn't have much leisure time to sunbathe on beaches as they do nowadays, but the rivers provided lots of recreation — swimming and rafting in the summer, and ice hockey and ice fishing in the winter. And if people had a few moments to bask in the sun on the riverbank, they didn't have to worry about the ozone layer, ultraviolet rays, or what sunscreen protection factor they should be wearing on their face.

There were fishing boats aplenty in times past with dories, scows, and rafts, and schooners using wind power. Ferries provided reliable and regular service.

There was no fear of oil pollutants entering the waters. Even noise pollution was unknown.

Many jobs were and still are related to the logging industry on the Miramichi, but the horse and wagon or horse and sled of the past made less impact on the environment than the huge exhaust-spewing tandem trucks of today. Horse manure at least was biodegradable.

Students even discovered that the infamous outhouse was environmentally friendly. No raw sewage ran into local rivers and streams in years gone by. When excessive, the sewage was treated with lime and buried, and the outhouse was moved to new ground. The outhouse was the perfect spot to recycle paper, too, especially the outdated catalogs.

With declining fish stocks, fishing regulations they see as unreasonable, expensive licenses, and precious few clean and safe beaches in the area, these kids felt envious of the rather carefree and unspoiled environment their grandparents once knew.

Isaac Erb Collection, Provincial Archives of New Brunswick

this is the framework that will be used to assess the local information they are to collect in this project.

4. Have students list under "Positive" the favorable aspects of the technology, under "Minus" the negative aspects, and under "Interesting" any comments they have that are neither positive nor negative.

5. Ask for a show of hands by students who changed their mind about whether their item of technology was good or bad.

Collecting the data

The next step is to establish a process for collecting the data. Ask students how they might find information about life in their area some 50 years previous. Some students, it is hoped, will suggest that print resources such as newspapers or local history books would be useful; others might mention such human resources as their grandparents. Indicate that, in this instance, they will be interviewing their grandparents or other older people in the area to collect the required information.

Before doing so, however, they need to learn something about interviewing techniques. The first lesson is to make sure that they acquire relevant information, and to do this they must establish a list of topics that will be covered in the interview. With either small groups or the entire class, generate a list of interview topics and organize these under appropriate headings, such as environmental, social, and economic.

Once the broad topics have been identified, help students generate a list of questions that might guide their interview. Certain protocols are recognized as helpful in ensuring successful interviews and these provide a useful guide to this lesson (e.g., avoid questions that generate only a Yes or No answer). (See "Interviewing tips" below.)

Armed with the list of topics and potential questions, students can then undertake to interview their grandparents or other members of the community, and to compare their findings in class. (Those who wish to could tape their interview.)

Analyzing the data

The analysis of the data should take place in the classroom. Analysis can provide an opportunity for students to develop certain generic skills that are relevant in evaluating information gained from oral interviews. When assessing the information gathered, students might consider these questions:

- To what extent is the picture painted by their grandparents influenced by nostalgia (a longing for the good things of the past)?

- How balanced is the information provided? To what extent do political or other biases shape the perspective of the person who was interviewed?

- What information is missing? Are there relevant causes or consequences that have not been addressed in examining a topic?

- What criteria should be used in determining whether change has resulted in progress?

A framework for analysis and conclusions

It is important that students establish a framework or set of criteria that may be used to guide their evaluation of the information gathered to arrive at a conclusion, however tentative. In this particular study, the concept of

Isaac Erb Collection, Provincial Archives of New Brunswick

sustainable development may provide the required framework in discussing whether progress has occurred over the two generations involved in the study. In judging whether a particular strategy or era meets the requirements of a sustainable society, students should note that sustainable development is development that meets the needs of today's generation without jeopardizing the ability of future generations to meet their needs. Students should understand that, in this instance, growth does not equate with development, that the attention is on needs rather than wants, and that the definition encompasses the concept of intergenerational rights. A sustainable society is one that tries to reconcile the competing demands of the economy, the environment, and social justice.

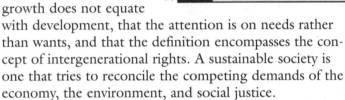

Isaac Erb Collection, Provincial Archives of New Brunswick

To provide a more concrete framework in which to make their assessment of the sustainability of the two societies involved, each student could collect his/her information under the headings of economic, environmental, and social. Students might organize their data using a chart like the following:

	Grandparents' Generation	My Generation
Economy		
Environment		
Social Justice		

Another approach to having students visualize a sustainable society is to have them draw three circles representing, respectively, the environment, the economy, and social justice. A Venn diagram in which the overlapping area is identified as sustainable development may serve to underline the need to reconcile the demands of the three sectors. (See example)

Whichever approach you use, you can draw out students' analytical conclusions through a discussion using guiding questions such as these:

- What are the main problems — environmental, social, or economic — in this region now?
- Were these same problems evident years ago?
- What present-day factors make these problems worse for us?
- What features of people's way of life in the past enabled them either to avoid or to solve these problems?
- What are the costs and benefits of the lifestyle described by the students' elders?
- Can we improve our life by returning to some of the lifestyle options of our grandparents' generation? If so, which options are still practical nowadays? What would be the costs and benefits of adopting them tomorrow?
- If we cannot solve present problems by returning to a past way of life, what new choices and actions can we take to work toward solving them?

Action

One component of citizenship education is to encourage students to assume the responsibilities that go with being a member of a community. Teachers may choose to take the opportunity offered by this study of the past and present by asking students to share their findings with the community or to undertake a specific action that will address one or more of the obstacles to sustainability that they identified in their study. In this way they will give visible evidence of their commitment to their concept of progress.

Once a teacher at Napan Elementary, Brian Loggie now teaches at St. Andrew's Elementary in Miramichi, New Brunswick. Jim Petrie is a retired teacher and educational consultant in Fredericton, New Brunswick.

Making Global Connections

Teaching and learning about interconnectedness through highly participatory activities

by Graham Pike and David Selby

Subject areas: social studies

Key concepts: interdependence

Skills: lateral and creative thinking, relational thinking, cooperation, using atlas

Location: indoors

Interconnectedness is the conceptual glue that binds together the ideas, fields, focuses, themes, and topics that fall within the orbit of global education. In economic, environmental, social, and political terms, global educators are concerned with the nature and effects of connections, propelled by movements of goods, people, and information that link all humanity together — albeit not always within relationships that are just and equitable. They are likewise at pains to show that any global issue is linked, to a greater or lesser degree, to all other global issues; that issues of development, environment, peace, and social justice are, in the final analysis, interwoven. Phases of time are also seen as interconnected: past, present, and future are not discrete periods but are deeply embedded, one within another. At a personal level, global education is concerned with the synergies that can arise from helping students mindfully connect their mental, emotional, physical, and spiritual potentials and their inner well-being to the well-being of the planet. A challenge for the global educator is how to help students think in a relational mode. The activities offered here suggest some practical ways forward.

the mechanics of the global system and the ways in which seemingly unconnected events and decisions can affect their lives. The development of relational thinking — seeing patterns and making connections — also helps students to perceive connections between different curriculum areas, and between the curriculum and the real world, thereby fostering a more holistic and relevant learning experience.

Time: 20 minutes

Materials: (per student) 5 slips of paper, pencils

Procedure:

1. Distribute five slips of paper to each student. Ask students to write the following category names, one on each slip of paper: a natural object, a human-made object, an animal, an emotion, a hope for the future.

2. On the reverse side of each slip, have students write one word that represents the category written on the front. (An animal, for example, could be "deer"; an emotion could be "gratitude.") Any word can be chosen for a category; the selections do not have to follow a theme or pattern.

3. Have students place the slips of paper on the table in front of them with the category names facing up.

4. Choose two students at random and ask them to turn over their "natural object" slips and state what they have written down. The two students then have ten seconds to think of at least one way in which the two natural objects are connected. Should they fail to do

Only connect

This enjoyable and lively activity encourages the development of lateral and creative thinking skills, and heightens students' sensitivity to potential connections between disparate phenomena. Such skills and awareness are important if students are to understand fully

Tom Goldsmith

so in the time allotted, other class members can contribute.

5. The two students then choose two classmates, whose challenge is to find connections between the two new objects that they reveal by turning over their "natural objects" slips.

6. Continue the activity, switching to another category at any time. The students' task is always to find connections between the two items written on the slips.

7. When the activity is progressing well, you can start to mix the categories randomly: connections can be sought between, for example, a human-made object and an emotion. As well as choosing a classmate, a student might also select a category. At this point, creative thinking will be required in abundance and any type of connection should be allowed: the goal is to develop and enhance creativity rather than to discover the optimum connection.

Globetrotting

This lively activity assesses and reinforces students' knowledge of North America's global connections and the geographical location of various countries. The whole group's success depends on the degree of cooperation shown, not only in matching countries with connections but also in helping each other to form appropriate groups. The activity refines the skills of non-verbal communication and develops a sense of group cohesiveness.

Location: an open indoor space in which students can move about freely

Time: 30 minutes

Materials: set of self-adhesive labels, index cards, atlases

Preparation: Write the names of the countries listed in the Country Connections chart (see page 216) on adhesive labels, one country per label. Write (or photocopy and glue) the "connections" from the second column of the chart on index cards.

Procedure:

1. Ask students to form a circle, close their eyes, and remain silent.

2. Stick an adhesive "country" label on the backs of half of the students. Give the other half of the students "connections" cards. Ask students to open their eyes but not to speak.

3. Instruct students with "connections" cards to read their cards and, without speaking, find the student who has the matching country label on his/her back. Atlases can be used at any time.

4. Have students use the country names to form groups, *still without speaking,*

according to each of the following criteria:
- northern and southern hemispheres
- rich and poor countries (by GDP, per capita income, or degree of industrialization)
- continents
- coastal, island, and land-locked countries
- population (e.g., less than 100 million, 100 to 999 million, over 1 billion)
- population density

5. Have students refer to the "connections" to form groups according to connections that have a direct impact on students' lives, and those that do not.

6. Finally, ask the students who have country labels on their backs to inform their partner which country they think they represent.

Extensions:
- As a final challenge to their global sense of place, ask each pair of students to organize themselves, by country, into a human world map. You can take the position that represents Canada and the United States and invite student pairs to adopt relative positions around you.

- As a research task, student pairs can be given a country name and asked to find out some relevant connections to Canada or the United States, or perhaps the country of origin of one of the students. Once these connections are written on blank labels or index cards, the activity can proceed, as described above.

Graham Pike is Dean of the Faculty of Education, University of Prince Edward Island in Charlottetown, Prince Edward Island. David Selby is Professor of the Faculty of Education at the University of Plymouth in England.

Tom Goldsmith

Country Connections

Country	Connections
Australia:	Much of the interior is hot desert or dry grasslands. Exports meat and dairy products to North America. Aboriginal peoples lived here for thousands of years before European settlers arrived.
Bangladesh:	A country that exports clothing and yarn to North America. Experiences tropical cyclones every year. Its coastline is formed by the huge delta of a river flowing from India.
Bosnia:	A European country that used to be part of Yugoslavia. A civil war took place here in the 1990s, after which Canadian soldiers served there as peacekeepers.
Brazil:	A South American country that exports coffee, rubber, footwear, and automobile parts to North America. Its main physical feature is a massive river system flowing through one of the largest forests in the world.
China:	This country has the largest population in the world. It exports salt, chemicals, clothing, toys, and food to North America. The Great Wall is located here.
England:	This country has a mild climate because of an Atlantic Ocean current from the Caribbean. Settlers from here helped form the first European colonies in North America. Soccer, sailing, and cricket are popular sports.
France:	The country from which North America's first European fur traders came. It now exports wines and spirits to North America. The language is also an official language of Canada.
Hong Kong:	The newest territory of China, this former British colony exports clocks, toys, plastics, and electronics to North America.
Japan:	This nation composed of four main islands exports photographic and electronic products, steel, machinery, and vehicles to North America. Known for tranquil art and for food made from rice, seaweed, and raw fish.
Kenya:	An East African country that exports coffee, tea, and spices to North America. Its wildlife and parks on the savanna grasslands attract many tourists. The equator runs through this country.
Mali:	The Niger River runs through this poor West African country. Droughts are frequent. North American scientists are helping the people to prevent soil degradation, so that they can continue herding livestock and growing crops.
Mexico:	This mountainous country sits between the Atlantic and Pacific oceans. It is a member of the North American Free Trade Association.
Netherlands:	One of the most densely populated countries in the world. Extra land has been reclaimed from the sea, and dykes keep the North Sea from flooding coastal lands. Many North American families originated from here.
Russia:	Part of the former Union of Soviet Socialist Republics. Exports iron, steel, diamonds, and metals to North America. Famous for hockey, ice skating, and ballet.
Saudi Arabia:	A large and wealthy country in the Middle East with a rapidly increasing population. Exports oil to North America. Mecca, the holiest city of Muslims, is here.

Press Agent for a Day

This activity provides students with an opportunity to consider events from different perspectives

by Adrienne Mason

Subject areas: language arts, science, geography

Key concepts: communication, different perspectives, environmental effects of oil

Location: indoors (classroom)

Time: 1 to 2 hours

Materials (optional): glass jars with lids, water, detergent, motor oil

In this activity, students read about an oil spill and then write a press release from a particular perspective. Press releases are written by organizations, governments, businesses, and individuals in order to provide information to the media. As such, press releases often emphasize or de-emphasize events and information, depending on their bias and perspective. This activity provides students with an opportunity to consider events from differing perspectives.

Press releases are short — usually one or two pages — and provide journalists with information, including quotes, that could form the basis of a news article or report. All press releases include a contact name and information, so that journalists can obtain more information from this person or conduct an interview. Sometimes press releases are used as a form of advertising or promotion; at other times, they are used to respond to an issue or to attempt to get accurate information to the public through the media.

Warm-up activities (optional):

1. Fill a glass bottle with water and add a few drops of motor oil. Put on the lid and tighten. Shake the bottle. Ask students to observe whether the oil and water mix. Then add a few drops of detergent and shake again. Ask the students if the oil is still there or if it has dispersed. Repeat using more oil.

This activity demonstrates that detergents disperse oil by breaking it into tiny droplets and spreading it throughout the water. Discuss

whether this would be a good way of dealing with oil spills. Have students suggest or try other clean-up methods, such as putting oil and water in a bowl and using a cotton swab to collect the oil or "corralling" the oil with a string.

2. Dip a feather in some oil. Ask students to observe what happens to it. Would a feather covered in oil be able to insulate a bird? Research some environmental effects of oil spills.

Procedure:

1. Read aloud, or provide for students to read, the following account of an oil spill:

On July 23, 1989, the S.S. Bunker Queen, owned by the Oily Oil Company of Vancouver, British Columbia, was traveling south from Alaska with a full load of oil destined for Vancouver. During the evening of

Tom Goldsmith

the 23rd, the Bunker Queen hit a large rock about three kilometers (two miles) offshore, close to the small fishing community of Squeaky Clean Cove. The rock was clearly shown on the ship's charts. The ship began to lose oil. There are rumors that the captain of the ship had not slept for more than 24 hours, owing to poor weather, and was playing rock music at full volume to help him stay awake.

The ship's crew immediately contacted the Coast Guard and began trying to contain the oil spill. However, millions of liters of oil had escaped and begun to come ashore on remote beaches. Many of the local residents, including fishermen, have been hired by the Oily Oil Company to help with the cleanup. They are being paid $25 per hour. A seabird breeding area is near the site where the ship hit the rock.

2. Discuss the situation described, using some of these ideas as prompts:
   - A rumor is mentioned: is this something that should be stated in a newspaper or magazine article?
   - What might have contributed to the accident?
   - Very few people live in the area where the accident happened. Does this make the oil spill an environmental disaster?
   - What significance might this oil spill have to people who live a great distance from where the accident happened?

3. Have the students write a press release of two to three paragraphs about this accident. They could work in pairs or small groups. Suggest that they begin writing what they consider to be the most important points. Have students write the release from the perspective of one of the following:
   - a representative of a local environment group
   - the president of the local birdwatching group
   - a member of a fishing crew
   - a public relations person for the Oily Oil Company
   - the mayor of Squeaky Clean Cove

4. Ask students to read aloud their press releases. Compare the various points of view and the different things emphasized in each press release. Were some things omitted by some people?

Extensions:

- For one week, have students collect stories on environmental issues from magazines, newspapers, and the Internet (e.g., from websites of environmental organizations). You could also contact an organization involved in an issue to request its press releases, so that students can see what a real press release looks like. (Sometimes they are posted on a website and can be printed.) Have students collate the information they have gathered under various headings such as the types of issues, the people involved, and which organizations are represented. Hold a discussion of students' impressions of the stories. Did one issue dominate the week's news? Did journalists have different points of view on the same issue?

- Research ways in which oil spills are actually cleaned up.

- Discuss whether we, as consumers, are in any way responsible for oil spills or other environmental disasters, such as tire fires. After this discussion, read the class this quote from the Southam News Environment Project: "Close to 300 million liters [80 million U.S. gallons] of motor oil vanish into the Canadian environment each year, much of it carelessly poured down sewers by do-it-yourself mechanics. That's almost eight times more oil than spilled when the *Exxon Valdez* ran aground off Alaska."

Adrienne Mason is the author of many education books, including The Green Classroom: 101 Practical Ways to Involve Students in Environmental Issues *(Pembroke Publishers, 1991), from which this activity was adapted. She lives in Tofino, British Columbia.*

Computers in Environmental Learning

Incorporating 21st century computer skills in environmental studies

by Sue LeBeau

Subject areas: mathematics, language arts, social studies, science

Skills: word processing, navigating the Internet, working with templates, creating electronic graphs, designing multimedia presentations and web pages, desktop publishing, summarizing and synthesizing facts and concepts, problem solving, letter writing, comparing data, higher order thinking, understanding points of view, oral reports, newspaper writing

Location: indoors

Time: not applicable

Materials: computers, various software programs, Internet access

Studies worldwide have shown that the integration of computer technology throughout the curriculum increases learning at all levels and provides students with skills that they are almost certain to need in the future. One area in which we can use computer technology to its full potential is environmental studies. Here are some generic activities that can be used to teach students the use of different computer applications, while increasing their understanding of environmental topics. Activities are suggested for various applications, and they span numerous skills that are within the scope of most environmental studies curricula. The general level of computer skill (i.e., beginner, intermediate, or advanced) that is needed to complete the activity is indicated as a guide for the teacher. The activities are not in any particular order; however, since word-processing software is probably the most common and the easiest to use, activities using it are presented first.

Skill levels are denoted as follows:

B — Beginner
I — Intermediate
A — Advanced

Using word-processing software

Stories and essay writing (B, I): Have students develop keyboarding and editing skills by writing stories or essays related to environmental issues that the class is studying.

Letter writing (B, I, A): After students have learned about famous environmentalists, have them a write letter to one of them, asking what inspired him/her to work toward improving the environment. Students can include in their letters their personal opinion of what the environmentalist did to help protect the environment, and state what they have done, or might do, in similar situations. Teachers can extend this activity by having students exchange letters and take on the role of the environmentalists in replying to them.

Daily logs or journals (B, I): Keeping daily logs is a quick and easy use of a computer. For a study of waste

Sue LeBeau

and recycling, for example, students could keep a log of what they throw away. They could also keep a log of daily observations in nature, daily temperatures, or other environmental data.

Book summaries (B, I, A): After reading environmental stories, have students write summaries in a word-processing document and find clip art or other graphics to illustrate the summary. Students will learn how to manipulate clip art, as well as the importance of selecting graphics that are appropriate and relevant to the text. (A list of environmental and science picture books can be found at <www.suelebeau.com>.)

Newspaper articles (I, A): Ask students to write a news article that summarizes the outstanding contributions of a famous environmentalist, past or present. Students could also work in small groups to create newspapers devoted to a specific environmental issue that the class is studying. Many word-processing applications have newsletter or newspaper templates that students can use to design their pages.

Sue LeBeau

Dictionaries (B, I): Starting a new environmental topic often exposes students to new vocabulary. Ask students to create a glossary for each environmental topic by keeping a running list of new terms in a word-processing document. This document could include the terms and their definitions, as well as appropriate graphics to illustrate them. At the end of the school year, students can print out all of their glossary pages to create their own environmental dictionary. Other vocabulary-building activities using different software include having students create crossword or word-search puzzles using vocabulary terms. There are many puzzle-creation tools on the Internet to help with this activity; for examples, see <www.puzzlemaker.com>, <www.genuineclass.com/games/wordsearch.html>, and <http://teachers.teachnology.com/web_tools/crossword>.

Using spreadsheet and database software

Comparisons (I, A): Students can use spreadsheet and database software to compare a variety of data they

encounter in environmental studies. For example, they might compare the uses and types of renewable energy or the quantities of materials that are recycled in different jurisdictions, or the actions that different states/provinces are taking to prevent air or water pollution.

Chronological dates (I, A): Have students use a spreadsheet to create a chronological list of seasonal occurrences or a list of observations on a field trip.

Data comparisons and graphs (I, A): Using a spreadsheet, students can compare data from different countries, such as the land area that is occupied by landfill or the per capita energy usage. Have students create a bar graph from their data using the chart wizard tool. They could write a summary of their findings in a word-processing document.

Cost comparison of environmental products (I, A): Ask students to collect information on the costs of products that are environmentally friendly and of comparable products that are not. They can then set up a spreadsheet that has columns for the names and prices of products and a column for calculating and displaying the differences. Have students examine the cost differences and discuss the benefits of using environmentally friendly products, even though their initial cost may be higher.

Using multimedia applications

Travel guide (B, I, A): Have students gather photos and information on the Internet in order to create a pictorial travel guide to an area in need of environmental restoration or to areas where successful projects have been undertaken. Remind students to use only material in the public domain and to cite the accredited source of photos, maps, and other artwork used in their presentation.

Cause and effect (I, A): Using a multimedia program, students can create a presentation to demonstrate the causes of pollution and the remedial effects that a recycling or renewable energy program can have in a particular situation. Students can find the latest information concerning these problems on the Internet.

Multimedia presentations (I, A): After doing research on a particular environmental topic, ask students to present their findings in the form of a multimedia presentation that includes appropriate sound, music, images, animation, and, if possible, a video clip.

Web pages (I, A): Research findings on any number of environmental topics can be combined and summarized in the form of a web page. Students can add appropriate graphics and background, as well as animation and digital photos. Many word-processing programs (such as Microsoft Word) can be used to create web pages.

Sue LeBeau

Points of view
(I, A): Ask students to create a multimedia presentation on the points of view of different stakeholders in an environmental issue or topic. Students could use the presentation as an outline for an oral report that they present to the class.

Using desktop publishing and graphic software

Posters (B, I, A): Students can create a persuasive poster on an environmental topic, for instance, to urge people to recycle or to use renewable resources and technologies. Posters could be designed using the features available in the software, such as graphics, borders, and stylish lettering. Have students display the posters around the school.

Bumper stickers and bookmarks (B, I, A): Have students compose short messages or sayings urging people to behave in an environmentally friendly way and then create bumper stickers or bookmarks to convey these messages to the community. Graphic illustration can be done in a drawing program, such as Paint, and then imported into the publishing program. Black and white samples could be printed for younger students to color with crayons or markers.

Business cards (I, A): Have students create business cards for themselves, for historical persons in the environmental field, or for components of natural ecosystems that provide essential services (e.g., decomposers, photosynthesizing organisms, wetlands). The business cards could include a logo or design that represents the person or service provider. Contact information (i.e., address, telephone number, e-mail address) should be fictitious and could be humorous.

Greeting cards (B, I, A): Have students create custom-made greeting cards in celebration of Earth Day or another environmental event. Remind students to use images and other graphics that are appropriate and relevant to the event as well as to the person who will receive the card.

Trash coupons (B, I, A): To raise awareness of waste in the classroom, have students design trash coupons that they must use each time they throw something away. The coupons can include space for filling in the name of the item disposed of. After an agreed period of time (e.g., a week), count how many coupons have been used and discuss whether any of the items thrown away could have been reused or recycled. Reuse the coupons in subsequent weeks, gradually reducing each student's weekly allotment.

Using the World Wide Web

Hotlists (B, I, A): It is extremely time consuming for students to type a long and complicated URL (Uniform Resource Locator, or website address) to reach a specific page within a website. One solution is to make hotlists of useful Internet sites for research projects, enabling students to go immediately to an intended site by clicking on the URL in the hotlist document. Each URL can be inserted into a word-processing document, which is saved in a place where all students can easily access it. Give a brief description below the URL so that students know what is on that site. A wonderful search tool for compiling hotlists for students is Filamentality at <www.kn.pacbell.com/wired/fil>.

Scavenger hunts (B, I, A): Have students go on website scavenger hunts to find facts or answers to environmental questions. Scavenger hunts help to increase students' abilities to navigate websites and to read for a specific purpose. Teachers can easily create their own scavenger hunts, or use those that have been designed by other teachers, such as "Our Environment: How Important Is It? Scavenger Hunt" at <www.iss.k12.nc.us/schools/scavenger/bshab.html>.

WebQuests (B, I, A): WebQuests are inquiry activities in which students work in cooperative groups to derive solutions to problems using information from the Internet. WebQuests have very specific components: an introduction, a task, a process, resources, evaluation, and a conclusion. Because of their association with concepts that affect us in the real world, WebQuests are very well suited for environmental topics. See, for example, Acid Rain at <www.swlauriersb.qc.ca/english/edservices/pedresources/webquest/rainwq.htm>. For more information, visit <www.suelebeau.com/webquests.htm>.

Virtual field trips (B, I, A): Have students go on a virtual field trip on the Internet to learn about a particular ecosystem or environmental issue. "Take a Walk in the Rainforest — A Self-Guided Tour" at <www.pbs.org/tal/costa_rica/rainwalk.html> is an excellent example of an environmental field trip; for other examples, visit <www.suelebeau.com/cybertrips.htm>. Many virtual field trips are highly visual and sometimes interactive.

Environmental monitoring (B, I, A): Internet-based environmental monitoring programs provide students with opportunities to interact with scientists and share ideas with students in other regions. For example,

Journey North has students monitoring the progress of spring in North America by observing local environmental changes and reporting sightings of migratory animals (see <http://www.learner.org/jnorth/>). An international example is The GLOBE Program through which students use scientific protocols to gather and report environmental data and have opportunities to collaborate with other schools in ecosystem studies (see <http://www.globe.gov/fsl/welcome.html>). Such programs provide extensive support materials to aid educators in the classroom.

Online expeditions (B, I, A): Have students use the Internet to follow the daily progress and field dispatches of expeditions by scientists and explorers. The Global Schoolhouse (<http://www.globalschoolhouse.org/expeditions/>) is a gateway to numerous opportunities for students to engage in and interact with live real-world, real-time expeditions all over the world.

Sue LeBeau has over 30 years teaching experience in the elementary and middle school grades. She is presently a Technology/Distance Learning Advisor for the Long Branch Public School District in New Jersey, a regional editor of Green Teacher magazine, an adjunct instructor for Monmouth University, and an online instructor of graduate courses for Walden University. Visit Sue's website at: <www.suelebeau.com>.

The Greening of Home Economics

Examining interconnections in our everyday lives

by Robin Ruff

Key concepts: consumer choices have global impacts; personal well-being is embedded in the health of the larger environment

Skills: analyzing product life cycles, creatively reusing materials, making environmentally and socially responsible consumer choices

In 1892, American chemist and educator Ellen Swallow Richards proposed an interdisciplinary science of "right living" that she called Oekology.[1] A pioneer in the field of public health and sanitation, Richards advocated the application of principles of biology, chemistry, and engineering to the tasks of everyday life in order that people might live healthy lives in a healthy relationship with the environment. She saw this new discipline — later known as home economics — as one that would meet women's needs for efficiency and economy in the home as the transition to an industrial society was shifting their role from producers to consumers.

Today, home economics is a particularly relevant area for environmental education. An interdisciplinary and integrative field, it promotes wise living, care, and connectedness in everyday life; as such, it is well suited to the development of practical skills and knowledge that are necessary for living in balance with the environment. In recent years, home economics education, like environmental education, has broadened to include a global perspective[2] that includes systems consciousness and respect for diversity. The synergistic potential of integrating these two disciplines is clear; and drawing on this potential, home economics teachers can encourage students to reflect on ways to establish a more balanced and healthy relationship with the Earth. This article presents ideas for integrating environmental education into four areas within home economics: food studies, textiles, consumer studies, and health and well-being.

Food studies

Food is an excellent vehicle for exploring complex relationships between people and the environment. One strategy is to have students take a close look at the energy, materials, people, and places involved in producing, processing, and transporting food from the farm to the dinner table.[3] A food system analysis can also take into account the waste and recycling that follows all aspects of food production, as well as the potential environmental impacts of such agricultural practices as irrigation or the use of genetically modified crops and chemical pesticides. Encouraging students to analyze factors beyond the price, nutritional value, and convenience of a food item can lead them to consider how human values — such as those underlying organic gardening, voluntary simplicity, or the slow-food movement — have consequences for the social, economic, and ecological dimensions of food.

Food studies can also be revitalized as a means for relearning how to grow, cook, and eat food in ways that are economically, ethically, and ecologically sound. Learning to grow food develops knowledge and skills that reduce reliance on energy-intensive agriculture, and fosters an

By the seat of the pants: an ottoman upholstered with the sturdy rear ends of old denim jeans, designed by a home economics student in Medicine Hat, Alberta.

Shelley Lukasowich, Crescent Heights HS

understanding of how natural systems function. Composting improves the soil and keeps organic waste out of landfill, while also teaching that simple actions can help to reduce our ecological footprint. Exploring traditional indigenous diets and designing meal plans that take local foods into account can increase students' awareness of indigenous plants and animals of their bioregion, and teach them the wisdom inherent in a diet that follows local seasonal cycles.

Peggy Hensley, Clay County HS, Manchester, KY

Home economics meets environmental education in a school garden, where students can grow herbs for cooking, soap-making, and tea.

The integration of environmental education into food studies can also provide opportunities for interacting with the community and connecting emotionally with nature. Walking around the neighborhood to map backyard gardens can help in planning a food garden, while also meeting objectives of environmental education. The smell of fresh herbs and flowers, the sounds of wind and birds, and the sight of seedlings emerging from the soil can forge emotional connections that precipitate a lifelong appreciation of and desire to care for the environment.

> *A food system analysis can take into account the waste and recycling that follows all aspects of food production, as well as the potential environmental impacts of such agricultural practices as irrigation or the use of genetically modified crops and chemical pesticides.*

Textile studies

Textile studies in home economics provide a context for exploring how everyday decisions connect consumers to other people and ecosystems. As the textile industry becomes increasingly global and mechanized, few people know how, by whom, and under what conditions their clothing is made. Textile studies can encourage students to consider the social, economic, and ecological costs of textile products, so that they can think critically about what clothing labels do and do not say about garments. Awareness-raising research topics may include the environmental impacts of producing and caring for different types of textiles.

Textile studies that build students' sewing skills enable them to mend and reuse their textile items rather than perpetuating a wasteful cycle of consuming and discarding. By teaching students to replace buttons and zippers, and to patch or design textile items from scraps and used materials, textile studies can

---

Be Proud to Wear It

At Eric Hamber Secondary School in Vancouver, students of home economics teachers Judy Chan and Nina Ho apply the concepts of reducing, reusing, and re-forming with inspiring results. In 2003, the students transformed samples from a local fabric importer into creative fashion apparel for themselves, and into scarves and hats that they sold as a fundraising venture for the class. In past years, students turned fleece scraps from Mountain Equipment Co-op into hats for the homeless, and re-formed upholstery samples into cosmetic bags that were given to a women's shelter. As a design project, students wove ribbons from a flower shop to create unique garments that they modeled in the school fashion show. Senior students' final textile project was to redesign two old items of clothing into one new item, with the stipulation that they had to be "proud to wear it." By providing opportunities for creative use of textile resources, these teachers are integrating environmental education into the home economics classroom.

Nina Ho

Nina Ho

Left: Students sort through knit samples donated by a fabric importer to find the perfect pieces for their creative fashions. Right: Elegantly woven dresses fashioned from ribbons donated by a flower shop.

224

promote zero waste and encourage creativity.

Other ideas for bringing an environmental ethic into textile studies include composting such natural fibers as cotton, linen, silk, and wool, or making paper from scraps of fabric. Producing cloth lunch bags or grocery bags as introductory sewing projects can reduce the use of plastic and paper bags.[4] Textile projects can also become a form of environmental activism: students could, for example, design a class quilt that tells their individual or collective stories as a creative way to express themselves on environmental issues that they care about.

Consumer studies

As the main subject area for consumer education, home economics is the ideal class for promoting an environmental ethic in students as consumers.[5] Consumer studies can raise awareness of consumption habits that deplete the planet's resources, while enabling students to make more environment-friendly choices in the products they purchase and use.

A helpful starting point is to have students assess the true environmental costs of products they consume — costs that are seldom reflected in product

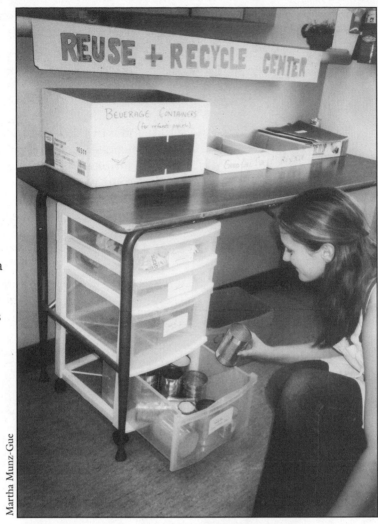

Martha Munz-Gue

A classroom recycling center is a continuous teacher, encouraging choices at the point of discard and a recognition that there is no "out" to which things can be thrown.

prices. Students could conduct a life-cycle analysis of a product, assessing all the natural resources and energy used in its manufacture, distribution, and disposal, as well as social costs such as impacts on health.[6] Comparing the materials and processes used in producing "green" products with those used in making conventional products can raise awareness of the implications of the choices students make as consumers.

Individually or as a class, students can estimate their own environmental impact by calculating their ecological footprint (see page 84), and then brainstorm simple changes they can make to reduce it. A strategy for exploring students' values as consumers is to have them compare the value of goods they buy to the value of things that do not have a price tag — a sunrise, fresh air, clean water, or the haunting call of a loon.

Family studies: health and well-being

Family studies programs can also forge links between natural and human systems. Studies of health and well-being could consider ways in which lifestyle choices affect our personal and family health, as well as the health of the natural environment. This approach builds on the "family as ecosystem" framework proposed by Nancy Hook and Beatrice Paolucci in 1987.[7] In response to the growing awareness of environmental problems, Hook and Paolucci suggested that home economists

Peggy Hensley

Planting herbs in a school garden.

> *As the textile industry becomes increasingly globalized and mechanized, few people know how, by whom, and under what conditions their clothing is made. Textile studies can encourage students to consider the social, economic, and ecological costs of textile products, so that they can think critically about what clothing labels do and do not say about garments.*

consider the interdependence and interconnectedness between humans and natural systems:

The family as a life support system is dependent upon the natural environment for physical sustenance and upon the social organizations which are related to man's humanness and give quality and meaning to life. Home economists for some time have emphasized the social-emotional environment. It is necessary for the field (as it focuses on the family) to link both the natural environment and the social environment. Therein lie its uniqueness and strength.[8]

Home economics teachers can help students to link the natural and social environment by having them consider how local green spaces and wilderness contribute to healthy lifestyles. In discussing and experiencing the benefits of natural spaces, students can become more aware of how their health and the well-being of their families and communities is linked to the health of the environment. The environmental impact of transportation choices can also be examined within studies of health and well-being, by considering the personal and environmental benefits of walking and cycling compared to other forms of recreation and transportation.

True to its origins as a science of "right living," home economics today is an important subject area for environmental education. As we become more conscious of the impact of our lifestyles on the environment, and we make stronger connections between environmental health and our own well-being, home economics can take a leading role in educating for sustainability. It is one of the few subjects where hands-on skills are emphasized and the means for achieving health and well-being are addressed.

By encouraging students to examine critically the everyday choices they make about food, clothing, consumption, and health, home economics can help them to develop an ecocentric worldview that is vital for learning to live well with less impact on the planet. As home economics teachers become attuned to the many ways in which environmental education can be integrated into their programs, there is a potential for great transformations in the ways in which students, families, and schools interact with the natural environment.

Robin Ruff is working toward a master's degree in environmental education at the University of Victoria, British Columbia, where she is exploring the relationship between environmental education and home economics.

Elizabeth Martin

Elizabeth Martin's eighth grade home economics students at New Windsor Middle School in Maryland made cloth "squirrel bags" for injured and abandoned squirrels living at a local wildlife shelter. Each bag provides a soft and cozy retreat for up to eight young squirrels.

Notes

1 R. Clarke. *Ellen Swallow: The Woman Who Founded Ecology.* Follett Publishing Company, 1973.

2 G. Smith and L. Peterat. *Developing Global/Development Perspectives in Home Economics Education.* Canadian Home Economics Association, 1992.

3 See *Green Teacher,* issue 65 (Summer 2001) for activity ideas and resources for teaching about food systems in middle schools.

4 These ideas are from Vancouver School Board, *Bringing the World Into Your Classroom,* 1996.

5 Sue L.T. McGregor. "Status of Consumer Education in Canada." Paper presented at the Inaugural Colloquium on Consumer Protection: Globalization, Deregulation and Impoverishment of Consumers, March 2000. On-line in January 2004 at <www.consultmcgregor.com>, Research paper 17.

6 See J. Ryan and A. Durning, *Stuff: The Secret Lives of Everyday Things,* Northwest Environment Watch, 1997, for examples of the hidden environmental costs of everyday products.

7 Nancy Hook and Beatrice Paolucci. "The Family as Ecosystem." In ed. B. Rader. *Home Economics Teacher Education Yearbook 7 — Significant Writings in Home Economics: 1911–1979.* American Home Economics Association, 1987, pp. 315–17.

8 Hook and Paolucci, p. 316.

Twenty Leaden Rules to Make Sure Your Project Sinks!

The author prepared this satirical list while he and his students were developing wildlife habitat around a sewage lagoon adjacent to their school

by John Perry

 Do not involve students in your initial plans. Students are apathetic and not willing to help the environment.

2. Keep the long-term view to yourself. Today's students are concerned only with the immediate future.

3. If a student makes a suggestion, ignore it. It is your plan, and if it needed any improvement you would have thought of it yourself.

4. If a student offers a resource such as a parent's help, ignore the offer. What practical insight can a parent who spends his/her lunch break helping geese at the company's lagoon have to offer? Your lagoon is a school lagoon. There is a big difference.

5. Be sure to divide activities on the basis of gender. Let only the boys do the cutting, hammering, and nailing of the dock. Let the girls do only the "girl stuff."

6. Keep the project under wraps from your custodian. Custodians have enough to do inside the school and they might have a few suggestions. You definitely do not want to find out that your head custodian helped to save and restore a disappearing marsh that is now an international educational tourist attraction.

7. When you want to build the components of a floating dock in your classroom, do not discuss your building plans with the cleaning staff. It is possible that they will not notice what you are doing. If they do notice, be sure to leave pieces of lumber and flotation devices lying all over the place. After all, it is their job to clean up your room.

8. Your school administration should not know about your plans. Administrators like to be able to tell parents, central administration, and elected school trustees that they do not know what is happening in their school. Administrators are also more likely to give you moral and financial support if they do not know anything about the project.

9. If you have to get permission from divisional maintenance or the school board, do not follow proper channels. The people you bypass have enough to do and would not be able to help your project anyway.

Tom Goldsmith

10. Conservation groups and owners of private wildlife sanctuaries are not willing to come out and make suggestions, so why bother asking them in the first place?

11 Doing research on successful stewardship projects is a waste of time. Each project is different.

12. Do not involve such groups as wildlife federations and government agencies, especially when they offer seed money to start your project. You do not need to use the fact that you have a grant from a national organization to give an extra boost to the students. Besides, having a grant will not help to convince people that you are serious and the project is worthwhile.

13. Once your site is usable, make sure that your classes have so many observing, sketching, and sample-taking assignments that they do not have time to enjoy the wonder of nature and the joy of sharing discoveries with you and their classmates. School is a serious business and students should not enjoy themselves.

14. Pre-teaching and explanation of what you want the students to accomplish should be done outdoors. When the weather is miserable, be sure to take extra time to make your explanations as detailed as possible. Students need to learn to overcome the adversity of sketching with shaking hands.

15. Followup in the classroom is to be avoided. You do not want students to be able to synthesize their experiences and see the larger environmental picture. They might get ideas.

16. Do not involve other teachers. They might want to "help." Worse, they might even see a use of your site for their classes. Even worse, there might be someone to continue the project if you leave the school.

17. Keep all the glory to yourself. Why should students and others feel good about their suggestions and work? It was your idea.

18. Try not to bother with a timetable. If you must have a timetable, make sure it is only for the short term. Long-term planning just invites long-term problems.

19. With your next environmental project, start from scratch. What you have learned from a habitat project has absolutely no relevance to any other possible environmental project.

20. Do not look around your own area for a potential outdoor classroom. To be good, an area must be located a great distance from your school.

Prior to retirement, John Perry taught Grade 3 to university in Manitoba. He is currently involved in a number of environmental education projects and lives in East St. Paul, Manitoba.

Glossary

acid mine drainage: acidic water containing high concentrations of heavy metals, resulting from the exposure during mining operations of rock containing sulfur compounds that are oxidized to form sulfuric acid.

acid: a substance that releases hydrogen ions (H+) when dissolved in water, or a solution that has a higher concentration of hydrogen ions than pure water. Acids taste sour and have a pH lower than 7.0; the higher the concentration of H+, the lower the pH and the more acidic.

acid rain: precipitation that has a pH below 5.6, as a result of the formation of sulfuric and nitric acids when water combines with sulfur and nitrogen oxides in the atmosphere.

adaptation: an inherited characteristic that has evolved through natural selection and results in the fitness of an organism for living in a particular environment; also, an advantageous modification of an organism in response to environmental conditions, such as the thickening of an animal's coat in winter.

adsorption: the adherence of a substance to the surface of a solid; in environmental remediation, the removal of contaminants such as heavy metals from air or water by collecting the contaminant on the surface of a solid material.

aeration: the exposure of water to air, often by mechanical means such as stirring or bubbling, in order to dissipate volatile contaminants; also, the introduction of air into soil by turning it over or by the action of earthworms.

amphibians: cold-blooded vertebrates adapted for life both on land and in water, e.g., frogs.

aquifer: an underground geological formation that contains water; aquifers are the water sources for springs and wells.

Bernoulli's principle: named after its discoverer, Daniel Bernoulli, the principle that the faster a gas or liquid moves, the less pressure it exerts.

biodiversity: the variety of life in all its forms, including the variability within a species (genetic diversity), the number and types of different organisms within an ecosystem (species diversity), and the variety of ecosystems within a region (ecosystem diversity).

biogeoclimatic zone: a geographic area that has relatively uniform vegetation, topography, soil, and climate, usually named for a dominant species in the zone, e.g., sub-boreal spruce zone.

biological indicator (also called bioindicator and indicator species): an organism that functions as a sign of environmental conditions because it is likely to occur only in environments with certain chemical, physical, or biological characteristics or it has an easily observable response to one or more environmental factors.

biome: a large ecological unit or community comprising a distinctive assemblage of plants, animals, and microorganisms that occurs over a wide area and is defined by vegetation, soils, and climatic factors that distinguish it from other major assemblages, e.g., desert, temperate grassland, and tropical rainforest.

biomonitor: an animal or plant that accumulates contaminants from air and water in its tissues, or is otherwise sensitive to changes in its environment and thereby helps us to assess changes in the overall health of its habitat over time.

bioregion: an area bounded by natural rather than artificial borders that has distinct soils, landforms, watersheds, climates, native plants and animals, and other particular characteristics.

carrying capacity: the maximum population size that any given environment can support indefinitely.

cash crop: a crop that is harvested and sold for money.

community ecology: the study of interactions among organisms that coexist in a given habitat, and the processes involved in these interactions.

competition: interaction between two or more organisms when they require the same resource (e.g., food, water, nesting space, ground space) and the resource is in limited supply.

compost: nutrient-rich material that results from the decomposition of organic waste; also called humus, it is a good soil conditioner and fertilizer.

conflict resolution: a process whereby conflict is resolved or reduced to an acceptable state for all parties involved.

consensus building: a process wherein individuals with varying interests work together to arrive at a mutually agreeable position on a given issue.

conservation: the planning and management of natural resources in order to ensure their long-term use and improve their quality, value, and diversity; a reduction in the use of energy and resources, either by using more efficient technologies or by changing wasteful habits.

constructed wetland: a human-made facility that exhibits wetland characteristics and is designed to perform wetland functions, such as removing heavy metals from water, treating sewage, or removing sediments.

consumerism: the purchase or "consumption" of goods and services as an end in itself, beyond what is required to meet human needs; the ideology that encourages consumption as an economic and social good.

convection: a thermal process that maintains atmospheric circulation through the upward or downward transfer of air masses of different temperature; the transference of heat in a gas or liquid resulting from unequal temperature and the consequent unequal densities.

dendrochronology: the study of the annual growth rings on trees in order to reconstruct past weather events and climate.

desertification: the degradation of vegetative cover to form a desert, caused by natural factors such as drought and — more often — human activities such as overgrazing livestock, and clearing land by cutting trees or burning it; the loss of trees and other vegetation exposes soil to erosion, evaporation, and salinization.

developing countries: generally poor, often indebted countries whose economies are based mostly on agriculture and primary resources, and do not have a strong industrial base; also called "less developed" and "underdeveloped" countries.

dispersal: the movement of animals from where they were born to other areas in order to mate with individuals from other populations of the same species.

DNA: deoxyribonucleic acid, the genetic material of living organisms through which the characteristics of an organism are inherited.

ecology: the study of interrelationships between organisms and their environment.

ecosystem: a dynamic complex of plants, animals, microorganisms, and their non-living environment, interacting as a unit in the cycling of energy and matter.

endangered species: plants or animals in immediate danger of extinction, due to habitat destruction or because of overexploitation, disease, or other factors.

environment: the physical, biotic, and chemical conditions that surround a living organism.

environmental assessment: a process of reviewing a proposed action or project to determine whether it is likely to have significant environmental impacts.

environmental monitoring: measuring environmental change, for example, in air or water quality, in order to guide public policies or remedial actions.

food systems: systems by which food is produced, processed, and distributed among people and/or countries, on a local or a global level.

food webs: the complex patterns of energy flow in an ecosystem based on who eats whom within that system.

gait pattern: the way in which an animal moves, determined by its morphology (form and structure).

gene: the basic unit of heredity; a sequence of deoxyribonucleic acid (DNA) on a chromosome that initiates or regulates the production of proteins that control the development of hereditary characteristics.

genetic diversity: differences in the genes of individuals within a population of organisms; genetic diversity improves the ability of a species to survive in a changing environment.

geometric progression: a progression in which each number is multiplied by a constant in order to obtain the next number; for example, 1, 4, 16, 64, 256 is the beginning of a geometric progression.

global awareness: an understanding of the systems and processes that determine the state of the world and how people, communities, and countries relate to each other and the environment around them

global citizenship: a recognition that we are all citizens of Earth, with responsibilities to each other and to the planet itself.

global perspective: a viewpoint that examines ideas and issues for their global connections, and recognizes our shared humanity in an interdependent world.

habitat: the natural place where an organism lives, including environmental factors (e.g., climate and availability of nutrients, water, space, shelter) that the organism requires in order to complete its life cycle and reproduce.

habitat fragmentation: the division of natural habitats into small, relatively isolated sections.

heavy metals: metals with high atomic weights and density, such as mercury and lead, that are toxic to living organisms and that tend to accumulate in the food chain.

higher-order thinking skills: cognitive skills that enable humans to comprehend experiences and information, apply knowledge, express complex concepts, make decisions, criticize and revise unsuitable constructs, and solve problems.

human rights: the rights that people are deemed to be entitled to simply because they are human, and that become enforceable when codified in domestic and international law.

inbreeding depression: a reduction of the fitness of offspring as the result of mating between closely related individuals in a population; by reducing genetic diversity, inbreeding increases the probability that harmful genes will occur homozygously and thus be expressed.

indicator species: a species of animal or plant whose presence is an indication of a particular set of environmental conditions; a species whose presence provides information about the overall condition of a habitat.

inquiry: learning through direct observation and exploration of the environment, often initiated through central questions that students answer by collecting and synthesizing data.

integrated teaching: instruction that draws on several or all academic disciplines simultaneously, rather than treating them as distinct subjects; often utilizes applied projects, thematic instruction, service learning projects, social-issue investigations, science-technology-society investigations and/or simulations. (See also "vertical integration of curriculum" below.)

interdependence: dependence on one another; the idea that the movement of goods, people, and information links all humanity together and that any global issue is linked, to a greater or lesser degree, to all other global issues.

interdisciplinary inquiry: thematic learning that integrates subject curricula and builds on students' interests and experiences.

invasive species: a species that, when introduced to an ecosystem outside of its natural range, quickly establishes itself and successfully competes with native species for space, food, or shelter, often causing the populations of native species to decline; once they are established, invasive species are difficult to eradicate.

life-cycle analysis: an examination of the total environmental impact of a product through every step of its "life," from the extraction of its raw materials, to its manufacture, packaging, transportation to a store, use, and disposal.

lift: aerodynamic force acting opposite to gravity, created by a pressure differential between the upper and lower surfaces of an airfoil (such as the wing of an aircraft) when air is flowing over it; see also Bernoulli's principle.

limiting factor: a particular environmental or habitat factor that a species needs to thrive and reproduce; e.g., temperature, precipitation, soil nutrients, sunlight, food, nesting sites.

materialism: a desire for wealth and material possessions; in philosophy, the belief that physical matter is the only reality.

monoculture: in agriculture, the cultivation of a single crop over a large area of land; due to lack of diversity, such crops are prone to disease and insect infestations and often require large quantities of chemical pesticides.

multiple intelligences, theory of: a theory of cognition, developed by Howard Gardner in 1983, that all humans are endowed to varying degrees with eight forms of intelligence (mathematical/logical, linguistic, musical, interpersonal, intrapersonal, spatial, kinesthetic, and naturalist) that offer different pathways to learning; by contrast, most schools emphasize linguistic and mathematical/logical intelligences. The theory emphasizes the need for educational strategies that address a variety of modes of learning.

non-point source pollution: pollution generated by diffuse land use activities rather than emanating from a single, identifiable source, and carried to waterways through runoff or groundwater seepage rather than by deliberate discharge; it can often be corrected by changes in land management practices.

nutrient cycling: the continuous transformation of chemical elements from inorganic form in the environment to organic form in living organisms, and back again to inorganic form through decomposition.

organic agriculture: crop and livestock production that excludes the use of synthetic fertilizers, pesticides, pharmaceuticals, and other chemicals, and that seeks to promote the health and integrity of agricultural ecosystems through management practices such as crop rotation, natural pest control, and animal and green manures.

paleobotany: the study of fossil plants and of plant populations, distribution, diversity, and uses in the past, useful in reconstructing past environments and cultures.

paleoclimatology: the study of the Earth's climate throughout geological history, using such means as the analysis of tree rings and of atmospheric gases trapped in glacial ice, and the inference of past climate based on the fossil pollen record of past vegetation.

perspective: a view of facts, ideas, events, or other matters and their interrelationships, that is not universally shared.

pH: a logarithmic scale from 1 to 14 that indicates acidity and alkalinity as a measure of the relative concentrations of hydrogen ions ($H+$) and hydroxyl ions ($OH-$) in a solution. The scale is inversely related to the concentration of hydrogen ions ($H+$), so that 1-6.9 is acidic (more $H+$ than $OH-$), 7 is neutral ($H+$ and $OH-$ in equilibrium, as in pure water), and 7.1-14 is alkaline (more $OH-$ than $H+$).

phenology: the study of periodic events in nature, such as an organism's growth, development, and reproduction in relation to the seasons.

phytoremediation: the use of plants to take up through their roots, and hence remove, contaminants such as organic compounds and heavy metals from soil, sediments, and water.

pollination: the fertilization of plants by the transfer of pollen from (male) anthers to (female) stigmas.

population dynamics: variations in time and space in the size and density of populations.

precipitation (of metals): the separation and settling of a substance held in solution.

renewable energy: energy produced from regenerative or virtually inexhaustible sources such as the sun, the wind, falling water, biomass, and geothermal heat (as opposed to non-renewable sources of energy, such as fossil fuels).

renewable resources: natural resources that are continuously produced and can be replenished naturally on a time scale relevant to their use, e.g., forests and fish.

resource allocation: the apportioning of a resource to specific uses or to particular individuals, organizations, or species.

service learning: learning and developing skills through participation in projects that meet community needs; service learning programs coordinated by a school or school district are designed to support or enhance the academic curriculum.

soil degradation: a decrease in the productivity of soil due to the deterioration — usually human-induced — of its physical, chemical, or biological properties, e.g., erosion, compaction, salinization, or loss of water, nutrients, and organic matter.

straddle: in animal tracking, the widest point of a trail or group pattern, measured perpendicular to the line of travel and usually including the width of the tracks.

stride: in animal tracking, the distance from one track along an animal's trail to the next track made by the same foot.

subsistence farming: farming that meets the basic needs of the grower but does not generate surplus crops or livestock that can be sold in the market.

sustainable development: development that meets the needs of the present generation without compromising the ability of future generations to meet their needs (as defined by Brundtland Commission, 1987).

sustainability: able to be sustained over the long term, such as the use of a natural resource in a manner that does not damage or deplete it.

toponymy: the study of the origin of place names; knowing who named a place, when it was named, and what it was named for, can aid in interpreting cultural landscapes and investigating environmental history.

trophic level: the position an organism occupies in a food chain, determined by what it eats and what eats it, or by the number of energy-transfer steps it is from primary producers (plants); organisms at the same trophic level obtain energy in the same basic manner, either from the sun through photosynthesis (plants), by eating plants (herbivores), or by eating other animals (carnivores/omnivores).

wind turbine: a machine that converts the mechanical energy of the wind into electrical energy by means of propeller-like blades that are moved by the wind around a rotor hub, which in turn spins a drive shaft connected to a generator.

umbrella species: species of large, wide-ranging animals, such as grizzly bears, that are at the top of the food chain and thus indicators of ecosystem health; if a protected area is large enough to support a healthy population of an umbrella species, it is assumed that the area will protect most other species "under" the umbrella.

vermicomposting (also known as vermiculture): an intensive method of composting in which red wiggler worms digest food scraps and produce nutrient-rich waste, or castings, that can be used as fertilizer for plants.

vertical integration of curriculum: the structuring of curriculum so that it provides students with continuous experiences that build on one another, year after year; the result is reiteration without repetition.

wants vs. needs: an important distinction when examining consumerism; "needs" refer to goods and services that are necessary for survival; "wants" refer to goods and services that are desired, but not necessary for survival.

wastewater treatment: a mechanical, chemical, or natural process used to restore the quality of "used" water to acceptable human standards; the process of removing pollutants from water that has been used.

water cycle (also known as the hydrological cycle): the continuous circulation of water between the Earth (including the oceans) and the atmosphere through evaporation, condensation, precipitation, runoff, ground water storage and seepage, and re-evaporation into the atmosphere.

wind barb: a weather map symbol that indicates the direction from which a wind is blowing, how fast it is blowing, and the amount of cloud cover (if any) at that time.

wind meter: a device used for measuring wind speeds

watershed (also referred to as a drainage basin): all the land that drains water into a river system or other body of water.

wetlands: lands where the water table is at or near the surface of the land; neither fully terrestrial nor fully aquatic, wetlands perform important functions such as providing a habitat for migratory waterfowl and filtering wastes and contaminants.

Index

S

Sampling methods
fish populations, 74
plants, 14
shorelines, 53
Scavenger hunts, on-line, 221
School tree ordinances, 207
Schoolyard Special Interests activity, 59
Seals, harp, 72
Seasonal change, study of, 2-6
Sense of place, 175-179
Service learning, 108
Settling ponds, 25
Sex, invertebrates, 53
Shoreline studies, 50-54
Simulations (by topic)
basic needs, 89-91
genetic diversity, 61- 63
population and consumption, 96
rainforest debate, 47
Soil
degradation of, 64-67, 68, 116
erosion experiments, 68
Stalking wildlife, 29-34
Storywriting, 201
Stormwater runoff, 191
Straddle, in animal tracks 32
Straw balc construction, 123-128
Stride, in animal tracks, 32
Subsistence farming, 114-117
Superheroes, 159-162
Supermarket tour, 195
Surveys
plants, 14
birds and insects, 16
trees, 206-207
wetlands, 22
Sustainability, 7-12, 84, 140, 180-181
Sustainable
building, 123-128,
development, 114-117, 210-213,
food production, 107- 113, 114-117
living, 140
resource management, 70-75
Suzuki, David, 160
Swale, 191
Symbols, 176, 178
Systems thinking, 107-113, 210

T

Temperate rainforests, 44-49
Temperature, measuring, 21
Territorial limits, 70, 72-73
Territorial Tactics game, 38
Textile studies, 224-225
Thanksgiving Address, 177, 178
Thermometer response time, 21
Tidepools, exploring, 52
Tools of Hope board game, 114
Toponymy, 205
Topographic maps, 180, 200
Tracking, 29-34
Trailing activities, 31-32
Transects, 14, 51, 53
Trees, surveying and ordinance, 206-208
Turbidity, 23

U

Umbrella species, 63
Underwater Mountains, mapping activity, 200
UN Declaration of the Rights of the Child, 151

V

Valentine's Day, 166
Values clarification, 56, 141
Vermiculture, 118-122
Vertical integration of curriculum, 183
Visual arts, 172

W

Wackernagel, Mathis, 84
Wants vs. needs, 91, 140-144
Waste, food, 82, 118-122
Wastewater treatment, 104
Water
availability, 98-99, 102, 103
contamination, 98, 103
cycle, 104-105, 190
fast facts, 99
filters, making, 104
treatment and filtration, 24, 104-105
usage chart, 101
Water cycle activities, 105, 190
Water Fates activity, 102
Water quality, monitoring, 23, 24, 189-191

Curriculum Index

Green Teacher

Education for Planet Earth

A quarterly magazine by and for educators, *Green Teacher* provides inspiration, ideas and classroom-ready materials to enhance environmental and global education across the curriculum at all grade levels. Some of the themes covered since 1991 include:

waste reduction ☙ urban forestry
environmental monitoring ☙ sustainability
nature awareness ☙ waterways rehabilitation
humane education ☙ vecological footprints
transportation alternatives ☙ biodiversity
human rights ☙ peace education
sustainable agriculture ☙ climate change
habitat protection ☙ marine ecosystems

E-Packs: Collections of the Best of *Green Teacher*

E-Packs are collections of articles, delivered by e-mail, which contain some of the best of the curriculum ideas, perspectives and activities published in past issues of *Green Teacher* magazine:

• Green Teacher's Greatest Hits I & II, Transforming Schoolyards I & II,
• Science/Technology K-6 & 7-12, Social/Multicultural Studies K-6 & 7-12,
• Integrated High School Curriculum I & II, Language Arts/Art K-6 & 7-12.

Other Books by Green Teacher

Teaching About Climate Change: Cool Schools Tackle Global Warming
Des idées fraîches à l'école: Activités et projects pour contrer les changements climatiques
Greening School Grounds: Creating Habitats for Learning

For more information,
Please call (416) 960-1244 or visit our web site at
www.greenteacher.com

If you have enjoyed *Teaching Green, The Middle Years*, you might also enjoy other

BOOKS TO BUILD A NEW SOCIETY

Our books provide positive solutions for people who want to make a difference. We specialize in:

Sustainable Living • Ecological Design and Planning • Natural Building & Appropriate Technology
New Forestry • Environment and Justice • Conscientious Commerce • Progressive Leadership
Educational and Parenting Resources • Resistance and Community • Nonviolence

For a full list of NSP's titles, please call 1-800-567-6772 or check out our web site at:

www.newsociety.com

New Society Publishers

ENVIRONMENTAL BENEFITS STATEMENT

New Society Publishers has chosen to produce this book on Rolland Enviro 100, recycled paper made with 100% post consumer waste, processed chlorine free, and old growth free.

For every 5,000 books printed, New Society saves the following resources:[1]

62	Trees
5,599	Pounds of Solid Waste
6,161	Gallons of Water
8,036	Kilowatt Hours of Electricity
10,178	Pounds of Greenhouse Gases
44	Pounds of HAPs, VOCs, and AOX Combined
15	Cubic Yards of Landfill Space

---

[1]Environmental benefits are calculated based on research done by the Environmental Defense Fund and other members of the Paper Task Force who study the environmental impacts of the paper industry.

NEW SOCIETY PUBLISHERS